The Collected Works of

MARY SIDNEY HERBERT
COUNTESS OF PEMBROKE

Volume I

Corrected Reprint

The Collected Works of

MARY SIDNEY HERBERT

COUNTESS OF PEMBROKE

Volume I

POEMS, TRANSLATIONS, AND CORRESPONDENCE

Edited with Introduction and Commentary by

Margaret P. Hannay, Noel J. Kinnamon, and Michael G. Brennan

CLARENDON PRESS · OXFORD

1998

Oxford University Press, Great Clarendon Street, Oxford OX2 6DP
Oxford New York
Athens Auckland Bangkok Bogotá Buenos Aires Calcutta
Cape Town Chennai Dar es Salaam Delhi Florence Hong Kong Istanbul
Karachi Kuala Lumpur Madrid Melbourne Mexico City Mumbai
Nairobi Paris São Paulo Singapore Taipei Tokyo Toronto Warsaw
and associated companies in
Berlin Ibadan

Oxford is a registered trade mark of Oxford University Press

Published in the United States by
Oxford University Press Inc., New York

A catalogue record for this book is available from the British Library

Library of Congress Cataloging in Publication Data
Pembroke, Mary Sidney Herbert, Countess of, 1561–1621.
[Works. 1998]
The collected works of Mary Sidney Herbert, Countess of Pembroke /
edited with introduction and commentary by Margaret P. Hannay, Noel
J. Kinnamon, and Michael G. Brennan.
Includes bibliographical references and indexes.
Contents: v. 1. Poems, translations, and correspondence—
v. 2. The psalmes of David.
I. Hannay, Margaret P., 1944– . II. Kinnamon, Noel J.
III. Brennan, Michael G.   IV. Title.
PR2329.P2A12 1998 821'.3–dc21 97–25502
ISBN 0–19–811280–7 (v–1)
ISBN 0–19–818457–3 (v–2)

3 5 7 9 10 8 6 4 2

Printed in Great Britain
on acid-free paper by
Biddles Ltd,
Guildford and King's Lynn

12215437   ʨ

CONTENTS

Volume I Poems, Translations, and Correspondence

Acknowledgements	ix
References and Abbreviations	xiii
Editorial Procedure	xxv
Chronology	xxx

Introduction
Life	I
Origins, Early Reception, and Influence	21
Methods of Composition and Translation	55

Original Works

'A Dialogue betweene two shepheards, *Thenot* and *Piers*, in
    praise of *Astrea*'
Literary Context	81
Text	89

'Even now that Care'
Literary Context	92
Text	102

'To the Angell spirit of the most excellent Sir Phillip Sidney'
Literary Context	105
Text	110
Variant printed in Samuel Daniel's *Workes* (1623)	113

Disputed Work

'The Dolefull Lay of Clorinda'
Literary Context	119
Text	133

Translations

Antonius by Robert Garnier
Literary Context	139

Fidelity to Originals   147
Text   152

A Discourse of Life and Death by Philippe de Mornay
Literary Context   208
Fidelity to Originals   220
Text   229

The Triumph of Death by Francis Petrarch
Literary Context   255
Fidelity to Originals   268
Text   273

Correspondence

Manuscript Letters   285
Printed Letters Attributed to Mary Sidney Herbert, Dowager
Countess of Pembroke   298

Transmission and Authority of Texts   302

Commentary   319

Volume II   The Psalmes of David

References and Abbreviations   viii

Editorial Procedure   xx

The Psalmes
Literary Context   3
Textual Notes: MS *A*   33
Text   35
Text of Variant *Psalmes*   254

Manuscripts of the *Psalmes*   308

Relationship of the Texts of the *Psalmes*   337

Major Revisions of Psalms 1–43   358

Commentary   362

Glossary   460

Contents

Table of Verse Forms   469

Index of First Lines and Titles of Poems   485

General Index to Introductions and Textual Essays   491

ACKNOWLEDGEMENTS

Our collaborative work for this edition has been generously supported by many institutions and individuals. Valuable periods of leave of absence from teaching and administrative duties have been granted to Margaret Hannay by Siena College, to Noel Kinnamon by Mars Hill College, and to Michael Brennan by the School of English, University of Leeds. Support for this project from other sources has also been considerable. Margaret Hannay and Noel Kinnamon are grateful for support from the Andrew W. Mellon Foundation and the National Endowment for the Humanities. Noel Kinnamon has also been supported by the American Philosophical Society and the Faculty Scholars Program, University of Kentucky (James Still Fellowship). Michael Brennan is grateful to the British Academy for a period of Study Leave to allow uninterrupted work on the completion of this edition.

We have received much help and kindness from the staff of the many libraries in which we have worked. We are especially grateful to the librarians and governing bodies of those institutions which have allowed us to consult, cite, and quote from their printed and manuscript holdings, including the Beinecke Library (Yale University), the Bibliothèque Nationale (Paris), the Bibliothèque publique et universitaire (Geneva), the Bibliothèque de la Sorbonne (Paris), the British Library (London), the British Library Lending Division (Boston Spa), the Bodleian Library (Oxford), Boston Public Library, the Brotherton Library (University of Leeds), Cambridge University Library, the Codrington Library, All Souls College (Oxford), the Dyce Library of the Victoria and Albert Museum (London), Edinburgh University Library, Emmanuel College Library (Cambridge), the Folger Shakespeare Library (Washington), Glasgow University Library, the Hallward Library (University of Nottingham), Hatfield House Library (Hatfield), the Houghton Library (Harvard), the Huntington Library (California), the John Rylands Library (Manchester), Kent County Archive (Maidstone), the Kroch Library (Cornell University), Lambeth Palace Library (London), the Lee Library (Brigham Young University), the Leeds Library (Leeds), Leeds Public Library, the Library of the Inner Temple (London), Longleat

House Library (Warminster), Magdalen College Library (Oxford), the National Library of Wales (Aberystwyth), the National Library of Scotland (Edinburgh), the Newberry Library (Chicago), the New York Public Library, the Pierpont Morgan Library (New York), the Public Record Office (London), The Queen's College Library (Oxford), the Robert Taylor Collection (Princeton), Trinity College Library (Cambridge), Trinity College Library (Dublin), the University of Illinois Library, Wadham College Library (Oxford), Wellesley College Library (Massachusetts), and the Wilson Library (University of North Carolina at Chapel Hill). We also wish to thank specifically the following for allowing us unrestricted access to their manuscripts of the Sidney *Psalmes*: the librarians of the Bibliothèque de la Sorbonne, the Bodleian Library, the British Library, the Huntington Library, and the National Library of Wales; and the Provost and Fellows of Queen's College (Oxford), the Masters and Fellows of Trinity College (Cambridge), and the Warden and Fellows of Wadham College (Oxford).

The generosity of several private owners of manuscripts has also made this edition possible. In particular, we wish to thank the following: (the late) Viscount De L'Isle, VC, KG, and the present Viscount De L'Isle, MBE, for allowing us to use their manuscript of the Sidney *Psalmes* (MS *A*) as our copy-text; Dr Bent E. Juel-Jensen, DM, FRCP, for allowing us to print the unique texts of the two dedicatory poems ('Even now that Care' and 'To the Angell Spirit') from the Tixall MS; and Robert H. Schaffner of Johannesburg for granting access to his manuscript of the *Psalmes* (MS *Q*). We have also incurred similiar debts in collecting together the Countess of Pembroke's correspondence. Permission to print these letters has been granted by the Marquess of Bath (Longleat House, Warminster, Letter I), the Marquess of Salisbury (Hatfield House, Hatfield, Letters VII, VIII, IX, X, XVI), the British Library (Letters II, IV, XI, XII, XIII, XIV), Lambeth Palace Library (Letters III and XV), the Public Record Office (Letter VI), and the Robert Taylor Collection, Princeton University (Letter V). We are also grateful to the Masters and Bench of the Inner Temple for permission to print the Countess of Pembroke's translation of Petrarch's *The Triumph of Death*.

We have incurred numerous obligations to other individuals while working on this edition. Our research would have been impossible without the pioneering scholarship of William A. Ringler, Jr., and John Rathmell on the manuscripts of the Sidney *Psalmes*; and in other areas, we are no less indebted to the work of those many scholars whose works are cited in this edition. We are grateful to all those who have replied to our queries, read typescript drafts, and guided our research. Their contributions to this edition, so freely given, have been immense. These scholars include Gavin Alexander, Peter Beal, Elaine Beilin, L. Glenn Black, Patrick Cheney, Pamela Clements, James A. Devereux, SJ, Sir William Dugdale, Celia Diamond, Katherine Duncan-Jones, Kate Forhan, John Gouws, Elizabeth Hageman, Kate Harris, W. Speed Hill, Christopher Hodgkins, Martin Kauffmann, Hilton Kelliher, William Kennedy, Roger Kuin, Carole Levin, Harold Love, William A. McQueen, Steven W. May, Mary Meany, Jerry Mills, Richard A. Muller, Luther Peterson, Oliver Pickering, John Pitcher, Anne Prescott, John Rathmell, Emma Rees, Josephine Roberts, Michael Sham, John T. Shawcross, Christopher Sheppard, Victor Skretkowicz, Marvin Spevack, Theodore Steinberg, David Steinmetz, Deborah Hannay Sunoo, Janet Todd, Germaine Warkentin, Timothy Wengert, Franklin Williams, Robin Harcourt Williams, Susanne Woods, and Henry Woudhuysen. We are also much indebted to Frances Whistler, Jason Freeman, and Andrew Lockett, all of the Oxford University Press, for their expert guidance and support. In preparing the typescript for printing, we are very grateful to have had the benefit of the skills and advice of our copy-editor, Dorothy McCarthy. Invaluable personal assistance of various other kinds has been offered to us by Anthony Aycock, Robert Ballance, Bernadette Barnett, Carol Boggess, Geraldine Brennan, Mary W. Dickson, Dragan Djukic, Betty F. Hughes, Paul and Florence Kinnamon, Harold McDonald, Jr., Jason Ross Martin, James and Elaine Moorefield, Rebeccah K. Neff, Mattie E. Newsom, James and Cynthia Phillips, Jeanette Proffitt, Barbara Robinson, Thomas Sawyer, and Eric Smith. Inevitably, we may have inadvertently omitted others from this list. To these, we both readily apologize and offer our thanks. Any errors remaining in this edition are entirely the responsibility of its editors.

Two individuals have played key roles in the production of this edition. David Hannay has been a constant and reliable source of expert advice on all matters concerning the technical production of the typescript and computer disks for this edition. Elizabeth Paget of the School of English, University of Leeds, has over several years assimilated the challenges of the various (and sometimes incompatible) computer programs used by the editors, to produce with unfailing efficiency, expertise, and good humour the numerous drafts, as well as the final typescript and disk versions, of this edition. In a very real sense, the editors readily acknowledge that David Hannay and Elizabeth Paget have been no mere occasional contributors but rather constant and invaluable collaborators in this literary project. This sense of collaborative endeavour has also been of crucial importance to the three editors of this edition, which has relied heavily on the new technology and rapid interchange of communications offered by the Internet. As we have regularly exchanged texts and drafts by computer disk, and then discussed them by e-mail and fax, so our geographical distance from one another has been counterbalanced by the immediacy of our electronic communications. Just as the writings of the Countess of Pembroke owed much to her shared intellectual involvements with her brother, Sir Philip Sidney, so it is perhaps fitting that the first complete edition of her literary works is the product, from the point of view of its three editors at least, of a rewarding and stimulating collaboration. This edition is dedicated to our families and to the memory of Paul J. Kinnamon, Florence Newsom Kinnamon, William John Barnett, Kenneth Patterson, Emma Rogers Hannay, and George A. Hannay.

M. P. H.	N. J. K.	M. G. B.
Westerlo,	*Mars Hill,*	*Leeds,*
New York	*North Carolina*	*Yorkshire*

REFERENCES AND ABBREVIATIONS

Aggas, *Defence* — Philippe de Mornay, *The Defence of Death. Contayning a Most Excellent Discourse Written in Frenche. And Doone into English by E. A[ggas]* (1576), *STC* 18136.

APC — *Acts of the Privy Council.*

Arundel Harington MS — *The Arundel Harington Manuscript of Tudor Poetry*, ed. Ruth Hughey (Columbus, Ohio: Ohio State UP, 1960).

Attridge, *Syllables* — Derek Attridge, *Well-Weighed Syllables: Elizabethan Verse in Classical Metres* (London: Cambridge UP, 1974).

Aubrey, *Brief Lives* — *Aubrey's Brief Lives*, ed. Oliver Lawson Dick (London: Secker & Warburg, 1949).

Barnes, *P and P*, ed. Doyno — Barnabe Barnes, *Parthenophil and Parthenophe 1593*, ed. Victor A. Doyno (Carbondale: Southern Illinois UP, 1971).

Baxter, *Ouránia* — Nathaniel Baxter, *Sir Philip Sydneys Ouránia, that is, Endimions Song and Tragedie. Containing all Philosophie* (1606), *STC* 1598.

BC — *The Book Collector*

Beal — Peter George Beal, *Index of English Literary Manuscripts, I: 1450–1625*, 2 vols. (London: Mansell, 1980).

Beilin, *Redeeming Eve* — Elaine Beilin, *Redeeming Eve: Women Writers of the English Renaissance* (Princeton: Princeton UP, 1987).

Bèze — Théodore de Bèze, *The Psalmes of David, truly opened and explaned by paraphrasis, according to the right sense of everie Psalme.* Trans. Anthony Gilby (1581), *STC* 2033.

Bishops' Bible — *The holie bible conteynyng the olde testament and the newe* (1568), *STC* 2099.

BL — British Library.

Bloch, *Spelling* — Chana Bloch, *Spelling the Word: George Herbert and the Bible* (Berkeley: U of California P, 1985).

Bodenham, *Bel-vedére* — John Bodenham, *Bel-vedére or the Garden of the Muses*, [ed.], A. M.[unday?] (1600), *STC* 3189.

Brennan (D.Phil. diss.)   Michael G. Brennan, 'The Literary Patronage of the Herbert Family, Earls of Pembroke, 1550–1640', University of Oxford, D.Phil. diss., 1982.

Brennan, *Literary Patronage*   Michael G. Brennan, *Literary Patronage in the English Renaissance: The Pembroke Family* (London: Routledge, 1988).

Breton, *Pilgrimage*   Nicholas Breton, *The Pilgrimage to Paradise, Joyned with the Countesse of Penbrookes Love* (Oxford, 1592), *STC* 3683.

Breton, *Poems*   *Nicholas Breton Poems not Hitherto Reprinted*, ed. Jean Robertson (Liverpool: Liverpool UP, 1967).

Breton, *Wits Trenchmour*   Nicholas Breton, *Wits Trenchmour* (1597), *STC* 3713.

Breton, *Works*   *The Works in Verse and Prose of Nicholas Breton*, ed. Alexander B. Grosart (1879; rpt. New York: AMS P, 1966).

Briquet   Charles Moïse Briquet, *Les Filigranes: Dictionnaire historique des marques du papier dès leur apparition vers 1282 jusqu'en 1600*, 4 vols. (2nd edn., Leipzig: Hiersemann, 1923).

Bullough, *Sources*   Geoffrey Bullough, *Narrative and Dramatic Sources of Shakespeare* (New York: Columbia UP, 1966).

Buxton, *Sidney*   E. M. John Buxton, *Sir Philip Sidney and the English Renaissance* (London: Macmillan, 1954; rpt. 1964).

Calvin   *The Psalms of David and others. With M. John Calvins Commentaries*, trans. Arthur Golding (1571), *STC* 4395.

Camden, *Historie*   William Camden, *The Historie of the Most Renowned and Victorious Princesse Elizabeth ...Composed by way of Annals*, trans R. N.[orton] (1630), *STC* 4500.

Cary, *Mariam*   Lady Elizabeth Cary (Carey, Carew), *The Tragedie of Mariam, the Faire Queene of Jewry* (1613), *STC* 4613.

Cary, *Mariam*, ed. Weller and Ferguson   Elizabeth Cary, *The Lady Falkland, The Tragedy of Mariam the Fair Queen of Jewry with The Lady Falkland Her Life by one of her daughters*, ed. Barry Weller and Margaret W. Ferguson (Berkeley: U of California P, 1994).

Chamberlain, *Letters* The Letters of John Chamberlain, ed. Norman Egbert McClure, 2 vols. (Philadelphia: American Philosophical Society, 1939; rpt. Westport, Conn.: Greenwood P, 1979).

Churchyard, *Conceit* Thomas Churchyard, *A Pleasant Conceit penned in verse. Collourably sette out, and humblie presented on New-yeeres day last, to the Queenes Majestie at Hampton Court* (1593), *STC* 5248.

Constable, *Poems* The Poems and Sonnets of Henry Constable, ed. John Gray (London: Ballantyne P, 1897).

Creation of a Legend *Sir Philip Sidney: 1586 and the Creation of a Legend*, ed. Jan Van Dorsten, Dominic Baker-Smith, and Arthur F. Kinney (Leiden: J. J. Brill and Leiden UP, 1986).

Crowley Robert Crowley, *The Psalter of David Newely Translated into English metre* (1549), *STC* 2725.

CSP *Calendar of State Papers.*

Daniel, *Delia* Samuel Daniel, *Delia. Contayning Certayne Sonnets* (1592), *STC* 6253.

Daniel, *Delia & Cleopatra* Samuel Daniel, *Delia and Rosamond Augmented. Cleopatra* (1594), *STC* 6254.

Daniel, *Philotas* Samuel Daniel, *Certaine Small Poems lately printed: with the tragedie of Philotas* (1605), *STC* 6239.

Davies, *Muses Sacrifice* John Davies, *The Muses Sacrifice, or Divine Meditations* (1612), *STC* 6338.

Davies, *Poems* The Poems of Sir John Davies, ed. Robert Krueger (Oxford: Clarendon P, 1975).

Davies, *Works* The Complete Works of John Davies of Hereford, ed. Alexander B. Grosart (Edinburgh: Edinburgh UP, 1878).

Davison, *Rapsody* Francis Davison (ed.), *A Poetical Rapsody Containing Diverse Sonnets, Odes, Elegies, Madrigalls, and other Poesies, both in Rime, and Measured Verse* (1602), *STC* 6373.

De L'Isle MS De L'Isle and Dudley Papers, Penshurst Place, Kent and Kent County Records Office.

DNB *Dictionary of National Biography.*

Donne, *Divine Poems* John Donne: The Divine Poems, ed. Helen Gardner (Oxford: Clarendon P, 1952).

Drayton, *Works* The Works of Michael Drayton, ed. J. William Hebel. Introductions, notes, and variant readings, ed. Kathleen Tillotson and Bernard Newdigate, 5 vols. (Oxford: Basil Blackwell, 1931–41).

EHR   *English Historical Review.*

ELH   *English Literary History.*

ELR   *English Literary Renaissance.*

England   Martha Winburn England, 'Sir Philip Sidney and François Perrot de Méssières: The Verse Versions of the Psalms', *Bulletin of the New York Public Library* 75 (1971), 30–54, 101–10.

Esplin (Ph.D. diss.)   Ross Stolworthy Esplin, 'The Emerging Legend of Sir Philip Sidney 1586–1652', University of Utah, Ph.D. diss., 1970.

Fisken, 'Education'   Beth Wynne Fisken, 'Mary Sidney's *Psalmes*: Education and Wisdom', in *Silent but for the Word*, 166–83.

Fisken, 'Parody'   Beth Wynne Fisken, ' "The Art of Sacred Parody" in Mary Sidney's *Psalmes*', *Tulsa Studies in Women's Literature* 8 (1989), 223–9.

Fisken, 'World of Words'   ' "To the Angell spirit . . . ": Mary Sidney's Entry into the "World of Words" ', in *Renaissance Englishwoman*, 263–75.

Fraunce, *Emanuel*   Abraham Fraunce, *The Countesse of Pembrokes Emanuel* (1591), *STC* 11339.

Fraunce, *Ivychurch*   Abraham Fraunce, *The Countesse of Pembrokes Ivychurch. Containing the Affectionate life, and unfortunate death of Phillis and Amyntas: That in a Pastorall; This in a Funerall; both in English Hexameters* (1591), *STC* 11340.

Fraunce, *Ivychurch. Third Part*   Abraham Fraunce, *The Third Part of the Countesse of Pembrokes Ivychurch. Entitul'd Amintas Dale. Wherein are the most conceited tales of the Pagan Gods in English Hexameters together with their auncient descriptions and Philosophicall explications* (1592), *STC* 11341.

Freer, *Music*   Coburn Freer, *Music for a King: George Herbert's Style and the Metrical Psalms* (Baltimore: Johns Hopkins UP, 1972).

Geneva   *The Bible and Holy Scriptures* (Geneva, 1560). Facsimile. (Madison: U of Wisconsin P, 1969).

Great Bible   *The byble in Englysche, that is to saye the content of all the holy scrypture* [First Great

Bible]. Revised by M. Coverdale (1539), *STC* 2068.

Greville, *Prose Works*   *The Prose Works of Fulke Greville, Lord Brooke*, ed. John Gouws (Oxford: Clarendon P, 1986).

Hannay, *Philip's Phoenix*   Margaret P. Hannay, *Philip's Phoenix: Mary Sidney, Countess of Pembroke* (New York and Oxford: Oxford UP, 1990).

Harington, *Letters*   John Harington, *The Letters and Epigrams of Sir John Harington*, ed. Norman Egbert McClure (Philadelphia: U of Penn. P, 1930).

Harvey, *Letter*   Gabriel Harvey, *A New Letter of Notable Contents. With a Straunge Sonet, intituled Gorgon, or the wonderful yeare* (1593), *STC* 12902.

Harvey, *Pierces Supererogation*   Gabriel Harvey, *Pierces Supererogation or A New Prayse of the Old Asse. A Preparative to certaine larger Discourses, intituled Nashes S. Fame* (1593), *STC* 12903.

Harvey, *Works*   *The Works of Gabriel Harvey, D.C.L.*, ed. Alexander B. Grosart (1888; rpt. New York: AMS P, 1966).

Heawood   Edward Heawood, *Watermarks, Mainly of the 17th and 18th Centuries*, Paper Publication Society (Hilversum, 1950).

Heywood, *Gynaikeion*   Thomas Heywood, *[Gynaikeion]: or, Nine Bookes of Various History. Concerning Women* (1624), *STC* 13326.

Hiller   Geoffrey G. Hiller, ' "Where thou doost live, there let all graces be": Images of the Renaissance Woman Patron in Her House and Rural Domain', *Cahiers Elizabèthains* 40 (1991), 37–52.

HLB   *Harvard Library Bulletin.*

HLQ   *Huntington Library Quarterly.*

HMC   Historical Manuscripts Commission.

Howell, *Devises*   Thomas Howell, *Howell his Devises for his owne Exercise, and his Friends Pleasure* (1581), *STC* 13875.

Howell, *Devises*, ed. Raleigh   *Howell's Devises. 1581*, ed. Walter Raleigh (Oxford: Clarendon P, 1906).

Hunnis   William Hunnis, *Psalmes chosen out of the Psalter of David, and drawen fourth into English meter by William Hunnis* (1550), *STC* 2727.

JEGP	*Journal of English and Germanic Philology.*
JES	*Journal of European Studies.*
JMRS	*Journal of Medieval and Renaissance Studies.*
Jonson, *Poems*	*Ben Jonson: The Complete Poems*, ed. George Parfitt (New Haven: Yale UP, 1982).
Kay, *Melodious Tears*	Dennis Kay, *Melodious Tears: the English Funeral Elegy from Spenser to Milton* (Oxford: Clarendon P, 1990).
King, *Iconography*	John N. King, *Tudor Royal Iconography* (Princeton: Princeton UP, 1989).
King, *Reformation*	John N. King, *English Reformation Literature: The Tudor Origins of the Protestant Tradition* (Princeton: Princeton UP, 1982).
Lamb, *Gender*	Mary Ellen Lamb, *Gender and Authorship in the Sidney Circle* (Madison: U of Wisconsin P, 1990).
Lamb, 'Myth'	Mary Ellen Lamb, 'The Myth of the Countess of Pembroke: The Dramatic Circle', *Yearbook of English Studies* 11 (1981), 194–202.
Lamb, 'Patronage'	Mary Ellen Lamb, 'The Countess of Pembroke's Patronage', *ELR* 12 (1982), 162–79.
Lamb (Ph.D. diss.)	Mary Ellen Lamb, 'The Countess of Pembroke's Patronage', Columbia U, Ph.D. diss., 1976.
Lanyer, *Poems*	*The Poems of Aemilia Lanyer: Salve Deus Rex Judaeorum*, ed. Susanne Woods (New York: Oxford UP, 1993).
Lanyer, *Salve Deus*	Aemilia Lanyer, *Salve Deus rex Judæorum. Containing, the passion of Christ* (1611), *STC* 15227.
Leaver, '*Ghoostly Psalmes*'	Robin Leaver, '*Ghoostly Psalmes and Spirituall Songes*': *English and Dutch Metrical Psalms from Coverdale to Utenhove 1535–1566* (Oxford: Clarendon P, 1991).
Lewalski, *Protestant Poetics*	Barbara Kiefer Lewalski, *Protestant Poetics and the Seventeenth-Century Religious Lyric* (Princeton: Princeton UP, 1979).
Lewalski, *Writing Women*	Barbara Kiefer Lewalski, *Writing Women in Jacobean England* (Cambridge, Mass.: Harvard UP, 1993).
Lok	Anne Lok [Prowse], 'A Meditation of a Penitent Sinner: Written in Maner of a Paraphrase upon the 51. Psalme of David', in

	Sermons of John Calvin, upon the Songe that Ezechias made after he had bene sicke and afflicted by the hand of God, trans. Anne Lok (1560), *STC* 4450.
Lok, *Ecclesiastes*	Henry Lok, *Ecclesiastes, otherwise called the Preacher. Containing Salomons Sermons or Commentaries* (1597), *STC* 16696.
Love, *Scribal Publication*	Harold Love, *Scribal Publication in Seventeenth-Century England* (Oxford: Clarendon P, 1993).
Martz, *Meditation*	Louis Martz, *Poetry of Meditation* (New Haven: Yale UP, 1962).
May, *Courtier Poets*	Steven W. May, *The Elizabethan Courtier Poets: The Poems and Their Contexts* (Columbia: U of Missouri P, 1991).
Mind's Melodie	Alexander Montgomerie, *The Mindes Melodie, Contayning Certayne Psalmes of the Kinglie Prophet David applyed to a new pleasant tune* (Edinburgh, 1605), *STC* 18051.
MLN	*Modern Language Notes.*
Moffet, *Nobilis*	Thomas Moffet, *Nobilis or a View of the Life and Death of a Sidney and Lessus Lugubris*, ed. Virgil B. Heltzel and Hoyt H. Hudson (San Marino, Calif.: Huntington Library, 1940).
Moffet, *Silkewormes*	Thomas Moffet, *The Silkewormes and their Flies: Lively described in verse, by T.M. a Countrie Farmar, and an apprentice in Physicke* (1599), *STC* 17994.
Montgomery, *Symmetry*	Robert L. Montgomery, Jr., *Symmetry and Sense: The Poetry of Sir Philip Sidney* (Austin: U of Texas P, 1961).
Morton (Ph.D. diss.)	Lynn Moorhead Morton, ' "Vertue cladde in constant love's attire": The Countess of Pembroke as a Model for Renaissance Women Writers', U of South Carolina, Ph.D. diss., 1993.
N&Q	*Notes & Queries.*
New Ways	*New Ways of Looking at Old Texts: Papers of the Renaissance English Text Society, 1985–91*, ed. W. Speed Hill, Medieval and Renaissance Texts and Studies, in conjunction with the Renaissance English Text Society (Binghamton, NY, 1993).

NLH	*New Literary History*
North	Plutarch, *The lives of the noble Grecians and Romanes. Translated out of Greeke into French by J. Amyot, out of French by T. North* (1579), *STC* 20065.
OED	*The Oxford English Dictionary*, 2nd edn., prepared by J. A. Simpson and E. S. C. Weiner, 2 vols. (Oxford: Clarendon P, 1989).
Old Version	*The whole booke of psalmes collected into English meter by Thomas Sternhold, J. Hopkins and others* (Geneva, 1569), *STC* 2440.
Osborne, *Memoires*	Francis Osborne, *Historical Memoires on the Reigns of Queen Elizabeth and King James* (1683), Wing O515.
Parker	Matthew Parker, *The Whole psalter translated into English Metre, which contayneth an hundreth and fifty Psalmes* (1575), *STC* 2729.
Parry, *Victoria Christiana*	Henry Parry, *Victoria Christiana* (1594), *STC* 19336.
PBSA	*Papers of the Bibliographical Society of America.*
PMLA	*Publications of the Modern Language Association of America.*
PQ	*Philological Quarterly.*
Prescott, *French Poets*	Anne Lake Prescott, *French Poets and the English Renaissance: Studies in Fame and Transformation* (New Haven: Yale UP, 1978).
PRO	Public Records Office.
Psaumes	Clément Marot and Théodore de Bèze, *Les Psaumes de David mis en rime Francoise* (Geneva, 1562).
Rathmell (Ph.D. diss.)	John C. A. Rathmell, 'A Critical Edition of the Psalms of Sir Philip Sidney and the Countess of Pembroke', University of Cambridge, Ph.D. diss., 1964.
Renaissance Englishwoman	*The Renaissance Englishwoman in Print: Counterbalancing the Canon*, ed. Anne M. Haselkorn and Betty S. Travitsky (Amherst: U of Massachusetts P, 1990).
RES	*Review of English Studies.*
Rosenberg, *Leicester*	Eleanor Rosenberg, *Leicester: Patron of Letters* (New York: Columbia UP, 1955).
RQ	*Renaissance Quarterly.*

Schanzer, *Problem Plays*	Ernest Schanzer, *The Problem Plays of Shakespeare: A Study of 'Julius Caesar', 'Measure for Measure', 'Antony and Cleopatra'* (London: Routledge & Kegan Paul, 1963).
SEL	*Studies in English Literature 1500–1900.*
Shakespeare, *Works*	*William Shakespeare: The Complete Works*, ed. Stanley Wells and Gary Taylor (Oxford: Clarendon P, 1986).
Sidney, *Arcadia*	*The Countesse of Pembrokes Arcadia. Written by Sir Philip Sidney Knight. Now since the first edition augmented and ended* (1593), STC 22540.
Sidney, *Astrophel*	*Sir P.S. His Astrophel and Stella. Wherein the excellence of sweete Poesie is concluded* (1591), STC 22536.
Sidney, *Miscellaneous Prose*	*Miscellaneous Prose of Sir Philip Sidney*, ed. Katherine Duncan-Jones and Jan van Dorsten (Oxford: Clarendon P, 1973).
Sidney, *New Arcadia*	*The Countess of Pembrokes Arcadia [The New Arcadia]*, ed. Victor Skretkowicz (Oxford: Clarendon P, 1987).
Sidney, *Old Arcadia*	*The Countess of Pembrokes Arcadia [The Old Arcadia]*, ed. Jean Robertson (Oxford: Clarendon P, 1973).
Sidney, *Poems*	*The Poems of Sir Philip Sidney.* ed. William A. Ringler, Jr. (Oxford: Clarendon P, 1962).
Sidney, *Psalms*	*The Psalms of Sir Philip Sidney and the Countess of Pembroke*, ed. J. C. A. Rathmell (New York: New York UP, 1963).
Sidney, Mary. *Antonie*, ed. Freer	*The Tragedy of Antony by Robert Garnier. Translated by Mary Herbert, Countess of Pembroke*, ed. Coburn Freer, in *Women Writers*, 481–521.
Sidney, Mary. *Antonie*, ed. Luce	*The Countess of Pembroke's Antonie. 1592*, ed. Alice Luce (Weimar: Verlag von Emil Felber, 1897).
Sidney, Mary. *Discourse*, ed. Bornstein	*The Countess of Pembroke's Translation of Philippe de Mornay's Discourse of Life and Death*, ed. Diane Bornstein (Detroit: Michigan Consortium for Medieval and Early Modern Studies, 1983).
Sidney, Mary. *Triumph*	*The Triumph of Death and Other Unpublished and Uncollected Poems by Mary Sidney,*

	Countess of Pembroke (1561–1621), ed. Gary F. Waller (Salzburg: U of Salzburg, 1977).
Sidney, Robert. *Poems*	*The Poems of Robert Sidney*, ed. P. J. Croft (Oxford: Clarendon P, 1984).
Silent but for the Word	*Silent but for the Word: Tudor Women as Patrons, Translators, and Writers of Religious Works*, ed. Margaret P. Hannay (Kent, Ohio: Kent UP, 1985).
SP	State Papers.
SP	*Studies in Philology*.
Spenser, *Astrophel*	Edmund Spenser, *Astrophel. A Pastorall Elegie upon the death of the most Noble and valorous Knight, Sir Philip Sidney* (1595), STC 23077.
Spenser, *Colin Clouts*	Edmund Spenser, *Colin Clouts Come Home Againe* (1595), STC 23077.
Spenser, *Complaints*	Edmund Spenser, *Complaints. Containing sundrie small poemes of the worlds vanitie* (1591), STC 23078.
Spenser, *Faerie Queene*	Edmund Spenser, *The Faerie Queene* (1590), STC 23080.
Spenser, *Mother Hubberds Tale*	Edmund Spenser, *Prosopopoia. Or Mother Hubberds Tale* (1591), STC 23078.
Spenser: Poetical Works	*Spenser: Poetical Works*, ed. J. C. Smith and E. de Selincourt (Oxford: Oxford UP, 1912; rpt. 1983).
Spenser, *Shepheardes Calender*	Edmund Spenser, *The Shepheardes Calender* (1579), STC 23089.
Spevack	*A New Variorum Edition of Shakespeare: Antony and Cleopatra*, ed. Marvin Spevack (New York: MLA, 1990).
STC	*A Short-Title Catalogue of Books Printed in England, Scotland, & Ireland...1475–1640*, completed by A. W. Pollard and G. R. Redgrave, 2nd edn. revised & enlarged by W. A. Jackson, F. S. Ferguson, and K. F. Pantzer, *Vol. I, A–H* (London: The Bibliographical Society, 1986), *Vol. II, I–Z* (1976).
Strigelius	Victorinus Strigelius, *A Third Proceeding in the Harmony of King Davids Harp* [Psalms 45–61]. Trans. Richard Robinson (1595), STC 23361.
Taffin, *Children of God*	Jean Taffin, *Of the Markes of the Children of God, and of their Comforts in Afflictions...*

	Overseene againe and augmented by the Author, and translated out of French by Anne Prowse (1590), *STC* 23652.
TLS	*Times Literary Supplement.*
Vatablus	*Liber Psalmorum Davidis. Annotationes in eosdem ex Hebraeorum commentariis* (Paris, 1546).
Wall, *Gender*	Wendy Wall, *The Imprint of Gender: Authorship and Publication in the English Renaissance* (Ithaca: Cornell UP, 1993).
Waller, *Mary Sidney*	Gary Waller, *Mary Sidney, Countess of Pembroke: A Critical Study of Her Writings and Literary Milieu* (Salzburg: U of Salzburg, 1979).
Watson, *Amintae Gaudia*	Thomas Watson, *Amintae Gaudia* (1592), *STC* 25117.
Wing	*Short-Title Catalogue of Books Printed in England, Scotland, Ireland, Wales, and British America and of English Books Printed in Other Countries 1641–1700*, compiled by D. Wing, 3 vols. (New York: Index Society, Columbia UP, 1945–51; revised edn. New York: Index Society, Modern Language Association of America, 1972–88).
Witherspoon, *Garnier*	Alexander Maclaren Witherspoon, *The Influence of Robert Garnier on Elizabethan Drama* (New Haven: Yale UP, 1924).
Women in the Middle Ages	*Women in the Middle Ages and Renaissance: Literary and Historical Perspectives*, ed. Mary Beth Rose (Syracuse: Syracuse UP, 1986).
Women Writers	*Women Writers of the Renaissance and Reformation*, ed. Katharina M. Wilson (Athens, Ga: U of Georgia P, 1987).
Woods, *Natural Emphasis*	Susanne Woods, *Natural Emphasis: English Versification from Chaucer to Dryden* (San Marino, Calif.: Huntington Library, 1984).
Wroth, *Love's Victory*	*Lady Mary Wroth's Love's Victōry. The Penshurst Manuscript*, ed. Michael G. Brennan (London: The Roxburghe Club, 1988).
Wroth, *Poems*	*The Poems of Lady Mary Wroth*, ed. Josephine A. Roberts (Baton Rouge: U of Louisiana P, 1983).
Wroth, *Urania*	Mary Wroth, *The Countesse of Mountgomeries URANIA. Written by the right honourable the*

Lady MARY WROATH. Daughter to the right Noble Robert Earle of Leicester. And Neece to the ever famous, and renowned Sr. Phillip Sidney Knight. And to the most exelent Lady Mary Countesse of Pembroke Late Deceased (1621), *STC* 26051.

Wroth, *Urania*, ed. Roberts   *The First Part of The Countess of Montgomery's Urania by Lady Mary Wroth*, ed. Josephine A. Roberts (Binghamton, NY: MRTS, 1995).

Wyatt   Thomas Wyatt, *Certayne psalmes chosen out of the psalter of David, commonly called thee vii. penytentiall Psalmes* (1549), *STC* 2726.

Yates, *Astraea*   Frances A. Yates: *Astraea: The Imperial Theme in the Sixteenth Century* (London: Routledge & Kegan Paul, 1975; rpt. Peregrine Books, 1977).

Young, *Mary Sidney*   Frances Berkeley Young, *Mary Sidney, Countess of Pembroke* (London: David Nutt, 1912).

Zim, *Psalms*   Rivkah Zim, *English Metrical Psalms: Poetry as Praise and Prayer, 1535–1601* (Cambridge: Cambridge UP, 1987).

EDITORIAL PROCEDURE

Transcription

1. The original spelling and punctuation of the copy-texts have been retained except for 'long s', 'VV' and 'vv' used for 'W' and 'w', typographical ligatures (excluding digraphs, which are preserved), and the abbreviations noted below, which have been silently expanded.

2. The use of 'i', 'j', 'u', and 'v' has been regularized, except where specific forms of these letters have been used in acrostics (e.g. Psalm 117. 4). Incidental use of capitals within words has also been regularized.

3. Deletions are printed in the textual notes within angle brackets: < >.

4. Interpolations are printed in the textual notes within slashes: \ /.

5. In MS *A* of the *Psalmes* all four sides of the pages are ruled in red, with a second rule used to align the text on the left. However, the gold majuscules used in the MS often extend to the left of this second rule so that all subsequent lines (including rhyming lines) are slightly indented. These left-hand indentations have been regularized in the texts.

6. All other departures from the copy-texts are acknowledged in the textual notes and the commentary; cruces are explained in the commentary; because many of the letters are holographs, the interpolations and deletions in the correspondence have been retained in the text (and printed in superscript) rather than moved to the textual notes.

Abbreviations

Abbreviations have been silently expanded, except for special cases in the textual notes where the relationship of particular manuscripts would otherwise be obscured.

1. Standard abbreviations:
   ampersand;
   tilde used for 'n' and 'm';
   tilde used for 'i' in '-cion';
   the symbol resembling a figure eight used in the manuscripts for final 'es';

superscripted letters such as 'th' (in 'with'), 'ch' (in 'which'), 'r' (in 'Sir', 'our', 'your', '-our'), 't' (in 'Knight');

superscripted letters (such as 't' and 'e') used with 'y' for words like 'that' and 'the' (the latter is also substituted for 'ye' where Woodforde uses it for the definite article in his transcript of the *Psalmes*, MS *B*).

2. Additional scribal abbreviations:

'Psal:' and 'Ps.' for 'Psalm' in MSS *A* and *B*, respectively (and variously in other manuscripts);

forms used by Woodforde in MS *B*: 'exp.' for 'expunged', 'Q' for 'quære', 'v' with a bisecting virgule for 'verse';

the special character used for '-que' in Latin texts;

two abbreviations used more than once in the endorsements to the letters: 'ex.' for 'examination' and 'touch.' for 'touching'.

3. Additional abbreviations, especially in the holograph letters:

superscripted letters such as 'w' used with 'y' for 'yow' (in addition to superscripted 'r' in 'yowr', as in the scribal practice cited above; the forms with 'w' are the preferred holograph spellings);

the special characters used for 'pre-' and 'pro-' and similar combinations involving 'p' and 'r';

'ld', 'Ld', 'L:', 'Lo:' and superscripted 'rd' (with 'L') used for 'lord' and 'lordship', depending on context;

superscripted 'pe' with 'L' for 'Lordship';

superscripted 'tie', 'ty' for 'Majesty' and 'ties' for 'Majesty's';

'Ph:' for 'Philip' (as also in some title pages of the *Psalmes* manuscripts).

Textual Notes

1. Limitations of space normally allow only verbal variants in manuscripts or editions other than the copy-texts to be reported in the textual notes; most variations in spelling, punctuation, indentation, and paragraphing are thus ignored. This principle applies especially to the *Psalmes* (and in particular to MS *I*, with its highly eccentric spelling, which is discussed in 'Manuscripts of the *Psalmes*'); fully reporting the divergences in all seventeen of the extant copies would amount to a nearly complete transcription of each of the manuscripts (the choice of MS *A* as the copy-text for the *Psalmes* is justified in 'Relationship of the Texts of the *Psalmes*'):

all substantive variants involving single words, phrases, and lines are noted, but obvious scribal errors (e.g. 'th' for 'the' in 73. 49

and 'strangr' for the rhyme word 'strange' in 68. 42 [variant version], MS *I*, and 'rembraunce' for 'remembrance' in 45. 60, MS *H*) and routine, isolated corrections (e.g. 'right' corrected to 'ritch' in 49. 34, MS *K*) are usually ignored;

the main principle used in selecting substantive variants to report is whether a word is given a separate, full entry in the *OED* in its regular form (e.g. 'sperit' is treated as simply another spelling of 'spirit', but 'sprite' or 'spright' is considered to be a distinct form and is thus cited as a substantive variant in the textual notes); however, we do not apply the principle mechanically and uncritically, but are guided by the context and sources of each work and thus generally ignore unambiguous spelling variants such as 'be' and 'bee', 'we' and 'wee', since citing them would unnecessarily swell the textual notes;

to ensure the reporting of the complex transmission history of the *Psalmes*, including the late rhymed versions of Psalms 120 to 127, we discuss the seventeen extant manuscripts in 'Relationship of the Texts of the *Psalmes*' and provide a multi-level presentation of the texts themselves: the paraphrases as preserved in MS *A*, the copy-text, with all emendations reported in the textual notes and noted in the commentary; significant variants in the other manuscripts reported in the textual notes and, when it is useful to do so, noted in the commentary; and the alternative Psalm paraphrases, whether authorial or not, preserved in manuscripts other than *A*, printed in their entirety;

other differences are cited to help establish the text in the copy-texts or to clarify the relationship of the various editions and manuscripts (to the copy-texts and to one another);

cruces are fully described;

emendations are noted and justified in the commentary (previous editors are cited for support in the commentary when necessary, but disagreements are usually passed over in silence);

lack of punctuation is indicated by a caret, and repeated text is normally replaced by a tilde, except for complex cases (especially involving other variants), such as Pss. 64. 26, 69. 103, and 78. 161;

press variants are discussed in the introductions to the individual works.

2. Handling of the *Psalmes* manuscripts requires additional comment, for not all of them are substantive witnesses:

two manuscripts, *L* and *P*, are ignored because *P* is copied from *L*, which is a copy of *E*;

two others, *F* and *J*, are cited selectively because *J* and Psalms 27–150 in *F* were copied from *A*;

the Greek letter χ represents the members of the χ tradition (*I*, *K*, *O*, *D*, *H*, *Q*, *E*, *L*, *P*, *G*, *M*) when there is no disagreement among them; θ similarly represents *O* and *D*, and σ represents *H*, *Q*, *E*, *L*, and *P*;

we have normally not reported minor variations in spelling (e.g. final 'y' vs. 'ie');

we have not reported in detail the verse numbers which were added later to *K* from the Prayer Book Psalter (even when it is clear that the source of the paraphrase was Geneva or another text) or the rubrics for morning and evening prayer added later to both *K* and *I*; the special features of these and the other *Psalmes* manuscripts are noted in 'Manuscripts of the *Psalmes*';

variants in the alternative Psalms are reported more fully, especially in the case of *G* and *M* because of the doubtful authority of those manuscripts in relation to one another (although *M*, which seems generally to preserve the latest state of the text, has been chosen as the copy-text for the rhymed Psalms 120–7, *G* occasionally appears to be a more reliable witness and is thus reported so that readers may make their own judgements).

Emendation

The need for and method of emendation vary for each work:

'Astrea' and 'Dolefull Lay': Correction of obvious printing errors (including one probable omission) adopted from subsequent editions.

Triumph of Death: Correction of scribal errors based on examination of context and comparison with the Italian text.

'Even now that Care' and 'Angell Spirit': Correction of scribal (and 1623 printing) errors based on examination of context.

Discourse: Silent reversal of turned characters and noted deletion of one obviously mistaken repetition.

Antonius: Silent reversal of turned letters, spacing within words, and font substitution; noted correction of obvious printer's misspellings (including faulty abbreviation of speech prefixes and mistaken punctuation); noted correction of other errors based on examination of context and comparison with the French text.

Psalmes: Correction of scribal errors based on comparison with sources and other manuscripts.

Spelling in the Holograph Letters

The correspondence reveals some distinctive, though not unique, spellings. For instance, 'w' is frequently used for 'u', especially in forms of the second person personal pronoun, hence, our expansion to 'yow' and 'yowr' when those forms are abbreviated. Other examples include the following: retention of 'e' before 'ing' ('loveing', Letter II; 'haveing', V, VII, XII; etc.), spelling of [i] without 'i' ('perceve', I; 'conceved', V, VI; etc.) or 'a' ('leve', IX, XVI; 'Cretur', IX, XV; etc.), use of 'i' for the now standard 'e' ('knowlidg', VII, VIII, XV; 'chaling', VII; 'Inglands', IX), use of 'e' for 'i' ('testemony', V, VII, XV; 'happenes' VII, X, XVI; etc.), use of 'c' for 's' ('beeching', I; 'bace', XII, XV; etc.), use of 's' for 'c' ('presious', VI, IX; 'embrased', VII; 'partisepating', IX; etc.), use of 'w' for 'u' in other words besides 'yow' and 'yowr' ('dowt', II; 'dwe', VIII, X, XV; 'trwth', XIII; etc.), 'oo' for 'ou' in the modal auxiliaries, 'could', 'should', and 'would' ('coold', II, V; 'shoold', V; 'woold', II; etc.), 'bin' and 'bine' for 'been' (I, II, VIII). A number of notable, but again not necessarily unique, spellings occur only once: 'hard' for 'heard' (I), 'faute' for 'fault' (I), 'unusiall' for 'unusual' (II), 'god' for 'good' as in some *Psalmes* manuscripts (II), 'arrant' for 'errand' (V), 'aughter' for 'author' (VIII), 'phelows' (XIII), among others. The use of 'o' for 'u' occurs in 'retorne' for 'return' (V, VI, X) and in 'most' for 'must' (I), which helps solve a crux in line 18 of 'Even now that Care', where 'must' appears as 'most'. Two distinctive features of the Italian hand used in these holographs could have led to scribal confusion: a single-stroke 't' (with the cross stroke made from the left after a long downward swoop without lifting the pen) sometimes resembling a fully looped 'long s', and an angular, cursive 's' sometimes resembling both secretary 'c' and secretary 'r'.

CHRONOLOGY

1554	(30 Nov.) Philip Sidney born
1559–86	Henry Sidney Lord President of the Council of Wales
1561	(27 Oct.) Mary Sidney born at Tickenhall near Bewdley, Worcestershire
1563	(19 Nov.) Robert Sidney born
1564?	Ambrosia Sidney born
1565–71	Henry Sidney Lord Deputy of Ireland
1569	(25 Mar.) Thomas Sidney born
1575–8	Henry Sidney Lord Deputy of Ireland
1575	(22 Feb.) Ambrosia dies at Ludlow
	(Spring) Mary Sidney invited to Elizabeth's court
1577	(21 Apr.) Mary Sidney marries Henry Herbert, 2nd Earl of Pembroke
1580	(8 Apr.) William Herbert born
1581	(15 Oct.) Katherine Herbert born
1583	(9 Mar.) Anne Herbert born
1584	(16 Oct.) Katherine Herbert dies; Philip Herbert born
1586	(5 May) Sir Henry Sidney dies
	(9 Aug.) Lady Mary Dudley Sidney dies
	(17 Oct.) Philip Sidney dies
1587	(16 Feb.) Philip Sidney's funeral
?	(18 Oct.) Mary Sidney (later Lady Wroth) born
1588	(Summer) MSH at Wilton during attack of Spanish armada
	(4 Sept.) Robert Dudley, Earl of Leicester, dies
	(Nov.) MSH and children return to London for Accession Day
1589–1616	Robert Sidney Governor of Flushing
1590	*The Countesse of Pembrokes Arcadia* first published
1592	Publication of *A Discourse of Life and Death* and *Antonius*
1593	MSH produces edition of *The Countesse of Pembrokes Arcadia*
1595	(26 July) Thomas Sidney dies
	Publication of 'The Dolefull Lay' in *Astrophel*

1598	*The Countesse of Pembrokes Arcadia* published with *Defence of Poetry*; the first complete edition of all the *Astrophil* poems also published
1599	Transcription of Tixall MS of Sidneian *Psalmes*
1600	Transcription of *Triumph of Death*
1601	(19 Jan.) Henry Herbert, Earl of Pembroke, dies
1602	Publication of 'Astrea' in Davison's *Poetical Rapsody*
1603	(24 Mar.) Death of Queen Elizabeth
	(13 May) Robert Sidney created Baron Sidney of Penshurst
	Robert Sidney appointed Chamberlain to Queen Anne
	(Aug.–Nov.) King James intermittently at Wilton
1604	(27 Sept.) Mary Sidney marries Sir Robert Wroth
	(4 Nov.) William Herbert marries Mary Talbot
	(27 Dec.) Philip Herbert marries Susan de Vere
1605	(4 May) Philip Herbert created Earl of Montgomery by King James
	Robert Sidney created Viscount L'Isle
1606?	Anne Herbert dies
1607 to 1614	Hiatus in biographical records for MSH
1614–16	MSH on Continent
1618	Portrait engraved by Simon van de Passe
	(2 Aug.) Robert Sidney created Earl of Leicester
1619	(13 May) MSH participates in funeral of Queen Anne
1621	(21 July) King James visits Houghton House
	(25 Sept.) MSH dies of smallpox at her home on Aldersgate Street, London

INTRODUCTION

Life

Mary Sidney Herbert, Countess of Pembroke, was well placed to become the first Elizabethan woman to achieve public acclaim as a literary figure, for she was not only intelligent and well educated, but also wealthy and part of a powerful family alliance.[1] By her marriage, she was allied with the Herbert family, whose members were of major political and financial importance in both England and Wales. By her birth she was a member of the Dudley/Sidney family, whose fortunes vacillated spectacularly, but whose alliances controlled more than a third of the land under Elizabeth's rule. Her paternal grandfather, Sir William Sidney, had served as chamberlain for the infant Prince Edward, while her grandmother, Anne Pagenham, served as the prince's governess; their rewards included Penshurst Place, still the primary seat of the Sidney family. Their son Henry was educated with Edward and was given positions of honour during his brief reign; he was also permitted to marry Lady Mary Dudley, a woman considerably above his rank, on 29 March 1551. The daughter of the powerful Duke of Northumberland, Mary Dudley had probably known Henry Sidney since childhood, for her brothers Ambrose and Robert had studied with him and Prince Edward. When the young king died in his arms on 6 July 1553, Henry Sidney's fortunes took a downward turn from which they never fully recovered.

Mary Sidney's maternal grandfather, John Dudley, Duke of Northumberland, had also risen to prominence under King Edward. Unwilling to give up his power under the Catholic Mary Tudor, he married his son Guildford to Lady Jane Grey on 21 May 1553 and engineered the attempt to place them on the throne after Edward's death. On 9 July Lady Jane was declared queen, but within eleven days Mary Tudor had replaced her. The familiar sequel led to the immediate execution of Northumberland and to the imprisonment of Lady Jane and all five of Northumberland's sons. The family was convinced that they suffered for their faith; both the eldest son

[1] Two full-length biographies are available: Young, *Mary Sidney*; and Hannay, *Philip's Phoenix*.

John, Earl of Warwick, and his brother Robert so identified their cause with God's that they translated Psalms of vengeance during their imprisonment.[2] In February 1554, after the uprising led by Sir Thomas Wyatt the younger, Guildford and Lady Jane were executed. Although the duchess and the Sidneys procured the release of the other sons in October 1554, John was so ill that he died shortly after he arrived at Penshurst. The widowed duchess did not long survive him, dying on 22 January 1555; Henry Dudley died at the Battle of St Quentin in August 1557. During this period, the only cheerful family news was the birth on 30 November 1554 of Philip Sidney, astutely named in honour of his godfather, King Philip.

Only two sons remained, Ambrose and Robert, who were still under attainder. The fortunes of the Dudley family were in the hands of the two daughters, Mary, Lady Sidney, and Katherine, who had been just 7 years old in May 1553 when her father married her to Henry Hastings, later Earl of Huntingdon, another Protestant with a remote claim to the throne. Surprisingly, the union not only produced an important political alliance for the Dudleys, but also apparently became a happy marriage. Although she never had children of her own, the Countess of Huntingdon became 'another mother' to her Sidney nieces and nephews and raised many other children of the Protestant nobility.[3] When Elizabeth came to the throne on 17 November 1558, the Dudley/Sidney family once again prospered, largely because the queen favoured her childhood friend Robert Dudley, making him her Master of Horse (a position that his brother John had held under King Edward), inducting him into the Order of the Garter, and granting him extensive honours and properties, including Kenilworth.

The Sidneys were considered so influential with the queen that they were courted by European diplomats, including the Spanish ambassador Alvarez de Quadra, Bishop of Aquila.[4] In 1562 Lady Sidney nursed the queen through smallpox. Henry Sidney later wrote, 'When I went to Newhaven [Le Havre] I lefte here a full faire Ladie in myne eye at least the fayerest, and when I returned I found her as fowle a ladie as the smale poxe could make her.'[5] Philip Sidney later

---

[2] *Arundel Harington MS*, I. 338–41, nos. 289 and 290, *Psalms* 55 and 94.

[3] Daniel Rogers, quoted in Jan Van Dorsten, *Poets, Patrons, and Professors: Sir Philip Sidney, Daniel Rogers, and the Leiden Humanists* (Leiden: Leiden UP, 1962), 62.

[4] *CSP*, I. 95–6, 107, 113–17, 178–80.

[5] Sir Henry Sidney to Sir Francis Walsingham, 1 Mar. 1583, PRO SP 12/159, f. 38ᵛ.

reworked the story in the figures of Argalus and Parthenia in his *Arcadia*, but the reality was less satisfying.[6] Unlike Argalus, Sir Henry was dismayed by his wife's disfigurement and, unlike Parthenia, Lady Sidney never did recover her beauty or her health. She never wavered in her love for her 'owen deare Lord', as she habitually called him, and he continued to seek her advice; nevertheless, Henry Sidney records that she spent much of her time in solitude, like a 'nicticorax', an owl of the desert, sometimes even living apart from her family.[7] Although she had once been one of the queen's closest friends, by the mid 1570s her influence had so much declined that she had difficulty even obtaining suitable rooms at court.[8]

Mary Sidney was born on 27 October 1561 at Tickenhall near Bewdley, Worcestershire. Because of Henry Sidney's concurrent positions as Lord President of the Council of Wales (1559–86) and Lord Deputy of Ireland (1565–71 and 1575–8) during her childhood, she lived at Tickenhall and his other official residences of Dublin Castle, Ludlow Castle, and Shrewsbury, as well as at Penshurst. While Philip, Robert (born 1563), and little Thomas (born 1569) prepared for the university, Mary and her younger sister, Ambrosia (born *c.*1564), studied with tutors at home. They received an outstanding education, following the standard humanist curriculum of the classics, the Church Fathers, and Latin, French, and Italian language and literature; they may also have studied the other learned languages of Greek and Hebrew, although the evidence is inconclusive.[9] The countess's later writing suggests that they may also have studied rhetoric. Their education had a strong Protestant emphasis on the scriptures and on personal piety; the accounts list '2 bookes of prayer for Mrs Marye and Mr Robert' and 'two books of Martirs', probably Foxe's *Actes and Monuments*.[10] Like most aristocratic girls, Mary and Ambrosia learned practical medicine and the typically feminine accomplishments of needlework, lute playing, and singing. The

---

[6] Sidney, *New Arcadia*, 28–33, 42–5. See also Dennis Kay, ' "She was a Queen, and therefore beautiful": Sidney, His Mother, and Queen Elizabeth', *RES* ns 43 (1992), 18–39.

[7] Sir Henry Sidney to Sir Francis Walsingham, 1 Mar. 1583, PRO SP 12/159, f. 38ᵛ, quoting Ps. 102. 6.

[8] Lady Sidney to Earl of Sussex, 1 Feb. 1574, BL Cotton MS, Vespasian, F.xii, f. 179.

[9] Abraham Fraunce's Greek lines in his dedication to Pembroke suggest that she may have had at least a rudimentary knowledge of that language: *The Arcadian Rhetorike*, ed. Ethel Seaton (Oxford: Basil Blackwell, 1950), 2. On Pembroke's access to Hebrew scholarship, see *Psalmes*: 'Literary Context'.

[10] De L'Isle MS U1475 A56 (3), 1575–7; A4/5, 1573–4.

Sidneys were particularly careful of their daughters, since two girls had already died in childhood, Mary (Margaret) in 1558 at 'one yere and three quarters old' and Elizabeth in 1567 at the age of 8.[11] After Ambrosia died from an illness at Ludlow on 22 February 1575, Queen Elizabeth wrote to Henry Sidney, inviting him to send his only surviving daughter away from the 'unpleasant ayre' of Wales into the 'better' air of the court.[12]

It was a time of great promise for the Sidneys. Philip was the acknowledged heir of both surviving Dudley uncles: Ambrose, who had been permitted to succeed his brother as Earl of Warwick; and Robert, whom Queen Elizabeth had created Earl of Leicester in 1564. The queen's progress that summer of 1575 included Leicester's famous festivities at Kenilworth, and the entertainments at Woodstock, where Mary was presented with her first poetic tribute, a posy with an attached verse praising her lineage and intellect:

> Tho yonge in yeares yet olde in wit, a gest dew to your race,
> If you holde on as you begine who ist youle not deface?[13]

She served Elizabeth at court for less than two years before Leicester arranged a marriage to the recently widowed Earl of Pembroke, an important political ally and a fellow-soldier with the Dudleys at St Quentin. Despite her father's difficulty in raising her dowry of three thousand pounds, he was delighted with the match.[14] On 21 April 1577, when she was just 15, Mary Sidney became the Countess of Pembroke. The only hints of how the young bride felt about marriage to this wealthy widower in his mid-forties are contained in a trembling letter she wrote to Leicester (Correspondence: Manuscript Letter I) and in the advice she gives to a bride of an arranged royal marriage in her paraphrase of Psalm 45. 37–64. She quickly assumed her duties as hostess at Pembroke's Wiltshire estates of Wilton, Ivychurch, and Ramsbury, as well as their London residence, Baynards Castle. She welcomed frequent visits from her own family, including

---

[11] Margaret Sidney's brass in the Sidney Chapel of Penshurst Church; epitaph for Elizabeth Sidney, Nov. 1567, BL Egerton MS 2642, f. 197.

[12] Queen Elizabeth to Sir Henry Sidney, 1575, PRO SP 40/1, f. 83.

[13] *STC* 7596, unique (but imperfect) copy in the BL; printed in J. W. Cunliffe, 'The Queenes Majesties Entertainment at Woodstocke', *PMLA* 26 (1911), 99–100.

[14] Sir Henry Sidney to Earl of Leicester, 4 Feb. 1577, De L'Isle MS U1475 C7/3 and Z53/11 (Arthur Collins's transcript). A jointure manuscript, detailing an impressive range of properties and land settled on Mary Sidney for life at her marriage, is preserved at the Houghton Library, Harvard University, fms Eng 725. See Hannay, *Philip's Phoenix*, 41–2.

her brother Philip, who had recently offended Elizabeth by his oppo-
sition to the match with the French Catholic duc d'Alençon (after
1574 duc d'Anjou). During his visits to Wilton, Sidney apparently
began writing his *Arcadia*, which he said was written 'in loose sheetes
of paper, most of it in your presence'.[15] His sonnet sequence, *Astrophil
and Stella*, was circulated at Wilton, and he may have begun paraphrasing the Psalms there as well. He may also have left several of
his manuscripts with his sister since, as W. A. Ringler has suggested,
she probably supplied the texts of *Certain Sonnets*, *Astrophil and
Stella*, and the *Lady of May* for inclusion in the 1598 edition of the
Arcadia, as well as one or more manuscripts of the *Arcadia*, including
the *Old Arcadia* foul papers used in printing *The Countesse of Pembrokes Arcadia* (1593).[16]

The countess's primary duty was to produce an heir for the Pembroke estates. The ageing earl was so elated at the birth of his first son,
William, on 8 April 1580, that he installed a stone plaque in St Mary's
Church, Wilton, commemorating the event, and he invited the entire
parish to dinner.[17] William succeeded his father as third Earl of Pembroke on 19 January 1601, shortly before his twenty-first birthday.
The Pembrokes had three other recorded children. Katherine, born
15 October 1581, died at 'threyeare old and one daie, a child of promised much excellencie if she mought have lived', as the Sidney
Family Psalter poignantly records.[18] Anne, born 9 March 1583, died
unmarried in 'the flower of her age' (probably in 1606).[19] Philip, born
on 16 October 1584, the same day that his sister Katherine died, was
created Earl of Montgomery by King James on 4 May 1605 and succeeded his brother William as fourth Earl of Pembroke on 10 April

---

[15] 'To my Deare Ladie and Sister, the Countesse of Pembroke', Sidney, *Arcadia*, sig. A3.
George Carleton says that it was composed at Wilton in his elegy '*D. Philippus Sidnaenus.
Silva*' in *Exequiae illustrissimi Equitis, D. Philippi Sidnaei gratissimae memoriae ac nomini
impensae* (Oxford: 1587), *STC* 22551, sig. L1ᵛ–2.

[16] The textual history of the *Old* and *New Arcadia* is complex, obscure, and still con-
tested. See Sidney, *Poems*, 373–4; *Old Arcadia*, p. lxiv, and *New Arcadia*, pp. lxiv, lxxviii.

[17] James M. Osborn, *Young Philip Sidney (1572–1577)* (New Haven: Yale UP, 1972),
540.

[18] Sidney Family Psalter, Trinity College Library, Cambridge, R.17.2, f. 5ᵛ. The marginal notations of family births, marriages, and deaths are written in two hands, one using a
regular, perhaps professional hand, and the other (only for 16 Oct. 1584) using an irregular
hand, perhaps that of Mary Dudley Sidney. See Michael G. Brennan, ' "First rais'de by thy
blest hand, and what is mine | inspird by thee": the "Sidney Psalter" and the Countess of
Pembroke's Completion of the Sidneian *Psalms*', *Sidney Newsletter & Journal* 14 (1996),
3–10.

[19] Camden, *Historie*, sig. Bbbb4ᵛ.

1630. William and Philip Herbert eventually both achieved prominence under James I.

In the first ten years of her marriage, the Countess of Pembroke devoted her time to her family and to her young children. But these happy days came to an abrupt end. Sir Henry Sidney died on 5 May 1586, after taking a chill during a boat trip from Bewdley to Worcester; Lady Sidney soon followed her husband, dying on 9 August. By that autumn Mary Sidney herself was desperately ill, according to the Pembroke family physician, Thomas Moffet; her brother Philip, serving under Leicester's command in the Low Countries, was much distressed by reports that she was dying.[20] She recovered, only to learn that Philip had been wounded on 23 September at Zutphen. Although he had been expected to survive, he developed gangrene and died on 17 October.

As a woman, the countess could not participate in the public mourning for her brother, neither in the series of elegies issued by English and Dutch universities, nor at the magnificent funeral held on 16 February 1587. (See 'Angell Spirit': 'Literary Context'.) She remained quietly in the country for two years after this devastating series of deaths. While all England prepared for the Spanish attack in the summer of 1588, she kept her sister-in-law Barbara and her little niece Mary with her at Wilton as her husband prepared the defence of the Welsh ports and her brother Robert served at Tilbury.[21] Then, in November 1588, she and her children rode into London for the Accession Day festivities in a magnificent procession of about 100 servants, who were dressed in her blue livery and wearing gold chains.[22]

Virtually all of the patronage, the translation, and the original writing for which she is known were accomplished between this triumphal return and the death of her husband in January 1601. She seems to have begun her literary work to honour her brother, celebrated in England and on the Continent as a Protestant martyr: she wrote elegiac verses for him, completed his paraphrase of the Psalms, encouraged many of the poets who celebrated him, and assumed

---

[20] Moffet, *Nobilis*, 85–6.
[21] Privy Council to Earl of Pembroke, 4 Jan. 1588, *Calendar of Wynn (of Gwydir) Papers, 1515–1690, in the National Library of Wales and Elsewhere* (Aberystwyth: National Library of Wales, 1926), 106; Earl of Pembroke to John Wynn, 20 June 1588, *Wynn Papers*, 110; Robert Sidney to Lady Sidney, 24 May–6 Aug. 1588, De L'Isle MS U1475 C81/3–8.
[22] *CSP Spanish*, IV. 488.

responsibility for publishing his works. Her efforts to stabilize the text of Sidney's works served to present him primarily as a writer rather than as a soldier or courtier. The printed editions of Sidney's works (and of her own translations) also helped to mitigate the 'stigma' of print for other writers, even though Pembroke restricted the circulation of the *Psalmes* to scribal publication.[23] Her efforts to present a scholarly text may be contrasted with those, for example, of John Bodenham (or his editor), who produced a printed miscellany by rearranging and rewriting poetic texts by a variety of authors, including Sidney and Pembroke, to fit under topical headings.[24]

Believing that Fulke Greville's 1590 edition of Sidney's unfinished revision of *The Countesse of Pembrokes Arcadia* was blemished, perhaps because the work had been divided into chapters with inaccurate headings and the eclogues had been rearranged, she had another edition of the *Arcadia* published in 1593.[25] Although the Pembrokes' secretary Hugh Sanford himself apparently undertook the more tedious parts of the editor's task, he claimed that it was 'most by her doing, all by her directing', concluding that, 'it is now by more than one interest *The Countesse of Pembrokes Arcadia*: done, as it was for her: as it is, by her'.[26] Then in 1598 she authorized another edition that collected Sidney's works, reprinting the 1593 edition and including the *Defence of Poetry*, *Certain Sonnets*, the *Lady of May*, and the first complete edition of all the Astrophil sonnets, one that corrected Thomas Nashe's corrupt edition of 1591.[27]

Because Sidney never completed his revision of the *Arcadia*, all of these editions were composites, printing his revised Books I–III and the original Books IV–V. The original, unrevised *Old Arcadia* was

---

[23] See J. W. Saunders, 'The Stigma of Print: A Note on the Social Bases of Tudor Poetry', *Essays in Criticism* 1 (1951), 139–64; Arthur F. Marotti, *John Donne, Coterie Poet* (Madison: U of Wisconsin P, 1986), 3; Love, *Scribal Publication*, 35–140; Wall, *Gender*, 23–60.

[24] Bodenham, *Bel-vedére*.

[25] The countess's dissatisfaction with Greville's 1590 text (apparently edited with the assistance of Matthew Gwinne and John Florio) was confirmed by the uncompromising opening sentence of Hugh Sanford's preface to the 1593 edition: 'The disfigured face, gentle reader, wherewith this work not long since appeared to the common view, moved that noble lady, to whose honour consecrated, to whose protection it was committed, to take in hand the wiping away those spots wherewith the beauties thereof were unworthily blemished.' For the subsequent controversy, see Sidney, *New Arcadia*, pp. lviii–xiii.

[26] H.S., 'To the Reader', Sidney, *Arcadia*, sig. A4.

[27] On the editions of *Astrophil and Stella* as a struggle over patronage, see Arthur Marotti, *Manuscript, Print, and the English Renaissance Lyric* (Ithaca, NY: Cornell UP, 1995), 312–14.

lost for several centuries. When Bertram Dobell rediscovered three manuscripts of the *Old Arcadia* in 1907, he concluded that Pembroke 'allowed herself a good deal of freedom in dealing with her brother's work', not only rearranging and revising sections of Books I–III, but also 'suppressing portions' to eliminate the less virtuous actions of the princes.[28] Many other scholars castigated her bowdlerization.[29] More recent studies, however, including those by Jean Robertson, conclude that the major alterations in the *New Arcadia* 'are interrelated, and were probably either made or their nature indicated by Sidney himself' as he revised his work.[30] Despite that earlier controversy, it now appears that Pembroke was fairly conservative in editing the *Arcadia*, evidently believing, as Sanford said, that 'Sir Philip Sidneies writings' could not be 'perfected without Sir Philip Sidney'.[31]

Yet the countess may have made some revisions in the forty-three Psalms that he had written. In 'Angell Spirit' she describes his Psalms

> As goodly buildings to some glorious ende
> cut of by fate, before the Graces hadde
> each wondrous part in all their beauties cladde. (64–6)

Although she says that he had 'so much done, as Art could not amende' and claims that 'no witt can adde' to 'thy rare workes' (67–8), someone, probably Pembroke, altered occasional phrases and revised the endings of some of his Psalms. (See 'Major Revisions of Psalms 1–43'.) From the surviving manuscripts there is no way to prove whether those changes were original, or whether she was following her brother's intentions, given orally or in written form.

---

[28] Bertram Dobell, 'New Light Upon Sir Philip Sidney's "Arcadia"', *Quarterly Review* 211 (1909), 75.

[29] Young, *Mary Sidney*, 131; Feuillerat, *The Countess of Pembrokes Arcadia*, in *The Complete Works of Sir Philip Sidney* (Cambridge: Cambridge UP, 1912), I. vii; Mario Praz, 'Sidney's Original *Arcadia*', *London Mercury* 15 (1926–7), 503–14; R. W. Zandvoort, *Sidney's Arcadia: A Comparison Between the Two Versions* (Amsterdam: Swets and Zeitlinger, 1929), 28–38; A. G. D. Wiles, 'Parallel Analyses of the Two Versions of Sidney's *Arcadia*, Including the Major Variations of the Folio of 1593', *SP* 39 (1942), 197. Hannay, *Philip's Phoenix*, 237, n. 71.

[30] Sidney, *Old Arcadia*, p. lxii. See also Mona Wilson, *Sir Philip Sidney* (London: Duckworth, 1931), 154; Kenneth Thorpe Rowe, 'The Countess of Pembroke's Editorship of the *Arcadia*', *PMLA* 54 (1939), 138; William Leigh Godshalk, 'Sidney's Revision of the *Arcadia*, Books III–V', *PQ* 43 (1964), 171–84; Joan Rees, 'Fulke Greville and the Revisions of *Arcadia*', *RES* 17 (1966), 54–7; Waller, *Mary Sidney*, 86–7; Richard A. Lanham, *The Old Arcadia* (New Haven: Yale UP, 1985), 190; Jon S. Lawry, *Sidney's Two Arcadias: Pattern and Proceeding* (Ithaca, NY: Cornell UP, 1972), 154–5; and Sidney, *Poems*, 378.

[31] Sidney, *Arcadia*, sig. A4.

Those changes, however, as recorded by Samuel Woodforde (MS *B*), parallel her revisions on her own Psalms and may indicate that she learned her poetic craft from these endeavours.[32] (See II. 358.)

Because of her publication of Sidney's works, her completion of the *Psalmes*, and primarily because poets wished her to assume her brother's role as patron, most dedications written to her stress her resemblance to her brother, as does Edmund Spenser, who finds 'His goodly image living evermore | In the divine resemblaunce of your face'. As usual, the resemblance is stressed in order to appeal for patronage: 'For his, and for your owne especial sake, | Vouchsafe from him this token in good worth to take'.[33] Abraham Fraunce makes a similar appeal for patronage when he praises her as '*morientis imago Philippi*' and asks that she favour his work.[34] Henry Constable, who admits that he knows her only 'by reportes', addresses her because 'Thou art his Sister whom I honour'd so'. Observing 'Thy minde all say like to thy Brother is', he claims that he has already 'praysed thyne by praysing his'.[35] Poets such as John Donne, William Gager, William Browne, Nicholas Breton, and Aemilia Lanyer also linked the siblings in their praise of Pembroke. (See pp. 27 ff.) During her life, references to Pembroke's connection with Sidney are invariably combined with compliments to her virtue, her learning, or her own writing. Lanyer even praises her as superior to her brother in 'virtue, wisedome, learning, dignity', and poets like Barnabe Barnes promise that after her 'mortall pilgrimage' she would ascend to the heavens with her 'late sainted brother to give light'.[36] In Michael Drayton's *Pastorals. Contayning Eglogues* (1619), Gorbo complains that there are none left that follow virtue. Perkin replies, 'Vertue is not dead … But to a Nymph, for succour she is fled', identifying that 'Nymph' as a shepherdess of Wilton, sister to Elphin (Sidney), 'To whom she was of living things most deare'.[37] So intertwined had their reputations become that an eighteenth-century manuscript of Sidney's epitaph identified him as the 'brother of the Countess of Pembroke'.[38]

---

[32] Freer, *Music*, 73, 100–1; Fisken, 'Education', 166–83; Zim, *Psalms*, 186; Waller, *Mary Sidney*, 161–78.

[33] 'To the right honourable and most vertuous Lady, the Countesse of Penbroke', Spenser, *Faerie Queene*, sig. Qq4ᵛ.

[34] Fraunce, *Ivychurch. Third Part*, sig. A2.

[35] 'To the Countesse of Pembroke', Constable, *Poems*, p. lvi.

[36] Lanyer, *Poems*, p. 28; Barnes, *P and P*, ed. Doyno, 132.

[37] Michael Drayton, 'The Eighth Eglogue', in *Works*, II. 560–1.

[38] Thomas Archer, 1760, BL Additional MS 5830, f. 179ᵛ.

The most notorious of such identifications with her brother was part of the Royalist slander directed at her son Philip Herbert, Earl of Pembroke and Montgomery, who had altered his allegiance from king to Parliament in the civil war. During the reign of Charles II, nearly a century after Sidney's death, John Aubrey recorded that Mr Long of Draycot told him that he had heard old men say that 'there was so great love' between Sir Philip Sidney and 'his faire sister that...they lay together, and it was thought the first Philip Earle of Pembroke was begot by him'.[39] Other Royalist propaganda portrayed Herbert as illiterate and of low intelligence, but Aubrey adds a twist to the familiar libel by saying his defects were the result of incestuous union: 'he inherited not the witt of either brother or sister'. Royalists frequently called Herbert a cuckold and accused him of drunken revelry and indiscriminate slaughter, but little was made of his open adultery with Lady Elizabeth Norris, the niece of his first wife Susan de Vere, suggesting that the charges were formulaic rather than specific.[40] Aubrey, writing in the midst of a feud with Mary Sidney's great-grandson over an election at Sarum, mixed into his factual accounts other sexual innuendoes against the Herberts, including the suggestion that the countess was salacious in

---

[39] Aubrey, *Brief Lives*, 139. Although Aubrey's charge of incest is 'scandalously unfounded on any public fact', as Gary Waller observes (Sidney, Mary. *Triumph*, 53 and Waller, *Mary Sidney*, 100), some modern critics have speculated that the charge reflects 'psychological' truth. See Waller, 'The Countess of Pembroke and Gendered Reading', in *Renaissance Englishwoman*, 327–46; John Briley, 'Mary Sidney—a 20th Century Reappraisal', *Elizabethan and Modern Studies: Presented to Professor Willem Schrickx on the Occasion of his Retirement* (Gent: Seminarie voor Engelse en Amerikaanse Literature, 1985), 47–56; Jonathan Crewe, *Hidden Designs: The Critical Profession and Renaissance Literature* (London: Methuen, 1986), 82–7, 166; and Janet MacArthur, 'Ventriloquizing Comfort and Despair: Mary Sidney's Female Personae in *The Triumph of Death* and *The Tragedy of Antony*', *Sidney Newsletter and Journal* 11 (1990), 3–13.

[40] For Herbert's reputation, see such documents as the fictional 'Earl of Pembroke's speech in the House of Peers when the Lords were accused of High Treason', BL Additional MS 47112; the supposedly supportive *An impartial account of the misfortune that lately happened to the Right Honourable Philip Earle of Pembrooke and Montgomery. Together with a true and just relation taken not only from that Constable that was then upon the Watch, but from sober and eminent Citizens of London that went down on purpose to know the bottom of that barbarous Injury* (1680), Wing, I71, sig. A1ʳ⁻ᵛ; and the crude satire published anonymously as *The Last Will and Testament of Philip Herbert, Burgess for Back-shire, Vulgarly called the Earl of Pembroke and Mongomery. Who dyed of Fool-Age. Jan 23. 1650...also His Elegy, taken verbatim, in time of his sicknesse, and published to prevent false Copies, By Michael Oldisworth* ('Nod-Nol, Printed in the Fall of Tyranny, and Resurrection of Loyalty, 1650'), Wing L524. The accompanying fictional elegy by 'Michael Oldisworth' admonishes those 'that will mourne his death at the Grave' to 'Draw neere and make Water upon an old Knave' (sig. 4ᵛ).

supervising the mating of Wilton's famous racehorses.[41] Aubrey's unreliability on such matters is demonstrated by his assertion that William Herbert, first Earl of Pembroke, warned his son to keep young Mary at home lest he be cuckolded—but William Herbert had died in 1570, seven years before the marriage, when Henry Herbert was married to Catherine Talbot and Mary Sidney was a small child.[42]

Pembroke is usually introduced by her own self-designation, 'Sister of Sir Philip Sidney'. That phrase comes from a business letter, one in which she is seeking justice at the Star Chamber against jewel thieves and murderers. After a formal request written by her secretary, she adds a proud postscript: 'it is the Sister of Sir Philip Sidney who yow ar to right and who will worthely deserve the same' (Correspondence: Manuscript Letter XII). This usage clarifies her self-identification as Philip Sidney's sister: it was not only a statement of love, but also of self-assertion. Twentieth-century critics have often dismissed her writing as derivative, as though it was motivated solely by blind devotion for her brother.[43] Without attention to literary genre, it is easy to exaggerate her poetic mourning. For example, Pembroke certainly does describe Sidney's apotheosis (as in 'Angell Spirit', 57–63), but that is a standard topos, one employed in elegies for Sidney by Lodowick Bryskett and others. Her praise of her brother is extravagant, but hardly more so than Ralegh's calling him the '*Scipio*, *Cicero*, and *Petrarch* of our time'.[44] Nor is her expression of grief more extreme than other poems printed with 'Astrophel', which claim, for example, that Sidney's death is 'the cause of all this woe . . . And endles griefe, which deads my life, yet knowes not how to kill'.[45] The point of elegy is that 'every one did make exceeding mone, | With inward anguish and great griefe opprest'. All the poets 'did weep and waile, and mone, | And meanes deviz'd to shew his sorrow

---

[41] Aubrey, *Brief Lives*, 138.

[42] On similar slanders directed at Philip Herbert's widow, Lady Anne Clifford, see Margaret P. Hannay, 'Literary Reconstruction: Written Texts and Social Contexts of Aristocratic Englishwomen', in *Attending to Women in the Renaissance*, ed. Betty Travitsky and Adele Seeff (Newark, NJ: U of Delaware P, 1994), 44–6.

[43] See particularly the critical reception of *Antonius*, discussed in 'Origins, Early Reception, and Influence', but even her *Psalmes* have been dismissed as 'a devotional act: to her brother more than to God' because to her 'Sidney was literally an expression of the divine': Freer, *Music*, 106.

[44] 'An Epitaph upon the right Honourable sir Phillip Sidney knight: Lord governor of Flushing', Spenser, *Astrophel*, sig. K2.

[45] 'Another of the same', Spenser, *Astrophel*, sig. K4.

best'. The sorrow for Sidney was so great, Spenser says, that never 'was ... like mourning seen'.[46]

One reason that poets so grieved for Sidney is that they had sought his patronage; after his death, they turned to other patrons, including his sister. Because of this transference of patronage, Pembroke became the first non-royal woman in England to receive a significant number of dedications.[47] Following the example of Sidney's title, *The Countesse of Pembrokes Arcadia*, other writers incorporated her name into their own work, thereby hoping to appeal to her patronage and to increase sales. Abraham Fraunce presented to her *The Countesse of Pembrokes Emmanuel* (1591), *The Countesse of Pembrokes Ivychurch* (1591), and *The Third Part of the Countesse of Pembrokes Ivychurch* (1592). *Englands Helicon* includes a poem entitled 'The Countess of Pembrokes Pastoral' by 'Shep. Tonie' (Antony Munday).[48] With these precedents, and Nicholas Breton's own poem entitled 'The Countesse of Penbrookes love', it is surprising that the title of his poem, 'The Countess of Pembrokes Passion', was long taken for a signal of authorship and so misattributed to the countess herself. (See p. 55.)

Although the extent of her patronage has sometimes been exaggerated, the Countess of Pembroke does seem to have encouraged other writers, particularly those in her family or household.[49] Samuel Daniel, looking back on his time at Wilton, recalled that he had 'been first incourag'd or fram'd' as a poet by her and had received 'the first notion for the formall ordering of those compositions at Wilton, which I must ever acknowledge to have beene my best Schoole'.[50]

---

[46] 'Astrophel', Spenser, *Astrophel*, sig. F4.

[47] Franklin Williams demonstrates that the only aristocratic woman to receive more dedications than Pembroke was her second cousin Lucy Russell, Countess of Bedford, who received 38: 'The Literary Patronesses of Renaissance England', *N&Q* 207 (1962), 364–6. See also Williams's invaluable *Index of Dedications and Commendatory Verses in English Books Before 1641* (London, 1962) and Supplement, *The Library* (London, 1975).

[48] *Englands Helicon 1600*, ed. Hyder Edward Rollins (Cambridge, Mass.: Harvard UP, 1935), I. 167–70.

[49] Stanley D. Johnson, 'The Literary Patronage of Sir Philip Sidney and his Family', (Yale U, Ph.D. diss., 1943); Buxton, *Sidney*, 173–204; Pearl Hogrefe, *Tudor Women: Commoners and Queens* (Ames: Iowa State UP, 1975), 124–33; Lamb (Ph.D. diss.); Lamb, 'Myth', 194–202; and 'Patronage', 162–79; D. M. Bergeron, 'Women as Patrons of English Renaissance Drama', in *Patronage in the Renaissance*, ed. Guy Fitch Lytle and Stephen Orgel (Princeton: Princeton UP, 1981), 274–90; Brennan, *Literary Patronage*, 59–82; Hannay, *Philip's Phoenix*, 106–42; Hiller, 37–52; Louise Schleiner, *Tudor and Stuart Women Writers* (Bloomington: Indiana UP, 1994), 52–81.

[50] Samuel Daniel, 'To William Herbert Earle of Pembroke', *A Panegyrike Congratulatorie ... with a Defence of Ryme* (1603), *STC* 6259, sig. G3.

Thomas Churchyard similarly praises her because she 'sets to schoole, our poets ev'ry where' and John Aubrey later echoed his description of Wilton as a 'College'.[51] When dedicating to her *The Countesse of Pembrokes Arcadia*, her brother Philip said that he wrote it because 'you desired me to doo it, and your desire, to my heart is an absolute commaundement'.[52] Her younger brother Robert wrote a manuscript of poems and addressed it 'For the Countess of Pembroke'.[53] Her son William wrote poetry, later collected and published by John Donne the younger.[54] Her daughter Anne died in her early twenties; although no works are extant, Lady Anne may also have been a writer, for Moffet describes her as partaking in story-telling sponsored by the countess at Wilton, and the Bright MS includes anonymous poems possibly written by a woman in the Sidney circle, whether Lady Anne or one of Pembroke's nieces.[55] Perhaps her most important literary protégé was her niece and goddaughter, Mary Sidney, Lady Wroth, daughter of Robert Sidney and Barbara Gamage.[56] Except for her husband, who provided the financial and political backing that constituted her patronage, most of the family wrote poetry. And so did her children's tutors, the secretaries, the family physician, and even old retainers like Thomas Howell.[57]

Her role as a catalyst for writing is emphasized by Nicholas Breton, who compares her to 'the Duchesse of Urbina', saying that she has more 'servants' writing poetry to her than did Elizabetta Gonzaga, celebrated in Castiglione's *Courtier*.[58] Breton, who had lost her patronage, evidently looks back on Wilton as a paradise for poets: 'God [was] daily served, religion trulie preached, all quarrels avoyded,

[51] Churchyard, *Conceit*, sig. B1v; Aubrey, *Brief Lives*, 138.

[52] 'To my Deare Ladie and Sister, the Countesse of Pembroke', Sidney, *Arcadia*, sig. A3.

[53] Robert Sidney, BL Additional MS 58435. This inscription may have been an address, rather than an abbreviated dedication.

[54] *Poems Written by the Right Honorable William Earl of Pembroke, Lord Steward of his Majesties Houshold, Whereof Many of Which are answered by way of Repartee, by Sir Benjamin Ruddier, Knight, with Several Distinct Poems, Written by them Occasionally, and Apart* (1660), Wing P1128.

[55] Moffet, *Silkewormes*, sig. F4v. Mary Ellen Lamb discusses the slight possibility that Lady Anne is the author of three poems in the Bright MS in Lamb, *Gender*, 194–8.

[56] See Margaret Hannay, '"Your vertuous and learned Aunt": The Countess of Pembroke as a Mentor to Lady Wroth', in *Reading Mary Wroth: Representing Alternatives in Early Modern England*, ed. Naomi Miller and Gary Waller (Knoxville, Tenn.: U of Tennessee P, 1991), 15–34; and Lewalski, *Writing Women*, 243.

[57] Thomas Howell said that he wrote 'at ydle times in your house, to avoyde greater ydlenesse or worse businesse': Howell, *Devises*, ed. Raleigh, 6.

[58] Breton, *Pilgrimage*, sig. A2; rpt. *Works*, I. b. 4.

peace carefully preserved.' Equally important, 'a table fully furnished'
and 'a house richly garnished' were provided for poets.[59] But not all
was peaceful among the poets who vied for her patronage. Breton
claims that envy had driven him from her presence, and there were
unseemly squabbles among others who sought her favour at Wilton,
just as there were among those courtiers who sought Queen Elizabeth's favour. As Mary Ellen Lamb has demonstrated, Abraham
Fraunce's portrayal of the countess as Pembrokiana 'resonates with
the power of the patronage relationship'.[60] When Pembrokiana kills
a whelping bear, the poet identifies his own poetic works with the
bear's cubs, portraying his patron not only as a midwife delivering
the works, but also a more menacing figure, a violent huntress.
Thomas Nashe demonstrates similar resentment. In his 1591 edition
of *Astrophil and Stella,* he sought her favour.[61] When he did not
receive the patronage he sought, probably because his edition of *Astrophil* was unauthorized and corrupt, he attacked female patrons: 'I hate
those female braggarts that contend to have all the Muses beg at their
doores' but never open their purse except to 'pedanticall Parasites'.[62]

Of the poets in her household, Samuel Daniel was by far the most
accomplished; perhaps because her achievement did not threaten his
own, he seems to have considered her not just as a patron, but as a fellow poet. He said that she not only inspired his rhymes, the traditional
female role, but also encouraged him to attempt a higher form of
poetry, 'To sing of state, and tragick notes to frame'.[63] In dedicating
to Pembroke his *Civile Wares,* Daniel pays her the ultimate compliment—he discusses the intent of his historical work with her as

---

[59] Breton, *Wits Trenchmour,* sig. F2ᵛ; rpt. *Works,* II. b. 19. Neither Wilton nor the countess are mentioned by name, but the passage appears to refer to them.

[60] Lamb, *Gender,* 34.

[61] Thomas Nashe, 'Somewhat to reade for them that list', Sidney, *Astrophel,* sig. A4. See
Christopher R. Wilson, '*Astrophil and Stella*: A Tangled Editorial Web', *The Library* 6th
ser. 1 (1979), 336–46, 338–9. (See p. 27.) Lisa Klein suggests that, despite his disclaimer,
Samuel Daniel may have 'had a hand in Newman's surreptitious publication' that included
sonnets from his *Delia* with *Astrophil and Stella: The Exemplary Sidney and the Elizabethan
Sonneteer* (Newark, Del.: U of Delaware P, forthcoming).

[62] Nashe, Dedication to Elizabeth Cary of *Christs Teares* (1593) in *Works,* ed. R. B.
McKerrow, rev. F. P. Wilson (Oxford: Blackwell & Mott, 1958), II. 10–11. See Hiller,
46. In his dedication to Humfrey King of *Lenten Stuffe* (1599) Nashe alludes to the pig
and marjoram device on the title page of the *Arcadia,* satirizing Hugh Sanford and presumably Pembroke as 'his Empresse'. Nashe, *Works,* III. 147.

[63] Daniel, 'To the Right Honourable, the Lady *Marie,* Countesse of Pembroke', *Delia &
Cleopatra,* sig. H6. Cf. Baxter, who also says that she asks him for a 'higher straine' of
poetry, sacred verse in this case: *Ouránia,* sig. B4ᵛ.

with his poetic equal.[64] From his dedications and from the fact that an early draft of Pembroke's 'Angell Spirit' was found among his papers, we may surmise that the two writers exchanged works in progress. We know that she did circulate her works among her household. Moffet, for example, obviously knew her translations of Petrarch and the *Psalmes* before they were complete. In presenting to her his *Silkewormes*, he instructs her to amuse herself with her ladies and (speaking as her physician) to rest occasionally from her poetic labours:

> Vouchsafe a while to lay thy taske aside,
> Let Petrarke sleep, give rest to Sacred Writte,
> Or bowe or string will breake, if ever tied,
> Some little pawse aideth the quickest witte.[65]

Previously, learned English women had usually confined their work to the family circle or to anonymous translation. Pembroke, however, achieved public reputation for her writing. Her contemporary stature as a literary figure is revealed not only through the many poems and dedications which praise her as muse and as writer (see p. 26), but also in the extent of manuscript circulation of her *Psalmes*. (See 'Relationship of the Texts of the *Psalmes*'.) Daniel inverted the usual promise that his verse would immortalize his patron, saying instead that she would be immortalized by her own religious verse:

> Those *Hymnes* that thou doost consecrate to heaven ...
> Unto thy voyce eternitie hath given ...[66]

Among her contemporaries, Pembroke was acclaimed both for her poetic achievement and for her virtue. She, or at least her public image, apparently fulfilled the Elizabethan ideal, but it was an ideal enlarged to include her writing. By confining her works to the approved genres of translation and encomium—of the queen, of her martyred brother, of her God—she produced a substantial body of poetry without openly challenging cultural restrictions on women. (See p. 25.) Although she was far from silent, contemporary

---

[64] Samuel Daniel, 'To the Right Noble Lady, the Lady Marie, Countesse Dowager of Pembroke', *The Civile Wares betweene the Howses of Lancaster and York* (1609), *STC* 6245, sig. A2–3ᵛ. A copy of Daniel's *A Panegyrike Congratulatorie to the King's Majestie* (1603), *STC* 6260, at the Pierpont Morgan Library bears a supposed but unproved signature of Pembroke.

[65] Moffet, *Silkewormes*, sig. A2.

[66] Daniel, *Delia & Cleopatra*, sig. H6ʳ⁻ᵛ.

dedications and references construct her as the embodiment of all feminine virtue and accomplishment. (Even those qualities which modern readers find abrasive, such as her aristocratic hauteur and her hot temper, would not have been considered inappropriate to her rank and wealth.) She was praised for her music, her needlework, her knowledge of medicine, celebrated for her devotion to her family, her piety, and her commitment to the Protestant cause. As a member of the aristocracy she was asked to support public works, such as rebuilding the bridge across the river Medway, and to finance voyages of exploration, such as those of Martin Frobisher.[67] She was also involved in court politics, assisted her husband with his business correspondence, interceded for her brother Robert when he was in Flushing and delivered his private correspondence during the Essex rebellion,[68] sought justice for her servants and positions at court for her children, sponsored church ministers like Gervase Babington to provide spiritual instruction for her family and retainers, and oversaw the household administration for several estates. After her husband succeeded her father as Lord President of the Council of Wales in 1586, she also performed the tasks that had been her mother's at Ludlow Castle and the other official residences. Instead of mentioning these duties, typical for an aristocratic woman, dedications praised her for her feminine accomplishments in music and needlework, for her learning, or for her writing. John Taylor, for example, varies the usual declaration that the poet will immortalize the patron by declaring that her worth will be 'recorded in the mouth of fame | (Untill the world shall end)' not because of his words, but because 'She wrought so well in Needle-worke, that she | Nor yet her workes, shall ere forgotten be'. Of Pembroke he puns, 'A Patterne, and a Patronesse she was | Of vertuous industry, and studious learning'.[69] That is, even as she served as a patron to artists, she provided a model to other women for her industry and her learning, her needle and her pen.

---

[67] Thomas Wotton to Pembroke, 6 Dec. 1583, *Thomas Wotton's Letter-Book 1574–1586*, ed. G. Eland (London: Oxford UP, 1960), 59–60. This is the only extant letter to Pembroke, because it survives in a copy book; her other correspondence may have been lost to fire. Brennan (D.Phil. diss.), 318; Hannay, *Philip's Phoenix*, 151–2. *APC*, X. 414–15.

[68] Robert Sidney to Sir John Harington, undated (1600), says 'my sister beareth this in privacy, and therefore so safe', in Harington, *Letters*, 389.

[69] John Taylor, *The Needles Excellency. A New Booke wherin are divers Admirable Workes wrought with the Needle. Newly invented and cut in Copper for the pleasure and profit of the Industrious* (1634), *STC* 23776, sig. A3ᵛ.

Her role as a religious figure is also repeatedly stressed in dedications. Gervase Babington, for a time the chaplain at Wilton, praises her support of religious education even as he admonishes her to continue in 'the studie of his worde, and all other good learning' and 'of the practise of duty to your God', duty that includes 'incouragement to your servants' and 'honorable clemencie to all men'.[70] Nicholas Breton also presents a series of religious works to her. Addressing her as 'the Right Honourable, discreete, and vertuous Lady, the Nourisher of the Learned and favorer of the Godly', he declares that 'the wise admire, the learned followe, the vertuous love and the honest serve' her.[71] Breton asks her to patronize only religious works: 'thinke not of the ruines of Troie, but helpe to builde up the walles of Jerusalem', a reference to Psalm 51: 8 that had become part of the Protestant code.[72] Walter Sweeper praises her 'learning humane and divine'.[73] In an epitaph, William Browne declares that there was 'so much divinity' in her that her loss would injure 'Our Age, too prone to Irreligion'.[74]

Other Protestant noblewomen were so praised and so admonished. What is unprecedented is the recurrent emphasis on Pembroke's own role as writer as well as patron. (See p. 27.) Barnes, for example, says that she is both 'great favourer of Phoebus of-spring' and herself one 'in whom even Phoebus is most florishing'.[75] Baxter similarly calls her the 'Divine Mistresse of Elocution' and asks her to accept the verse of

[70] Gervase Babington, *A Brief Conference betwixt mans Frailtie and Faith* (1584), *STC* 1081, sig. A5. See also his admonitions in *A Profitable Exposition* (1588), *STC* 1090, sig. A6–8ᵛ.

[71] Nicholas Breton, *The Ravisht Soule, and the Blessed Weeper* (1601), *STC* 3648, sig. A2; rpt. *Works*, I. j. 3. On Breton's presentation of feminine virtue, see Suzanne Trill, 'Engendering Penitence: Nicholas Breton and "the Countess of Pembroke"', in *Voicing Women: Gender and Sexuality in Early Modern Writing*, ed. Kate Chedgzoy, Melanie Hansen, and Suzanne Trill (Keele: Keele UP, 1996), 25–44.

[72] Breton, *Pilgrimage*, sig. A2; rpt. *Works*, I. b. 4. Cf. Richard Taverner, *An Epitome of the Psalmes* (1539), *STC* 2748, sig. F6; and Anne [Lok] Prowse: 'Everie one in his calling is bound to doo somewhat to the furtherance of the holie building; but because great things by reason of my sex I may not doo, and that which I may, I ought to doo, I have according to my duetie, brought my poore basket of stones to the strengthening of the walls of that Ierusalem, whereof (by grace) wee are all both Citizens and members.' From her 'Dedication to the Countess of Warwick', in Taffin, *Children of God*, sig. A3ᵛ–4.

[73] Walter Sweeper, *Israels Redemption by Christ wherin is confuted the Arminian Universall Redemption* (1622), *STC* 23527, sig. A2ᵛ.

[74] William Browne, 'An Elegy on the Countess Dowager of Pembroke', BL Lansdowne MS 777, f. 44.

[75] 'To the Most Vertuous Learned and bewtifull Lady Marie Countesse of Penbrooke', Barnes, *P and P*, ed. Doyno, 132.

a rude shepherd, even as he praises her 'skill, in mightie Poesie', say-
ing that 'Poets Laureat crowne [her], with lasting Bayes, | In Songs of
never dying Memorie'.[76] Drayton, who chose to be portrayed wearing
the poet's laurel wreath himself, also describes her as 'learnings
famous Queene', one who wears 'the Lawrell crowne'.[77]

Pembroke's poetic endeavours were interrupted by the death of her
husband on 19 January 1601. Thereafter she was much occupied with
the administration of the estates that were part of her jointure and
those that she held for her son until he came of age. These duties
involved her in lawsuits with pirates, jewel thieves, and murderers
(Correspondence: Manuscript Letters X– XV), as well as in less dramatic cases involving what she perceived as the abuse of her property
by various tenants. She also wanted to keep her children out of the
Court of Wards, find a suitable position for young William at court,
and arrange the marriages of all three of her children. Her obsequious
letter to Queen Elizabeth, written in January 1601 while her husband
was dying, praises the queen in terms even more extravagant than her
'Astrea' or her dedicatory poem, as she reminded the queen of her
own service at court and sought a similar position for William (Correspondence: Manuscript Letter IX). Unfortunately, young William
did not distinguish himself as a courtier. Instead, he seduced one of
the queen's Maids of Honour, Mary Fitton; after she became pregnant, he refused to marry her. The queen was so infuriated that she
had him thrown into the Fleet Prison. When he was released, he
was sent home to Wilton in ignominy. Not until Elizabeth died and
James came to the throne did William achieve the position his mother
had sought for him. An ambiguous phrase in a letter from Robert Sidney to his wife ('I thinck my Lord of Pembroke wil bee with us, if his
mothers being there doe not stay him'), written when the countess
was at Penshurst, suggests that William became estranged from his
mother during this time.[78]

---

[76] Baxter, *Ouránia*, sig. B4ᵛ.

[77] Drayton, 'The sixth Eglog', *Idea: The Shepheards Garland*; rpt. *Works*, I. 74, 76.

[78] Sir Robert Sidney to Lady Sidney, 12 Sept. 1604, De L'Isle MS U1475 C81/111.
Sidney's letter was written during the midst of her legal battle against Edmund Mathew,
who may be the 'monster' as hath devided myne owne from me ('he that was held the deerest
part of me)' (Correspondence: Manuscript Letter XV). See Hannay, *Philip's Phoenix*,
173–84. Briley speculates that this estrangement (which he tentatively attributes to 'some
romantic or sexual relationship—actual or alleged'), may have lasted ten years, because of
the hiatus in the records of Pembroke's life between 1604 and 1614 (except for one business
letter in 1607, Correspondence XVI): John Richard Briley, 'A Biography of William Herbert, Third Earl of Pembroke, 1580–1630' (Ph.D. diss., U of Birmingham, 1961), 472. See

In the second year of James's reign, the countess's eldest niece and both of her sons made advantageous marriages: young Mary Sidney married King James's hunting companion Sir Robert Wroth on 27 September 1604; William married Mary Talbot, daughter of the Earl of Shrewsbury, on 4 November; and Philip married Susan de Vere, the granddaughter of Lord Burghley, on 27 December. Although arrangements had begun in 1599 for Lady Anne's marriage to Edward Seymour, Earl of Hertford, she never did marry, perhaps because of a recurring illness. Despite her mother's attempts to procure the best medical care, Anne died in her early twenties, probably in December 1606.[79]

Except for Pembroke's request for a wardship, written from Sir Henry Lee's estate at Ditchley in 1607 (Correspondence XVI), there is a hiatus in the known records of her life from 1604 to 1614. Her journey to Spa in 1614 is well documented, through her brother's business correspondence, the correspondence of Dudley Carleton and John Chamberlain, and even a poetic reference by William Basse.[80] Her amusements in Spa reportedly included taking tobacco, playing cards, shooting pistols, dancing, and flirting with her handsome and learned doctor, Sir Matthew Lister, a romance reflected in the courtship of Simeana and Lissius in Lady Wroth's pastoral drama *Love's Victory*.[81] (This Continental sojourn, as well as the use of her name in the title of Sidney's *Arcadia*, may have contributed to her seventeenth-century reputation in France as one who loved '*la galanterie et les belles choses*'.)[82] The letters from Pembroke to Sir Tobie

also Andreas Gebauer, *Von Macht und Mazenatentum Leben und Werk William Herberts, des dritten Earls von Pembroke* (Heidelberg: Carl Winter Universitätsverlag, 1987), 78–82; and Gary Waller, *The Sidney Family Romance: Mary Wroth, William Herbert, and the Early Modern Construction of Gender* (Detroit: Wayne State UP, 1993), 79–80. If there had been a ten-year estrangement, however, it would probably have been the subject of gossip in contemporary correspondence.

[79] Lady Anne's final illness is mentioned in a letter from John Chamberlain to Sir Dudley Carleton, 21 Dec. 1606, Chamberlain, *Letters*, I. 239–40.

[80] Sir John Throckmorton to Robert Sidney, 25 June–4 Oct. 1614, De L'Isle MS U 1475 C9/ 346–66; 24 Feb. 1615, C9/ 398; William Basse, 'Eclogue V', in *The Poetical Works of William Basse*, ed. R. Warwick Bond (London: Ellis and Elvey, 1893), 209–12.

[81] Sir Dudley Carleton to John Chamberlain, 2 Aug. 1616, *Dudley Carleton to John Chamberlain, 1603–1624: Jacobean Letters*, ed. Maurice Lee, Jr. (New Brunswick, NJ: Rutgers UP, 1972), 209. Wroth, *Love's Victory*. See also Aubrey, *Brief Lives*, 139.

[82] François Boisrobert, '*Advis au Lecteur*', *La folle gageure ou les divertissements de la comtesse de Pembroc* (Paris, 1653), sig. e1ᵛ. Boisrobert adapts the Spanish work, moving the setting from Naples to London, and replacing the role of the queen with the Countess of Pembroke as the one who listens to verses and encourages poets. The queen, he says, '*ne*

Matthew, if authentic, would indicate that she continued her translation and her writing, exchanging manuscripts with Matthew as she had done with Daniel years before (Correspondence: Printed Letters I–III.)

As the Dowager Countess of Pembroke, she continued to assert her individuality. When her signature, 'M. Pembroke', was adopted by her daughter-in-law Mary Talbot, she signed her name simply 'Pembroke', differentiating it from that of her son by the surrounding 'S fermé', or closed S, to represent Sidney. (The 'S fermé' was also frequently used by her niece, Lady Mary Wroth.) Instead of continuing to use the simple Sidney pheon to seal her letters, she designed her own device—two pheons intersecting to form an M for Mary and crossed by an H for Herbert. She was no longer the mistress of Wilton or Baynards Castle, but she did maintain a London home, and the king granted her land to build a country house in Bedfordshire. A graceful brick mansion with a classical marble loggia, Houghton House was decorated with a stone frieze with a recurring pattern of badges—the Sidney porcupine, the Dudley bear with ragged staff, and her own device. There she entertained her friends, defended her property in a series of lawsuits, and continued to enjoy the company of Matthew Lister.[83] Although she appeared at court less frequently than in her younger days, she was honoured as the mother of the Earls of Pembroke and Montgomery, and as the sister of Sir Philip Sidney. In 1619 she was one of the countesses who marched in the funeral procession for Queen Anne; there she would have talked with friends and relatives, including Lady Wroth and Lady Anne Clifford. The king visited Houghton House in July 1621. On 25 September she died of smallpox at her home on Aldersgate Street in London. Her funeral was 'made according to her quality' in St Paul's Cathedral, and then her body was taken 'with a great store of coaches and torch-light' to Wilton; she was buried with her husband under the choir steps in Salisbury Cathedral.[84]

---

devoit pas permettre tant de familiarité. See also Albert W. Osborn, *Sir Philip Sidney en France* (Paris: Librairie Ancienne Honoré Champion, 1932), 151.

[83] On Pembroke's architectural innovations at Houghton House, see Alice T. Friedman, 'Architecture, Authority, and the Female Gaze: Planning and Representation in the Early Modern Country House', *Assemblage: A Critical Journal of Architecture and Design Culture* 18 (1992), 41–56; 55, 57.

[84] Robert Sidney, Earl of Leicester, to Robert Sidney, Viscount L'Isle, Sept. 1621, De L'Isle MS U1475 Z53/81; Chamberlain to Carleton, 13 Oct. 1621, Chamberlain, *Letters*, II. 400.

Although she was known in her own day as a writer, she was eulogized in William Browne's famous phrase as 'Sydneys sister Pembrokes mother', a description that largely defined her future reputation.[85] It is not the full epitaph that she would have chosen, for it ignores her own accomplishments. In 1618, when she was considered aged, she had her portrait engraved by Simon van de Passe. In what is apparently her self-presentation, she is identified in the Latin and English inscriptions as a Sidney and as the Countess of Pembroke, but she is also represented as a writer. Dressed richly in ermine, silk, lace, and pearls, she holds out to the viewer her paraphrase of 'Davids Psalms'. The Sidney pheon is prominently displayed at the top of the architectural frame, crowned by a coronet to demonstrate her rank and by a laurel wreath to symbolize her poetry. She chose to be portrayed as the poets had described her, with 'the Lawrell crowne'.[86]

Origins, Early Reception, and Influence

The image of Pembroke holding her *Psalmes* in the portrait crowned with the poet's laurel wreath conforms, as we have seen, to her contemporary reputation. During her lifetime she was celebrated as a patron and praised for her virtue, as was customary in dedications addressed to women, but she went beyond these traditional roles to make significant contributions to the literary scene. By printing her brother's works and encouraging those who celebrated him, she helped to establish his reputation not only as a Protestant martyr, but also as an exemplary writer. An important, although probably unintentional, result of printing his works and some of her own, was to help break down the stigma against print. By importing Continental literary forms and practices in her own works, she contributed to the flowering of English verse that her brother had longed to see. And by presenting herself publicly as a writer, she encouraged younger women like Aemilia Lanyer and Mary Wroth.

Although her works did not receive the extraordinary manuscript and print circulation of works by her brother Philip, they were certainly read by her contemporaries and were acknowledged as models by seventeenth-century writers in several genres: drama, religious

---

[85] William Browne, 'On the Countesse Dowager of Pembroke', BL Lansdowne MS 777, f. 43ᵛ.

[86] Drayton, 'The sixth Eglog', *Idea: The Shepheards Garland*; rpt. *Works*, I. 76.

verse, and the personal letter. The best indication of Pembroke's literary reputation outside the circle of her family and friends is the circulation of her works. *Antonius* was reprinted once during her lifetime, and *A Discourse of Life and Death* was reprinted three times and reissued once. Her original pastoral dialogue 'Astrea' was included in Francis Davison's *A Poetical Rapsody*, a verse collection that was printed four times between 1602 and 1621. 'The Dolefull Lay', which may be hers, was similarly printed and reprinted in Edmund Spenser's *Astrophel*. Although her *Psalmes* were not printed during her life, they circulated widely in manuscript, as was considered appropriate for aristocratic verse. (See 'Transmission and Authority of Texts' and 'Relationship of the Texts of the *Psalmes*'.)

Another indication of her contemporary reputation is that the editor of John Bodenham's printed verse miscellany, entitled *Bel-vedére* (1600), listed her as a writer alongside Spenser, Sidney, and Shakespeare without any notice of her gender.[1] The only other woman included is Elizabeth—and the queen of England was understandably praised with King James of Scotland rather than treated as parallel to other writers, male or female.

Such presentation of a non-royal woman author was unprecedented in England, for women were admonished to be silent, not to write and publish.[2] In the *Instruction of a Christian Woman*, for example, Juan Luis Vives explains why women should be barred from public demonstration of learning: 'if she be good, it were better to be at home within and unknown to other folks, and in company to hold her tongue demurely, and let few see her, and none at all hear her'.[3] Vives's prohibition, symptomatic of a society that enjoined women to be 'chaste, silent and obedient', was internalized by generations of learned women, for it was consistently reinforced by their culture.[4] Chastity and silence were often linked, as in the familiar proverb, 'An eloquent woman is never chaste', and by Thomas Bentley in his

---

[1] Bodenham, *Bel-vedére*, sig. A4ᵛ.

[2] For lists of works by Renaissance women, see Elaine Beilin, 'Current Bibliography of English Women Writers, 1500–1640', in *Renaissance Englishwoman*, 347–60; and Charlotte F. Otten, 'Bibliography of Women Writers, 1540–1700', in her *English Women's Voices, 1540–1700* (Miami: Florida International UP, 1992), 393–415.

[3] Juan Luis Vives, *Instruction of a Christian Woman* (*c*.1529), STC 24856, sig. C6, printed in *Daughters, Wives and Widows: Writings by Men about Women and Marriage in England, 1500–1640*, ed. Joan Larsen Klein (Urbana: U of Illinois P, 1992), 102.

[4] See works intended for women as discussed in Suzanne W. Hull, *Chaste, Silent & Obedient: English Books for Women 1475–1640* (San Marino, Calif.: Huntington Library, 1982).

Monument of Matrones: 'There is nothing that becommeth a maid better than sobernes, silence, shamefastnes, and chastitie, both of bodie and mind. For these things being once lost, shee is no more a maid, but a strumpet in the sight of God.'[5] Even when writing was not presented as a violation of a woman's chastity, it was usually presented as a male prerogative, as when Nicholas Breton outlines in *The Praise of Virtuous Ladies* the virtues of each gender: 'if hee be valiaunt, shee is vertuous... and ... if hee can write, shee can reade'.[6]

The few English women writers who preceded Pembroke usually wrote or translated religious works. Most famous were Anne Askew and Pembroke's aunt, Lady Jane Grey, both of whom spoke boldly for their faith as they faced martyrdom. For women in less extreme circumstances, translation of religious works became a privileged genre, since it was also justified by religious duty.[7] Such translation was thought to be so appropriate for aristocratic women that Princess Elizabeth was given devotional works to translate as a school exercise; someone must have known that her stepmother Katharine Parr would be particularly pleased by a translation of a religious meditation by a royal woman, Marguerite de Navarre.[8] When women channelled their learning into the translation and dissemination of Continental texts deemed essential for partisan religious struggles, such as Anne Cooke Bacon translating Bernardino Ochino's sermons or Anne Lok translating sermons by Calvin and Jean Taffin, they could justly feel that they were serving God. But even that service had to be muted. To forestall the charge of immodesty, Margaret Roper's one extant work, her translation of Erasmus's *A Devout Treatise Upon the Pater Noster*, was published anonymously; Anne Lok hid her gender by using only her initials to sign the dedication of her anonymous translation of Calvin; and Anne Cooke Bacon's editor claimed that her translation of John Jewel's *Apologia ecclesiae anglicanae* was published without her knowledge.[9]

---

[5] Thomas Bentley, *The Monument of Matrones* (1582), *STC* 1892, 'Fift Lampe', sig. A2.

[6] Nicholas Breton, *The Wil of Wit*, in *Works*, II. c. 59.

[7] Hannay, 'Introduction', in *Silent but for the Word*, 1–14; Mary Ellen Lamb, 'The Cooke Sisters: Attitudes toward Learned Women in the Renaissance', in *Silent but for the Word*, 107–25; Tilde Sankovitch, 'Inventing Authority of Origin: The Difficult Enterprise', in *Women in the Middle Ages*, 234.

[8] Anne Prescott, 'The Pearl of the Valois and Elizabeth I: Marguerite de Navarre's *Miroir* and Tudor England', in *Silent but for the Word*, 61–76.

[9] [Margaret More Roper], *A Devout Treatise Upon the Pater Noster... turned into englishe by a yong vertuous and well lerned gentylwoman of xix yere of age* (*c*.1526), *STC* 10477; Lok, 'A Meditation of a Penitent Sinner'; and Taffin, *Children of God* (Lok's name, by then Anne

Secular translation, a standard part of the humanist curriculum, was sometimes also encouraged as part of a woman's education. For example, Elizabeth had translated works by Petrarch, Seneca, Plutarch, Boethius, and Horace, and Joanna Lumley translated Euripides' *Iphigeneia at Aulis*, but these were private exercises.[10] Apparently, the only English woman to publish a secular translation before Pembroke was Margaret Tyler; obviously anticipating censure for translating a Spanish romance, she included a preface attempting to justify secular translation for women.[11]

We should not underestimate Pembroke's boldness in permitting the publication of two secular translations and an original pastoral dialogue under her own name, without apology for her subject or her gender, and without the conventional declaration that they were published without her knowledge or permission. Her translations were not a feminine amusement, but part of a deliberate effort to transplant Continental genres into England and to support the Protestant cause on the Continent. Her translation of Robert Garnier's *Marc Antoine* helped to naturalize Continental political drama in England and served as both a precursor and a source for Shakespeare's Roman history plays; her translation of Philippe de Mornay's *Excellent discours de la vie et de la mort* was part of an international effort to aid the Huguenot cause; her translation of Petrarch's *Trionfo della Morte* presented a vibrant, speaking Laura in contrast to the silent female figure in most of the English Petrarchan tradition, thereby helping to empower her niece Lady Wroth, the first English woman to write a secular sonnet sequence, a prose romance, and a full pastoral drama.[12] (See *Triumph of Death*: 'Literary Context'.)

Before Pembroke, no woman had achieved such a prominent public literary identity in England, although she may well have looked to France and Marguerite de Navarre as a role model. She may also

Prowse, was included on the title-page of this translation); Anne Cooke Bacon, trans., *Sermons of Barnardine Ochine of Siena* (1548), *STC* 18764, and John Jewel, *An Apologie or answere in defence of the Church of Englande* (1564), *STC* 14591.

[10] Lady Lumley, trans., 'The Tragedie of Euripides called Iphigeneia translated out of Greake into Englisshe' (holograph), BL MS Reg. 15. A. See *Iphigenia at Aulis, Translated by Lady Lumley*, ed. Harold H. Child and W. W. Greg, Malone Society Reprint Series (London: Charles Whittingham and Co., 1909); Beilin, *Redeeming Eve*, 153–7; Cary, *Mariam*, ed. Weller and Ferguson, 26–7.

[11] Margaret Tyler, trans., *The Mirrour of Princely Deedes and Knighthood*, by Diego Ortuñez de Calahorra (London, 1578), *STC* 18859.

[12] On Pembroke's influence as a role model to other women writers, see Morton (Ph.D. diss.).

have felt empowered by her mother's reputed verbal excellence, by her aunt Lady Jane Grey's words as recorded in John Foxe's *Actes and Monuments*, and by the translations of her mother's friends, the Cooke sisters. And of course, any Elizabethan woman was to some extent empowered by Elizabeth herself. As Anne Bradstreet later wryly observed in her elegy on the queen, 'Let such as say our sex is void of reason, | Know 'tis a slander now but once was treason'.[13] Appropriately, two of Pembroke's extant original works are written in honour of the queen. Since the Petrarchan and heroic modes usually addressed to the queen were inappropriate to a woman's voice, she applied the myth of Astrea to the queen, and she presented that myth in a dialogue format that obscured her own gender. Her dedicatory poem, as appropriate to the genre, is more personal, speaking directly on behalf of her brother and herself as writers. In that poem she turns to Genevan models, praising Elizabeth as the David of her people. (See 'Even now that Care': 'Literary Context'.)

Pembroke's position as a Sidney, and as an avatar of her brother, gave her a voice, as many who sought her patronage recognized. Thomas Churchyard, for example, emphasizes her Sidneian heritage when he implicitly urges her to defy the usual restrictions on female speech: Pembroke is 'a *Sidney* right' who 'shall not in silence sit'. In her 'bookes, and verses' are revealed all the muses and all the graces.[14] As a grieving relative, an appropriate female role, she wrote at least one original elegy to honour her brother. But her most effective poetic strategy was to speak through the words of the Psalmist and therefore through the Word of God in her paraphrases of the Psalms.

Pembroke never apologizes for her role as a woman writer and rarely comments on it. Her identification as a woman poet is seen most clearly in an excised version of Psalm 68 wherein 'we' apparently becomes the women poets who sing praises to God as David brings the Ark to Jerusalem (1 Chronicles 15). Although her final version has been altered, the original version depicts the women singers as liberated from their usual confinement to house and distaff:

11.   A virgin army there, with chastness armed best
       While armys fledd, by Thee was taught this triumph Song to sing.

[13] 'In Honour of that High and Mighty Princess Queen Elizabeth of Happy Memory', *The Works of Anne Bradstreet*, ed. Jeannine Hensley (Cambridge, Mass.: Harvard UP, 1967), 198. See also Diana Primrose, *A Chaine of Pearle. Or a Memoriall of the peerles Graces, and Heroick Vertues of Queene Elizabeth, of Glorious Memory* (1630), *STC* 20388.

[14] Churchyard, *Conceit*, sig. B1ᵛ.

12.   These Kings, these Sons of Warr, lo, lo they fly they fly
         Wee house=confined maids with distaffs share the spoyle

13.   Whose hew though long at home the chimnys glosse did foyle
         Since now as late enlarged doves wee freer skyes do try
         As that gold-featherd fowle so shall our beautys shine
         With beating wavy aire with oare of silverd winge
         So dasleth gazing eyes that eyes cannot define
         If those sweet lovely, glittring streames from Gold or Silver spring.

Pembroke tolerates the cultural cliché that chastity is a woman's best armour, but she does not accept the injunctions to silence; indeed, she chooses to follow the tradition that renders the rest of the Psalm as the words of the women singers rather than the words of the Psalmist.[15] And she seems to identify with the women, who are discussed in the second person in her sources: we women, she says, we poets who sing God's praise, we who have been confined to the household. Like the women who were freed from domestic duties to sing before the Ark of the Covenant, Pembroke was freed to soar into the skies of poetic composition, singing songs of praise to God. By her careful use of appropriate rhetorical strategies, by appearing to stay within gender boundaries even while she challenged them, Pembroke created a literary role for herself and yet retained the respect of her contemporaries.

Contemporary references to Pembroke's 'verse', although disappointingly vague, are usually enthusiastic. The rhetoric is often coloured by an appeal for patronage, but even so, Pembroke seems to have had a considerable reputation as a writer, one who is often compared to Sappho. Thomas Heywood says, for example, that he will 'onely bestow upon her Muse' that character which Horace bequeathed to Sappho:

Vivuntque commissi Calores
Æoliae fidibus Puellae.[16]

---

[15] Vatablus comments in his note on Psalm 68. 13 that some say the words are those of the women and some say they are the words of the Psalmist: '*Sunt qui dicunt hoc loco verba esse mulierum renuntiantium partam victoriam: alii affirmant verba esse psalmographi.*' Calvin specifically rejects the women's voice in this Psalm in his commentary on v. 12. See Fisken, 'Education', 174–80; Margaret Hannay, '"House-confined maids": The Presentation of Woman's Role in the *Psalmes* of the Countess of Pembroke', *ELR* 24 (1994), 20–35.

[16] Heywood, *Gynaikeion*, sig. Mm1ᵛ. Heywood also praises Wroth ('the most ingenious Ladie, the late composer of our extant *Urania*'), and mentions John Harington's praise of the four daughters of Sir Anthony Cooke in his allegory on the 37th book of Ariosto.

Although Michael Drayton's 'Sixth Eglog' praises her primarily for her virtue and for her patronage, 'Erecting learnings long decayed fame', he also praises her 'rare quill' as the equal of Sappho's.[17] Curiously, Drayton once describes Pembroke not as patron, but as a competitor, for he writes to Henry Cavendish as his '*Maecenas*' in *Piers Gaveston*, asking him to turn from *Meridianis* (his anagram for Mari Sidnei, used in 'Amour 51' of *Ideas Mirror*) to his own works:

> lend thine eyes awhile,
> From *Meredian's* sun-bred stately straine:
> And from thy rare and lofty flying stile,
> Looke downe into my low and humble vaine.[18]

Poets often connected her with her brother in their search for patronage. In a typical configuration, Francis Meres identifies her as the sister of Sir Philip Sidney, praises her as both patron and writer, compares her to Sappho, and implies that she is the tenth muse: The 'noble sister of immortall Sir *Philip Sidney*, is very liberall unto Poets; besides shee is a most delicate Poet, of whome I may say, as *Antipater Sidonius writeth of Sappho: Dulcia Mnemosyne demirans carmina Sapphus, | Quaesivit decima Pieris unde foret*'.[19] Barnabe Barnes says that she is both 'great favourer of Phoebus of-spring' and herself one 'in whom even Phoebus is most florishing'.[20] Thomas Nashe, in his corrupt 1591 edition of *Astrophil and Stella*, says that those who mourn Sidney can gain some comfort from other 'goodly branches' of that 'house of honor'. Among these the 'fayre sister of *Phoebus*, and eloquent secretary to the Muses' is counted as 'a second *Minerva*', who is also extolled by 'our Poets . . . as the Patronesse of their invention'. He also compares her to Sappho: 'in thee, the Lesbian *Sappho* with her lirick Harpe is disgraced'. Like her brother, Nashe says, she is a patron, one who 'entertainest emptie handed *Homer*', so all 'learning, wisedom, beautie' seek her approval and, most importantly, 'the smiles of [her] favor'. Nashe openly admits his search for patronage, accurately noting that 'I shall be counted a mercenary flatterer'. Sounding as if he has never met her, he concludes that the 'generall report that surpasseth my praise, condemneth my rethoricke of

[17] Michael Drayton, 'The sixth Eglog', *Idea: The Shepheards Garland*, in *Works*, I. 73–4.

[18] *Works*, I. 207. See Jean Robertson, 'Drayton and the Countess of Pembroke', *RES* 16 (1965), 49; Jean R. Brink, *Michael Drayton Revisited* (Boston: Twayne, 1990), 8, 76.

[19] Francis Meres, *Palladis Tamia* (1598), *STC* 17834, sig. Oo4ᵛ.

[20] Barnabe Barnes, 'To the Most Vertuous Learned and bewtifull Lady Marie Countesse of Penbrooke', *P and P*, ed. Doyno, 132.

dulnesse for so colde a commendation'.[21] Even more exploitative is
Nathaniel Baxter's device of having the ghost of Philip Sidney promise 'Tergaster' (Baxter) that though 'Fates denie me learning to
advance' because he is dead, 'Yet Cinthia [Pembroke, 'my deerest Sister'] shall afford thee maintenance'. Cynthia herself promises, 'Cast
feare away, Ile be thy Patronesse'.[22] Thomas Moffet, the Pembroke
family physician, mocks such appeals in his *Silkewormes*:

> Vouchsafe from brothers ghost no niggards almes,
> Now to enrich my high aspiring layes.[23]

His own evocation of Sidney is more subtle when he praises Pembroke as 'inheritor of [Sidney's] wit and genius'.[24] In *Silkewormes*
Moffet stresses a family context for her writing, praising not only
Pembroke but also Robert Sidney and Philip Sidney's daughter Elizabeth, Countess of Rutland, as inheritors of Sidney's muse, although
he tactfully gives the most honour to his own patron:

> *Sydneian Muse*: if so thou yet remaine,
> In brothers bowels, or in daughters brest,
> Or art bequeath'd *the Lady of the plaine*,
> Because for her thou art the fittest guest.[25]

When Michael Drayton pictures 'the *Arcadian* Swaines' adoring
'*Pandoras* poesy' they are not entirely disinterested in their praise.[26]
Like most patrons, Pembroke is praised for her generosity and compared to gold or jewels, thereby symbolizing the rewards that the poet
hoped to receive. Gabriel Harvey, for example, calls her published
translations an '*Electuary of Gemmes*' and Edmund Spenser praises
her 'brave mynd' as 'a golden cofer' containing 'All heavenly gifts
and riches' that are more valuable than 'pearles of *Ynde*, or gold of
Opher'.[27] Even William Smith, who admits that he does not know
her, compares her to a marigold, with its pun on 'Mary's gold', a

[21] Thomas Nashe, 'Somewhat to reade for them that list', Sidney, *Astrophel*, sig. A4.
[22] Baxter, *Ouránia*, sig. N1, B4ᵛ.
[23] Moffet, *Silkewormes*, sig. G1.
[24] Moffet, *Nobilis*, 74.
[25] Moffet, *Silkewormes*, sig. B1.
[26] Drayton, dedication of *Ideas Mirror*, in *Works*, I. 97.
[27] Harvey, *Letter*, sigs. A4ᵛ–B1. Spenser, *Colin Clouts*, sig. C3. Cf. Robert Herrick's
praise of her son Philip as one who will 'turn [the poets'] lines to gold', 'To the right
honourable, Philip, Earle of Pembroke, and Montgomerie', *Hesperides*, in *The Complete
Poems of Robert Herrick*, ed. Alexander B. Grosart, 3 vols. (London: Chatto & Windus,
1876), II. 63.

reference also used by Michael Drayton, William Browne, and others.[28]

The terms of their praise are instructive. Given the conventions of encomia, there is surprisingly little stress on her beauty—although she was beautiful, if the portraits are at all realistic. Even those who do stress her beauty give equal emphasis to her learning: William Gager combines ritual praise of her beauty and bright eyes with praise of her learning in his appeal for patronage; similarly, Abraham Fraunce addresses his work to this patron, *'piae, formosae, eruditae'*.[29] She is rarely praised by the usual mythological comparisons; Fitzjeffery is a notable exception, saying that she surpasses Venus (both in virtue and in beauty), Pallas Athena, and Calliope.[30] Instead, she is typically praised for her learning and for her writing. William Camden calls her 'a friend to the *Muses*, and a Lady most addicted to delightfull studies'.[31] Nathaniel Baxter praises her 'wisedome' and 'learning', says that 'rare are her gifts full of *Sydneian*-fyres', declares that she is 'for learning had in admiration', calls her 'Divine Mistresse of Elocution' and asks her to accept the verse of a rude shepherd, even as he praises her 'skill, in mightie Poesie' as demonstrated by 'her learned Poems, and her Layes'.[32] Like many others, Drayton connects her poetry with her brother's, saying that she is the sister to Elphin [Sidney] who 'To her bequeath'd the Secrets of his Skill'.[33] Similarly, Francis Osborne claims that 'her *Pen'* is 'nothing short of his'.[34]

---

[28] William Smith, 'A new Yeares Guifte. made upon Certen Flowers', BL Additional MS 35186, f. 6; Drayton, *Ideas Mirror*, 'Amour 51', *Works*, I. 124; William Browne, 'An Elegy on the Countess Dowager of Pembroke', in *Poems of William Browne of Tavistock*, ed. Gordon Goodwin (London: Routledge, 1893), 249. On the identification of the marigold in Drayton see *Works*, V. 17–18.

[29] William Gager, '*Nobilissimae Ac Doctissime Heroine, Domine Marie Penbrochie Comitissa*', *Ulysses Redux: Tragoedia Nova* (Oxford, 1592), *STC* 11516; the dedication appears in the Huntington Library copy, without signature number. Fraunce, *Ivychurch. Third Part*, sig. A2.

[30] Charles Fitzjeffery, '*Ad Illustrissimam Heroinam Mariam Pembrochiae Comitissam*', *Affaniæ: sive Epigrammatum libri tres* (1601), *STC* 10934, sig. G7. Cf. Thomas Howell, although he compares himself, rather than the countess, with various mythological figures. In this, the first work dedicated to her, the old family retainer affectionately praised qualities appropriate to a young woman, her 'honorable curtesie and sweete behaviour'; that is the last mention of her sweetness, and, even then, Howell also noted her virtue and wisdom: Howell, *Devises*, ed. Raleigh, 6.

[31] Camden, *Historie*, sig. Bbbb4[v].

[32] Baxter, *Ouránia*, sig. A2, B1, B4[v], N2[v].

[33] Drayton, *Works*, II. 561.

[34] Osborne, *Memoires*, sig. Gg2.

One of the most intriguing presentations of Pembroke as a writer is by her niece, Lady Mary Wroth, who shadows Pembroke as the Queen of Naples in the quasi-autobiographical fiction of *Urania*. That queen is 'as perfect in Poetry, and all other Princely vertues as any woman that ever liv'd, to bee esteemed excellent in any one, [but] shee was stor'd with all, and so the more admirable'.[35] *Urania* includes 'Verses framed by the most incomparable Queene, or Lady of her time, a Nightingale most sweetly singing, upon which she grounded her subject'. Because the queen represents Pembroke and because we know that a poem in *Urania* attributed to Amphilanthus (who represents William Herbert) is included in various seventeenth-century miscellanies as the work of William Herbert, there is a slight possibility that this lyric, attributed to the Queen of Naples, is one of the lost works of the Countess of Pembroke.[36] Josephine Roberts has suggested that the poem, which is extant in two significantly different versions, may be 'an example of collaborative composition by the Sidney women, whereby Wroth reworked her aunt's original verse'.

> O That I might but now as senselesse bee
> Of my felt paines, as is that pleasant Tree,
> Of the sweet musique, thou deare Byrd dost make,
> Who I imagine doth my woes partake.
> Yet contrary we doe our passions moove,
> Since in sweet notes thou dost thy sorrowes proove.
> I but in sighs, and teares, can shew I grieve,
> And those best spent, if worth doe them beleeve.
> Yet thy sweet pleasures makes me ever finde
> That happinesse to me, as Love is blinde,
> And these thy wrongs in sweetnesse to attire,
> Throwes downe my hopes to make my woes aspire.
> Besides, of me th'advantage thou hast got,
> Thy griefe thou utter'st, mine I utter not.

[35] Wroth, *Urania*, sig. R3ᵛ; *Urania*, ed. Roberts, 371. Roberts suggests that Wroth also 'shadows' Pembroke in the characters of Clorina, the mother of Laurimello, and perhaps Melissea: ibid., pp. lxxxiv–lxxxvi.

[36] The poem 'Had I lov'd but at that rate', included in *Urania*, is attributed to Pembroke in BL MS Harley 6917, ff. 33ᵛ–34; Additional MS 21433, ff. 119ᵛ–120ᵛ; Additional MS 10309, ff. 25ʳ⁻ᵛ. See Wroth, *Poems*, 217. On the significance of the Nightingale as female poet in Sidney's *Arcadia*, see Cheryl Hinson, 'Sidney's Enticing Song: The Philomela Myth and the Rewriting of the *Arcadia*' (Penn State, Ph.D. diss., 1995), 82–90.

> Yet thus as last we may agree in one,
> I mourne for what still is, thou, what is gone.[37]

The queen's verses are received with extravagant praise. Perissus says 'that he never had heard any like them, and in so saying, he did right to them, and her who knew when she did well, and would be unwilling to lose the due unto her selfe, which he gave her, swering he never heard any thing finelier worded, nor wittilier written on the sudden'. The characterization of the poet as one 'who knew when she did well, and would be unwilling to lose the due unto her selfe' does seem to fit what we know of the Countess of Pembroke.[38] Self-abnegation is far from the mind of the Queen of Naples, who expects and receives great praise for her compositions. Given the torrent of praise that Pembroke apparently expected and certainly received from her contemporaries, we may deduce that an abject humility was not one of her faults.

Allusions to specific works are less frequent than the general praise of her pen. Her original works are rarely mentioned by her contemporaries. Except for Spenser's introductory stanza in *Astrophel* and his apparent references to 'The Dolefull Lay' in the 'Ruines' (see 'Dolefull Lay': 'Literary Context') few specific allusions to this work have been discovered. Lynn Moorhead Morton has recently suggested that Wroth alludes to 'The Dolefull Lay' in the opening lament of *Urania*, that Wroth adopts Pembroke's persona of a grieving shepherdess in songs interspersed in *Pamphilia and Amphilanthus*, and that Lanyer paraphrases the poem in her dedication to Queen Anne.[39] 'The Dolefull Lay' was thought significant enough to be excerpted in John Bodenham's *Bel-vedére*.[40] The anthology is of no help in

---

[37] Wroth, *Urania*, sig. Fff3ᵛ; *Urania*, ed. Roberts, 490. Wroth's holograph MS presents the poem without distinguishing it from Wroth's other work, except that it is given no title or number, Folger MS V.a.104, f. 49ᵛ. *Urania*, ed. Roberts, 776. On the Countess of Pembroke and Lady Wroth, see ibid., pp. lxxxiv–lxxxvi.

[38] H. T. R. was one of the first critics to challenge Lodge, who had said, 'as a poet she was spoiled by adulation, and complimented into conceit and carelessness': 'Mary Sidney and Her Writings', *Gentlemen's Magazine* 24 (1845), 369.

[39] Morton (Ph.D. diss.), 126, 142–4, 167–8.

[40] None of the sources of the paraphrased excerpts in *Bel-vedére* is identified in the volume itself. Charles Crawford first identified the borrowings from the 'Lay' (16 and 49, sigs. [K7] and Q4, respectively), in '*Bel-vedere, or The Garden of the Muses*', *Englische Studien* 43 (1910–11), 206. Crawford overlooked three passages adapted from *Antonius* (1427–8 and 1429–30 on sig. [I7], and 1507–8 on sig. O2ᵛ), which is probably the work the writer of the letter to the reader had in mind when he cited Pembroke as one of the authors represented in the anthology.

determining authorship, however, since no works are given individual attribution and since both Spenser and Pembroke are listed among the authors included. (See 'Dolefull Lay': 'Literary Context'.)

The poems dedicating the Sidneian *Psalmes* to Queen Elizabeth and to Philip Sidney apparently rarely circulated with the *Psalmes* manuscripts. Now extant in only one copy, the Tixall manuscript (MS *J*), they were probably also included in the Penshurst manuscript, now lacking pages so that it begins with Psalm 4. 'Even now that Care' does not seem to have been known to Pembroke's contemporaries, but the early draft of 'To the Angell Spirit of the most excellent Sir Phillip Sidney' found in Samuel Daniel's papers suggests that Pembroke may have shown that poem to at least one reader.

Angel references, ubiquitous in references to sacred poetry, were nonetheless employed with unusual frequency in poems presented to the countess in the late 1590s and early seventeenth century; such references may hint at knowledge of this dedication to Sidney. John Davies of Hereford, mentioning his transcription of the Penshurst MS ('My Hand once sought that glorious WORKE to grace; | and writ, in Gold, what thou, in Incke hadst writ'), declares that her *Psalmes* will live eternally, for 'when the *Spheares* shall cease their gyring sound, | the *Angels* then, shall chaunt it in their *Quires*'.[41] The phrasing closely echoes Pembroke's own, calling Sidney's *Psalmes* 'high Tons...which Angells sing in their cælestiall Quire' (12–13). Baxter mentions her work penned with 'Angells quill'.[42] Michael Drayton's *Idea* promises that 'Millions of Saints shall thy lives prayses sing, | Pend with the quill of an Archangels wing'.[43] Likewise Aemilia Lanyer portrays a company singing Pembroke's 'holy Sonnets' that 'Their musicke might in eares of Angels ring'.[44] Often such references connect her with her famous brother, co-author of the *Psalmes* paraphrases. Henry Lok, for example, may allude to 'Angell Spirit' in his dedicatory sonnet in *Ecclesiastes*:

> that pregnancie of spright,
> Whereby you equall honour do attaine,

[41] Davies, *Muses Sacrifice*, in *Works*, II. 4.

[42] Baxter, *Ouránia*, sig. N2ᵛ. Yet note that Henry Constable uses a similar phrase to praise King James, comparing him to David and saying that his pen is 'Made of a quill pluckt from an angell's winge': 'To the K. of Scots, whome as yet he had not seene', *Poems*, p. xli.

[43] Drayton, *Works*, I. 76.

[44] Lanyer, *Salve Deus*, sig. D1ᵛ.

To that extinguist Lampe of heavenly light,
Who now no doubt doth shine midst Angels bright.[45]

John Donne, praising the Sidneian *Psalmes* with a typical metaphysical conceit, shows the Angel choirs learning to sing those Psalms 'by what the Church does here'.[46] More striking is Samuel Daniel's deliberate echo in *Delia* 1 of Pembroke's phrasing in 'Angell Spirit'. As Lars-Håkan Svensson notes, both poems include a transition from 'ocean/river imagery to accountancy terminology' and employ similar terminology, such as feudal language and the Protestant term 'zeale', a term also used to speak of the commemoration of Sidney in the *Astrophel* elegies. Daniel's concluding couplet, Svensson suggests, 'reads like a condensed version of ll. 47–49 (1623: ll. 54–56) in the Countess's poem' (45). *Delia* thus opens with 'an exquisite literary compliment' to Pembroke's own work that Daniel had read in draft.[47]

Yet her dedicatory poems could not have circulated very widely. Thomas Heywood, at least, did not know of Pembroke's elegies for her brother. He compares 'The beautifull and learned Ladie *Mary*, Countesse of Penbrooke' with the 'great Italian Ladie, called *Vittoria* [Vittoria Colonna], who writ largely and learnedly in the praise of her dead husband', but specifically says that Pembroke wrote 'not in that Funerall Elegeick straine'.[48]

Her original 'Dialogue . . . in praise of Astrea', probably written in 1599, was given wide circulation under her name after it was anthologized by Francis Davison in 1602. Sir John Davies may have seen a manuscript version, for there are many parallels to Pembroke's 'Astrea' in his *Hymnes of Astraea*, twenty-six acrostic poems presented to the queen on Accession Day, 17 November 1599. (See 'Astrea': 'Literary Context'.)

Although it was reprinted three times (1600, 1606, 1608) and reissued once (1607), Pembroke's *Discourse* enlarged Mornay's reputation rather than her own, for it is rarely mentioned by her contemporaries. A year after her translations of Mornay and Garnier had been

---

[45] Lok, *Ecclesiastes*, sig. Y1ᵛ.

[46] Donne, 'Upon the translation of the Psalmes by Sir Philip Sydney, and the Countesse of Pembroke his Sister', in Donne, *Divine Poems*, 34.

[47] Lars-Håkan Svensson, *Silent Art: Rhetorical and Thematic Patterns in Samuel Daniel's Delia*, Lund Studies in English 57 (1980), 35–49.

[48] Heywood, *Gynaikeion*, sig. Mm1ᵛ. Heywood is here amplifying John Harington's praise of Pembroke in his allegory on the 37th book of Ariosto, also cited by Bathsua Makin, *An Essay to Revive the Antient Education of Gentlewomen* (1673), Wing M309, 20.

published together, Gabriel Harvey does refer to both works, although he does not mention Pembroke by name:

What *Dia margariton*, or *Dia ambre*, so comfortative, or cordiall, as *Her Electuary of Gemmes* (for though the furious Tragedy *Antonius*, be a bloudy Chaire of estate, yet the divine *Discourse of life, and Death* is a restorative Electuary of Gemmes) whom I do not expresly name, not because I do not honor *Her* with my hart, but because I would not dishonour *Her* with my pen, whome I admire, and cannot blazon enough.[49]

Another reference is Drayton's graceful allusion to the concluding motto of the *Discourse*, 'Die to live | Live to die'. Using the image of death as the beginning of life, stressed in her translations of Mornay and of Petrarch (2. 22–4), he declares 'by thy death, thy life shalbe begun'. Then she will listen to the music of angels, while earth resounds with her fame:

> Upon thy toombe shall spring a Lawrell tree,
> Whose sacred shade shall serve thee for an hearse,
> Upon whose leaves (in golde) ingrav'd this verse,
> *Dying she lives, whose like shall never be.*[50]

Shakespeare, who seems to be indebted to the *Discourse* for some of the Senecan elements in *Measure for Measure*, may echo the motto in Claudio's paradox:

> To sue to live, I find I seek to die,
> And seeking death, find life.[51]

Wroth may also allude to the motto in her pastoral romance. Urania recounts how, through Melissea's magic, she and Steriamus died to their old loves and then 'we from death in shew rose unto a new love'. Steriamus then presents Urania with a poem that concludes, 'Who dies to live, finds change a happy grace'.[52]

Although it was only reprinted once, Pembroke's translation of Garnier's *Marc Antoine* was far more influential than her translation

[49] Harvey, *Letter*, sigs. A4^v–B1.

[50] Drayton, *Idea: The Shepheards Garland*, in *Works*, I. 74, 76. The reference to the gold leaves may indicate that Drayton had seen, or at least knew of, a manuscript of her work decorated with gold, such as John Davies of Hereford's transcription of the *Psalmes* (MS *A*).

[51] Shakespeare, *Measure for Measure*, I. iii. 43–4, in *Works*, 907. See Katherine Duncan-Jones, 'Stoicism in *Measure for Measure*: A New Source', *RES* 28 (1977), 441–6.

[52] Wroth, *Urania*, sig. Nn2v; *Urania*, ed. Roberts, 332. The poem also mentions love triumphing ('Love mild to you, on me triumphing sits'), in what may be an allusion to Pembroke's translation of Petrarch. Wroth, *Urania*, sig. Nn2^v. On possible allusions to *The Triumph of Death* in *Pamphilia and Amphilanthus*, see Morton (Ph.D. diss.), 134–8.

of Mornay's *Excellent discours*. *Antonius* raises the question of Pembroke's connections with Shakespeare and the popular stage, long a matter of debate. One of the most eccentric of these speculations is Gilbert Slater's contention that she was one of seven people who actually wrote the works of Shakespeare. Since she was the only woman among this Shakespeare consortium, he proposes that her hand can be seen in *Antony and Cleopatra*, which 'showed feminine rather than masculine intuition'.[53] Naturally, she has also been put forward as a candidate for Shakespeare's 'dark lady', despite the fact that she was blonde—and far beyond Shakespeare's social class.[54] She is also identified as the mother of 'Mr. W. H.' in Shakespeare's third sonnet when 'W. H.' is believed to be William Herbert.[55]

Almost as misleading as Slater's theory has been Alexander Witherspoon's influential 1924 presentation of Pembroke as a 'fastidious' bluestocking who 'found the tragedy of the popular stage rough, uncouth, and unlearned', and determined to honour her dead brother by reforming the English drama in accordance with the precepts set forth in his *Defence*. 'With something of the zeal of the early Christian ascetics', she and her 'little coterie of academic tragedians withdrew from the world of the popular stage, and separated themselves from its naughtiness to work out their own salvation, and the salvation of English tragedy.'[56] For more than fifty years critics continued to say that the countess, misled by her blind devotion to her brother's ideas on drama expressed in his *Defence*, fostered closet drama in order to attack the popular stage. The conspiracy theory was fostered by Witherspoon's misreading of Samuel Daniel's praise of the countess and her brother as combatants against literary 'Barbarism'. In Daniel's 1592 prose dedication of *Delia*, he praises the countess as the one

---

[53] Gilbert Slater, *Seven Shakespeares: A Discussion of the Evidence for Various Theories with Regards to Shakespeare's Identity* (London: Cecil Palmer, 1931), 217.

[54] Rudolph Holzapfel, *Shakespeare's Secret* (Dublin: Doleman, 1961) argues that Shakespeare was the father of her son, William Herbert.

[55] John Padel, for example, proposes that the countess commissioned Shakespeare's *Sonnets* as a means of persuading her son, William, to marry: *New Poems by Shakespeare: Order and Meaning Restored to the Sonnets* (London: The Herbert Press, 1981), 28–53.

[56] Witherspoon, *Garnier*, 73, 75. See also T. S. Eliot, 'Seneca in Elizabethan Translation', in *Selected Essays: New Edition* (New York: Harcourt, 1950), 77; Virginia Walcott Beauchamp, 'Sidney's Sister as Translator of Garnier', *Renaissance News* 10 (1957), 12–13; H. B. Charlton, *The Senecan Tradition in Renaissance Tragedy* (Manchester: Manchester UP, 1946), 176–200. Steven May notes that Fulke Greville's tragedies conform more closely to Sidney's *Defence* than does Pembroke's *Antonius*: *Courtier Poets*, 170.

'whome the fortune of our time hath made the happie and judiciall Patronesse of the Muses...to preserve them from those hidious Beastes, Oblivion and Barbarisme'.[57] In his 1594 dedication of *Cleopatra* he amplifies this idea:

> Now when so many pennes (like Speares) are charg'd,
> To chace away this tyrant of the North:
> *Gross Barbarism*, whose powre growne far inlarg'd,
> Was lately by thy valiant Brothers worth,
> First found, encountred, and provoked forth:
> Whose onset made the rest audacious,
> Whereby they likewise have so well discharg'd,
> Upon that hidious Beast incroching thus.[58]

Daniel promises to use his pen to 'Resist so foule a foe in what I may: | And arme against oblivion and the grave', the greatest foes of poets, and he appeals for her patronage as one 'Who doost with thine owne hand a Bulwarke frame | Against these Monsters'. Like Sidney and Spenser, he implies that he and Pembroke are poets who will equal 'those *Po*-singers' of 'Declyned Italie'. The dedication, signed by one 'C. M.' (usually identified as Christopher Marlowe), of Thomas Watson's *Amintae Gaudia* also praises her for combating barbarism and ignorance.[59] While these dedications may indicate that the countess was part of a conscious campaign to improve English letters, they make no mention of the drama. Nor can the countess possibly be combating Shakespeare in her *Antonius*, for he had only recently begun his career by the time she completed her translation in 1590. Yet four years later Daniel may well be praising Shakespeare, who had written significant dramas in those intervening years, complimenting him through the pun on his name in the 'many pennes

---

[57] Daniel, *Delia*, sig. A2[v].

[58] Daniel, 'To the Right Honourable, the Lady Marie, Countess of Pembrooke', in *Delia & Cleopatra*, sig. H5[v].

[59] Watson, *Amintae Gaudia*, sig. A2. The dedication is attributed to Marlowe by Roma Gill in *The Complete Works of Christopher Marlowe* (Oxford: Clarendon P, 1987), I. 218–19. Although Watson and Marlowe almost certainly knew each other (M. Eccles, *Christopher Marlowe in London* (Cambridge, Mass.: Harvard UP, 1934), 167–9; P. Henderson, *Christopher Marlowe* (London: Longman, Green & Co., 1952; rpt. 1974), 28–34), the assertion that he dedicated to the countess his friend's posthumous work may be rendered somewhat problematic by R. B. Wernham's finding that Marlowe was arrested in 1592 on the authority of Sir Robert Sidney in Flushing on a charge of counterfeiting coinage: 'Christopher Marlowe at Flushing in 1592', *EHR* 91 (1976), 344–5. But see Patrick Cheney, *Marlowe's Counterfeit Profession: Ovid, Spenser, Counternationhood* (Toronto: U of Toronto P, 1997), 67, 223.

(like Speares)' raised against barbarism, analogous to Jonson's eulogy praising his efforts to 'shake a lance' at ignorance.[60]

Given the Dudley/Sidney family's long tradition of support for the popular drama and the Earl of Pembroke's nominal sponsorship of a dramatic troupe during the early 1590s, it is more likely that the countess would have encouraged the work of the rising dramatist than opposed him. Her uncle Leicester not only lent his protection to the troupe of players bearing his name, but also was connected with the Children of Chapel Royal and the children's company at St Paul's.[61] Her father also encouraged a variety of dramatic performances. The accounts of Ludlow Castle during his term as Lord President of the Council of the Marches of Wales include listings 'for the chylderne which did play in the Casttell' on 26 May 1562; Lord Sussex's players in 1569 and 1570; Lord Stafford's players 'In the Ester weeke that played in the Castell' (1577), as well as minstrels, singers for May day, and actors performing the life of Robin Hood.[62] When her husband assumed the position as Lord President, he evidently continued to encourage dramatic productions, for in the 1590s there was a flurry of performances at Ludlow: the Queen's Men in June 1590 and August 1596; Lord Strange's Men in August 1593; Worcester's Men in 1595 and 1596; Essex's Men in 1596; and Pembroke's Men during the summer tour of 1593. During this period ten companies, including Pembroke's Men and Lord Strange's Men, also performed at Shrewsbury, another primary residence of the Lord President.[63] There has been speculation that Shakespeare was, for a short time, a member of Pembroke's Men; whether or not he acted with them, the troupe did perform several of his plays.[64] That the countess herself had some responsibility for the players is indicated by the will of

[60] Ben Jonson, 'To the Memory of my Beloved, the Author Mr. William Shakespeare: and What He Hath Left Us', in Jonson, *Poems*, 263.

[61] In 1574, for example, Leicester's Men requested permission to wear his livery for added protection (Longleat House MSS, Marquis of Bath, Dudley Papers III, f. 125). His players travelled to the Low Countries, probably for his inauguration as governor. See Rosenberg, *Leicester*, 301–8; Paul Whitfield White, *Theatre and Reformation: Protestantism, Patronage, and Playing in Tudor England* (Cambridge: Cambridge UP, 1993), 62–6.

[62] De L'Isle MS U1475 A56 (2).

[63] See the Ludlow and Shrewsbury accounts in John Tucker Murray, *English Dramatic Companies* (London: Constable, 1910), II. 324–5, 389–93; Gerald Eades Bentley, *The Profession of Player in Shakespeare's Time, 1590–1642* (Princeton: Princeton UP, 1984), ch. 7; E. K. Chambers, *The Elizabethan Stage* (Oxford: Clarendon P, 1923), II. 128.

[64] Many of the players in Lord Strange's Men, including Shakespeare, left that company in 1594 to form the Chamberlain's Men. Brennan summarizes the critical opinion for and against Shakespeare's earlier membership in Lord Pembroke's Men: *Literary Patronage*, 95.

the actor Simon Jewell, which bequeathed 'my share of such money as shalbe givenn by my ladie Pembrooke or by her meanes'.[65] She was probably also involved in the elaborate Christmas feast held in Ludlow Castle in 1596, during which the guests performed an Arthurian entertainment.[66]

Shakespeare's later connection with the Herbert family is well established. As Lord Chamberlain, William Herbert, Earl of Pembroke, had control over the King's Men (formerly the Lord Chamberlain's Men), the company that included Richard Burbage and William Shakespeare. This company performed for King James at Wilton on 2 December 1603, although it is unclear whether Shakespeare himself was present. (See the unsubstantiated reference cited by Cory in Printed Letters IV.) William Herbert took a personal interest in the company, as indicated by his mourning for the death of Richard Burbage. As he wrote to Viscount Doncaster, Lennox 'made a great supper to the french Embassador this night here. And even now all the company are at the play which I being tender harted could not endure to see so soone after the [death] of my old acquaintance Burbadg.'[67] The First Folio edition of Shakespeare's works was dedicated to 'The Most Noble and Incomparable Pair of Brethren', William and Philip Herbert, because they had 'prosequuted both them, and their author, living, with so much favor'.[68] None of this proves the countess's patronage, of course, but it is less likely that she was an antagonist of Shakespeare than that he did, as Alice Luce suggests, 'come within the circle of her patronage', or at least that of her family.[69]

Pembroke's *Antonius* prefigured Shakespeare's Roman history plays. By translating *Marc Antoine* she was importing a Continental model that emphasized political commentary, as she later did in her *Psalmes*. Philip Sidney had praised *Gorboduc* for its 'notable morality, which it doth most delightfully teach, and so obtain the very end of poesy'.[70] *Antonius*, like *Gorboduc*, presents the conflict for the ruler between passion and public duty, focuses on the dangers of civil

[65] Will of Simon Jewell, proven 23 Aug. 1592, in Mary Edmond, 'Pembroke's Men', *RES* 25 (1974), 130. On sponsorship of drama by the Dudley/Herbert family, see Hannay, *Philip's Phoenix*, 119–29.

[66] Penry Williams, *The Tudor Regime* (Oxford: Clarendon P, 1979), 368.

[67] William Herbert, Earl of Pembroke, to Viscount Doncaster, 'this 20th of May' [1619], BL Egerton MS 2592, f. 81.

[68] Shakespeare, *Works*, p. xlii.

[69] Sidney, Mary. *Antonie*, ed. Luce, 11.

[70] Sidney, *Miscellaneous Prose*, 113.

war, and ends with the destruction of the princely line. By choosing to translate *Marc Antoine*, the countess helped to naturalize Continental tragedy that used classical history to comment on contemporary events. Garnier, who said that through his lamentations for the Greeks and Romans Cissé was '*Pleurant nos propres maux sous feintes etrangeres*', was equally explicit about his own intention in *Marc Antoine*.[71] His dedication to Monseigneur de Pibrac discusses the topical relevance of '*des guerres civiles de Rome*' to the French, '*qui avez en telle horreur nos dissentions domestiques, et les malheureux troubles de ce Royaume, aujourd'huy despouillé de son ancienne splendeur, et de la reverable majesté de nos Rois, prophanée par tumultueuses rebellions*'.[72] Lest the drama present the lovers too sympathetically, the chorus gives the perspective of the Egyptian people, who mourn that the passion of their ruler brings them, as Pembroke translates, 'Warre and warres bitter cheare' (231). Similarly, Philotas laments that love 'hath ashes made our towns . . . with deaths our lands have fil'd' (286–8). Garnier wrote in the midst of the French religious wars, but the topic was relevant to England as well. The potential for civil war was never far from English minds in the 1590s, as the ageing queen refused to name a successor; France was too close and the dynastic Wars of York and Lancaster too vividly remembered for them to be complacent. By importing Garnier's topical use of Roman history, Pembroke paved the way for explicitly political history plays in English, including those of Shakespeare and Daniel.

The influence of her translation may be seen in Shakespeare's *Antony and Cleopatra*, which echoes structural and thematic elements of *Antonius* as well as occasional phrasing. Shakespeare's Antony, like Garnier's, fears being taken in Caesar's triumph, accuses Cleopatra of treachery, and resolves to commit suicide before he is told of Cleopatra's (feigned) death. Like Garnier, Shakepeare uses Antony's identification with Hercules to draw a parallel between his unmanning by Cleopatra and that of Hercules by Omphale. (Both Pembroke and Shakespeare emphasize Antony's cross-dressing, a detail absent from Garnier.) Similarly, Shakespeare's Cleopatra, like that of *Antonius*, is motivated by fear of being taken in Caesar's triumph, a fear

---

[71] Robert Garnier, '*A. M. de Cissé*', in Jacques Courtin de Cissé, *Les hymnes de Synese* (Paris, 1581), sig. F4.
[72] Robert Garnier, *Les Tragedies de Robert Garnier* (Paris: Robert Estienne, 1585), sigs. F12^v–G1.

emphasized in Daniel's *The Tragedie of Cleopatra*. In both plays Plutarch's description of the fishing expedition is transformed so that Cleopatra's baited fish hook becomes a metaphor for the pleasure that captures Antony. The poets give similar lists of the realms that Antony gave to Cleopatra and her children at the Donations. In both plays she appears to die when she hears of Antony's death, but her women are able to revive her from a faint. Both plays emphasize the exertion of Cleopatra and her women in drawing Antony into the tomb. Cleopatra's description of Antony, in each case, emphasizes his eyes like suns and identifies him with Mars.

Verbal parallels establish that Shakespeare knew Garnier in Pembroke's translation. For example, both mention that Antony married Octavia to bring 'amity' between him and Octavius. Antony must break off from the enchanter; thus he flees at Actium because his soul is enchained to hers. He also appeals to his grey hair when he bemoans the triumph of the youthful, and (as he says) cowardly, Octavius. Shakespeare also follows Pembroke's use of 'disaster' as a verb form, refers to the fertile 'slime' of the overflowing Nile, and to Antony's fear that Cleopatra will 'practize' with Caesar. Pembroke refers to Hercules as a 'Demy-god' in connection with his bearing the world for Atlas, while Shakespeare speaks of him as a 'demy-Atlas'. In both plays, Cleopatra says that she and Antony will haunt Hades together. Shakespeare's Antony requests the thousands of kisses given by Pembroke's Cleopatra.[73] The parallels are too numerous to be coincidental.

The Countess of Pembroke's translation of Garnier's *Marc Antoine* is one of her most influential works, not only because of its use of Roman history to comment on contemporary political events, but also because of its versification (see *Antonius*: 'Fidelity to Originals') and its genre of the Senecan closet drama (see *Antonius*: 'Literary Context'). Although it may be an exaggeration to say that she 'initiated the courtly Senecan movement which led several members

---

[73] Ernest Schanzer, '"Antony and Cleopatra" and the Countess of Pembroke's "Antonius"', *N&Q* 201 (1956), 152–4, and *Problem Plays*, 150–1, 180–1; Kenneth Muir, 'Elizabeth I, Jodelle, and Cleopatra', *Renaissance Drama* 2 (1969), 197–206; Michael Steppat, 'Shakespeare's Response to Dramatic Tradition in *Antony and Cleopatra*', in *Shakespeare—Text, Language, Criticism: Essays in Honour of Marvin Spevack*, ed. Bernhard Fabian and Kurt Tetzeli von Rosador (Hildesheim: Olms-Weidmann, 1987), 254–79. Bullough, *Sources*, 230–1, lists some parallels but includes *Antonius* as an 'analogue' rather than a 'source' for Shakespeare, like Daniel's *Cleopatra*. For a summary of the critical controversy about Shakespeare's debt to Pembroke, see *Shakespeare—Text, Language, Criticism*, 475–9.

of her circle to write Roman tragedies within the next ten or fifteen years',[74] she does seem to have encouraged a vogue for 'closet drama'. With its discussion of moral issues presented in set speeches rather than stage action, the genre would have been particularly suited to reading aloud by the assembled guests at an English country house like Wilton. *Marc Antoine* was successfully staged in France; however, there is no record that Pembroke's translation was ever performed, even at Wilton, despite the phrase 'the Stage supposed Alexandra' in her 'Argument'. A supplement to the public stage, rather than an attack on it, *Antonius* should be read in the context of 'the general re-awakening of interest in classical models for Elizabethan literature' with particular emphasis on the works of Seneca, as Coburn Freer observes.[75] The genre was also particularly suited for women who desired to write plays but would not be permitted to write for the public arena.

The only such Senecan closet drama dedicated to Pembroke is *Cleopatra*, which Samuel Daniel calls 'the worke the which she did impose', encouraging him to ascend from love poems like *Delia* 'To sing of state' in the higher genre of tragic drama. He claims that he would have remained content with 'an humble song... had not thy well grac'd *Anthony*... Requir'd his *Cleopatras* company'.[76] Inspired by the countess in his choice of form and topic, Daniel may also have drawn on her *Antonius* in his 1607 revision of *Cleopatra*.[77] (Daniel's 'A Letter from Octavia' (1599) meditates on the same story from the perspective of the virtuous but abandoned wife.)

Although the form and topic are similar, the characterizations in *Antonius* and *Cleopatra* are quite different. Except for her concern for her children, Daniel's Cleopatra is much less appealing than Pembroke's and may obliquely shadow male frustration with female rule in the declining years of Queen Elizabeth. A fading beauty with 'new-appearing wrinkles of declining', she has used feminine wiles to destroy Antony, who was virtuous, unsuspecting, and loved her truly. Whereas in Plutarch and Pembroke Antony was a drinker and a womanizer long before he met Cleopatra, Daniel's Antony was 'in

[74] Bullough, *Sources*, 229.

[75] Sidney, Mary. *Antonie*, ed. Freer, 484.

[76] Daniel, *Delia & Cleopatra*, sig. H5[v].

[77] Schanzer, *Problem Plays*, 231. On structural parallels between *Antonius* and the 1594 *Cleopatra*, see Russell E. Leavenworth, *Daniel's Cleopatra: A Critical Study* (Salzburg: Universität Salzburg, 1974), 5–7.

womans wiles unwittie' and virtually without fault until she corrupted
him.[78] In *Antonius*, she loves Antony and scorns her maid's suggestion
that she save herself and Egypt by seducing Octavius; in *Cleopatra*,
her seduction attempt is rejected by Octavius because 'neither is |
Shee as shee was, nor wee as she conceives'.[79] Daniel portrays her
as the ultimate disdainful mistress, who has treated men with lust
and condescension and now deserves such contempt. Not until Antony is dead does she finally love him, but she then has no way to
demonstrate new love except by dying with him. In *Antonius*, however, Cleopatra is a consistent character, recognizing her own fault
from the outset and demonstrating her love for Antony in life as
well as in death. Cleopatra's suicide is motivated by wifely love for
Antony and is presented in almost erotic terms, for she will 'be in
one selfe tombe... wrapt with thee in one selfe sheete to rest'
(1989–90). In *Cleopatra*, the wanton woman of Acts 1–3 becomes
ennobled by her concern for her children in Act 4 and by her death
in Act 5. Suicide may unite her with Antony, but more importantly,
it is the only way she can demonstrate virtue and thereby regain her
lost dignity.[80] As even Caesar recognizes, the wanton woman has
died as a Queen.

Both plays stress the duties of the ruler to the people and the
destruction of Egypt by Cleopatra's passion.[81] In Daniel's companion
play, as well as in the countess's rendering of *Antonius*, the voice of the
people is heard, possibly at Pembroke's request. Once again the
chorus laments that her passion destroys her people: '[She] Likewise
makes us pay | For her disordred lust, | The int'rest of our blood'.[82]
Although it is always difficult to separate the translator's own voice
from her source, we can nevertheless see how the countess emphasizes
the concern for the people inherent in her originals. And by choosing
to translate the *Discourse of Life and Death*, the *Psalmes*, and *Antonius*,
Pembroke speaks of the dangers of power misused—to the rulers
themselves, to the aristocracy, and to the people.

The tale of Antony and Cleopatra inspired the same interest in
England as it did on the Continent. *Antonius* was republished within

---

[78] Daniel, *Delia & Cleopatra*, sig. I5.

[79] Ibid., sig. L2.

[80] Lucy Hughes-Hallett, *Cleopatra: Histories, Dreams and Distortions* (New York: Harper
& Row, 1990), ch. 4.

[81] Barbara J. Bono, *Literary Transvaluation: From Vergilian Epic to Shakespearean Tragicomedy* (Berkeley: U of California P, 1990), 116.

[82] Daniel, *Delia & Cleopatra*, sig. I6ᵛ.

three years, and Daniel's *Cleopatra* rapidly went through six editions. Other closet dramas on historical and political themes followed, although the evidence for their direct connection to Pembroke is somewhat tenuous: Thomas Kyd's translation of Garnier's *Cornelie* (1594); Samuel Brandon's *The Tragicomoedi of the Vertuous Octavia* (1598); the four *Monarchiche Tragedies* of William Alexander (1603–7); Elizabeth Cary's *The Tragedie of Mariam, the Faire Queene of Jewry* (pub. 1613); and Fulke Greville's *Alaham* and *Mustapha*. Most intriguing is the *Antony and Cleopatra* of Fulke Greville, which he said was 'sacrificed in the fire' because its presentation of their 'irregular passions in foresaking empire to follow sensuality' could be 'construed or strained to a personating of vice in the present governors and government', apparently a reference to the fall of his kinsman Essex, mentioned in his next paragraph.[83]

Daniel's *Philotas*, a play that may have been ultimately inspired by the countess, did create a furore because of its apparent allusions to Essex. Its dedication 'To the Prince' explained, as Garnier had done, that 'these ancient represantments of times past' are applicable to 'The tenure of our state'.[84] In the early years of the Stuart reign William Herbert, a leader of the anti-Spanish party at court, continued to be associated with highly charged political drama, such as *The Isle of Dogs*, Ben Jonson's *Sejanus*, and Thomas Middleton's *A Game at Chess*. Like *Antonius*, these plays commented on the duties of the monarch to the people.

Antonius also served as a model for women playwrights. Nancy Cotton has argued that it inspired *The Tragedie of Mariam, the Faire Queene of Jewry*, the first extant original tragedy known to be written by an English woman.[85] Elizabeth Tanfield Cary, Viscountess Falkland, found in *Antonius* not only a semi-private genre deemed (barely) suitable for a female pen, but also her subject. The tale of Herod is closely linked to that of his Roman superior, Mark Antony, both in

---

[83] Greville, 'Dedication to Sir Philip Sidney', in Greville, *Prose Works*, 93. See also Frank L. Lucas, *Seneca and Elizabethan Tragedy* (Cambridge: Cambridge UP, 1922).

[84] Daniel, *Philotas*, sig. A4^v.

[85] Nancy Cotton, *Women Playwrights in England c. 1363–1750* (Lewisburg: Bucknell UP, 1980), 36. See also Marta Straznicky, ' "Profane Stoical Paradoxes": *The Tragedie of Mariam* and Sidnean Closet Drama', *ELR* 24 (1994), 104–34. Cary had written an earlier but now lost play, set in Syracuse, Sicily. The play is mentioned by her former tutor, John Davies of Hereford, in the dedication to his *Muses Sacrifice*, in *Works*, II. 5, and in Cary's dedication of *Mariam* to 'my worthy sister [in-law]', also named Elizabeth Cary: Cary, *Mariam*, ed. Weller and Ferguson, 66.

Plutarch's tale of the traitor Alexas and in accounts of Cleopatra's treachery by Flavius Josephus, *The Antiquities of the Jews*. Both plays focus on strong and beautiful women of royal lineage, whose personal life is closely intertwined with national and international politics in the Roman Empire. Each woman has replaced an abandoned wife, each suffers the loss of her closest relatives, each ultimately accepts responsibility for her own actions, and each demonstrates heroism in her noble death. The morally complex depiction of Cleopatra in *Antonius* probably influenced not only Cary's portrayal of Mariam but also that of her antagonist Salome, as Weller and Ferguson suggest.[86] Less directly connected than *Mariam* to *Antonius* in form and content, but perhaps inspired by the example of the countess's drama, is *Love's Victory* by her niece, Mary Lady Wroth. Probably written for performance in a great household, the pastoral drama includes characters who allude to members of the Sidney circle, including Philip Sidney, his Stella (Penelope Devereux), and Pembroke herself as the lover of Lissius (her physician Sir Matthew Lister).[87] Wroth, who titles her prose romance *Urania*, a name long associated with Pembroke, echoes *Antonius* in such passages as her description of Cleopatra, and in her adaptation of Pembroke's bilingual pun, 'thou art | The armorer of my heart', as Roberts notes.[88]

In contrast to Pembroke's widely read *Antonius*, her translation of Petrarch's *Trionfo della Morte*, extant only in a transcription of a copy which Sir John Harington of Kelston sent to Lucy, Countess of Bedford (see 'Transmission and Authority of Texts'), may have circulated among a literary coterie.[89] Her physician, Thomas Moffet, obviously knew it, for he instructs her to rest occasionally from her poetic labours: 'Let *Petrarke* sleep, give rest to *Sacred Writte*'.[90] Lanyer may be alluding to *The Triumph of Fame* in her dream vision dedicated to Pembroke, wherein the countess is pictured seated in

[86] Ibid., 29. Morton (Ph.D. diss.) traces possible connections between the Wilton House circle and Cary, 67–73, and notes possible references to Philip and Mary Sidney in Cary's dedication, 79–81.

[87] These identifications were first proposed by Josephine Roberts, 'The Huntington Manuscript of Lady Mary Wroth's Play, *Loves Victorie*', *HLQ* 46 (1983), 156–74. See also Hannay, *Philip's Phoenix*, 201–2; Wroth, *Love's Victory*, 9–15; and Lewalski, *Writing Women*, 306–7.

[88] Wroth, *Urania*, ed. Roberts, 715, 735, 785.

[89] Lucy, Countess of Bedford, was the daughter of Lucy Sidney, Sir Henry Sidney's sister, and of Sir John Harington, first Lord Harington of Exton, who was a cousin of John Harington of Kelston.

[90] Moffet, *Silkewormes*, sig. A2.

'Honors chaire' surrounded by nine worthy ladies. A 'brasen Trumpet' sounds 'Throgh al the world that worthy Ladies praise' and then Pembroke is crowned 'by Eternall Fame'.[91] Drayton, who alludes to her translation of Mornay and perhaps to her 'Angell Spirit' in 'The Sixth Eglog' of *Idea: The Shepheards Garland* (1593), may also allude to her translation from Petrarch's *Trionfi* when he describes the pageant of the triumph of eternity over death:

> To adorne the triumph of eternitie,
> Drawne with the steedes which dragge the golden sunne,
> Thy wagon through the milken way shall runne,
> Millions of Angels still attending thee.[92]

It is quite possible that she had also translated at least *The Triumph of Fame* and *The Triumph of Eternity* as well as the still extant *The Triumph of Death*, since its preservation in a single manuscript copy was so fortuitous. Gabriel Harvey, in an unspecific reference, may also be alluding to that work when he refers to 'the fine dittyes of an other *Petrarch*' immediately before his statement on *Antonius*.[93]

Despite the influence of *Antonius*, the Countess of Pembroke is best known for her magnificent verse paraphrases of the *Psalmes*. Agreeing with Philip Sidney's classification of the Psalms as 'a divine poem', Pembroke and her contemporaries believed that her metrical paraphrase of the *Psalmes* was her most significant poetic achievement.[94] As we have seen, she chose to be portrayed holding 'Davids *Psalmes*' in the familiar portrait by Simon van de Passe, paralleling Théodore de Bèze's portrait with his Psalms translation.[95] Her *Psalmes* were praised by such writers as John Donne, Samuel Daniel, Aemilia Lanyer, John Davies, Henry Parry—and even Sir Edward Denny, who praised her translation of 'the holly psalmes of David' in order to rebuke her niece. Saying that Pembroke 'now...sings in the quier of Heaven', he demonstrates Pembroke's reputation as a religious writer and makes the connection between Psalm translation

---

[91] Lanyer, 'The Authors Dreame to the Ladie *Marie*, the Countesse Dowager of *Pembrooke*', 21–2. Morton (Ph.D. diss.) suggests that the genre of the dream vision itself may be an allusion to Pembroke's translation of Petrarch, 187.

[92] Drayton, *Works*, I. 76.

[93] Harvey, *Letter*, sig. A4ᵛ.

[94] Sidney, *Miscellaneous Prose*, 77.

[95] The portrait of Théodore de Bèze, at the Bibliothèque Nationale, is reproduced in George A. Rothrock, *The Huguenots: A Biography of a Minority* (Chicago: Nelson Hall, 1979).

and virtue that the Earl of Surrey had made in praising Sir Thomas
Wyatt's Psalms, that Thomas Moffet and Pembroke herself had
made in praising Sidney's *Psalmes*, and that is repeatedly made in dedications to the countess.[96] For example, Sir John Harington of Kelston terms them 'the devine, and trulie devine translation...Donne
by that Excellent Countesse, and in Poesie the mirrois of our Age',
to whom he compares the Countess of Bedford's 'admirable guifts,
of the mynde, that clothe Nobilitie with vertue'.[97] Most familiar is
Samuel Daniel's assurance that her words have won both human
and divine approval:

> Those *Hymnes* that thou doost consecrate to heaven,
> Which *Israels* Singer to his God did frame:
> Unto thy voyce eternitie hath given,
> And makes thee deere to him from whence they came.
> In them must rest thy ever reverent name,
> So long as *Syons* God remained honoured.[98]

Although Pembroke's *Psalmes* are presented as a translation, they
paradoxically also offer considerable scope for her own voice. (See
p. 77.) As Daniel says, 'this is that which thou maist call thine
owne', work that will keep her 'fresh in fame' even after '*Wilton* lyes
low levell'd with the ground'. Using the same architectural metaphor
that Pembroke had used for Sidney's *Psalmes* ('Angell Spirit', 65–77),
he promises that 'This Monument cannot be over-throwne'.[99] Harington also uses the architectural metaphor as he asserts divine
approval for her work. His epigram 'in prayse of two worthy Translations, made by two great Ladies' compares her *Psalmes* translation to
the work of rebuilding a college. Both efforts defeat death and time,
both win fame, and both do God's work:

> Two *Maryes* that translate with divers arte
> Two subjects rude and ruinous before....
> Both have ordaynde against deaths dreadfull darte
> A Sheeld of fame enduring evermore.

[96] Sir Edward Denny to Lady Mary Wroth, 26 Feb. 1621/22, cited in Wroth, *Poems*,
239; 'A Tribute to Wyatts Psalms', *The Poems of Henry Howard, Earl of Surrey* ed. Frederick Morgan Padelford (Seattle: U of Washington P, 1928), 97; Zim, *Psalms*, 183; Moffet,
Nobilis, 74; Pembroke, 'Even now that Care' and 'To the Angell Spirit of Sir Phillip Sidney'.
[97] Sir John Harington of Kelston to Lucy, Countess of Bedford, 19 Dec. 1600, Inner
Temple Petyt MS 538.43.14, f. 303ᵛ.
[98] Daniel, *Delia & Cleopatra*, sig. H6. See Beilin, *Redeeming Eve*, 126.
[99] Daniel, *Delia & Cleopatra*, sig. H6ᵛ.

> Both works advance the love of sacred lore,
> Both helpe the soules of sinners to convarte.
> Their learned payn I prayse, her costly almes;
> A Colledge this translates, the tother Psalmes.[100]

Several other dedications portray her *Psalmes* as extending her fame from earth to heaven. For example, Davies promises that the angels will sing her *Psalmes*, and Lanyer says that her songs of 'Hallalu- iah' will write her praise 'in th'eternall booke | Of endlesse honour, true fames memorie'.[101] Moffet claims that, 'The heav'ns themselves are scarce inough to praise' her 'sweet and heav'nly-tuned Psalmes'.[102] Similarly, Henry Parry praises her effort in completing and refining the Sidneian *Psalmes* in *Victoria Christiana*:

cuius vigiliis et invictis laboribus sacrum illud et à fratre Phillippo *priùs inchoa- tum poëma Davidicum hoc totum debet, quod limatum iam tandem, quod egregio pertextum artificio, quod suis numeris absolutum, quod carminum omni genere ornatum* Angliae *populares populari maternaque lingua alloquatur.*[103]

Although the Sidneian *Psalmes* were not published until the nine- teenth century, in the sixteenth and seventeenth centuries they circu- lated among a literary coterie.[104] In addition to the seventeen extant manuscripts, three Psalms (51, 104, and 137) are included with *The Triumph of Death* in transcriptions which John Harington of Kelston sent to Lucy, Countess of Bedford; seven Psalms were found in Har- ington's papers, later printed in *Nugae Antiquae*; and two penitential Psalms (51 and 130) were set for treble voice and lute in the fragment- ary BL Additional MS 15117.[105] A manuscript copy of Psalm 137 that

---

[100] Harington, *Letters*, 310. Harington apparently refers to two Marys who were each Countess of Pembroke, Mary Sidney and Mary de Valence, who founded Pembroke Col- lege, Cambridge, on Christmas Eve 1347. We are grateful to Mrs Judd, the College Librar- ian, for this information. Franklin Williams, 'Sir John Harington', *TLS*, 4 Sept. 1930, 697.

[101] Davies, *Muses Sacrifice*, in *Works*, II. 4; Lanyer, *Salve Deus*, sig. D1[v].

[102] Moffet, *Silkewormes*, sig. G1.

[103] Parry, *Victoria Christiana*, sig. A3[v]-4. Michael G. Brennan, 'The Date of the Coun- tess of Pembroke's Translation of the Psalms', *RES* 33 (1982), 434–6.

[104] Shortly after Sidney's death Fulke Greville mentions only the '40' Psalms done by Sidney (PRO SP 12/195/33), but in the seventeenth century the completed *Psalmes* circu- lated under her name, sometimes to the exclusion of her brother. Ben Jonson, for example, remarked that some of the Psalms circulating under Pembroke's name were actually written by Sidney. William Drummond of Hawthornden, National Library of Scotland MS 2060, f. 150, cited in Sidney, *Poems*, 500.

[105] Sir Richard Steele reprints Psalm 137 (attributing it to Philip Sidney) in the 'Pro- spect of Death', *The Guardian* 1 (1714), 73–7. To note only one other example of the con- tinuing interest in the Sidneian *Psalmes* in the early eighteenth century, this text of Psalm 137 was transcribed (not entirely accurately) from *The Guardian* into a copy of *The Book of*

may also have been enclosed in correspondence is at the University of Nottingham (MS Cl Lm 50). A similar text of the same Psalm is found along with Psalms 51 and 104 in a manuscript at All Souls College, Oxford (MS 155), that was copied in the later seventeenth century from a miscellaneous collection of papers belonging to Sir Christopher Yelverton (*c*.1535–1612). (See 'Relationship of the Texts of the *Psalmes*'.)

The Countess of Pembroke stands at a liminal position in the shift from a manuscript to a print culture. The printed *Arcadia* which she supervised, particularly the 1598 edition that was virtually a *Collected Works of Philip Sidney*, did much to legitimize print.[106] She also permitted her own translations and at least one poem to be printed under her own name, as we have seen. Yet she evidently chose to circulate the *Psalmes* only through manuscript, although many of her contemporaries believed that the Sidneian *Psalmes* should be printed. John Harington, who evidently owned *Psalmes* MS *I* and perhaps MS *K*, rephrases Daniel's familiar words to argue that the poems should be published:

seeing it is allredy prophecied those precious leaves (those hims that she doth consecrate to Heaven) shall owtlast Wilton walls, meethinke it is pitty they are unpublyshed, but lye still inclosed within those walls lyke prisoners, though many have made great suyt for theyr liberty.[107]

Among those who 'made great suyt for theyr liberty' was Francis Davison, who sought to print the *Psalmes*; his list of 'Manuscripts to gett' included 'Psalmes by the Countes of Pembroke. Qre. If they shall

---

Common Prayer (Oxford, 1679) and headed: 'done by Sʳ Philip Sidney knᵗ' (p. 75 of MSS additions), possibly by a member of the Gough family. In 1686 William Dugdale (1664–1714) married Judith Gough, the daughter of John Gough of Bushbury Hall. We are grateful to Sir William Dugdale of Merevale Hall for allowing access to this text of Psalm 137. In contrast to Steele's belief that this version of Psalm 137 was by Sir Philip Sidney, George Ballard attributes all the *Psalmes* to Pembroke in *Memoirs of Several Ladies of Great Britain Who Have Been Celebrated for Their Writings or Skill in the Learned Languages, Arts and Science* (Oxford: W. Jackson, 1752; rpt. ed. Ruth Perry, Detroit: Wayne State UP, 1985), 249–52.

[106] On the presentation of Sidney in the 1598 *Arcadia*, see Wall, *Gender*, 51–9, and Arthur F. Marotti, *Manuscript, Print, and the English Renaissance Lyric* (Ithaca and London: Cornell UP, 1995), 228–38.

[107] John Harington, 'Treatise on play', *Nugae antiquae*, ed. Henry Harington (1769–75), II. 6, cited in Love, *Scribal Publication*, 55. On Harington's connections with the Sidneys, see Michael G. Brennan, 'Sir Robert Sidney and Sir John Harington of Kelston', *N&Q* 34 (1987), 232–7.

not bee printed.'[108] Pembroke had evidently given him permission to print her 'Astrea', but she presumably refused him permission to print the *Psalmes*. John Davies of Hereford, who transcribed the Penshurst manuscript of her *Psalmes*, emphasizes her choice to restrict their publication:

> And didst thou thirst for Fame (as al *Men* doe)
> thou would'st, by all meanes, let it come to light.

After her death, some time between 1643 and 1648, John Langley, an official licenser of printed books, approved the printing of Trinity College, Cambridge, MS R.3.16 (MS *G*), but there is no such edition known to be extant.[109]

Although they remained in manuscript, the Sidneian *Psalmes* strongly influenced the seventeenth-century religious lyric, as John Donne acknowledges. In his poem 'Upon the translation of the Psalmes by Sir Philip Sydney, and the Countesse of Pembroke his Sister' Donne refers to the superiority of the Sidneian *Psalmes* to previous English versions (see *Psalmes*: 'Literary Context'), but he is also acknowledging their work as a model for English devotional verse.

> And who that Psalme, *Now let the Iles rejoyce*,
> Have both translated, and apply'd it too,
> Both told us what, and taught us how to doe.
> They shew us Ilanders our joy, our King,
> They tell us *why*, and teach us *how* to sing.[110]

Donne pictures the Sidneys singing the Psalms in heaven after God 'translated those translators' and prays that after death, 'We may fall in with them, and sing our part'. Many poets did not wait until they reached heaven to 'fall in with them'. The influence of the *Psalmes* can be seen most readily in the devotional poetry of Donne himself, Aemilia Lanyer, and George Herbert.[111]

---

[108] BL Harleian MS 298, f. 159ᵛ. Pembroke's Psalms are listed under the category 'Poems of all sorts: Divine/Humane', along with Psalms by 'Josuah Silvester' and 'Sir John Harrington', cited in *Davison's Poetical Rhapsody*, ed. A. H. Bullen (London: George Bell and Sons, 1890), II. lii.

[109] Davies, *Muses Sacrifice*, dedication; rpt. Davies, *Works*, II. l. 4. Michael G. Brennan, 'Licensing the Sidney Psalms for the Press in the 1640s', *N&Q* 31 (1984), 304–5.

[110] Donne, *Divine Poems*, 34. See also Heather Asals, '*Davids* Successors: Forms of Joy and Art', *Proceedings of the PMR Conference* 2 (1977), 34–6.

[111] For a detailed analysis of the influence of the Sidney *Psalmes* on these three writers, see Debra Rienstra, 'Aspiring to Praise: The Sidney-Pembroke Psalter and the English Religious Lyric' (Rutgers U, Ph.D. diss., 1995).

Donne's most direct use of the Sidneian *Psalmes* as a poetic model
is his poetic paraphrase, 'The Lamentations of Jeremy, for the most
part according to Tremelius', a work that, like the Sidneian *Psalmes*,
relies on a variety of biblical translations.[112] Stylistic similarities may
also be found throughout Donne's poetry, including his characterist-
ically dramatic openings, which he may have learned from Psalms that
retained the immediacy of the Hebrew original, as 'Tyrant whie
swel'st thou thus' (Ps. 52. 1), 'Not us I say, not us' (Ps. 115. 1),
'What? and doe I behold the lovely mountaines' (Ps. 121. 1). Donne
may also have been influenced by the argumentative structure of
Psalms such as 73, and by imagery that is virtually metaphysical, particularly the embryo image in Psalm 58. 22–4 and Psalm 139. 43–56.
(See p. 72.)[113]

Aemilia Lanyer conflates the work of the original Psalmist and of
Pembroke when she praises 'Those rare sweet songs which *Israels*
King did frame | Unto the Father of Eternite', with a marginal
note 'The Psalms written newly by the Countesse Dowager of Penbrooke'.[114] Perceiving this divine verse as authorizing her own sacred
poetry in *Salve Deus Rex Judaeorum*, she presents her religious poem
with decorous humility and implores Pembroke to appoint her as her
literary heir.[115]

George Herbert's debt to the Sidneian *Psalmes* has long been recognized. A cousin of William Herbert, Earl of Pembroke, he was granted
the living of Bemerton, a pleasant walk from Wilton. He also very
probably had ready access to a manuscript of the *Psalmes* there.
Louis Martz concludes that Sidney's *Psalmes* are 'the closest approx-
imation to the poetry of Herbert's *Temple* that can be found anywhere
in preceding English poetry', and surely the same can be said of Pembroke's *Psalmes*, especially with regard to their wit, 'metrical ingenu-
ity', clarity of structure, 'logical movement', and their creation of 'a
sense of familiar presence'.[116] Barbara Lewalski observes that Psalms

[112] Lewalski notes that, as one would expect from the title, Donne bases his work closely
on the Latin translation of Franciscus Junius and Immanuel Tremellius, although he also
consults the Vulgate, the Authorized Version, and the Geneva Bible: *Protestant Poetics*,
275–6.

[113] Ibid., 241–3; Rathmell (Ph.D. diss.), pp. xx–xxii.

[114] Lanyer, *Salve Deus*, sig. D1^v.

[115] Ibid., sig. D3^{r-v}. See Lewalski, *Writing Women*, 213–42, and Lanyer, *Poems*, pp.
xv–xlii.

[116] Martz, *Meditation*, 273–9. See also Rathmell (Ph.D. diss.), pp. l–li, lxxvi ff.; Woods,
Natural Emphasis, 171; Bloch, *Spelling*, 233–5; Alicia Ostriker, 'Song and Speech in the
Metrics of George Herbert', *PMLA* 80 (1965), 62–8; Heather Asals, 'The Voice of George

of affliction foreshadow Herbert in 'tone, stance of speaker, rhythmic effects, and deceptively simple formulations of staggering religious paradoxes', and lead to such poems as 'Grief', 'Denial', 'Affliction' (II), (III), and (IV).[117] More specifically, Lewalski notes the formal similarities between such poems as Pembroke's acrostic Psalm 117 and Herbert's 'Coloss. 3: 3' and the possible direct imitation of the opening of Psalm 106 in the parallel questions of Herbert's 'Dulnesse' (17–18). Numerous other parallels have been found. For example, Herbert's cry to 'My God, my king' in 'Jordan I' echoes Pembroke's Psalm 59. 88, and 'the accentual elegiac couplets' of Psalm 111 may be reflected in Herbert's 'Thanksgiving'.[118] Gary Waller finds other 'probable echoes' between Psalm 104 and 'Providence', Psalm 116 and 'Praise II', Psalm 103 and 'The Flower', and Psalm 95 and 'The Pulley'.[119] Rathmell suggests a parallel between Psalm 88. 43–54 and 'Affliction' (IV).[120] Psalm 88, a much freer paraphrase than most of Pembroke's *Psalmes*, anticipates the form of Herbert's psalm-like lyrics, such as 'Longing', 'Home', 'Dullnesse', 'Gidiness', 'The Method', 'Complaining', and 'The Glance'. In addition, Herbert may have been influenced in composing the two-part 'Easter' by an awareness of the two versions of Pembroke's Psalm 108, as well as her Psalm 57, where he would have read both 'consort' and 'beare a part', as well as her adaptation of Wyatt's phrase, 'awake my lute' (Pembroke, 'my lute awake', Ps. 57. 34–6).[121]

The Sidneian *Psalmes* were part of a movement to combine personal and scriptural elements in religious verse, including not only verse by Donne, Lanyer, and Herbert, but also such works as Barnabe Barnes's *Divine Centurie*, Robert Southwell's *Saint Peters Complaint* and *Marie Magdalen's Funeral Teares*, Joshua Sylvester's *Devine Weekes*, and the devotional poems of Henry Vaughan, Thomas Traherne, Richard Crashaw, Edward Taylor, Thomas Campion, and ultimately

---

Herbert's "The Church"', *ELH* 36 (1969), 511–28. See also Bloch's chart of his references to specific Psalms: *Spelling*, 308–10.

[117] Lewalski, *Protestant Poetics*, 244. See particularly Pss. 38. 1–4; 77. 1–4, 17–20, 41–8; and 88. 37–54.

[118] Freer, *Music*, 240; Woods, *Natural Emphasis*, 171.

[119] Waller, *Mary Sidney*, 226–7.

[120] Sidney, *Psalms*, pp. xviii–xix.

[121] Noel Kinnamon, 'A Note on Herbert's "Easter" and the Sidneian Psalms', *George Herbert Journal* 1 (1978), 44–8; Bloch, *Spelling*, 250–1; Woods, *Natural Emphasis*, 171, suggests a parallel between the first stanza of Psalm 92 and 'Easter'. See also Noel Kinnamon, 'Notes on the Psalms in Herbert's The Temple', *George Herbert Journal* 4 (1981), 10–29.

John Milton.[122] (See *Psalmes*: 'Literary Context'.) Metrical Psalters written after 1600 were usually written for congregational singing and therefore tend to be less metrically complex and less scholarly than the Sidneian *Psalmes*, like George Wither's *The Psalmes of David Translated into Lyrick Verse* (1632), George Sandys's *A Paraphrase upon the Psalmes of David* (1636), Francis Rous's *The Booke of Psalmes in English Meeter* (1638), *The Whole Booke of Psalmes Faithfully Translated into English Metre* [The Bay Psalm Book] (1640), and Watt's *Psalms of David Imitated in the Language of the New Testament* (1719).[123] That the Sidneian *Psalmes*, although too complex for congregational singing, were seen as part of this tradition is indicated by the possible adaption of three of Sidney's *Psalmes* (40, 41, and 42) and perhaps parts of Pembroke's Psalm 97 (ll. 10, 15, 32, 38) in *All the French Psalm Tunes with English Words* (1632).[124] The simplified variants of Pembroke's *Psalmes* 120–7 may have been similarly revised for congregational singing. (See 'Relationship of the Texts of the *Psalmes*'.)

Interest in the Sidneian *Psalmes* revived in the nineteenth century, with their publication in 1823 by the Chiswick Press. Either Charles Lamb or Samuel Coleridge (the hand is uncertain) wrote in a copy of Daniel's *Poetical Works*, after the misattributed early version of 'To the Angell Spirit', that the Sidneys' paraphrases are 'elegant', and 'Anglo-courtly' (though 'not... true Hebrew, like Milton's').[125] Selections from the *Psalmes*, usually attributed solely to Sidney, appeared in nineteenth-century studies and anthologies such as Nathan Drake's *Mornings in Spring* (1828), John Holland's *The Psalmists of Britain* (1843), George Macdonald's *England's Antiphon* (1868), and Edward Farr's *Select Poetry, chiefly Devotional, of the Reign of Queen Elizabeth* (1845). John Ruskin included 44 selected Psalms in *Rock Honeycomb*, praising the accuracy of the paraphrase, especially

[122] Rathmell (Ph.D. diss.), pp. lvii–lxxvi; Lewalski, *Protestant Poetics*, 253–426.

[123] Rathmell (Ph.D. diss.), pp. lxxxix–xcvii.

[124] Jim Doelman, 'A Seventeenth-Century Publication of Three of Sir Philip Sidney's Psalms', *N&Q* 38 (1991), 162–3. William Drummond of Hawthornden mentions this edition of 'some psalms of David' composed 'to the french Tunes, in Meter' by Philip Sidney and others, printed by John Standish. National Library of Scotland MS 2060, f. 150, cited in Sidney, *Poems*, 500.

[125] Cecil C. Seronsy, 'Coleridge Marginalia in Lamb's Copy of Daniel's *Poetical Works*', *HLB* 11 (1953), 112. Coleridge also commented: 'Daniel caught and recommunicated the Spirit of the great Countess of Pembroke, the glory of the North—he *formed* her mind, and her mind inspirited him.' *Collected Letters of Samuel Taylor Coleridge*, ed. Earl Leslie Griggs, 4 vols. (Oxford: Clarendon P, 1959), III. 55.

the vivid language used 'to say precisely in English what David said in Hebrew'.[126] After this flurry of attention, the Sidneian *Psalmes* once again passed into obscurity, to be recovered with J. C. A. Rathmell's edition in 1963.[127] In 1972 Coburn Freer characterized the Sidneian *Psalmes* as 'one of the best but most underrated achievements in the Renaissance lyric'.[128] No longer underrated, the *Psalmes* are now seen as central to the Protestant lyric tradition.

Like Pembroke's *Psalmes*, her correspondence was praised by her contemporaries. Rowland Whyte, Robert Sidney's agent, believed that her business letters had persuasive power: 'The copies of her letter [to the Lord Treasurer on Robert Sidney's behalf] she did vouchsafe to send unto me of her own hand writing. I never reade any thing that could express an earnest desire like unto this.'[129] Such a skill was particularly useful for an aristocratic woman, whose duties in the web of patronage included interceding at court for relatives and friends. (In this case, her suit was successful and Robert was given leave to return home from Flushing.) Scattered throughout the correspondence of Robert Sidney and of Rowland Whyte are references to her personal letters, all but two of which have been lost (Correspondence: Manuscript Letters I and II), as have the letters from Philip Sidney to her that are praised by Thomas Moffet.[130] In the seventeenth century Francis Osborne refers to some 'incomparable *Letters* of hers' that he had seen, and John Donne the younger says that he printed her letters to Sir Tobie Matthew as examples for composition. (See Correspondence: Printed Letters.)[131]

---

[126] John Ruskin, Preface, *Rock Honeycomb: Broken Pieces of Sir Philip Sidney's Psalter*, in *The Complete Works of John Ruskin* , ed. E. T. Cook and Alexander Wedderburn (London: George Allen, 1907), XXI. 117. Ruskin singles out Pembroke's Psalm 91 for particular praise, although he attributes it to Philip Sidney (117–18). See J. C. A. Rathmell, 'Hopkins, Ruskin, and the Sidney Psalter', *London Magazine* 6 (1959), 51–66.

[127] Excerpts from the Sidneian *Psalmes* have been included in several recent anthologies, including *The Penguin Book of Renaissance Verse 1509–1658*, ed. David Norbrook and H. R. Woudhuysen (London: Penguin, 1992), 667–80. A modern spelling edition was edited by R. E. Pritchard, *The Sidney Psalms* (Manchester: Carcanet, 1992).

[128] Freer, *Music*, 73. On the literary significance of the Sidneian *Psalmes*, see Martz, *Meditation*, 273–9; Lewalski, *Protestant Poetics*, 241–5, 275–6; Richard Todd, ' "So Well Atyr'd Abroad" ': A Background to the Sidney-Pembroke Psalter and Its Implications for the Seventeenth-Century Religious Lyric', *Texas Studies in Literature and Language* 29 (Spring 1987), 74–93; Waller, *Mary Sidney*, 152–256, and Sidney, Mary. *Triumph*, 36–44; Woods, *Natural Emphasis*, 169–75, 290–302; Fisken, 'Education', 166–83, and 'World of Words', 263–75; Zim, *Psalms*, 185–210.

[129] Rowland Whyte to Robert Sidney, 14 Jan. 1598, De L'Isle MS U1475 C12/ 121.

[130] Moffet, *Nobilis*, 74.

[131] Osborne, *Memoires*, sig. Gg2.

In addition to those lost letters, apparently much of what she wrote and translated has disappeared. One reason for the loss may have been some reluctance to put her original works into print, despite her boldness in printing her translations under her own name. John Davies of Hereford observed to three women writing in the early seventeenth century (Pembroke, Lady Cary, and the Countess of Bedford), 'that you presse the *Presse* with little you have made', explaining the aristocratic disdain of print:

the *Presse* so much is wrong'd
by abject *Rimers* that great Hearts doe scorne
To have their *Measures* with such *Nombers* throng'd
as are so basely *got, conceiv'd,* and *borne.*[132]

This stigma of print was, as Harold Love observes, 'particularly hard on women writers', for Renaissance writers often found 'a metaphorical equation . . . between an eagerness to appear in print and sexual immorality'.[133] Manuscript circulation was the preferred form of publication. Hiring the famous calligrapher, John Davies of Hereford, to produce the gilded Penshurst manuscript was a statement of the importance of the Sidneian *Psalmes*; allowing the *Psalmes* to be repeatedly copied ensured their preservation. Yet the fact that Pembroke printed little has undoubtedly contributed to the loss of additional work alluded to by her contemporaries, as did her occasional neglect in having copies made. Her letters to Sir Edward Wotton and, if authentic, to Sir Tobie Matthew, indicate that she sometimes sent the unique copy of a poem or translation to a friend; not surprisingly, many of these works are no longer extant. No names of lost works survive, but Gabriel Harvey makes the statement that his mysterious gentlewoman, whom he wishes his readers to believe is the Countess of Pembroke, could publish more in a month than the prolific Thomas Nashe in a lifetime 'or the pregnantest of our inspired Heliconists can equall'.[134] Sir Edward Denny's comment that Pembroke had 'trans-

---

[132] Davies, *Muses Sacrifice*, in *Works*, II. 5.

[133] Love, *Scribal Publication*, 54–5. Cf. Richard Lovelace's description of a woman who 'Powders a Sonnet as she does her hair, | Then prostitutes them both to publick Aire', *The Poems of Richard Lovelace*, ed. C. H. Wilkinson (Oxford, 1953), 200.

[134] Harvey, *Pierces Supererogation*, in *Works*, II. 321. The identification of his gentlewoman with Pembroke is confirmed by his reference to 'Meridianis', an anagram for Mary Sidney used by Drayton; see Jean Robertson, 'Drayton and the Countess of Pembroke', *RES* 16 (1965), 49. On lost and doubtful works, see Waller, *Mary Sidney*, 257–74. Waller suggests that anonymous poems in manuscripts such as those collected by John Finet and Sir Walter Aston might include some of her works: *Mary Sidney*, 267–9.

lated so many godly books' may also indicate that she did more sacred translation than the *Psalmes*.[135] There are, however, many explanations for the disappearance of such works: her own neglect in not keeping copies, the frequent suppression of works by women in the eighteenth and nineteenth centuries, and, most importantly, the fires that destroyed her primary residences of Wilton, Baynards Castle, and Ramsbury. Except for the holograph letters included here, all of her own papers have disappeared; the works that we have are copies, either in manuscript or in print. (See 'Transmission and Authority of Texts'.)[136] We thus lack the immediate access to the writer's own voice that we have in the holograph manuscript of Robert Sidney's poems, for example, or in the hundreds of extant letters written by Robert and Philip Sidney. The loss of her holograph drafts, her extensive correspondence, and probably of literary works, both original compositions and translations, intensifies the difficulty of historical reconstruction. The complete body of her works eludes us—and yet enough remains to sketch her probable methods of composition and translation.

Methods of Composition and Translation

The Countess of Pembroke employed a variety of Renaissance literary forms. An effective prose stylist, she translated Philippe de Mornay's philosophical treatise into balanced prose sufficiently popular to be reprinted several times. Her correspondence was recommended as a

---

[135] Sir Edward Denny to Lady Mary Wroth, 26 Feb. 1621/22, cited in Wroth, *Poems*, 239.

[136] Two poems were misattributed to her in the twentieth century: 'The Countess of Penbrooks Passion' by Nicholas Breton and 'The mighty JOVE beholding from above' said to be written by 'the divine *Urania*' in George Whetstone's *An Heptameron of Civill Discourses* (1582). Nicholas Breton, 'The Countess of Pembrokes Passion', BL Sloane MS 1303, ff. 60–71. The work was printed as Pembroke's in *A Poem on Our Savior's Passion from an Unpublished Manuscript in the British Museum* (London: John Wilson, 1862). On this work, a manuscript version of Breton's *The Passions of the Spirit*, see Young, *Mary Sidney*, Appendix B; Lamb, 'Patronage', 157; Michael G. Brennan, 'Nicholas Breton's *The Passions of the Spirit* and the Countess of Pembroke', *RES* 38 (1987), 221–7; Breton, *Works*, I. c. 3–10; and Breton, *Poems*, pp. liii–lxi.

On Whetstone, see Thomas C. Izard, *George Whetstone, Mid-Elizabethan Gentleman of Letters* (New York, 1942), 126; *A Critical Edition of George Whetstone's 1582 An Heptameron of Civill Discourses* ed. Diana Shklanka (New York: Garland, 1987), 252–3; Waller, *Mary Sidney*, 269–72, who also details the misattribution to her of 'If ever hapless woman had a cause', a song in John Bartlett's *Booke of Ayres* (1606), *STC* 1539. The song is attributed to Pembroke and given a modern setting by Ned Rorem, *Women's Voices: Eleven Songs for Soprano and Piano* (New York: Boosey and Hawkes, 1979).

model for composition, particularly her business letters that are appropriately assertive, affectionate, conciliatory, angry, or even blandishing, as occasion required. Like all genres, the letter had its own decorum, even to the placement of the signature according the relative ranks of sender and recipient.[1] Pembroke was widely praised for her skill in writing letters, but more important to modern readers are Pembroke's poetic works, notable for their variety of genre and form. Actively engaged in the effort to import Continental verse forms, she was the first English translator to retain the *terza rima* of Petrarch's *Trionfi*, and one of the first to use blank verse for drama, when she translated Garnier's *Marc Antoine*. She also composed a pastoral dialogue in caudate or tail-rhyme, and used different stanza forms in iambic pentameter for her two dedicatory poems.

Her most significant poetic achievement, however, is her completion of the Sidneian *Psalmes*. Using as their primary literary model the French *Psaumes* by Marot and Bèze,[2] the Sidneys composed elegant paraphrases that use 167 different verse forms. Pembroke alone used 126 different poetic forms, some of which are, as Woods observes, 'highly complex and even daring' although the metres are 'not usually very subtle' and some of the syntax is 'awkward'.[3] An early seventeenth-century manuscript of the Sidneian *Psalmes* emphasizes their variety in its lengthy title: 'THE Psalmes of David translated into divers and sundry kindes of verse, more rare, and excellent, for the method and varietie then ever yet hath bene don

---

[1] On the letter as literary form, see Claudio Guillén, 'Notes toward the Study of the Renaissance Letter', in *Renaissance Genres*, ed. Barbara Kiefer Lewalski (Cambridge, Mass.: Harvard UP, 1986), 70–101; and *Writing the Female Voice: Essays on Epistolary Literature*, ed. Elizabeth C. Goldsmith (Boston: Northeastern UP, 1989).

[2] Rathmell (Ph.D. diss.), 530, charts extensive parallels between the form used in the *Psaumes* and in Pembroke's *Psalmes*; on Sidney's use of Marot in Psalm 38, see Zim, *Psalms*, 172–6. Richard Todd, however, notes that only one of Pembroke's settings, Psalm 97, 'actually imitates its French counterpart formally': 'Humanist Prosodic Theory, Dutch Synods, and the Poetics of the Sidney-Pembroke Psalter', *HLQ* 52 (1989), 275.

[3] Woods, *Natural Emphasis*, 170. The Sidneys paraphrased 150 Psalms, along with the extra 21 forms for Psalm 119, making a total of 171 poems (Woods, *Natural Emphasis*, 170); there are, however, 167 different verse forms because there are 4 repetitions. See also Attridge, *Syllables*, 203–4; Zim, *Psalms*, 185–210; Waller, *Mary Sidney*, 159, 190–211; Freer, *Music*, 72–108, which praises the metric variety of Pembroke's *Psalmes* while simultaneously stating that she achieves her best effects 'as much by accident as by design' (97) and 'misses the second or third rank of Elizabethan lyricists' (107). See also Freer, 'The Countess of Pembroke in a World of Words', *Style* 5 (1971), 37–56; Sallye J. Sheppeard, 'On the Art of Renaissance Translation: Mary Herbert's Psalm 130', *Texas College English* 18 (1985), 1–3; Louise Schleiner, *Tudor and Stuart Women Writers* (Bloomington: Indiana UP, 1994), 58–60.

in English' (MS *C*). Throughout the *Psalmes*, there are only four exact repetitions in metre and rhyme. Pembroke uses Sidney's form of Psalm 8 in Psalm 118, and his form for Psalm 32 in Psalm 71; in addition, she repeats her own stanzaic form in Psalms 60 and 119S, and uses *rhyme royal* in Psalms 51 (with feminine rhymes) and 63.[4] This was an unprecedented achievement in English verse, leading Hallett Smith to call the Sidneian *Psalmes* a 'School of English Versification'.[5] (See 'Table of Verse Forms'.)

In their use of multiple verse forms, the Sidneys demonstrated an awareness of the various types of Psalms. These differences were suppressed in the most familiar English Psalter, the Sternhold and Hopkins version, which forced each Psalm into the procrustean bed of a common measure. Matthew Parker, however, had established that the poetic form should fit the content, when he offered eight tunes by Thomas Tallis and encouraged his readers to sing each Psalm to the tune they found most appropriate: 'ye ought to conjoyne a sad tune or song, with a sad Psalme, and a joyful tune and songe wyth a joyfull Psalme'.[6]

Pembroke's *Psalmes* are a compendium of Elizabethan verse forms, including *ottava rima* (Psalm 78), sonnets (Psalms 100, Spenserian, and 150, a variant of the Italian form), *rhyme royal* (Psalms 51 and 63 and with metric variation in Psalms 135 and 145), *terza rima* (Psalm 119H), and a complex variation of *terza rima* that may have been her own invention (Psalm 101).[7] She also includes a wide variety of stanzaic forms. Some are strikingly unusual, such as her seventy-two-line palindrome constructed of three rhymes in Psalm 55, her pattern of couplets alternating with a repeated rhyme in each twelve-line stanza of Psalm 73 (*abb acc add aee*), or her use of feminine rhymes in Psalm 138 in all lines except those that link rhymes between stanzas. (See 'Table of Verse Forms'.) She also used acrostics, both in

---

[4] Sidney, *Psalms*, p. xxvii (misnumbered in some copies as xvii).

[5] Hallett Smith, 'English Metrical Psalms in the Sixteenth Century and their Literary Significance', *HLQ* 9 (1946), 269. Ellen St Sure Lifschutz declares that Pembroke's 'technical virtuosity in inventing verse forms can scarcely be exaggerated' and suggests that had she chosen a different 'poetic matter' than the Psalms, 'her accomplishment might be better appreciated today': 'David's Lyre and the Renaissance Lyric: A Critical Consideration of the Psalms of Wyatt, Surrey and the Sidneys' (U of California, Berkeley, Ph.D. diss., 1980), 235, 237.

[6] Matthew Parker, *The Whole Psalter Translated into English Metre* (*c*.1567), *STC* 2729, sig. VVii.

[7] Sidney used *terza rima* in Psalm 7, adapted the form to iambic tetrameter in Psalm 30, and used interlinked stanzaic forms, as in Psalms 20 and 31.

Psalm 117 and in the twenty-two poems of Psalm 119. Most of her poems are iambic, but she also employs the dactyl, anapaest, and trochee; she frequently uses headless iambic tetrameter with a trochaic effect, as in Psalms 56, 119D, and Variant Psalm LXXXVI. She also makes effective use of unrhymed quantitative measure, including sapphics, elegiacs, anacreontics, and asclepiadic verse, metres that Sidney had used as part of a patriotic effort to make English verse the equal of the classics.[8] Quantitative metre is not often successful in English and the experimentation was soon abandoned, but several of Philip Sidney's poems do use that metre effectively, and so do Pembroke's Psalms 120–7. (As we argue in 'Relationship of the Texts of the *Psalmes*', someone other than the author may have later replaced these complex poems with paraphrases of the *Book of Common Prayer* in simple rhymed iambic metres.)

While there is not space here for a thorough study of Pembroke's style, even a brief summary should indicate that she did have considerable skill in handling rhetorical figures. Like her brother Philip, she used most of the rhetorical tropes approved in George Puttenham's *The Arte of English Poesie* (1589), with particular emphasis on figures of repetition.[9] One of her favourite techniques is polyptoton, using a word in two or more forms of speech, as 'lightning lighten' (*Antonius*, 400).[10] The figure occurs frequently in her *Psalmes*, as in 'restlesse rest', 'sleepie sleeplesse eies', and 'chang lies in his hand, | who changlesse sittes aloft' (Ps. 77. 19, 20, 51–2) or 'hastning their haste with spurr of hasty feare' (Ps. 104. 24). She also uses it in her prose translation, as 'they have joyes . . . and do not enjoy them' (*Discourse*, 183) or 'the end of our miseries, then the endlesse misery' (*Discourse*, 38–9). Less successful is 'Then doune she sate, and me sitt-doune she made' (*Triumph*, 2. 16).

Another of her most common usages is chiasmus, or reversal of terms, as in the 'sea of light' | the 'light of sea' (Ps. 148. 9–10), 'my

---

[8] Cf. the phalaecian hendecasyllables of Psalm 121 and Sidney's *Old Arcadia* 33, for example, or the asclepiadic verse of Psalm 122 Variant 1 [MS B] and *OA* 34 (Attridge, *Syllables*, 203–4). Richard Helgerson, 'Barbarous Tongues: The Ideology of Poetic Form in Renaissance England', in *The Historical Renaissance: New Essays on Tudor and Stuart Literature and Culture*, ed. Heather Dubrow and Richard Strier (Chicago: U of Chicago P, 1988), 273–92.

[9] On Sidney's style, see *Poems*, pp. li–lx; Montgomery and Veré L. Rubel, *Poetic Diction in the English Renaissance from Skelton through Spenser* (New York: MLA, 1941), 203–11.

[10] Ps. 88. 28–9 varies the phrase to 'lightning . . . lighted'. Cf. Sidney, Ps. 4. 7, 31 'in peace, and peacefull blisse'; Ps. 9. 15 'to endless end'; Ps. 9. 19 'Both ruines, ruiners, and ruin'd plott'.

crying call' | 'my calling cry' (Ps. 77. 1–2), 'my filthie fault, my faultie filthines' (Ps. 51. 9), 'Gods loved choise unto his chosen love' ('Even now', 54).[11] She also uses anadiplosis, in which the same word appears at the end of a unit and the beginning of the next, as in 'Salem resound, resound ô Sion hill' (Ps. 135. 56) or 'What heav'nly powrs thee highest throne assign'de, | assign'd thee goodnes suting that Degree' ('Even now', 13–14).

Occasionally she includes epizeuxis, or repetition of a word for emphasis, as in 'his name, the sweetest, sweetest thing' (Ps. 135. 7). But this figure may not always be as simple as it first appears, as in God's 'right right hand' in Psalm 63. 21, which is not a mere repetition, but a statement that God's 'right hand' is also righteous, protecting the Psalmist and punishing the wicked.[12] Similarly, Psalm 73. 74 repeats 'thee' in a form of epizeuxis, that simultaneously expands and builds upon the first phrase: 'with thee, thee good, thee goodnes to remain'. Psalm 47. 19 appears to be epizeuxis, but the repeated phrase refers to two different persons, 'hee, greatest prince, greate princes gaines'. Verbally more complex is 'remove I may not, move I may' (Ps. 62. 4), which becomes in line 20, 'remove? O no: not move I may'. Several of these figures may be combined in a single phrase, as 'my bones the grave, the grave expects my bones' (Ps. 141. 19), which, as Zim demonstrates, combines personification, zeugma, chiasmus, and epizeuxis.[13]

Other forms of repetition are ubiquitous, such as repeating a word to build on it, as in her use of 'hir warre's' and 'Foyl'd' in the opening of *The Triumph of Death*:

> Turn'd from hir warre's a joyefull Conqueresse:
> > Hir warre's, where she had foyl'd the mightie foe,
> > whose wylie strategems the world distresse,
> And foyl'd him, not with sword, with speare or bowe . . .   (ll. 4–7)

She will also repeat a word for emphasis, as in the heavy use of the word 'dead' in the ladies' lament for Laura:

> > Vertue is dead; and dead is beawtie too,
> > > And dead is curtesie . . .   (ll. 145–6)

---

[11] Chiasmus is the rhetorical figure most characteristic of Robert Sidney's poems, as in 'Of wretched monsters I most monstrous wretch', Sonnet 19. 3. See Sidney, Robert. *Poems*, 27–8.

[12] Cf. Sidney's repetition of 'ready' in Ps. 18. 11, discussed in Zim, *Psalms*, 159.

[13] Ibid., 192–3.

Another characteristic of Pembroke's style is the parenthetic statement. To clarify the meaning of her text she frequently adds parenthetical explanation, as 'Loe our goods (o changed case!) | spoil'd by them, that late we spoiled' (Ps. 44. 39–40), or a description of Laura's companions, 'But eache alone (so eache alone did shine)' (*Triumph*, 1. 17), or her frequent use in *Antonius* (including 10–11, 21, 60–1, 309, and 460). The parenthesis can also be used for confession, as in 'I was a foole (I can it not defend) | so quite depriv'd of understanding' (Ps. 73. 64). Psalm 86. 15 adds a caveat in the discussion of pagan gods, '(if gods be many)'. She also uses parenthetical expressions to intensify the emotional impact of the text, as in the lamentation of the godly in Psalm 129, interrupted in line 8 by '(ô height of woe)', or to honour her brother with the completed *Psalmes* in 'Angell Spirit' (22)—'Yet here behold, (oh wert thou to behold!)'—or to mourn for him in 'Even now' (23)—'Who better might (O might ah word of woe)'. In the *Discourse* she will frequently add parentheses to Garnier's text (as 258–9, 282, or 318–20) or occasionally remove them (as 107).

Enjambment, used extensively in her Psalms (as in Ps. 62. 1, 17, 30), in *Triumph* (as 1. 13, 26, 67, and 73), and in the choruses of *Antonius*, is most strikingly used between stanzas in 'Angell Spirit', 'To pay the debt of Infinits I owe | To thy great worth' (35–6).[14] Her verse occasionally employs internal rhyme, as 'fresh bleeding smart; not eie but hart teares fall' ('Angell Spirit', 20) or 'Then lett with heede, thy deedes' (*Triumph*, 2. 26), or the elaborate internal rhyme scheme of Psalm 140 (*ab/ bc/ cd/ de/ ef/ af*), wherein the opening line of each stanza is a cry to the Lord and the final line of each stanza has an internal rhyme with Lord. Her use of rhyme is inventive, including redundant rhyme as 'transform'd/form'd' ('Angell Spirit', Variant, 8/ 11), double rhyme as 'pleasure/measure' (Ps. 75. 9/ 12) or 'delights/ [en]vie bites' ('Angell Spirit', 60/63), and the mosaic effect, eliding two or more words to rhyme with one, as in 'stay in her' and 'staine her' ('Astrea', 21/24). Psalm 76 employs triple rhymes throughout, beginning with 'signify/dignify' and 'notorious/glorious'. She uses feminine rhymes frequently, as in Psalms 52, 84, 130, and 141 and *Antonius* (as 253, 297–8), although she avoids them in the *terza rima* of *Triumph*. Heavy alliteration is characteristic of her style. She must have realized that she had overdone the alliteration in the first

---

[14] Alice Luce has computed the proportion of unstopped lines as 1: 3.7 (Sidney, Mary. *Antonie*, ed. Luce, 45). On Sidney's enjambment in the *Psalmes*, see Freer, *Music*, 75–7.

version of Psalm 64. 6–7 ('wicked witts in wiles… working wrong'), for that wording is removed in the Penshurst manuscript, but Penshurst does contain, in addition to the ubiquitous alliterated adjective and noun, such as 'wittnest will' (Ps. 119N. 9) or 'slendrest slumbers' (Ps. 132. 10), many alliterative passages, including 'be buried breathing in theyr beare' (Ps. 55. 45); 'wittnesse this waterlesse this weary waste' (Ps. 63. 5); 'fiers flashed; | where swelling streames did rudely roare' (Ps. 66. 37–8); 'forgetting follies, faultes forgiving' (Ps. 130. 36); and 'formed, framed, founded' (Ps. 148. 21). Her translations of Mornay, Garnier, and Petrarch also add alliteration to her original, as *Discourse*, 'pleasures bought with paine and perill' (82); 'deep ditches, and dungeons' (284–5); or 'borne, bred and brought up' (345). In *Antonius* she uses such phrases as 'despisde', 'disdain'd', and 'despoilde' (13–15), 'wafted with wandring wings' (634), 'high and hawtie' (1412), 'blowes had bloudilie benumb'd' (1661), and repeated alliterative phrases in 1411–17. Similarly, her *Triumph* has such phrases as 'Pestring the plaine' (1. 75) and 'Could frye and freese in few nights changing cheere' (1. 128), as well as alliterated adjective and noun, like 'carefull crue' (1. 112) or 'sweete spright' (1. 162), and alliterative doublets, like 'moane and miserie' (1. 121) and 'ground and grasse' (1. 131).

Occasionally she will use a colloquial phrase, as 'pay them home' (Ps. 54. 10), 'sets it so close' (*Discourse*, 247) for '*si serré*' (*Excellent discours*, sig. B7ᵛ), and 'are borne in hande' (471) for '*on propose*' (sig. C6), or 'take's breath' for '*si riconforte*' (*Triumph*, 2. 49). Also typical of her style are exclamations, particularly *Ah!*, as in 'ah! cast me not from thee' (Ps. 51. 33) or 'ah! why delaies that happy while | when Sion shall our saver bring?' (Ps. 53. 21).[15] The phrase 'Ay me!' is used in *Antonius* (11, 460, 1007, 1905) and many of the Psalms, including 'Ay me, alas, I faint, I dy' (Ps. 88. 61); it also begins 'The Dolefull Lay' and is repeated in line 66. She also uses the vocative 'O' frequently, most strikingly when gilded in the Penshurst MS, as in the opening of Psalm 100, 'O all you landes the treasures of your joy', or of Psalm 102, 'O lord my praying heare'.

Like her brother Philip, Pembroke delights in word play of various kinds, including oxymorons like 'gladly sadd, and richly poore' (Ps. 69. 71).[16] The oxymoron of 'pleasing paines', familiar from

[15] Fisken, 'World of Words', 268.
[16] On Sidney's verbal wit, see Montgomery, *Symmetry*, ch. 2, and Zim, *Psalms*, 169–79.

Petrarchan sonnet tradition, is put to sacred use in Psalm 119T. 15, 'esteeming it but pleasing paines | to muse on that thy word containes'. She highlights paradoxes, as Sion's gates that are 'high in lowlinesse' (Ps. 87. 3) and the more profound paradox of Laura's spirit telling Petrarch, 'Alive am I: And thow as yett art dead' (*Triumph*, 2. 22). She also employs puns with Elizabethan zest, as the Psalmist who has been both created and instructed by God, 'conceiving all thou dost command' (Ps. 119K. 4). She makes several puns on 'fowl' and 'foul' in Psalms involving bird imagery. For example, in Psalm 140. 10 Pembroke expands the biblical metaphor of the snare laid by the wicked (v. 5) as a 'nett of fowle misshape'. (See also Ps. 141. 29.) More subtle is the word play of 'plaines shall plaine' (*Antonius*, 422), 'one disordred act at *Actium*' (*Antonius*, 1125), 'Rites to aright' ('Angell Spirit', Variant, 27), and the 'gracelesse' taunting at 'thy disgrace' (Ps. 139. 75–6). The pun on Pharaohs and Pharos (an island near Alexandria with a lighthouse that was one of the Seven Wonders of the ancient world) is more evident in Pembroke's translation (*Antonius*, 119) than in Garnier. She also renders the familiar proverb that 'the feare of the Lorde is the beginning of wisdom' (Ps. 111. 18) almost as a pun: 'Stand in his lawe, so understand you well'. That is, if you stand in, or under, his law, you will have understanding. Psalm 59. 41–2 puns on 'wait' as planning entrapment and as patient expectation, word play taken from Bèze (v. 9): 'wherefore though these do lye in waite about my house, so againe I will diligently waite for thy helpe'. (The unreliable MSS *G* and *M* often miss and delete such word play, as in the line 'Eye doth faile while I not faile' in Ps. 119Q. 9, changed to 'Eyes doe faile' to match the Psalter.)

As a translator, Pembroke retains much of the word play in her originals, such as 'the Covetouse in all his goodes, hath no good' (*Discourse*, 431) to render Mornay's '*l'avaricieux n'a point de bien avecques tous ces biens*' (sig. C4ᵛ). Similarly, '*d'abandonner un homme abandonné*' becomes 'A man forsaken fearing to forsake' (*Antonius*, 568). Sometimes the French word play is difficult to render into English. Her translation 'We folow solitarines, to flie carefulnes' (*Discourse*, 535–6), for example, omits Mornay's word play in '*Nous cerchons la solitude pour fuir la sollicitude*' (sig. C7ᵛ). She also eliminates Mornay's deliberate repetition when she alters '*le Chrestien*' (sig. E2ᵛ) to 'hee' for the third usage in a sequence (928). Yet her consciousness of Mornay's rhetorical devices is demonstrated by her attempts to replace them. When she removes the alliteration present in '*passion enterree' and *'raison eslargie'* (sig. D6ᵛ), rendering the phrases as 'passion buried' and 'reason in perfect libertie' (778), she adds alliteration later in the same sentence, the 'foule and filthie prison' (779) for *'orde et sale prison'* (sig. D6ᵛ). Similarly, when her translation eliminates word play, as *'songe'* and *'mensonge'* (sig. D7), she attempts to compensate by supplying a similar figure, as in 'we be disburthened of this earthlie burthen' (791–2). Sometimes she adds word play herself as 'fore-knowes' and 'forgoes' (575–6) for *'predira'* and *'perdra'* (sig. C8ᵛ). She also adds a pun to Mornay's *'sens'* and *'sentiment de la douleur'* (sig. D2), describing the aged losing all senses except the 'sence of paine' (620).

In her translations, she occasionally doubles a term, as when *'courroux'* becomes 'wrathfull rage' (*Antonius*, 532), *'gemme'* becomes 'pearle and stone' (*Triumph*, 1. 84), or *'elle dort'* becomes 'such must, such ought' to give both meanings of the French (*Antonius*, 555). A prominent feature of Mornay's style is the doubling of terms, such as *'ses illusions et enchantemens'* (sig. B5ᵛ) or *'chose d'exquis et de singulier'* (sig. B5ᵛ). Usually Pembroke does retain the doublet (as in *Discourse*, 163, 202–3, 483, 613–14, and 709–10), but she occasionally varies the style. Sometimes she alliterates the doublet, as in 'long and lothsome remorse' (83) or 'life and light' (796). When Mornay rhymes the doublet, she usually does not, as 'busieth and abuseth' (212) for *'amuse et abuse'* (sig. B6ᵛ). Sometimes she replaces a doublet with a single term, as when 'maister of himselfe' (65) replaces *'estre maistre et gardien de soy-mesme'* (sig. B2ᵛ) or *'attachez et liez'* (sig. B1) becomes simply 'tied' (6), or, in *Antonius*, *'magnamime et royal'* becomes 'Princelie' (894) or *'douceur debonnaire'* becomes 'goodnes' (1012). Sometimes the second term of a doublet will become a modifier, as 'an habite of crookednes' (*Discourse*, 780) for *'habituee et accroupie'* (sig. D6ᵛ).

More often, her wording takes on a distinctive, often compact, style. Frequently she will use an adjective to replace an entire phrase or clause, as in Psalm 119T. 1 where 'harty plaint' replaces the Geneva phrase, 'with my whole heart' (v. 145), or the 'self-deaff' adder of Psalm 58. 16 renders the phrase 'like the deafe adder that stoppeth his eare' (v. 4). She uses the compound epithet to similar effect, a usage associated with her brother's style by Joseph Hall, who called it 'that new elegance, | Which sweet *Philisides* fetch't of late from *France*'.[17]

---

[17] Joseph Hall, *Virgidemiarum, sixe bookes* (1597), *STC* 12716, sig. G7.

Sidney himself thought of the compound epithet as classical and praised those 'compositions of two or three words together' as 'one of the greatest beauties can be in a language'.[18] Pembroke's frequent usages include 'hoary-headed age' (*Antonius*, 1677), 'Glad-making oile' (Ps. 45. 27), 'ill-pleas'd eye' (Ps. 51. 29), 'shadow-clothed night' (Ps. 74. 86), God as 'thunder-hid' (Ps. 81. 22), 'never-numbred summe' (*Triumph*, 1. 74), 'dark-confused face' (*Triumph*, 2. 6), and 'woe-darkned skyes' (*Triumph*, 2. 87). Or she will use a phrase like 'eye taught' (Ps. 86. 47) to sum up the idea of the enemies of the godly being shown God's goodness, or 'short-glorious' (*Triumph*, 1. 103) to describe Laura's life. The inexpressibility topos is captured in her phrase 'praise past-praise' (Ps. 145. 6). She uses compound nouns for similar concision, as 'after goers' (Ps. 79. 62), 'god-serchers' (Ps. 105. 5), 'quarrell-pickers' (Ps. 72. 12). In Psalm 49. 1 she uses the compound 'World-dwellers', a more concise wording than Sidney's clause, 'And who abroad | Of world a dweller is' (Ps. 33. 29–30).

Sometimes her style can be difficult. Her use of possessives without apostrophes, for example, can be misleading for the modern reader. For example, 'statutes light' (Ps. 119C. 9) might look on first reading as if the statutes weigh little, rather than describing the light of God's statutes. Similarly, 'life joyes' means life's joys (Variant Ps. LXIII. 14). Also occasionally confusing are her pronouns, which may obscure the meaning, as when 'we' (instead of the impersonal French 'on') is used for the enemies of the godly (*Discourse*, 896). Recognizing that problem in her *Triumph*, she frequently interpolates 'quoth I' or 'shee said' (as 2. 172, 176). Sometimes in the *Psalmes*, however, the antecedent does change without warning, as in Psalm 112 where 'he' in line 13 is God, and 'he' in line 17 is the just man. Other difficult passages arise from her occasional Latinate structure, with verb at the end, as in Psalm 119H. 13–15.

Pembroke is inventive in coining new words and recycling old ones. Some of these are virtually transliterations of the French, as 'redoubt' (*Antonius*, 94, 576, 958; *Discourse*, 894; Ps. 121. 5), 'odiouse' (*Antonius*, 517), 'impackt' for wrapped up (*Antonius*, 1648). She occasionally retains the French form, as 'presse' (sig. C8) for crowd (*Discourse*, 551), or adapts the French spelling, as 'embushes' for ambushes (*Discourse*, 428). Yet sometimes her English word is more obscure to the twentieth-century reader than is the original French, as in

---

[18] Sidney, *Miscellaneous Prose*, 119.

'vizarde' (*Discourse*, 680) for '*masque*' or mask (sig. D3ᵛ), the 'down-falls of *Nilus*' (*Discourse*, 346) for '*cataractes*' (sig. C2), or 'without difference whatsoever' (*Discourse*, 239) for '*sans aucune discretion*' (sig. B7ᵛ).

The *OED* credits Pembroke with the first recorded use of twenty-seven words, such as 'dishedge', 'rebecome', 'impearl', and the more familiar terms 'maid of honour' and 'sea-monster'. More than forty words are cited as instance of the first use in particular senses, e.g. 'distort' ('misrepresent'), 'eternize' ('make eternal'), 'measure' ('turn into metre'), 'shallow' ('superficial'), 'vocal' (as applied to music), and 'winged' (applied to a ship with sails). In addition are words used by the countess before the earliest citations in the *OED*, such as 'disbrain', 'fieldeth', 'seatless', and 'thunderstrike'; and words used in particular senses before the earliest citation in the *OED*, as 'candy' ('cover or encrust with a crystalline substance'), 'oblivion' ('thing forgotten'), 'unsounded' ('unfathomed'), and 'void' ('vast empty space').

The use of archaic words in 'The Dolefull Lay' is Spenserian enough to have been cited as evidence of Spenser's authorship, but it might better be explained as appropriately pastoral, like the archa-isms in Sidney's 'On Ister banke'. She occasionally uses such diction in other pastoral contexts. For example, she will use an old word like 'heardsman' in Psalm 80. 1, as in George Joye's 1530 translation of Martin Bucer, instead of following the more contemporary 'shepherd' in the Psalter and Geneva.[19]

In her translations, Pembroke frequently expands metaphors to make them more vivid, as Mornay's references to a drunkard (*Dis-course*, 121–4), to navigation (932–7), and to a landlord (930). Unlike the only previous English translator of Mornay's *Excellent discours*, Edward Aggas, she expands metaphors, continuing the Penelope reference in the phrase 'weaving at this web' (15) instead of 'beeing at our woork'.[20] She also continues the metaphor of geometry in cor-rectly translating Mornay's '*poinct*' (sig. C1ᵛ) as 'a point' (320), used in its precise mathematical sense, rather than 'as nothing' (Aggas, sig. B7). Where she cannot work out a French pun in English, she at least continues the metaphor. When Mornay describes the

[19] *The Psalter of David in Englishe purely and faithfully translated after the texte of Feline: every Psalme havynge his argument before declarynge brefly thentente and substance of the whole Psalme* ([Antwerp,] 1530), *STC* 2370.

[20] Aggas, *Defence*, sig. A5.

avaricious man '*à un pied en terre*' (sig. D2) who is concerned to
'*enterre*' his money, she renders it 'The covetous man hath one foote
in his grave, and is yet burieng his money' (625–6), a connection
obscured in Aggas's phrase 'hoording up of treasure' (sig. D1$^\text{v}$).

She retains or expands the imagery in *Antonius*, such as the father
images for Nile (*Antonius*, 764–5). She also carries through metaphors, as 'fortunes flower' (841) maintains the image of Time scything
flowers (831–6), or 'begot'/'borne' (490–1) amplifies the idea of birth
in Garnier's '*ordonnees*'/'*nees*'. She also amplifies the courtly context
in *Antonius*. She adds the contrast between 'field tents' and 'courtly
bowers' (70), for example, and extends the appeals to blood and
rank, as in her phrase 'royall hart' (406).

Her *Psalmes* also make metaphors more vivid, as her phrase 'the
just may howses frame' (Ps. 140. 29) for the biblical 'the just shall
dwell in thy presence'; she adds drowning where the biblical text
has the wicked cast 'into the deepe pits' (Ps. 140. 10) and 'Mines' to
the biblical image of gold and silver (Ps. 119I. 23). Her description of
stars 'bedasht with raine' (Ps. 107. 67) amplifies the scriptural hyper-
bole of the storm that makes the ship 'mount up to the heaven, and
descend to the deep' (v. 26). She personifies abstractions, particularly
when the figure is present in the biblical sources, as in the 'Grace and
Honor' which are before the Lord in Psalm 96. 16, or when that trope
is expanded in her sources. For example, the personification implicit
in Psalm 55. 10–12 is somewhat developed by Calvin, who states that
'quarreling and brawling' walk the city walls, wickedness lives there,
and 'craft and decit' are in the streets. The metaphoric potential is
amplified in Pembroke's rendition: 'Mother Wrong' and 'daughter
Strife' walk around the walls of the city, while 'oppressions, tumults,
guiles of every kind' are the burgesses of that town, and 'Mischeif'
wears 'his masking robes' of 'deceit, with treason lin'd' (Ps. 55. 22–
9). Similarly, as part of a lengthy description of the plagues of
Egypt she says 'abroad goes Death . . . and men and cattell kills' (Ps.
78. 151–2). Death is also personified in *The Triumph of Death*, as in
Petrarch, and in 'The Dolefull Lay'. She follows her brother's example in his Psalm 16. 21 by personifying Night in Psalm 139. 36–9, but
she makes Night female rather than male, as does her niece Lady
Wroth in Sonnet 12 of *Pamphilia to Amphilanthus*.[21]

---

[21] For a listing of Sidney's use of personification, see Montgomery, *Symmetry*, 125–6.
Wroth frequently personifies Night in her *Pamphilia to Amphilanthus*, as in Sonnets
1[P1], 4[P4], 12[P13], 15[P17], 18[P20], 19[P22], 29[P33], 37[P43], 1[P63], 3[P65], and

Pembroke typically adds rhetorical questions to structure a work as a dramatic monologue. Such questions, incidentally, provide the structure of 'The Dolefull Lay' (1–7, 13, 32, 44, 55–6, 66), and are used in 'Even now' (41), and 'Angell Spirit' (54–6). She retains the device used by Mornay to involve the reader in the argument, as '*Or quel bien y a-il, je vous prie, en ceste vie*' (sig. B2), rendered 'Now what good, I pray you, is there in life' (*Discourse*, 43–4), or '*En somme, veux-tu savoir quelle difference il y a*' (sig. C1), rendered 'Lastly, will you knowe what the diversitie is' (303). Pembroke also retains his series of questions, as in 54–62, 69–71, and 702–4. In *Antonius* she adds rhetorical questions, as 'for why?' (510) and 'Who knowes it not?' (971), uses them frequently in *Triumph* (as 1. 82–3, 88, 94; 2. 13–15, 20–1), and adds them to many of her Psalms. Psalm 94. 1, for example, repeatedly asks the 'God of revenge' how long the wicked will remain unpunished; then the speaker turns to address the wicked directly before continuing the prayer to God. Psalm 129. 14 questions the wicked, 'what you thinck shalbe your end?' before telling them of their impending doom. Psalm 115 uses questions to establish both a rhetorical parallel and a theological difference. The ungodly ask, *Where* is your God? The godly reply with a question, *What* are your gods? That is, the invisible but omnipotent God is contrasted with the visible but impotent idols that having eyes cannot see and ears cannot hear. Rhetorical questions can also make sense of a difficult passage, like the opening of Psalm 121. In most English versions it is unclear why the Psalmist should look to the hills to find God, but Pembroke follows Bèze in looking toward the site of the temple. 'What? and doe I behold the lovely mountaines?' The answer is supplied, 'ô there abides the worlds Creator' (Ps. 121. 3).

A primary literary influence on her work was the poetry of her brother Philip, although critical study has often focused on the difference between the two writers. In his 1667 Psalter Samuel Woodforde, for example, claims to see a difference based on gender in the work of the two authors: 'This Paraphrase as I remember Dr. *Donne* calls by the name of Sir *Philips* and the Countess of *Pembroks* translation, and not without good reason, as far as I could judge by that cursory view I had of it, during the short time it remained in my hands; There appearing that difference as I conceived in the composition,

6[P100]. See Ann Rosalind Jones, *The Currency of Eros: Women's Love Lyric in Europe, 1540–1620* (Bloomington: Indiana UP, 1990), 145–7; and Wall, *Gender*, 331–2.

which is wont to be in the aires of Brother, and Sister, not so unlike, as to have no resemblance, nor yet so perfectly resembling, as to have nothing but the sex to distinguish them.'[22]

Certainly many of her usual rhetorical forms, including alliteration, polyptoton, chiasmus, and compound epithets, were also extensively used by her brother Philip in his Psalms and in his secular poems. Since she was preparing his works for publication during the same years that she produced most of her extant work, it would be more surprising if there were not similarities. The forms, however, are too typical of Renaissance verse to conclude that she is using her brother as her only literary model. Indeed, her wording and versification are often at least as Spenserian as Sidneian. (See 'Dolefull Lay': 'Literary Context'.)

But there are instances where she deliberately alludes to her brother's ideas or wording, most obviously in Psalm 73. As has long been noted, Pembroke begins that Psalm with a quotation from *Astrophil and Stella*, 5. 1, 'It is most true', in a technique that Louis Martz aptly terms 'sacred parody'.[23] The parallels are more significant than such verbal echoes, however, for both poems are sceptical of the power of Reason to solve life's problems: in the sonnet, Reason is undercut by Desire; but in the Psalm, Reason is surpassed by Faith. Sidney argues that Reason is inadequate to conquer his love for Stella, using his familiar pattern of 13 lines of logical argument undercut by a final statement: 'True, and yet true that I must *Stella* love'. Pembroke echoes her brother's phrasing frequently in her rendition of this Psalm, but she also relied on her usual textual sources for the interpretation of the Psalm, which presents a continual problem. Why do bad things happen to good people? Why do the wicked prosper? Pembroke's interpretation is closely connected to Bèze's Argument for Psalm 73 that Reason is inadequate to understand God's governance of the world and so Reason can work against 'the true wisdom' in spiritual matters. Reason would say that the good should prosper and the evil should be punished, but we see the evil

[22] Samuel Woodforde, *A Paraphrase upon the Psalms of David* (1667), Wing B2491, sigs. B4ᵛ–C1. Among twentieth-century critics some, such as Freer, *Music*, 73, conclude that Sidney 'far surpasses his sister in suiting form to meaning', while more recently Zim, *Psalms*, 185, states that most 'modern assessments . . . have tended to favour the Countess's literary achievement'. Freer, *Music*, 75, goes against gender stereotypes by praising Sidney's 'grace' and Pembroke's 'muscular logic'.

[23] Martz, *Meditation*, 186. See also Fisken, 'Parody', 226; Zim, *Psalms*, 199–200; Waller, *Mary Sidney*, 199.

flourishing. Yet God's wisdom teaches us that 'unto the evil men, good thinges are turned to evill: and on the contrarie unto the good men, even evill thinges turne to good'. Pembroke's parallel debts to scholarly biblical commentary and to her brother's secular poems are most evident in her first line, which both quotes the opening phrase of *Astrophil and Stella* 5 and also paraphrases Bèze's verse 1, 'It must needs be true and inviolable, that God can not be but favourable towardes Israel, that is, to them that worship him purely and devoutlie':

> It is most true that god to Israell,
>   I mean to men of undefiled hartes,
>   is only good, and nought but good impartes.

Sidney's 'from whose rules who do swerve' (3) becomes 'from this truth with straying stepps declin'd' (6). Thus, her first six lines directly parallel the first 5 lines of *Astrophil and Stella* and make a similar argument about the danger of straying from reason, although the problem presented in Psalm 73 is quite different from Astrophil's desire for Stella. She continues to echo the sonnet. Her phrase 'inward part' (63) combines her brother's phrases in line 2, 'inward light' and 'heavenly part'. 'Inward light' is also echoed in line 48, 'inward sight'. Other phrases in this Psalm that parallel Sonnet 5 include, 'I was a foole' (line 64), echoing reference to 'fooles' in Sidney's line 7; and 'whoorish Idolls' (line 81, echoing Sidney's line 6). The breast that 'did chafe and swell' (Ps. 73. 7) echoes *Astrophil*, 37. 1, 'My mouth doth water, and my breast doth swell'. Similarly, 'O what is he will teach me clyme the skyes?' (line 73) is perhaps a self-conscious reference to *Astrophil*, 31. 1, implying that 'Sidney was her teacher in the art of poesie of "that Lyricall Kind"', as Zim suggests.[24] Yet here it also directly contrasts the teaching of the godly with the teaching of the wicked in her second stanza, where the evil 'pronounce as from the skies'.[25]

Wording in other Psalms also occasionally echoes *Astrophil*. Psalm 126. 9 also uses the phrase 'Most true', once again combining an allusion to Sidney with Bèze's commentary. The reassurance that this is truth and not a dream comes from Bèze, 'and surelie so it is' (v. 3), but

---

[24] Zim, *Psalms*, 201.

[25] The idea for sky in this verse may come from *Psaumes*, this one by Bèze, '*De tout ce qu'au ciel j'apperçoy?*' Cf. Sidney's Ps. 19. 11, 'But of the skyes the teaching cryes', and Ps. 34. 22, God's 'Call the skyes did climb'.

the wording comes from *Astrophil* 5. Pembroke's phrase 'trewand soule' in Psalm 51. 21 echoes *Astrophil*, 1. 13, 'my trewand pen', in what Zim sees as a deliberate reference to the novice learning the poetic craft.[26] Other echoes of *Astrophil* are scattered throughout the *Psalmes*. Psalm 114. 20, for example, uses the Sidneian wording 'purling spring' from *Astrophil*, 15. 1. Echoes of *Astrophil* occur in her other works, such as the phrase 'beamie eyes' from *Astrophil*, 8. 9, used in the blazon of Cleopatra (*Antonius*, 723), and the phrase 'wood-musiques Queene' (*Antonius*, 333) which echoes Sidney's 'woodmusique's King' (*Arcadia*, 66. 13). And 'Who better might (O might ah word of woe)' ('Even now', 23) echoes 'I might, unhappie word, ô me, I might, | And then would not, or could not see my blisse' (*Astrophil*, 33. 1–2).[27] Pembroke's Psalms also echo phrases in her brother's versions. For example, Variant Psalm LIII. 15 picks up Sidney's description of the enemies of God as 'Canibals' (Ps. 14. 14), although Pembroke adds the intensification of bestiality in her phrase 'Wolvish Canibals'. She also follows Sidney in adding the idea of blushing where shame occurs in her biblical sources, as in Sidney's Psalms 34. 20 and 40. 52. Both may derive the usage from Bèze's *carmine*, as in 69. 6: '*Non erubescant mea causa*'. (See, for example, Pss. 69. 20; 119F. 24; and 129. 16.) Sidney also uses 'Blush...for shame' in *Arcadia*, 56. 5 and frequently in *Astrophil*. More subtle is her original phrase, 'hand-writyng' (Ps. 143. 26), which is probably developed from God's 'handworking' (4) in Sidney's Psalm 19. 15–16 where the skies become God's book: 'Their Words be set in letters great | For evry body's reading'. She also echoes Sidney's Psalms in *Triumph*, alluding to Psalm 42. 3, 'So my soul in panting playeth' in the 'panting soule' of 2. 49.

Another opportunity for direct comparison is Pembroke's rendition of Psalm 53, which is almost identical to Psalm 14 in the Hebrew original. Sidney renders the Psalm in tercets, while Pembroke employs a more complex eight-line stanza, rhyming *ababbcac* in the Penshurst version. Her original draft follows Sidney's ideas line by line and is far closer to Sidney's wording than is the revision in the Penshurst MS (*A*). God's 'peircing eye' in Sidney, line 7, becomes God's 'searching eye' in Pembroke, line 8. His line 'Not One that God discerneth' (12) is rendered by Pembroke with a direct quotation from

---

[26] Zim, *Psalms*, 200.
[27] *The Penguin Book of Renaissance Verse 1509–1659*, ed. H. R. Woudhuysen (1992; rpt. 1993), 132.

Geneva, 'Not one doth good, not one' (line 12). Although she intensifies the wording, she uses an exclamation to render verse 4, as he
does. For verse 8, Pembroke follows Sidney's opening words, 'Ah
when', although he follows the Psalter in treating the verse as a question, whereas she renders it with one of her typical exclamations, 'Ah,
when shall time' (line 22). The Messianic reading of the Psalm,
stressed by Bèze, is slightly clearer in Pembroke's Variant Psalm
LIII, where she refers to the 'Saviour' (line 23), than in the revision,
where she uses Sidney's word, 'saver' (line 22). In the opening line,
Sidney mentions that the fool is 'by flesh and fancy led', an idea Pembroke develops, explaining that even if the fool does not speak the
words, 'There is noe god', he evidences that idea in 'thought and
will'. His 'fancie' is soon revealed in 'rotten deedes' (lines 1–3).
Unlike Sidney, or any of her usual sources, in her revision Pembroke
adds the idea that once God has freed his people, they will 'daunce
and sing' (line 24) as they do in Sidney's translation of Psalms 30
and 42.[28]

Although her use of neologisms and compound words can make her
text more concise than her original, she also frequently expands her
text to develop a metaphor, as did her brother. For example, the
brief comparison of God to a shepherd leading his people in the wilderness in Psalm 78. 161–8 becomes virtually an epic simile.[29] She also
expands the pastoral imagery that concludes Psalm 78. 209–16. Similar expansions occur frequently, as in the description of the dogs in
Psalm 59. 70–9 and the birds in Psalm 91. 9–14. She also occasionally
adds metaphors from Nature, as in the description of Laura's 'leafe' in
Triumph, 1. 141.

Pembroke frequently develops details implicit in a metaphor. For
example, Psalm 49. 14 reads: 'and the righteous shal have dominacion
over them in the morning: for their beautie shal consume, *when they
shal go* from their house to the grave'. Pembroke intensifies the biblical image in a memorable statement that what is lovely in the house,
that is, the living prince, becomes abhorred as a decaying carcass (29–
30), like the familiar medieval *memento mori* tombs of princes, with a
skeleton carved below the lifelike sculpture on top of the tomb. More
often, she expands clothing metaphors, used so effectively in 'Even

---

[28] Fisken, 'Parody', 228, has compared the storm imagery used in Sidney's Psalm 18 and
Pembroke's Psalm 77, concluding that in Sidney the storm becomes a 'solemn pageant, a
stately show of authority', whereas in Pembroke the storm rages around the speaker.

[29] May, *Courtier Poets*, 209.

now' and 'Angell Spirit'. In the Psalms the metaphor is frequently used in connection with Nature, as in Psalms 74. 85–8, 85. 32, or 102. 82–4. The enemies of God may also be described in terms of their clothing. In Psalm 73. 3–6 the Psalmist considers the 'prosperitie of the wicked', declaring that because 'They are not in trouble as other men . . . Therefore pride is as a chaine unto them and crueltie covereth them as a garment.' Pembroke develops the allusion to the chain and robes of office worn by the wicked: they wear 'pride, as . . . a gorgious chaine' on 'their swelling necks' and are 'cloth'd in wrong, as if a Robe it were' (16–18). Psalm 109 prays that the wicked be clothed more appropriately, that 'wretchednes [may be] his cloake' and 'woe . . . his garment', that he will wear worse disgrace 'then ever clothed me, | trailing in trayne a synnfull shamefull gowne' (Ps. 109. 45, 49, 77–8). As the hypocrisy and the punishment of the wicked can be shown in terms of their clothing, so can God's power. Jehovah reigns 'Cloth'd with state and girt with might' (Ps. 93. 1–2), an idea developed in the courtly imagery of Psalm 104, wherein Pembroke follows Calvin in depicting the curtain of the heavens as a canopy of state. In Psalm 106. 10, Pembroke's speaker asks to wear God's 'liv'ry', an idea repeated in Psalm 74. 96.

Similarly, Pembroke expands agricultural metaphors, as in Psalms 44. 6–8, 85. 31–8, 90. 25, and 92. 20, 35–43. She develops metaphors from accounting in 'Angell Spirit', 43–5, as she does in several Psalms, including 51. 30, 89. 2 and 89. 94–5. She adds kinetic imagery (Ps. 82. 23–5), metaphors from the law (Pss. 51.30 and 138.14) and architecture (Ps. 115. 39 and Variant Ps. LXII. 7–12), and presents God as landlord (Ps. 132. 64).

She occasionally interpolates or expands from her own experience. As Calvin's preface compares his experience with that of David, and as Bèze's Argument for Psalm 91 becomes a moving statement about his 'one and thirtie' years of exile, so her Psalms reflect her own life. Significant expansions or additions from her own experience as an aristocratic woman include her descriptions of the women of the court and of arranged marriage in Psalm 45; her description of pregnancy and childbirth in Psalms 48. 17–18, 51. 15–18, and 113. 17–18,[30] her references to an embryo in Psalms 58. 21–4, 71. 19–24, and 139. 43–63, and to children in Psalms 131. 1–10 and 144. 9–12. Perhaps the most moving reference is her original reading of Psalm

[30] Sidney also expands the childbirth metaphor in Ps. 7. 37–9 and uses it in dedicating the *Arcadia* to his sister.

68 to show that 'wee house=confined maids' are now liberated and as doves 'freer skyes do try', in a use of the traditional bird motif for poetic composition. (Variant Ps. 68. 34–6.)

Her interest in science and discovery is also reflected in her *Psalmes*. For example, in Psalm 139. 34 Pembroke interprets the biblical phrase 'the uttermost partes of the sea' (Geneva, v. 9) as the 'West', or the New World. Here she is following Bèze (v. 9), 'the formost part of the west', but she is also expressing her interest in New World exploration.[31] Similarly, her interest in embryology, not only her experience of childbirth, is reflected in her expansion of the embryo images in the *Psalmes*. Developing the presentation of orderly foetal development from the commentaries of Calvin and Bèze, she emphasizes the delight of such knowledge:

> My god, how I these studies prize,
> that doe thy hidden workings show!   (Ps. 139. 64–5)

The study of science reveals God's working in Nature, a sophisticated view that she shared with her contemporary Francis Bacon. Yet, like Donne and Milton, she continues to use the Ptolemaic cosmos for poetic purposes, adding the 'starry Spheare' to Psalm 139. 24, for example, and emphasizing in Psalm 103. 42–3 the distance of 'the Sphere of farthest starre' from 'earthly Center'.[32]

Her identification with her own social class brings some striking differences in wording from her sources, for she identifies with the courtier, not with the poor. Class perspective could hardly be clearer than in Psalm 62. 10, '*if* riches increase, set not your heart thereon', which she renders (our italics) '*when* riches growes' (Ps. 62. 35). Psalm 45. 19 is particularly striking in its discussion of the 'meaner people' who must be controlled by force.[33] Yet she also emphasizes the responsibility of the powerful to protect the poor in her original adaptation of Psalm 104. 54–61. So evident is the upper-class perspective throughout Pembroke's work that the alteration of Psalm 123 from an aristocratic to a lower-class perspective may suggest

---

[31] For example, the Pembrokes subscribed to Martin Frobisher's voyages, *APC*, X. 414–15.

[32] See Margaret P. Hannay, ' "How I these studies prize": The Countess of Pembroke and Elizabethan Science', in *Women, Medicine and Science 1500–1700*, ed. Lynette Hunter and Sarah Hutton (Phoenix Mill, Gloucestershire: Sutton Publishing, 1997), 108–21.

[33] See May, *Courtier Poets*, 208, and Margaret P. Hannay, ' "When riches growes": Class Perspective in Pembroke's *Psalmes*', in *Women, Writing, and the Reproduction of Culture in Tudor and Stuart Britain*, ed. Jane Donawerth *et al.* (U of Syracuse, forthcoming).

that the revision is not authorial. (See 'Relationship of the Texts of the *Psalmes*'.)

Her versions of the Psalms are also set apart from her Geneva sources by their use of language of suits and courtiers, similar to that employed by Sidney and by Parker, as throughout Psalm 86. She also interprets the 'mighty man' of Psalm 78. 197 as a 'knight', expands the bird imagery of the Hebrew Psalm with references to falconry in Psalm 83. 7–12, describes the queen's clothing and the role of women at court in Psalm 45, and refers to aristocratic travel with the words 'pasport' (Ps. 72. 60) and the 'lords conduct' (Ps. 126. 2). Many Psalms refer to problems of envy and slander at court, as David experienced in the court of Saul; Pembroke typically expands such references in the Psalms, just as they were emphasized in elegies for Sidney.[34] (See 'Angell Spirit': 'Literary Context'.) Psalm 71. 32 even adds to her sources the concept of 'Spies' who have been watching the Psalmist and then debate how best to destroy him. Proper governance is an important issue in many of the Psalms, particularly the instruction to the prince 'who king hym self shalbe' in Psalm 72. 1, David's outline of how he will rule in Psalm 101, the question of legitimate rulers versus tyrants in Psalms 52 and 89, and the duty of princes to defend 'the folk of Abrahams god' in Psalm 47. 16–20. While these issues are present in the Hebrew Psalms and in her usual sources, she gives an apparently original allegorical interpretation of the cedars that tower over other plants as princes who should demonstrate *noblesse oblige* to 'the rest' (Ps. 104. 56).

Her patterns of composition can be illustrated by her revision of 'Angell Spirit', a more subtle reworking than in many of the Psalms drafts recorded by Woodforde. The rhyme scheme (*abbabba*) and metre (iambic pentameter) of the seven-line stanza remain unchanged, unlike many of her Psalms revisions such as 53, 58, 119H, S, and W; and the revision is longer than the original, unlike such Psalms as 50, 58, 80, and 86. (Psalm 89, however, is considerably longer in the revision.)

The major changes are the elimination of two stanzas on her grief (Variant, 22–35) and the addition of four stanzas on Sidney and on her role as writer ('Angell Spirit', 50–70, 78–84), with deliberate echoes of Sidney's own words. The excised stanzas employ images of ruins, like

---

[34] Cf. Anne Lake Prescott, 'Evil Tongues at the Court of Saul: The Renaissance David as a Slandered Courtier', *JMRS* 21 (1991), 163–86.

those in Spenser's 'The Ruines of Time' (Variant, 31) and allude to Petrarch's *Trionfo della Morte* (Variant, 35). The revised poem emphasizes her role as a writer as much as a grieving relative. For example, in the early draft, her love 'hath never dun, | Nor can enough, though justly here contrould' (Variant, 41–2). In the revision, her love still 'hath never done', but it is clearer that what is not complete is her written expression: 'Nor can enough in world of words unfold' (27–8). (The phrase also adds characteristic alliteration.) The 'joynt worke' becomes the 'coupled worke' (2), which may indicate a time sequence as Sidney first began the work and then inspired her to complete it. Instead of dwelling on the festered, bleeding wounds of her grief (Variant, 19–20), she develops the metaphor and uses it to describe the writing process. The *Psalmes* left unfinished by Sidney, 'This precious peece', become 'This halfe maim'd peece' (18). The wounds of her grief still fester and bleed (19–20), alluding to Sidney's own 'festred' wound, but Pembroke adds a stanza on her role as author (78–84), wherein that blood is 'dissolv'd to Inke', as the poems become 'theise dearest offrings of my hart' (78–9). She reworks a stanza on the inexpressibility topos (43–9), replacing a passive construction that presents the speaker as overcome with grief ('Sometime of rase my swelling passions know, | How work my thoughts' (Variant, 59)), with an active construction that presents the speaker as taking control of her emotions: 'I call my thoughts, whence so strange passions flowe' (45), echoing *Arcadia*, 41, 'Like those sicke folkes, in whom strange humors flowe'.[35] She adds a statement that Sidney's 'rare workes' are so well written 'as Art could not amende' them and 'no witt can adde' to them (67–8). That is, no writer is adequate to complete the *Psalmes*. Both versions emphasize that the problem of inability to express Sidney's worth is not hers alone: 'There lives no witt' that can sufficiently praise Sidney (49; Variant, 63). In the revision she removes the concluding description of the *Psalmes* as 'Made only thine' (Variant, 73), thereby allowing for her own agency. She adds a query, 'such losse hath this world ought | can equall it?' (75–6), echoing *Astrophil*, 21, 'Hath this world ought so faire as Stella is?'[36] Protesting that she writes only from 'simple love | not Art nor skill' (82–3), she employs the traditional modesty topos and also makes a graceful allusion to *Astrophil*, 1, wherein Astrophil

<hr/>

[35] May, *Courtier Poets*, 180.
[36] Ibid.

learns to write from the heart. By such references to her brother's words, she both celebrates his poetic works and situates herself as a writer.

Other changes include replacing the term 'Israels King', familiar from Protestant usage as a synonym for God, with the more inclusive term 'heavens King' (8); and removing the harsh condemnation of other metrical Psalters, replacing it with references to the angelic choir (10–14). She strengthens wording, as when 'My Muse with thine, it selfe dar'd' becomes 'So dar'd my Muse' (5), 'faire beames' become 'lightning beames' (7), 'And rest faire momuments' (Variant, 64) becomes 'Immortall Monuments' (71). She removes an unsuccessful pun on 'sole' and 'soul' (37; Variant, 51), removes the catalogue of qualities (40; Variant, 53), removes internal rhyme (Variant, 45), clarifies pronouns (3), adds characteristic rhetorical questions (75–6), and removes redundant parentheses (Variant, 72), using such parenthetic explanations more effectively in 22 and 25. She adds repetition in 'too too bold' (25) for 'overbold' (25; Variant, 39) and adds her characteristic exclamations 'Oh' (15, 43) and 'ah!' (75). Her syntax becomes even more complex, as Louise Schleiner has noted.[37] She amplifies the metaphor of the streams pouring into the sea (32–4; Variant, 46–7), which is connected to the outpouring of her heart's blood as ink, and the combination of her Muse with that of her brother, to describe her efforts to complete her brother's work in the *Psalmes*.[38] She also adds a stanza (64–70) to introduce the architectural metaphor, thereby clarifying the image in her revised lines 71–7. In her description of her brother, she allows for more praise on earth (39–42), adds the Phoenix image (38), and appeals to Truth, in an attempt to refute the charge that she is partial to her own 'blood' (50–6). An additional stanza (57–63) continues the angel reference, describes Sidney's apotheosis, and emphasizes the problem of envy, a recurrent theme in the *Astrophel* elegies. (See 'Angell Spirit': 'Literary Context'.) The final couplet, which may have been lost from the printed version (see 'Transmission and Authority of Texts'), concludes the poem with the conventional wish that she could join her brother in heaven.

In these revisions of 'Angell Spirit' and in Woodforde's recorded revisions of her *Psalmes* paraphrases, Pembroke demonstrates both a

---

[37] Schleiner includes a modernized version of the revised poem in her discussion of its syntax: *Women Writers*, 77–9.

[38] Ibid., 80.

growing mastery of poetic form and a gradual shift in self-definition. Although she may continue to identify herself as 'the Sister of Sir Philip Sidney', she increasingly asserts herself as a poet. Paradoxically, by speaking on behalf of her brother and by transmitting the words of the Psalmist, she found her own voice.

ORIGINAL WORKS

'A Dialogue betweene two shepheards, *Thenot* and *Piers*, in praise of *Astrea*'

Literary Context

The Countess of Pembroke spent comparatively little time at court after her marriage (see p. 4); nevertheless, she prudently sought to maintain a connection with her sovereign, demonstrated by her New Year's gifts and by her two poems in praise of Elizabeth—'A Dialogue betweene two shepheards, *Thenot* and *Piers*, in praise of *Astrea*', and the poem dedicating the Sidneian *Psalmes*, 'Even now that Care'. Both poems were apparently written in or about 1599, when the queen was expected to visit Wilton and when the countess was eager to place her young son William at court. (See her properly obsequious letter, endorsed 1601, to Queen Elizabeth, Correspondence: Manuscript Letter IX.) Both poems use Protestant iconography to praise Elizabeth: 'Astrea' uses the classical figure of that divine virgin, and 'Even now' the biblical figure of David.

Entertainments for the monarch were an outgrowth of the household revels in the early Tudor period, presented both to entertain and to influence their audience.[1] In Elizabethan performances, such as the ones Pembroke had witnessed at Kenilworth and at Woodstock in 1575, or the Earl of Hertford's entertainment at Elvetham in 1591, praise of the queen was expected to reflect glory on the aristocrat who commissioned and paid for the entertainment.[2] Pembroke boldly departed from convention in writing her own pastoral dialogue, so that Queen Elizabeth would be greeted at Wilton by her host's own words.

[1] Suzanne R. Westfall, *Patrons and Performance: Early Tudor Household Revels* (Oxford: Clarendon Pr, 1990), 2–3.

[2] Leicester's magnificent entertainments at Kenilworth were written by George Gascoigne, William Hunnis, Richard Mulcaster, and others. See Robert Langham, *A Letter*, ed. Roger J. P. Kuin (Leiden: E. J. Brill, 1983), 13–16. David Scott has proposed that this letter was written by William Patten and attributed to Robert Laneham as a jest: 'William Patten and the Authorship of "Robert Laneham's Letter"', *ELR* 7 (1977), 297–306. Susan Frye agrees with Scott, arguing that the fictional letter is a critique of court practice written by Patten 'to send up the Dudley agenda': *Elizabeth I: The Competition for Representation* (Oxford and New York: Oxford UP, 1993), 65. On Elvetham, see Curt Breight, 'Realpolitik and Elizabethan Ceremony: The Earl of Hertford's Entertainment of Elizabeth at Elvetham, 1591', *RQ* 45 (1992), 20–48.

Like her brother Philip's 'Lady of May', presented to the queen at Wanstead in May 1578 (or 1579), and the inconclusively attributed 'A Dialogue betweene two shepherds, utterd in a pastorall shew, at Wilton',[3] Pembroke's 'Astrea' is a singing match between two shepherds designed for presentation on the queen's summer progress. Its exact date is a matter of conjecture. John Nichols suggests that 'the Dialogue was probably written in 1600, when the Queen meditated a Progress into North Wiltshire'. Because that projected visit to Ramsbury was cancelled, the poem 'was perhaps recited in 1601 in *Aldersgate Street*', Pembroke's London residence.[4] The title as first printed by Francis Davison in *Poetical Rapsody* (1602), however, reads 'made by the excellent Lady, the Lady Mary Countesse of Pembrook, at the Queenes Maiesties being at her house at   Anno 15   ', suggesting that 1599 is the latest possible date of composition. E. K. Chambers doubtfully dates the poem as 1592, when the queen visited Ramsbury in August.[5] Mary Erler has more convincingly dated the poem to 1599, drawing on records of the intended August progress to Wilton and on numerous parallels with Sir John Davies's *Hymnes of Astraea*, twenty-six acrostic poems presented to the queen on Accession Day, 17 November 1599.[6]

Pembroke applies the imperial myth of the goddess Astraea (she Anglicizes the spelling) to Queen Elizabeth, a myth particularly appropriate to an August progress, for the Greek astronomical poet Aratos connects Astraea with the virgin Justice who became the constellation Virgo; hence August is her month.[7] Elizabeth was represented as the Virgo in such varied works as Christopher Saxton's

[3] Sidney, *Poems*, 343–4, 517. Since this poem (first included in the 1613 edition and reprinted in all subsequent folio editions of the *Arcadia*) was never suppressed, Ringler speculates that the family 'possibly accepted it as genuine'.

[4] John Nichols, *The Progresses and Public Processions of Queen Elizabeth* (London: John Nichols & Sons, 1788–1821), III. 529.

[5] E. K. Chambers, *The Elizabethan Stage* (Oxford: Clarendon P, 1923), III. 337. See 'Diary of Events by Burghley', *HMC Salisbury*, XIII. 466; and a meeting 'At the Court at Ramsbery, the 28th of August', *APC*, XXIII. 157–8.

[6] Mary C. Erler, 'Davies's *Astraea* and Other Contexts of the Countess of Pembroke's "A Dialogue"', *SEL* 30 (1990), 41–61. These parallels include both imagery and poetic form. See also May, *Courtier Poets*, 177–8.

The queen's projected itinerary is described in a letter by Sir Charles Danvers to the Earl of Southampton, 'Before July 24' 1599, *HMC Salisbury*, IX. 245–7 (the visit was cancelled). See Rowland Whyte's letters to Robert Sidney, 2–26 Aug. 1600, De L'Isle MS U1475 C12 / 264–272.

[7] Aratos, *Phaenomena*, 93–136. The connection was continued by Latin poets, including Seneca, *Hercules Oetaeus*, 69; cited in Yates, *Astraea*, 30–1.

Survey of England (1579) and a pageant play by the students of Grey's Inn called *The Misfortunes of Arthur* (1588). From Ovid's *Metamorphoses*, I. 149–50, Elizabethans adapted the story that Astrea fled the world in its Iron Age of war and greed. Spenser, for example, uses the Astrea/Virgo/August motif to open *Mother Hubberds Tale*:

> It was the month, in which the righteous Maide,
> That for disdaine of sinfull worlds upbraide,
> Fled back to heaven, whence she was first conceived.[8]

From Virgil's Fourth Eclogue, read as proto-Christian, Elizabethans adopted the promise that when Astraea returns, she will bring back the Golden Age.[9] *The Misfortunes of Arthur*, for example, concludes with the cry:

> Let Virgo come from Heaven, the glorious Starre...
> That vertuous Virgo borne for Brytain's blisse...
> Let her reduce the golden age againe.[10]

Because the myth spoke of departure and change, even as it promised that Astraea would return, bringing the Golden Age of eternal Spring, it seemed to be particularly appropriate for the waning days of Elizabeth's life. The Spring motif was used by Davies, for example, who portrays Elizabeth as decked with 'E ternall garlands of thy flowers, / G reene garlands never wasting'.[11] In his 'Hymnes of Astraea' Davies also includes praise of Elizabeth as the *'May of Majestie'* ('Hymne IV. To the Moneth of May') and as Flora ('Hymne IX. To Flora'). Pembroke incorporates the motif of eternal Spring when Thenot praises her as 'A field in flowry Roabe arrayd' and is corrected because 'That Spring indures but shortest time', but Astrea's Spring is eternal (38–42).

In Elizabethan encomia, the promise that Astraea would bring back the Golden Age was conflated with Astraea as the image of justice and imperial rule, and with the cult of the Virgin Queen which supplanted the cult of the Virgin Mary, to produce an image of Elizabeth as the

---

[8] Spenser, *Mother Hubberds Tale*, 1–3. See also *Faerie Queene*, V, Proem, 9–11, and VII. vii. 37.

[9] The image of Virgil as a proto-Christian was most familiar through Dante's representation of him as his guide through the Inferno.

[10] Thomas Hughes, *The Misfortunes of Arthur*, ed. H. C. Grumbine (Berlin, 1900), 190; Tudor Facsimile Texts 1911, 45–6; also quoted in Yates, *Astraea*, 62.

[11] 'Hymne III. To the Spring', Davies, *Poems*, 72. Davies maintains the paradox of eternal Spring and harvest by including 'To the Moneth of September', praising that fruitful month as the time of her birth, 76–7.

one who would usher in the Golden Age of reformed England. Praise of Elizabeth as Astraea was most frequent in the decade following the defeat of the Spanish Armada, often presenting her both as an imperial ruler who brought peace and prosperity and as a religious figure who vanquished the Catholic enemy and established Protestantism.[12] Supplementing the prevailing biblical iconography, Protestants compared her with Astraea as well as with David and other biblical figures. (See 'Even now that Care'.) For example, Jan van der Noodt, an aristocrat forced to flee to England from his home in Antwerp because of his Calvinist beliefs, adds the figure of Astraea to his list of biblical comparisons for Elizabeth, along with Israel's leaders 'Joshua, Juda, Gedeon, David', and women who have delivered God's people, such as Deborah, Jael, Michal, and Esther. In dedicating *A theatre ... [for] worldlings* (1569) to Elizabeth, he claims that 'the Golden worlde is come againe, and the Virgin *Astrea* is descended from heaven to builde hir a seate in this your moste happie countrey of *England*'.[13] The myth was also used to convey a Protestant message in such works as George Peele's *Descensus Astraeae* (the 1591 Lord Mayor's Show), in which Elizabeth is presented as Astraea with a sheep-hook, tending a Reformed England blessed by 'Great Israels God'.[14] Similarly, an elegy for Elizabeth mourned:

> Righteous *Astraea* from the earth is banish't ...
> Which did to us a radiant light remaine,
> But was a comet to the eye of *Spaine*:
> From whose chaste beames so bright a beautie shin'de,
> That all their whorish eyes were striken blinde.[15]

By linking Astrea with the figure of Piers, Pembroke places her dialogue in this Protestant tradition. Because of its association with Langland's *Piers Plowman*, read in the sixteenth century as a 'Protestant' text, the name Piers was usually used for satiric comments on abuses in the Church, as in Spenser's 'Maye'.[16] In 'October', Piers asks Cuddie to praise Eliza, thereby associating the name with encomia. The

---

[12] Yates, *Astraea*, 59.

[13] Jan van der Noodt, *A theatre wherein be represented as wel the miseries and calamities that follow the voluptuous Worldlings* (1569), STC 18602, sig. A6.

[14] George Peele, *Descensus Astraeae*, in *The Life and Minor Works of George Peele*, ed. David H. Horne (New Haven: Yale UP, 1952), 214–19; Yates, *Astraea*, 60–2; King, *Iconography*, 241–2.

[15] John Lane, *An Elegie upon the death of the high and renowned Princesse, our late Soveraigne Elizabeth*, Fugitive Tracts, 2nd ser., no. 2 (London, 1875); quoted in Yates, *Astraea*, 61.

[16] On Protestant 'kidnapping' of *Piers Plowman*, see King, *Reformation*, 322–39.

name may also allude to John Piers, who would have been well known to Pembroke because of his association with Leicester's militantly Protestant alliance at court and because he was Bishop of Salisbury from 1577 to 1589, during her residence at Wilton.[17] Thenot was a traditional pastoral name, most familiar in England through Spenser's *Shepheardes Calender*. Thenot serves as the voice of old age in 'Februarie' who recounts the tale of the oak and the briar.[18] Spenser also connects him with the encomium, for Thenot twice helps to introduce Colin's encomia, praising Elisa in 'Aprill' and Dido in 'November'.

The flattery of Elizabeth in 'Astrea' is extravagant for modern tastes, but Pembroke is following the advice of her brother's *Defence of Poetry*, that the 'right poets' should paint not 'what is, hath been, or shall be', but 'what may be and should be'.[19] Since the classical era, the epideictic tradition had been closely identified with ethics. Aristotle's *Rhetoric*, for example, defines epideictic oratory as that which praises noble acts or blames ignoble acts.[20] A public rather than a private genre, encomium is designed for a ceremonial occasion.[21] The epideictic mode is usually, as A. Leigh DeNeef demonstrates, 'a means of persuasion'.[22] By demonstrating that a person's actions were virtuous, the orator would move the audience to emulation. Sidney makes this point several times in the *Defence*. The task of the lyric poet is to give 'praise, the reward of virtue, to virtuous acts'. Because 'the ending end of all earthly learning' is 'virtuous action', the poet feigns 'notable images of virtues, vices, or what else, with that delightful teaching' to induce us to follow the example set before us.[23]

Flattery of the monarch was a subgenre of the epideictic that provided a decorous opportunity for admonition. The poet is not so naïve as to believe that the monarch exemplifies all virtues, but rather holds

---

[17] Paul E. McLane, *Spenser's Shepheardes Calender: A Study in Elizabethan Allegory* (Notre Dame, Ind.: Notre Dame UP, 1961; rpt. Notre Dame and London, 1968), 175–87.

[18] As 'E. K.' notes in 'Februarie', Thenot had been used as 'the name of a shepheard in Marot his *Æglogues*'.

[19] Sidney, *Miscellaneous Prose*, 80–1. O. B. Hardison, Jr. demonstrates just how traditional Sidney was in his insistence on ethics: *The Enduring Monument: A Study of the Idea of Praise in Renaissance Literary Theory and Practice* (Chapel Hill: U of North Carolina P, 1962), 44–67. See also Brian Vickers, 'Epideictic and Epic in the Renaissance', *NLH* 14 (1982–3), 497–537.

[20] Aristotle, *Rhetoric*, 1366a 24 ff.

[21] A. Leigh DeNeef, 'Epideictic Rhetoric and the Renaissance Lyric', *JMRS* 3 (1973), 203–31; 222, 227–8.

[22] Ibid., 204.

[23] Sidney, *Miscellaneous Prose*, 97, 83, 81.

up a mirror to the queen, to show what she should be, as Elizabeth herself recognized. After a particularly fulsome piece of flattery, she once responded, 'I now thank you for putting me in mynd of my duety, and that should be in me.'[24] Praising the divine Astrea's virtue and wisdom was a recognized (and safe) way for Pembroke to remind Elizabeth to rule wisely. 'Astrea' lacks specific admonitions, but 'Even now that Care' implies a specifically Protestant course of action. (See 'Even now that Care': 'Literary Context'.)

'Astrea' adapts the two primary strategies of encomia, the topoi of outdoing and of inexpressibility.[25] When Thenot praises Elizabeth by saying 'she is so good, so faire, | With all the earth she may compare' (13–14), Piers responds that she outdoes all earthly things:

> Compare may thinke where likenesse holds,
> Nought like her the earth enfoldes,
>   I lookt to finde you lying.   (16–18)

When Thenot says that 'Astrea is our chiefest joy', Piers disputes the superlative, for 'Where chiefest are, there others bee' (31, 34). Elizabeth has no peer.

The topos of inexpressibility, however, is far more important to the poem for, in what might be termed 'meta-panegyric', it becomes a commentary on the failure of the language of encomia. The poem raises the philosophical and theological issue of 'the poetic expression of divine or ineffable truth', the post-lapsarian problem of fitting human language to divine reality.[26] To express this theme, the poem uses the structure of the medieval *débat*, particularly the 'medieval lying match'.[27] Nine times Piers challenges Thenot by giving him the lie, beginning with the accusation:

> Thou needst the truth, but plainly tell,
> Which much I doubt thou canst not well,
>   Thou art so oft a lier.   (4–6)

Thenot does not defend himself by arguing Sidney's position in the *Defence*, that 'of all writers . . . the poet is the least liar . . . he nothing

---

[24] Quoted in James Garrison, *Dryden and the Tradition of Panegyric* (Berkeley, Los Angeles, and London: U of California P, 1975), 20.

[25] Ernst Robert Curtius, *European Literature and the Latin Middle Ages* (London: Routledge & Kegan Paul, 1953), 159–66.

[26] Beilin, *Redeeming Eve*, 139.

[27] Sallye J. Sheppeard, 'Mary Herbert's "A Dialogue Between Two Shepherdes": A Study in Renaissance Poetic Method', *Proceedings of the Conference of College Teachers of English of Texas* 46 (1981), 18.

affirms, and therefore never lieth'.[28] Instead, he allows Piers to pursue the problem of the ineffability of the divine to its logical conclusion— silence.

Waller argues that the 'neo-Platonic' Thenot believes that Astrea's divinity can be expressed through 'natural and cosmic phenomena', but his assertions are undercut by the 'conscientious, even iconoclastic, Protestant' Piers, who emphasizes God's transcendence and denies the truth of allegorical language.[29] We might therefore assume that Piers speaks for the countess, since he is consistently given the final word, but there is no necessity to identify her completely with his more extreme positions on the ineffectuality of language. Rather, as Beilin points out, both are 'working together on the central poetic problem of language', the chasm between divine truth and earthly expression.[30] Sidney's *Astrophil and Stella* raises the same problem in his inability to convey the divine truth represented by Stella. Astrophil sometimes cheerfully assumes, like Thenot, that all he need do to express 'What Love and Beautie be' is to copy 'what in her Nature writes'.[31] Yet occasionally he, like Piers, does confront the central problem of encomia: 'What may words say, or what may words not say, | Where truth it selfe must speake like flatterie?' (*Astrophil and Stella* 35) The inability of Astrophil to express the depth of his joy leads him to conclude, 'Wise silence is best musicke unto blisse' (*Astrophil and Stella* 70).

John Davies gives a comic treatment of the problem in his 'Hymne XII. To her Picture'. He begins by accusing the audacity of the painter, saying that he is ashamed because 'S o dull her counterfait should be, | A nd she so full of glory'. After describing the portrait, he concludes that the painter was not too bold after all: 'N or durst his eyes her eyes behold; | A nd this made him mistake her'.[32] That is, an inadequate comprehension of the divine may underlie the inability to portray it.

Thenot believes, however, that his frustration arises not so much from the inability to comprehend the truth as from the inability to express it, asking Piers to 'tell me why, | My meaning true, my words should ly' (55–6). That is, his meaning is separate from and

---

[28] Sidney, *Miscellaneous Prose*, 102.
[29] Sidney, Mary. *Triumph*, 61–3; Waller, *Mary Sidney*, 81–2.
[30] Beilin, *Redeeming Eve*, 140–1; 311, n. 24.
[31] Sidney, *Poems*, 166, *Astrophil and Stella*, 3. See also 1, 15, 55, and 90.
[32] Davies, *Poems*, 77–8.

prior to language. Pembroke expresses that same idea in her paraphrase of Psalm 139. 12–14:

> not yongest thought in me doth grow,
> no not one word I cast to talk,
> but yet unutt'red thou dost know.

That is, the Psalmist's idea is known to God before words can be
formed, implying that thought precedes language.[33] Piers agrees.
'Words from conceit do only rise', that is, words arise from thought,
while 'Above conceit her honour flies' (58–9). Elizabeth, as a symbol
of the divine, is beyond our capacity to imagine and therefore beyond
our capacity to praise.

Like most of the countess's works, 'Astrea' has both a religious and
a political dimension. It raises a theological problem, the inadequacy
of language to speak of the divine, but the dialogue is also a clever
political performance. 'Astrea' can easily be read as challenging its
own genre, flattering the queen by smiling with her at the outrageous
flattery offered her, pretending that it fails only by not being superlative enough. Pembroke thereby manages simultaneously to separate
herself from fawning courtiers and to praise the queen herself. The
dialogue evidently was never performed at Wilton, but the fact that
Davison had a copy indicates that it had some manuscript circulation;
it may have reached the queen even before it appeared in print in
1602.

---

[33] Here she echoes Sidney's idea in his *Defence* of the 'fore-conceit' (*Miscellaneous Prose*,
79), comically expressed in the *Old Arcadia*, when the 'general fancy' of the blazon, 'What
tongue can her perfections tell', comes into the mind of Pyrocles as he gazes at Philoclea
(*Old Arcadia*, 238, 242).

A DIALOGUE *betweene* two *shepheards*, Thenot, *and* Piers, *in praise of* ASTREA, *made by the excellent Lady, the Lady* Mary Countesse of Pembrook, *at the Queenes Majesties being at her house at   Anno* 15 .

<table>
<tr><td>*Then.*</td><td>I Sing divine ASTREAS praise,
O Muses! help my wittes to raise,
And heave my Verses higher.</td><td></td></tr>
<tr><td>*Piers.*</td><td>Thou needst the truth, but plainly tell,
Which much I doubt thou canst not well,
Thou art so oft a lier.</td><td>5</td></tr>
<tr><td>*Then.*</td><td>If in my Song no more I show,
Than Heav'n, and Earth, and Sea do know,
Then truely I have spoken.</td><td></td></tr>
<tr><td>*Piers.*</td><td>Sufficeth not no more to name,
But being no lesse, the like, the same,
Else lawes of truth be broken.</td><td>10</td></tr>
<tr><td>*Then.*</td><td>Then say, she is so good, so faire,
With all the earth she may compare,
Not *Momus* selfe denying.</td><td>15</td></tr>
<tr><td>*Piers.*</td><td>Compare may thinke where likenesse holds,
Nought like to her the earth enfoldes,
I lookt to finde you lying.</td><td></td></tr>
<tr><td>*Then.*</td><td>ASTREA sees with Wisedoms sight,
Astrea workes by Vertues might,
And joyntly both do stay in her.</td><td>20</td></tr>
<tr><td>*Piers.*</td><td>Nay take from them, her hand, her minde,
The one is lame, the other blinde,
Shall still your lying staine her?</td><td></td></tr>
</table>

'A Dialogue between two shepheards . . . in praise of *Astrea*'
Title: ASTREA] ASTREV *1611*   excellent] ex-cellent *1602 (line break)*   made . . . Anno 15 .] *om. 1608, 1611, 1621*
2 Muses!] muses‸ *1611*; Muses‸ *1621*   help] helpe *1608, 1611*; helps *1621*   4 needst] needs *1621*   8 Than] Then *1611, 1621*   15 Not] Nor *1611, 1621*   19 ff. *19, 22, 25, 28, 31, 34, 37, 40, 43, 46, 49, 52, 55, 58 slightly indented in 1602 (apparently because of speech prefixes)*

25 *Then.*   Soone as ASTREA shewes her face,
              Strait every ill avoides the place,
                  And every good aboundeth.
    Piers. Nay long before her face doth showe,
              The last doth come, the first doth goe,
30   How lowde this lie resoundeth!

    Then.   ASTREA is our chiefest joy,
              Our chiefest guarde against annoy,
                  Our chiefest wealth, our treasure.
    Piers. Where chiefest are, there others bee,
35   To us none else but only shee;
                  When wilt thou speake in measure?

    Then.   ASTREA may be justly sayd,
              A field in flowry Roabe arrayd,
                  In Season freshly springing.
40 *Piers.* That Spring indures but shortest time,
              This never leaves *Astreas* clime,
                  Thou liest, instead of singing.

    Then.   As heavenly light that guides the day,
              Right so doth shine each lovely Ray,
45   That from *Astrea* flyeth.
    Piers. Nay, darknes oft that light enclowdes,
              Astreas beames no darknes shrowdes;
                  How lowdly *Thenot* lyeth!

    Then.   ASTREA rightly terme I may,
50   A manly Palme, a Maiden Bay,
                  Her verdure never dying.
    Piers. Palme oft is crooked, Bay is lowe,
              Shee still upright, still high doth growe,
                  Good *Thenot* leave thy lying.

55 *Then.*   Then *Piers*, of friendship tell me why,
              My meaning true, my words should ly,
                  And strive in vaine to raise her.

26 Strait] Straight *1608, 1611, 1621*   34 there] there *1611, 1621*; three *1602*
44 shine] *1608, 1611, 1621*; thine *1602*   46 oft] of *1621*   enclowdes,] in clouds,
1608; in cloudes, *1611*; in cloudes. *1621*   57 her.] ~? *1608, 1611, 1621*

Piers.   Words from conceit do only rise,
          Above conceit her honour flies;
              But silence, nought can praise her.   60

                         Mary Countesse of Pembroke.

58 do only] doe onely *1611*; to onely *1621*

'Even now that Care'

Literary Context

By presenting a poetic meditation on the Psalms to Queen Elizabeth, Pembroke continued the tradition of identifying the monarch as a symbol of piety, an image that the Tudors had assiduously cultivated. After his victory over Richard III at Bosworth Field, Henry VII swore allegiance to Pope Innocent VIII, who declared him the lawful king (27 March 1486) and bestowed on him the title Defender of the Faith. As the deposed Richard III was presented as misshapen in body and spirit by Tudor writers, such as Thomas More in his *History of Richard III*, so the Tudors were presented as descendants of the 'saintly' Henry VI, whose tomb in St George's chapel had become a place of pilgrimage and who was popularly believed to have performed posthumous miracles of healing. Henry VII even obtained the authorization of Pope Julius II in 1504 to form a commission to canonize Henry VI, and Henry VIII continued the canonization process until the Reformation made Catholic sainthood a political liability.[1] Thereafter, the public piety of the ruler was connected to the Word of God.

In Protestant works, the monarch was often portrayed as receiving and disseminating the scriptures.[2] For example, the title page of the Great Bible (1539), the first authorized English translation, portrays Henry VIII giving a volume labelled '*Verbum Dei*' to Thomas Cromwell, his chief minister, and to Thomas Cranmer, Archbishop of Canterbury, who would then disseminate the scriptures to the people. For Henry VIII, such a portrayal is particularly ironic. Although Thomas Cromwell, on behalf of Henry, had issued an injunction to the clergy in September 1538 that the Great Bible should be placed in each church, the primary translators of that Bible were condemned as heretics under the king's authority. In 1536 William Tyndale had been executed as a heretic, and in 1540 Miles Coverdale was denounced and his books burned.[3] The irony was apparently not lost on Richard

---

[1] Pope Julius II to King Henry VII, 19 June 1504, University Library, Cambridge, MS Mm.I.45; cited in King, *Iconography*, 25.

[2] On the presentation of scripture to the monarch, King, *Iconography*, particularly ch. 2.

[3] An earlier compilation of their work was printed as *The Byble, which is all the holy Scripture: In whych are contayned the Olde and Newe testament truly and purely translated into Eng-*

Taverner, who discreetly compares Henry to 'kynge Ezechias' in his prayer that the king will perfect 'the true religion' and destroy 'all false religion'.[4]

The Psalms were thought particularly appropriate for the sovereign because they were believed to have been written by a king, David.[5] As Pembroke says, 'A King should onely to a Queene be sent' (53). George Sandys later made a similar connection in dedicating his *A Paraphrase upon the Divine Poems* (1638) 'To the Prince':

> Since none but Princes durst aspire
> To sing unto the Hebrew Lyre;
> Sweet Prince, who then your Selfe more fit
> To reade, what sacred Princes Writ?[6]

Because of this perceived connection between author and reader, psalters were frequently presented to royalty. For example, Taverner dedicated to Henry VIII *An Epitome of the Psalmes* (1539); John Fisher prepared a presentation copy of *Psalmes or prayers taken out of holye scripture* (1544) for him; and Sir Anthony Cope presented *A godly meditacion upon .xx. select and chosen Psalmes* (1547) to Queen Katherine Parr as a New Year's gift. (Sir Thomas Wyatt's *Certayne psalmes* (1549) were presented by John Harington of Stepney to Katherine's powerful brother, William Parr.)[7] Because Edward encouraged the composition, publication, and congregational singing of the metrical

---

lysh by Thomas [i.e. M. Coverdale and W. Tyndale] . . . *Set forth with the Kinges most gracyous lycence* (Antwerp, 1537), *STC* 2066. 'Thomas Matthew' is an alias for the editor, John Rogers, who was the first Marian martyr.

[4] 'An epistle to the Kynge', *An Epitome of the Psalmes, or briefe meditacions upon the same, with diverse other moste christian prayers, translated by Richard Taverner* (1539), *STC* 2748, sig. [*]4.

[5] The comparison was also widely used in France. See Anne Lake Prescott, 'Musical Strains: Marot's Double Role as Psalmist and Courtier', in *Contending Kingdoms*, ed. Marie-Rose Logan and Peter Rudnytsky (Detroit: Wayne State UP, 1990), 42–67. On Bèze's use of David to justify the Huguenot rebellion, see Edward A. Gosselin, 'David in *Tempore Belli*: Beza's David in the Service of the Huguenots', *Sixteenth Century Journal* 7 (1976), 31–54. On the Protestant David of Bèze (paralleling the David in the commentaries of Luther, Melanchthon, Calvin, and Bucer) and the Catholic David of Lefevre d'Etaples, see Edward A. Gosselin, 'Two Views of the Evangelical David: Lefevre d'Etaples and Theodore Beza', in *The David Myth in Western Literature*, ed. Raymond Jean Frontain and Jan Wojcik (West Lafayette, Ind.: Purdue UP, 1980), 56–67.

[6] George Sandys, *A Paraphrase upon the Divine Poems* (1638), *STC* 21725, sig. *3, 'To the Prince' (Folger Shakespeare library copy). This edition includes *A Paraphrase upon Job* and *A Paraphrase upon the Psalmes of David. Set to new tunes for private Devotion . . . By Henry Lawes.*

[7] Taverner, *STC* 2748; Fisher *STC* 3001.7; Cope, *STC* 5717; and Wyatt, *STC* 2726.

Psalms, Thomas Sternhold dedicated to him his *Certayne Psalmes*, a dedication that was reprinted in *Al such Psalmes of David* (1549), including Sternhold's metrical Psalms and seven by John Hopkins.[8] Even the Catholic Queen Mary was given works that included excerpts from the Psalms: Thomas Paynell dedicated to her *The Piththy and moost notable sayinges of al Scripture* (1550), and Thomas Bownell celebrated her accession with *A Godly Psalme, of Marye Queene* (1553).[9]

When Elizabeth was received into London on 14 January 1558/9, she dramatically identified herself with the effort to disseminate the vernacular scriptures by her reception of the gift of an English Bible. As is recorded in *The Quenes Majesties Passage*, 'she thanked the citie therefore, promysed the reading therof most diligentlie, and incontinent commaunded, that it shoulde be brought'. Taking the Bible in both hands, she kissed it, 'and lay it upon her brest to the great comfort of the lookers on'. So effective was the gesture that Mulcaster concludes, 'God will undoubtedly preserve so worthy a prince, which at hys honor so reverently taketh her beginning.'[10] Praising her work in promoting vernacular scriptures, her chaplain John Bridges presented her with a fifteenth-century manuscript of Wyclif's translation of the New Testament as an 'auncient president, for the warrantise of your Majesties doing, that it is not new and never h[e]ard of before this age (as some dare avouche) that the woord of God shoulde be translated into our mother tongue'.[11] During her reign she received numerous dedications of vernacular scriptural translations, primarily by those who sought her support for the Protestant cause. In 1559 the Anglo-Genevan exiles presented to her *The Boke of Psalms*, later incorporated into the 1560 Geneva Bible.[12] Like a Pauline letter, the dedication of the Geneva Bible is presented to

---

[8] Thomas Sternhold, *Certayne Psalmes chosen out of the Psalter of David, and drawen into Englishe Metre by Thomas Sternhold* (*c*.1549), *STC* 2419; *Al such Psalmes of David as Thomas Sternehold ... didde in his life time draw into English Metre* (1549), *STC* 2420. Their work was revised and enlarged in *The Whole Booke of Psalmes, collected into Englysh metre by T. Sternhold, J. Hopkins and others* (1562), *STC* 2430, a work that eventually became known as the Old Version. (See *Psalmes*: 'Literary Context'.)

[9] Paynell, *STC* 19494; and Bownell, *STC* 1655.

[10] *The Quenes Majesties Passage through the Citie of London to Westminster the Day before her Coronation.* Facsimile ed. James M. Osborn (New Haven: Yale UP, 1960), sig. E4ᵛ.

[11] *The Newe Testament of our Saviour Jesu Christe*, BL MS Royal 1 A.XII, ff. 2ᵛ–3. Bridges apologizes that this old translation is from the Latin rather than the Greek.

[12] *STC* 2384. See Zim, *Psalms*, 231.

Queen Elizabeth 'with grace and peace from God the Father through Christ Jesus our Lord'. Citing the difficulty of all worthy enterprise, the translators commend to her the task of 'building of the Lords Temple' like Zerubbabel, who was not deterred by 'foreyn adversaries' and 'domestical enemies' who sought to interrupt God's work. They pray fervently that God will 'bring to perfection this noble worke which he hath begon by you' for 'the advancement of his glorie, for your owne honour and salvation of your soule', and for the 'comfort' of God's people who are 'committed unto your charge to be fed both in body and soul'. Appealing to the example of King Asa, they contend 'that the quietnes and peace of kingdomes standeth in the utter abolishing of idolatrie, and in advancing of true religion'. (The queen would not need a gloss to understand their meaning of 'idolatrie' as Catholic or 'true religion' as Protestant.) Asa is ominously praised for enacting an edict 'that whosoever wolde not seke the Lord God of Israel, shulde be slayne'; similarly, Josiah is praised because he destroyed idols and burnt 'the idolatrous priests bones upon their altars'. These biblical precedents are given as examples to rulers, the translators say, 'to reforme their countreys and to establish the worde of God with all spede, lest the wrath of the Lord fall upon them for the neglecting thereof'.[13] Such dire warnings by these zealous Protestant exiles did not endear them to the young queen. Wary of them and of the politically charged English Bible that they had produced, Elizabeth authorized the Bishops' Bible (1568), translated under the direction of Matthew Parker. As Henry VIII had been portrayed on the title page of the Great Bible (1539) that he authorized, so Elizabeth is portrayed on the title page of the Bishops' Bible. In the biblical triad of Faith, Hope, and Charity, she is depicted as Hope; that is, she brings the hope of a peaceful Reformed faith, as John King has noted.[14]

Toward the end of her reign, Elizabeth received a cluster of dedications of works based on the Psalms. Many paraphrases from and meditations on the Psalms were included in the seven Lamps of Thomas Bentley's *The Monument of Matrones: conteining seven severall Lamps of Virginitie* (1582), including the Psalm translation attributed to

---

[13] *The Bible and Holy Scriptures Conteyned in the Olde and Newe Testament* (Geneva, 1560), *STC* 2093, sigs. ***ii–iii; also available as *The Bible and Holy Scriptures. Geneva*, 1560. Facsimile (Madison: U of Wisconsin P, 1969).

[14] King, *Iconography*, 107. For a description of Elizabeth's own bibles and devotional works, some with holograph annotations, see ibid., 107–15.

Elizabeth herself by John Bale. Henry Lok's 'Sundry Psalmes of David', printed with his *Ecclesiastes* (1597), contains five metrical Psalms. William Patten presented a metrical version of Psalm 21 to her to celebrate her forty years of rule, *Anno fœlicissimi Regni Augustæ Reginæ Elizabeth Quadragesimo primo* (1598).[15] Probably during the same year in which the Tixall manuscript of the Sidney *Psalmes* was transcribed (1599), Esther Inglis prepared an illuminated copy of the French version of the Psalms, bound in crimson velvet embroidered with the Tudor rose and crown.[16] Even Protestants who were not English dedicated Psalters to the queen, including Giulio Cesare Paschali, *De' Sacri Salmi di Davidde* (1592), and François Perrot, *Salmi di David* (1603).[17]

Thus in her detailed comparison of the queen to David, Pembroke draws on an extensive tradition, one claimed by both Richard III and his enemy Henry VII, and developed in scriptures presented to Henry VIII. Most poignant is Richard's self-representation in his private Book of Hours as David suffering the rebellion of Absalom.[18] Davidic comparisons for Tudor monarchs were ubiquitous, predictably including portrayals of Henry VII's conquest of Richard III as David over Goliath, as in the pageants staged for Henry's entry into York on 20 April 1486.[19]

The comparison was thought appropriate to Henry VIII. Partially because of his own musical compositions, which included masses as well as secular songs, 'Henry VIII's psalter' represents the king as David playing his lyre, as he is also represented in the Holbein

[15] Bentley, *STC* 1892; Lok, *STC* 16696; and Patten, *STC* 2368.5.

[16] Twenty-six of Esther Inglis's manuscripts are copies, extracts, or verse summaries of biblical passages. In addition to the psalter presented to the queen, she prepared scriptural manuscripts for Robert Sidney and Lucy, Countess of Bedford (1606). See A. H. Scott-Elliott and Elspeth Yeo, 'Calligraphic Manuscripts of Esther Inglis (1571–1624): A Catalogue', *PBSA*, 84 (1990), 10–86.

[17] The first half of Perrot's *Salmi di David* was printed with music in 1581; the complete edition was published in 1603; he prepared an elaborate dedication for the 1603 edition that was never presented to Elizabeth, whom he claimed as the true queen of France. See England, 36–8.

The tradition of dedicating Psalms to royalty continued into the seventeenth century. For example, William Temple dedicated his Psalms exposition, *A Logicall Analysis of Twentie Select Psalmes* (1605), *STC* 23870, to Henry, Prince of Wales, because the Psalter was regarded as an appropriate book of instruction for princes; and George Wither dedicated his Psalter, *The psalmes of David tr. into lyrick-verse* (1632) *STC* 2735, which he said was written at the king's request, to the Protestant Princess Elizabeth.

[18] Lambeth Palace MS 474, quoted in Pamela Tudor-Craig, *Richard III*, National Portrait Gallery Exhibition Catalogue, 27 June–7 Oct. 1973, 96–7.

[19] King, *Iconography*, 21–5, 27–8, 35–6.

engraving on the title page of the Coverdale Bible (1535).[20] Another miniature in the psalter portrays Henry as David triumphing over Goliath. Wearing his courtly garb, including his characteristic black velvet hat, he confronts a giant wearing full armour.[21] Often this comparison carries a specifically Protestant message, as when Morley says that the king triumphed over the Pope as David triumphed over Goliath.[22] The David comparison cannot be taken as exclusively Protestant, however, for 'Henry VIII's psalter' not only portrays Henry as David, but also portrays God as wearing the papal tiara.[23] Coverdale's comparison of King Henry to Josiah, Jehoshaphat, and Hezekiah as godly rulers was flattering and conventional, but he was less tactful when he spoke of Nathan's rebuke of David. That prophet, he said, reverenced King David and yet 'spared not to rebuke him, and that right sharply, when he fell from the word of God to adultery and manslaughter'; Henry could hardly miss the implied correspondence to his own conduct.[24] Hugh Latimer was more circumspect, waiting until 1549, during the reign of King Edward, to make explicit a parallel between David and Henry that must have occurred to many of Henry's subjects—their polygamy.[25]

The positive aspects of the Davidic comparison were thought to be most appropriate to Queen Elizabeth, for her life was seen to parallel his. The David narrative is set out in the Geneva 'Argument' to 2 Samuel:

this seconde boke declareth the noble actes of David, after the death of Saul, when he began to reigne, unto the end of his kingdome: and how the same by him was wonderfully augmented: also his great troubles and dangers, which he susteined bothe within his house and without: what horrible and danger-

---

[20] BL Royal MS 2 A. XVI, f. 63[v], illustrating Psalm 52. Presented by Jean Mallard, French orator, *c*.1540–1. King Henry is also portrayed reading the Psalter in his bedroom (illustrating Psalm 1, '*Beatus vir*'), f. 3. Henry's annotations in this psalter, as John King establishes, demonstrate his own identification with the godly king beset by the wicked: *Iconography*, 79–80.

[21] BL Royal MS 2 A. XVI, f. 30, illustrating Psalm 27, '*Dominus illuminatio*'.

[22] Henry Parker, Lord Morley, *The Exposition and declaration of the Psalme, Deus ultionum Dominus* [Ps. 94] (originally prepared 1534, pub. 1539), *STC* 19211, sig. A7. The work praises Henry in terms that are so hyperbolic as to be almost blasphemous. The Psalm '*Beatus homo*' is applied directly to the king, for example, sig. B4[v].

[23] God, wearing the tiara, looks down from the sky on angels playing instruments, BL Royal MS 2 A. XVI, f. 98[v], illustrating Psalm 80, '*Exultate Deo*'.

[24] Miles Coverdale, 'Dedication and Prologue to the Translation of the Bible', in *The Remains of Bishop Coverdale*, ed. George Pearson (Cambridge: Cambridge UP, 1846), 6–7.

[25] Hugh Latimer, *Selected Sermons*, ed. Allan G. Chester (Charlotteville, Va., UP of Virginia: 1968), 79–80; King, *Reformation*, 176–7.

ous insurrections, uprores, and treasons were wroght against him, partly by false counselers, fained friends and flatterers, and partly by some of his owne children and people: and how by Gods assistance he overcame all difficulties, and enjoyed his kingdome in rest and peace.

English Protestants applied the narrative to Elizabeth. For example, Thomas Rogers, in *A Golden Chaine* (1579), lists parallels between her and David:

Application hereof might aptly be made unto you Highnes, as his foiling of Goliath with your Majesties overthrowing the Pope; His rooting out of the Philistines with your Majesties suppressing the Papistes; his affliction with your imprisonment; his persecution with your trobles; his singing of godlie songes with your godlie bookes; his love of his God, with your promoting his glorie and defending of pure religion.[26]

Similarly, Edmund Bunny of York, writing in 1588, the year of the Spanish Armada, compares 'the attempt of this late forrein invasion' with the attacks of the Philistines on Israel, and predicts that Elizabeth, like David, will at length rule in peace.[27] Fulke Greville, writing in the Stuart era, nostalgically praises Elizabeth as England's 'she-David', who had 'ventured to undertake the great Goliath among the Philistines abroad (I mean Spain and the Pope)'.[28]

Like Greville, Bunny, Rogers, and the translators of the Geneva Bible, the Countess of Pembroke employs the standard Protestant comparison of the monarch to the biblical David, an image used both to flatter and to admonish the queen.[29] Pembroke addresses Elizabeth on public issues, advocating the queen's active involvement on behalf of Continental Protestants, and alluding to such contemporary events as the defeat of the Spanish Armada and the New World explorations.

Saying that all that is English belongs to the queen, Pembroke presents the Psalms to her as an act of patriotism. Although the 'Psalmist King' was 'Hebrue borne', the Sidneys hoped to see him 'denizend',

[26] Thomas Rogers, 'To the Queenes most sacred Majestie', *A Golden Chaine, taken out of the rich Treasure house the Psalmes of King David* (1579), STC 21235, sig. A5[r-v].

[27] Edmund Bunny of York, *The Coronation of David* (1588), STC 4090, sig. A3[v]. The work, published shortly after the Armada was defeated, offers an extended parallel between the sufferings of David and those of contemporary England, with the Spanish cast as Goliath and the Philistines (as in sigs. C4[v]-D1, L2–3, N2).

[28] Greville, *Prose Works*, 'Dedication to Sir Philip Sidney', 98–9.

[29] Note, for example, Rogers's reminder in his dedication that one day all rulers 'shal render an accompt unto the King of al Kings of their behavior in their places'; Elizabeth is not to imitate 'Caesar Borgias, as that infamous Florentine [Machiavelli] doth counsel', but rather David and Solomon (*A Golden Chaine*, sig. A4[v]). See also Hannay, *Philip's Phoenix*, particularly ch. 4.

or made a naturalized citizen, in English (29–30). Her clearest statement of poetic intent is given in terms of the clothing metaphor so frequently employed by translators, when she says that David would not
be displeased by the Sidneian version, 'Oft having worse, without
repining worne' (32).[30] The clothing metaphor also describes the
contributions of the two authors; Sidney provided the warp, or the
structural vertical threads, while she 'weav'd this webb to end' (27).
Now that the cloth is complete, the countess gives it to her queen as
a 'liverie robe' for her to give to others (34), yet these 'holy garments'
fit best the queen herself (63–4).

Pembroke appeals to Elizabeth as 'so meet a Patrones | for Authors
state or writings argument' (51–2). She is the appropriate patron of
any work in English, but particularly for the Psalms of David, for,
as Pembroke explains in lines 53 to 80, Elizabeth's condition so parallels that of David that she is the most fit recipient of the *Psalmes*. As
David was oppressed by Saul, so Elizabeth was 'nigh by wrong
opprest' under the reign of her sister Mary. As David 'at length'
was 'Possest of place...in peace', so Elizabeth took her rightful
place on the throne. In both cases, 'man crossing God in vaine' (66–
8), their enemies were defeated. As the Philistines attacked David, so
the Spaniards, those 'foes of heav'n', attacked Elizabeth. David was
blessed with 'great conquest', Pembroke claims, but Elizabeth was
blessed with a 'greater' (70–1) when the Armada was defeated with
the help of a storm sent, the English believed, by God: 'The very
windes did on thy partie blowe, | and rocks in armes thy foe men
eft defie' (77–8). In all these ways she is like David, Pembroke claims,
but Elizabeth surpasses him in the extent of her realm. Referring to
Virginia, the territories claimed for the queen by Sir Walter Ralegh
and others, Pembroke declares that 'two hemispheres' (75), the Old
World and the New, honour the queen.

In her comparison, Pembroke emphasizes the paradox of a woman's
rule, often stated in comparisons of the queen to Solomon. A familiar

---

[30] Cf. William Hunnis, 'The booke to his Readers':

> I being good, am not the woorse,
> though clothing mine be bad,
> He that bestowed the same on me,
> did give the best he had.

Seven Sobs of a Sorrowfull Soule for Sinne (1583), *STC* 13975, sig. A4. See also the translator
François Boisrobert, who boasts that in just 15 days he has '*habillée à la Françoise*', '*Advis au
Lecteur*', *La folle gageure* (Paris, 1653), sig. e1ᵛ.

Elizabethan proverb said, 'As a woman journeyed to see a man, so now men journey to see a woman'; that is, as the Queen of Sheba had journeyed to see King Solomon, so now men journey to see Queen Elizabeth.[31] Pembroke adapts that formulation, reversing gender roles:

> Kings on a Queene enforst their states to lay;
> Main=lands for Empire waiting on an Ile;
> Men drawne by worth a woman to obay;
> one moving all, herselfe unmov'd the while.   (81–4)

The paradox of a woman ruler will lead to all the characteristics of a successful reign:

> Truthes restitution, vanitie exile,
> wealth sprung of want, warr held without annoye.   (85–6)

The war that Pembroke optimistically believes could be held 'without annoye' is a glance back at the opening stanza, wherein she admonishes the queen to 'dispose | what Europe acts in theise most active times' (7–8). Her phrase 'active times' was part of the Protestant code, as indicated by Greville's later nostalgic praise of 'those active times' when Queen Elizabeth defended Continental Protestantism, in contrast to what Greville perceived to be the 'effeminate age' of the Stuarts.[32]

Pembroke continues the David metaphor in her concluding prayer. Presenting herself as but the 'handmaid' of the queen, Pembroke prays that Elizabeth will outlive her peers and 'Rivall . . . Judas Faithfull King' by a reign both longer and more triumphant than David's (94). The final phrase presents the queen, like David and like Pembroke herself, as a writer of divine poetry, one who has sung 'what God doth' (96), presumably in her translation of Marguerite de Navarre and in the translation of Psalm 13 attributed to her by John Bale.[33] And as a queen, Elizabeth should follow God's guidance, so that men 'may sing' (96) of her achievements. The poem thus ends with the same admonitory flattery with which it began, reminding the queen of her religious duty.

Like the works dedicated to Pembroke, this poem, dedicating the Sidneian *Psalmes* to the queen, is striking in its omissions. Pembroke

---

[31] Lynn Staley Johnson, 'Elizabeth, Bride and Queen: A Study of Spenser's April Eclogue and the Metaphors of English Protestantism', *Spenser Studies* 2 (1981), 78.

[32] Greville, *Prose Works*, 'Dedication to Sir Philip Sidney', 7.

[33] Queen Elizabeth, trans., Margaret of Angoulême, *A godly medytacyon of the christen sowle* (1548), *STC* 17320.

makes no reference here to the queen's beauty, her eternal youth, or even her chastity, nor does she employ the usual fulsome mythological references, not even to Astraea, as she does in her pastoral dialogue. Instead, Pembroke addresses her monarch in strictly religious and political terms, presenting her as the equal of the biblical David in her experience of God's grace. A woman placed by God above men, she is the divinely ordained ruler of England; because Elizabeth is empowered by God, Pembroke pays her the truest compliment by discussing her duty. Presenting herself and her poems with decorous humility, Pembroke addresses the queen as one placed by God on the 'highest throne' (13), one whose character and diligence fit her position.

[Dedicatory Poem in the Tixall Manuscript of the *Psalmes*]

Even now that Care which on thy Crowne attends
and with thy happy greatnes dayly growes
Tells mee thrise sacred Queene my Muse offends,
and of respect to thee the line outgoes,
5 One instant will, or willing can shee lose
I say not reading, but receiving Rimes,
On whom in chiefe dependeth to dispose
what Europe acts in theise most active times?

Yet dare I so, as humblenes may dare
10 cherish some hope they shall acceptance finde;
not waighing less thy state, lighter thy Care,
but knowing more thy grace, abler thy minde.
What heav'nly powrs thee highest throne assign'de,
assign'd thee goodnes suting that Degree:
15 and by thy strength thy burthen so defin'de,
To others toile, is Exercise to thee.

Cares though still great, cannot bee greatest still,
Busines most ebb, though Leasure never flowe:
Then these the Postes of Dutie and Goodwill
20 shall presse to offer what their Senders owe;
Which once in two, now in one Subject goe,
the poorer left, the richer reft awaye:
Who better might (O might ah word of woe.)
have giv'n for mee what I for him defraye.

25 How can I name whom sighing sighes extend,
and not unstopp my teares eternall spring?
but hee did warpe, I weav'd this webb to end;
the stuffe not ours, our worke no curious thing,
Wherein yet well wee thought the Psalmist King
30 Now English denizend, though Hebrue borne,

'Even now that Care'
Poem lacking in A. Preserved only in J, the copy-text.
16 toile] t *written over* s   19 these] r *altered to* s   22 reft] rest *J*   25 sighes]
signes *J*   30 denizend] n *written over erased* d

woold to thy musicke undispleased sing,
Oft having worse, without repining worne;

And I the Cloth in both our names present,
A liverie robe to bee bestowed by thee:
small parcell of that undischarged rent,   35
from which nor paines, nor paiments can us free.
And yet enough to cause our neighbours see
wee will our best, though scanted in our will:
and those nighe feelds where sow'n thy favors bee
unwalthy doo, not elce unworthie till.   40

for in our worke what bring wee but thine owne?
What English is, by many names is thine.
There humble Lawrells in thy shadowes growne
To garland others woold, themselves repine.
Thy brest the Cabinet, thy seat the shrine,   45
where Muses hang their vowed memories:
where Wit, where Art, where all that is divine
conceived best, and best defended lies.

Which if men did not (as they doe) confesse,
and wronging worlds woold otherwise consent: 50
Yet here who mynds so meet a Patrones
for Authors state or writings argument?
A King should onely to a Queene bee sent.
Gods loved choise unto his chosen love:
Devotion to Devotions President: 55
what all applaud, to her whom none reprove.

And who sees ought, but sees how justly square
his haughtie Ditties to thy glorious daies?
How well beseeming thee his Triumphs are?
his hope, his zeale, his praier, plaint, and praise,   60
Needles thy person to their height to raise:
lesse need to bend them downe to thy degree:
Theise holy garments each good soule assaies,
some sorting all, all sort to none but thee.

42 is] i *written over erased* b   47 where all] whereall *J*

65   For ev'n thy Rule is painted in his Raigne:
     both cleere in right: both nigh by wrong opprest:
     And each at length (man crossing God in vaine)
     Possest of place, and each in peace possest.
     proud Philistines did interrupt his rest,
70   The foes of heav'n no lesse have beene thy foes;
     Hee with great conquest, thou with greater blest;
     Thou sure to winn, and hee secure to lose.

     Thus hand in hand with him thy glories walke:
     but who can trace them where alone they goe?
75   Of thee two hemispheres on honor talke,
     and Lands and seas thy Trophees jointly showe.
     The very windes did on thy partie blowe,
     and rocks in armes thy foe men eft defie:
     But soft my muse, Thy pitch is earthly lowe;
80   forbeare this heav'n, where onely Eagles flie.

     Kings on a Queene enforst their states to lay;
     Main=lands for Empire waiting on an Ile;
     Men drawne by worth a woman to obay;
     one moving all, herselfe unmov'd the while:
85   Truthes restitution, vanitie exile,
     wealth sprung of want, warr held without annoye,
     Let subject bee of some inspired stile,
     Till then the object of her subjects joye.

     Thy utmost can but offer to hir sight
90   Her handmaids taske, which most her will endeeres;
     and pray unto thy paines life from that light
     which lively lightsome Court, and Kingdome cheeres,
     What wish shee may (farre past hir living Peeres
     and Rivall still to Judas Faithfull King)
95   In more then hee and more triumphant yeares,
     Sing what God doth, and doo what men may sing.

                                              1599

69 did] *second* d *written over* s   81 enforst] c *altered to* s   87 subject] a *altered to* e
92 lightsome∧] light some, *J*   93 What] With *altered to* What   96 doo] *second* o
added   1599] 6 *altered to* 5 *in darker ink*

'To the Angell Spirit of . . . Sir Phillip Sidney'

Literary Context

By eulogizing her brother, Philip Sidney, the Countess of Pembroke joined an extensive literary project. When Sidney, mortally wounded in the campaign to free the Protestant Netherlands from Spanish rule, died on 17 October 1586, he became an international hero. As John Foote records, Sidney was mourned by the Low Countries, England, the queen, the parliament, and the university:

> *Belgia Philippum defleat ducem suum,*
> *Anglia Philippum defleat patrem suum,*
> *Princeps Philippum defleat Martem suum,*
> *Curia Philippum defleat decus suum,*
> *Plangat Philippum Oxonia patronum suum,*
> *In hoc Philippo quanta spes uno iacet.*[1]

Similarly, his friend Lodowick Bryskett describes 'the cry that woful England made, / Eke *Zelands* piteous plaints, and *Hollands* toren heare / Would haply have appeas'd thy divine angry mynd'.[2] Poets vied to honour Sidney. In the Netherlands, where he had been seen as a future Governor General, the Protestant University of Leiden issued a commemorative volume by Sidney's friend Georgius Benedicti (Werteloo); more surprisingly, that volume was also issued by the Catholic University of Louvain.[3]

The commemoration of Sidney's death became a literary event unprecedented in England. His splendid funeral on 16 February 1587 was recorded by John Stow, Richard Lea, and most memorably by Thomas Lant, whose ten metres of engravings portray more than 700 mourners who marched in the procession.[4] Scholars, soldiers, and

---

[1] John Foote, '*Belgia Philippum defleat ducem suum*', *Exequiae illustrissimi equitis, D. Philippi Sidnaei, gratissimae memoriae ac nomini impensae* (Oxford, 1587), *STC* 22551, sig. K2.

[2] 'The Mourning Muse of Thestylis', in Spenser, *Astrophel* (published with *Colin Clouts*), sig. G3ᵛ.

[3] Marjon Poort, 'The Desired and Destined Successor', in *Creation of a Legend*, 34; and Dominic Baker-Smith, ' "Great Expectation": Sidney's Death and the Poets', ibid., 89. *Epitaphia in Mortem Nobilissimi et Fortissimi Viri D. Philippi Sidneii Equitis* (Leiden and Louvain: J. Paedts, 1587).

[4] John Stow, *Annales or a General Chronicle of England. Continued . . . unto the End of the Present Yeare 1631* (1631), *STC* 23340, 739–40. Richard Lea, Oxford, Bodleian Library, MS

popular writers joined in the mourning. Both Oxford and Cambridge issued collections of elegies in Latin and the other learned languages, the first such collections to be published in England; even King James VI of Scotland contributed a sonnet in Latin and English.[5] The university poets raised Sidney to mythological status, comparing him to legendary heroes such as Hector and Priam, and declaring that he died both *'pro patria'* and *'pro pietate'*.[6] In addition to these poetic tributes, those who claimed to be eyewitnesses recorded the manner of his death in hagiographic terms.[7] Popular ballads also mourned him, such as 'A Doleful Dyttie of the Death of Sir Philip Sidney' (22 February 1587), 'A Ballad of the Buriall of Sir Philip Sidney' (27 February 1587), and 'A Mirrour of the Life and Death and Vertues of Sir Philip Sidney' (15 June 1587).[8]

Ashmole, 818, item 9, ff. 40–1, published by B. H. Newdigate *et al.*, 'Mourners at Sir Philip Sidney's Funeral', *N&Q*, 180 (1941), 398–401, 444–5, and 463–4. Thomas Lant, *Sequitur celebritas & pompa funeris quemadmodum a Clarencio Armorum et Insignium rege institute est, etc.* (1587), *STC* 15224. For discrepancies in these accounts, see Sander Bos, Marianne Lange-Meijers, and Jeanine Six, 'Sidney's Funeral Portrayed', in *Creation of a Legend*, 38–61.

[5] King James, '*In Philippi Sidnaei interitum, Illustrissimi Scotorum Regis carmen*', *Academiae Cantabrigiensis Lacrymae Tumulo Nobilissimi Equitis, D. Philippi Sidneii Sacratae* (1587), *STC* 4473, sig. K1. *Lacrymae* was edited by Alexander Neville of St John's and published on the day of Sidney's funeral by Cambridge University. Shortly thereafter John Lloyd of New College, Oxford, edited *Peplus, Illustrissimi viri D. Philippi Sidnaei supremis honoribus dicatus* (Oxford, 1587), *STC* 22552; and later in 1587 William Gager edited the *Exequiae* volume for Christ Church, Oxford. See also Dominic Baker-Smith, ' "Great Expectation": Sidney's Death and the Poets', in *Creation of a Legend*, 83–103.

[6] '*Miles in Hispanos gemina ratione Philippus*', *Exequiae*, sig. E3ᵛ.

7 Several contemporary accounts of the battle were published, including those by George Whetstone, *Sir Philip Sidney* (1587), *STC* 25349, sigs. B4–C1, based on information supplied by his brother Bernard who fought at Zutphen; by Edmund Molyneux in Holinshed's *Chronicles* (1587), *STC* 13569, 1554–5; by Henry Archer in John Stow's *Annales* (1592), *STC* 23334, 1251–3; and George Carleton's accounts in '*Silva*', *Exequiae*, sigs. L2–3v, rpt. in *Heroici Characteres* (Oxford, 1603), *STC* 4636, sigs. G2v–3ᵛ. Thomas Moffet's account in *Nobilis* (Huntington Library MS HM 1337) remained unpublished until the twentieth century. Fulke Greville's 'Dedication to Sir Philip Sidney', the source of the legend that the wounded Sidney gave his water bottle to a common soldier, was not published until 1652. The veracity of Greville's account is a matter of debate. See particularly W. A. Ringler, Jr., 'Sir Philip Sidney: The Myth and the Man', in *Creation of a Legend*, 3–15, and John Gouws, 'Fact and Anecdote in Fulke Greville's Account of Sidney's Last Days', ibid., 62–82.

8 Other commemorative poems in England include 'Upon the Life and Death of Sir Philip Sidney' (believed to be by Angel Day, Nov. 1586); 'The Epitaph of Sir Philip Sidney, Lately Lord Governour of Flushing' by Thomas Churchyard (1587); and 'The Life and Death of Sir Philip Sidney, Late Lord Governour of Flushing' by John Philip (1587). On these commemorative verses, see Esplin (Ph.D. diss.) and Dominic Baker-Smith, ' "Great Expectation": Sidney's Death and the Poets', in *Creation of a Legend*, 83–103. On commem-

The mourning for Sidney was, for the most part, quite genuine but many poets also looked for patronage from his family, particularly from his powerful uncle, the Earl of Leicester. William Gager, for example, dedicated *Exequiae*, which he edited for Sidney's Oxford college, Christ Church, to Leicester; and although John Lloyd of New College dedicated *Peplus* to his brother-in-law, the Earl of Pembroke, that volume also stressed Sidney's position as Leicester's heir, as in Thomas Bastard's poem, '*HAERES occiso tibi quis*, Dudlaee, Philippo?' When Leicester died on 4 September 1588, the end of his patronage brought a sharp decrease in elegies for Sidney. Public mourning for Leicester himself was noticeably sparse. As Spenser later commented in 'The Ruines of Time':

> His name is worne alreadie out of thought
> Ne anie Poet seekes him to revive;
> Yet manie Poets honourd him alive.[9]

'The Ruines', praising the Sidney/Dudley family, was dedicated to the Countess of Pembroke in 1591, indicating a shift in patronage. Once again Sidney's name was celebrated, for throughout the 1590s poets sought to win the patronage of his sister and her wealthy husband by writing commemorative verses. Celebrations of Sidney presented to the countess in the early 1590s include Spenser's 'The Ruines'; Abraham Fraunce's *The Countesse of Pembrokes Emanuel* and *Ivychurch* and *The Third Part of the Countesse of Pembrokes Ivychurch*; and Michael Drayton's *Idea: The Shepheards Garland*. Thomas Moffet's hagiographic *Nobilis*, a manuscript presented to young William Herbert, included extravagant praise of the Countess of Pembroke no doubt intended for her eyes.[10] In addition, most of the dedications to the countess mention her brother, including those by Francis Meres, Charles Fitzjeffery, Henry Constable, Nathaniel Baxter, and Aemilia Lanyer.

Two writers who had lived at Wilton indicate that Pembroke deliberately set out to memorialize her brother by her patronage and her publication of his work. Hugh Sanford, in his preface to the 1593

orative verses in Leiden, see Jan Van Dorsten, *Poets, Patrons, and Professors: Sir Philip Sidney, Daniel Rogers, and the Leiden Humanists* (Leiden: Leiden University Press, 1962), 152–66.

[9] Spenser, *Complaints*, sig. B4ᵛ.

[10] Fraunce, *Emanuel*, STC 11339; *Ivychurch*, STC 11340; and *Ivychurch. Third Part*, STC 11341. Drayton, *Idea: The Shepheards Garland* (1593), rpt. *Works*, I. 45–94. Moffet, *Nobilis* (Huntington Library MS HM 1337). See also Rosenberg, *Leicester*, 350.

Arcadia, states: 'Neither shall these pains be the last (if no unexpected accident cut off her determination) which the everlasting love of her excellent brother, will make her consecrate to his memory.'[11] Similarly, Samuel Daniel emphasizes the dynastic nature of her role as 'the happy and judiciall Patronesse of the Muses, (a glory hereditary to your house)'.[12] As we have seen, her patronage of writers who celebrated her brother and her publication of his works encouraged the hagiography which has developed into the Sidney legend. (See p. 12.) She also wrote her own poems of mourning, including 'To the Angell Spirit' and an unidentified early elegy mentioned in her letter to Sir Edward Wotton (Correspondence: Manuscript Letter III), possibly 'The Dolefull Lay of Clorinda'.

In this dedication Pembroke deliberately adopts the voice of the grieving female relative, modelled on classical precedents, such as Niobe's speech in Aphthonius' *Progymnasmata*, as Lisa Jardine has noted.[13] As in 'The Dolefull Lay of Clorinda', the woman speaks primarily to lament the death of her brother. Yet the apparent self-abnegation of the speaker is somewhat illusory. Of course Pembroke did mourn her brother, and of course she did honour him by completing his work, but it is disingenuous to claim that the work was addressed only to him, that 'it hath no further scope to goe, | nor other purpose but to honor thee' (29–30). Her statement is immediately contradicted by her placement of this dedicatory poem beside one to Queen Elizabeth, implying a royal audience, and by her circulation of the Sidneian *Psalmes* through the aristocratic medium of scribal publication.

Furthermore, as Beilin reminds us, when the countess praises Sidney, she also praises him as a poet. Adopting the voice of a grieving relative, she implicitly casts her brother as her muse in a dedicatory poem that employs such Petrarchan poetic conventions as, in Wendy Wall's words, 'broken bodies, monetary expenditure, emotional reckoning, eternizing conceits, and hyperbolic praise'.[14]

Pembroke honoured her brother by completing the Psalms which he had begun; his voice therefore authorized her own. As she says, the Sidneian *Psalmes* are 'First rais'de by thy blest hand, and what is mine | inspird by thee' (3–4). Because of that inspiration, her muse could dare to complete the work. As her sorrow is 'dissolv'd

---

[11] 'To the Reader', Sidney, *Arcadia*, sig. A4; rpt. Sidney, *Old Arcadia*, l.

[12] Daniel, *Delia*, sig. A2.

[13] Lisa Jardine, *Reading Shakespeare Historically* (London: Routledge, 1996), 143–6.

[14] Beilin, *Redeeming Eve*, 148; Wall, *Gender*, 315.

to Inke' (79), she becomes a writer. 'To the Angell Spirit' is thus not only her eulogy for Sidney; it is also a meditation on her own role as a writer. Not only his own words but hers will become the 'Immortall Monuments' of Sidney's fame (71). The humility topos is frequently invoked—her muse is mortal while his is divine, her work is like the little streams and his like the great sea. She declares that her poetic abilities are insufficient to complete Sidney's work, or even to express her grief. Yet we must be careful not to overstate her use of the conventional topos. She apologizes for her 'presumption too too bold' (25) in completing her brother's work, but she presents almost two-thirds of the Sidneian *Psalmes* as her own. Like Spenser and other elegists of Sidney, she emphasizes the conventional inexpressibility topos, admitting that her own words are inadequate to praise Sidney. Like Astrophil, she may have neither 'Art nor skill which abler wits doe prove' (83), but neither art nor skill would suffice; she insists that 'There lives no witt' able to give adequate praise (49).[15] That is, she places herself in an equal predicament with other writers—a strategy that masks 'the assertiveness of her style with the self-abnegation of her subject matter', as Fisken notes.[16] Significantly, she never uses the humility topos in connection with her gender; for her position as a woman writer, she never makes apology. The underlying problem here, as in 'Astrea', is the ineffability of language.

[15] Sidney also explores the inability of his words to express his thought, as in sonnets 1, 3, and the opening of *Astrophil*, 69, 'O joy, too high for my low stile to show'.
[16] Fisken, 'World of Words', 266. See Louise Schleiner, *Tudor and Stuart Women Writers* (Bloomington: Indiana UP, 1994), 75–81.

[Dedicatory Poem in the Tixall Manuscript of the *Psalmes*]

To the Angell spirit of the most excellent
Sir Phillip Sidney

To thee pure sprite, to thee alone's addres't
    this coupled worke, by double int'rest thine:
    First rais'de by thy blest hand, and what is mine
inspird by thee, thy secrett power imprest.
5   So dar'd my Muse with thine it selfe combine,
      as mortall stuffe with that which is divine,
Thy lightning beames give lustre to the rest,

That heavens King may daigne his owne transform'd
    in substance no, but superficiall tire
10   by thee put on; to praise, not to aspire
To, those high Tons, so in themselves adorn'd,
    which Angells sing in their cælestiall Quire,
    and all of tongues with soule and voice admire
Theise sacred Hymmes thy Kinglie Prophet form'd.

15 Oh, had that soule which honor brought to rest
    too soone not left and reft the world of all
    what man could showe, which wee perfection call
This halfe maim'd peece had sorted with the best.
    Deepe wounds enlarg'd, long festred in their gall
20   fresh bleeding smart; not eie but hart teares fall.
Ah memorie what needs this new arrest?

Yet here behold, (oh wert thou to behold!)
    this finish't now, thy matchlesse Muse begunne,
    the rest but peec't, as left by thee undone.
25 Pardon (oh blest soule) presumption too too bold:
    if love and zeale such error ill=become
    'tis zealous love, Love which hath never done,
Nor can enough in world of words unfold.

'To the Angell Spirit'
*Poem lacking in A. This version preserved only in J, the copy-text. Lines 3 and 5 not indented,
line 4 indented in stanza 1 in J.*
    27 'tis] ti's *J*   28 words] l *erased after* r

And sithe it hath no further scope to goe,
    nor other purpose but to honor thee,   30
    Thee in thy workes where all the Graces bee,
As little streames with all their all doe flowe
    to their great sea, due tributes gratefull fee:
    so press my thoughts my burthened thoughtes in mee,
To pay the debt of Infinits I owe   35

To thy great worth; exceeding Natures store,
    wonder of men, sole borne perfections kinde,
    Phoenix thou wert, so rare thy fairest minde
Heav'nly adorn'd, Earth justlye might adore,
    where truthfull praise in highest glorie shin'de: 40
    For there alone was praise to truth confin'de;
And where but there, to live for evermore?

Oh! when to this Accompt, this cast upp Summe,
    this Reckoning made, this Audit of my woe,
    I call my thoughts, whence so strange passions flowe;   45
Howe workes my hart, my sences striken dumbe?
    that would thee more, then ever hart could showe,
    and all too short who knewe thee best doth knowe
There lives no witt that may thy praise become.

Truth I invoke (who scorne else where to move   50
    or here in ought my blood should partialize)
    Truth, sacred Truth, Thee sole to solemnize
Those precious rights well knowne best mindes approve:
    and who but doth, hath wisdomes open eies,
    not owly blinde the fairest light still flies   55
Confirme no lesse? At least 'tis seal'd above.

Where thou art fixt among thy fellow lights:
    my day put=out, my life in darkenes cast,
    Thy Angells soule with highest Angells plac't
There blessed sings enjoying heav'n=delights   60
    thy Makers praise: as farr from earthy tast
    as here thy workes so worthilie embrac't
By all of worth, where never Envie bites.

29 no further] nofurther *J*   33 due tributes] duetributes *J*   34 in mee,] im mee. *J*
35 owe₍ₐ₎] ~. *J*   56 'tis] ti's *J*   57 Where] n *altered to* re

As goodly buildings to some glorious ende
65   cut of by fate, before the Graces hadde
      each wondrous part in all their beauties cladde,
Yet so much done, as Art could not amende;
      So thy rare workes to which no witt can adde,
      in all mens eies, which are not blindely madde,
70 Beyonde compare above all praise, extende.

Immortall Monuments of thy faire fame,
      though not compleat, nor in the reach of thought,
      howe on that passing peece time would have wrought
Had Heav'n so spar'd the life of life to frame
75   the rest? But ah! such losse hath this world ought
      can equall it? or which like greevance brought?
Yet there will live thy ever praised name.

To which theise dearest offrings of my hart
      dissolv'd to Inke, while penns impressions move
80   the bleeding veines of never dying love:
I render here: these wounding lynes of smart
      sadd Characters indeed of simple love
      not Art nor skill which abler wits doe prove,
Of my full soule receive the meanest part.

85 Receive theise Hymnes, theise obsequies receive;
      if any marke of thy sweet sprite appeare,
      well are they borne, no title else shall beare.
I can no more: Deare Soule I take my leave;
      Sorrowe still strives, would mount thy highest sphere
90   presuming so just cause might meet thee there,
Oh happie chaunge! could I so take my leave.

                  By the Sister of that
                  Incomporable Sidney

70 above all] aboveall *J*   73 have wrought] havewrought *J*   87 they borne]
theyborne [y *added in lighter ink and a slightly different hand*] *J*

To the Angell Spirit of the most excellent, Sir Phillip Sidney.

[Variant]

To the pure Spirit, to thee alone addrest
Is this joynt worke, by double intrist thine,
Thine by his owne, and what is done of mine
Inspir'd by thee, thy secret powre imprest.
My Muse with thine, it selfe dar'd to combine   5
As mortall staffe with that which is divine:
Let thy faire beames give luster to the rest.

That Israels King may daygne his owne transform'd
In substance no, but superficiall tire:
And English guis'd in some sort may aspire   10
To better grace thee what the vulgar form'd:
His sacred Tones, age, after age admire
Nations grow great in pride, and pure desire
So to excell in holy rites perform'd.

O had that soule which honour brought to rest   15
To soone not leaft, and reaft the world of all.
What man could shew, which we perfection call,
This precious peece had sorted with the best.
But ah! wide festred wounds that never shall
Nor must be clos'd, unto fresh bleeding fall,   20
Ah memory, what needs this new arrist.

Yet blessed griefe, that sweetnes can impart
Since thou art blest. Wrongly do I complaine,
What ever weights my heavy thoughts sustaine
Deere feeles my soule for thee. I know my part   25
Nor be my weaknes to thy rites a staine
Rites to aright, life, bloud would not refraine:
Assist me then, that life what thine did part.

Time may bring forth, what time hath yet supprest
In whom, thy losse hath layd to utter wast   30
The wracke of time, untimely all defac't,

Remayning as the tombe of life disceast:
Where, in my heart the highest roome thou hast
There, truly there, thy earthly being is plac't
35   Triumph of death: in life how more then blest.

Behold, O that thou were now to behold,
This finisht long perfections part begun
The rest but peic'd, as leaft by thee undone,
Pardon blest soule, presumption overbold:
40   If love and zeale hath to this error run
Tis zealous love, love that hath never dun,
Nor can enough, though justly here contrould.

But since it hath no other scope to go,
Nor other purpose but to honour thee,
45   That thine may shine, where all the graces be;
And that my thoughts (like smallest streames that flow,
Pay to their sea, their tributary fee)
Do strive, yet have no meanes to quit nor free,
That mighty debt of infinits I owe

50   To thy great worth which time to times inroule
Wonder of men, sole borne, soule of thy kind
Compleat in all, but heavenly was thy mind,
For wisdome, goodnes, sweetnes, fairest soule:
To good to wish, to faire for earth, refin'd
55   For Heaven, where all true glory rests confin'd;
And where but there no life without controule.

O when from this accompt, this cast-up somme,
This reckning made the Audit of my woo,
Sometime of rase my swelling passions know,
60   How work my thoughts, my sense, is striken dombe
That would the more then words could ever shew;
Which all fall short. Who knew thee best do know
There lives no wit that may thy prayer become.

And rest faire momuments of thy faire fame,
65   Though not complete. Nor can we reach, in thought,
What on that goodly peece, time would have wrought.

'To the Angell Spirit' [Variant]
39 presumption] prespmption 1623   49 owe‸] ~. 1623

Had divers so spar'd that life (but life) to frame
The rest: alas such losse the world hath nought
Can equall it, nor O more grievance brought,
Yet what remaines must ever crowne thy name.   70

    Receive these Hims, these obsequies receive,
    (If any marke of thy secret spirit thou beare)
    Made only thine, and no name els must weare.
    I can no more deare soule, I take my leave,
    My sorrow strives to mount the highest Sphere.   75

DISPUTED WORK

'The Dolefull Lay of Clorinda'

Literary Context

While university poets were publishing their elegies soon after Sidney's death (see 'Angell Spirit'), the Countess of Pembroke apparently composed her own poem and sent a copy to her brother's 'deere and spetial frende' Sir Edward Wotton. By the time she wrote to Wotton, she had misplaced the original, so she asked him to return his copy of her 'Idle passion', her 'toy', such a trifle that she does not know any 'reason ~~whie~~ yow should yeld me any account of'. Yet her self-deprecation, paralleling her brother's references to his *Arcadia*, does not mask her 'earnest desire' that she obtain a copy of that poem sent to him 'loonge since'. Although the poem may be 'unworthy of the humour that then possest me', none the less she wishes 'to review what the Image could be of those sadd tymes'. To spur his co-operation, she promises 'other things better worth your keepinge', perhaps copies of poems by her brother or more polished versions of her own compositions. (See Correspondence: Manuscript Letter III.) Because no title or identifying description is given, she may refer here to a poem which is no longer extant, but the date '1594' inscribed on the letter (if added by either the countess or someone with first-hand knowledge of its composition) suggests that the poem she needed back may have been a manuscript draft of 'The Dolefull Lay', attributed to Sidney's 'sister that *Clorinda* hight' by Edmund Spenser in the 1595 *Astrophel* (sig. F4ᵛ). In 'The Ruines of Time' Spenser also speaks of an elegy written by Pembroke for her brother:

> Then will I sing: but who can better sing,
> Than thine owne sister, peerles Ladie bright,
> Which to thee sings with deep harts sorrowing,
> Sorrowing tempered with deare delight.
> That her to heare I feele my feeble spright
> Robbed of sense, and ravished with joy,
> O sad joy made of mourning and anoy. (sig. C2)

Writing here for publication in 1591, Spenser refers to an early poem in which Pembroke mourned for Sidney; if it is not 'The Dolefull

Lay', then she must have written one or more elegies lost to us, mentioned here and in her letter to Wotton.

Like numerous other Elizabethan writers, Pembroke may have first practised her poetic skill in the elegy. The Renaissance elegy was a form 'accessible to writers of all ages and abilities... a kind of laboratory' in which they practised 'the components of art and the disciplines of the craft', as Dennis Kay notes.[1] This may have been even more true for women, since the need to commemorate the dead could override gender restrictions, making the elegy one of the few forms of original writing open to women. Pembroke might have known such works as the 104 Latin distichs honouring Marguerite de Navarre by Anne, Margaret, and Jane Seymour, daughters of the Lord Protector Somerset (published 1551); or the poem by Lady Elizabeth Cooke Russell, inscribed on her husband's tomb (1584); or an elegy composed by Anne Dacre Howard, Countess of Arundel (1595).[2] The pretence that elegies did not require extensive rhetorical training is dramatized in Bryskett's 'Pastorall Aeglogue', wherein Lycon apologizes for his 'rude' verse and Colin replies, 'what need skill, to teach | A grieved mynd powre forth his plaints?... No, no, each | Creature by nature can tell how to waile' (sig. H2^v).

'The Dolefull Lay' was first published in 1595 as a companion poem to Spenser's personal lament for Sidney, 'Astrophel'. Scholars continue to debate whether it is the early elegy mentioned in Pembroke's letter to Wotton, and whether the 'Lay' was written by Pembroke, by Spenser, or in collaboration.

Spenser had celebrated Philip Sidney on the title page of *The Shepheardes Calender* and had commemorated the Sidney/Dudley family

[1] Kay, *Melodious Tears*, 6.

[2] Anne, Margaret, and Jane Seymour, *Hecatodistichon* (Paris, 1550), reprinted as *Le tombeau de Marguerite de Valois Royne de Navarre* (Paris, 1551); see Brenda M. Hosington, 'England's First Female-Authored Encomium: The Seymour Sisters' *Hecatodistichon* (1550) to Marguerite de Navarre. Text, Translation, Notes, and Commentary', *SP* 93 (1996), 117–63. The poems by Russell and Howard are printed in *The Paradise of Women: Writings by Englishwomen of the Renaissance*, ed. Betty Travitsky (Westport, Conn.: Greenwood P, 1981), 23–4, 33–4. Women's poems of personal mourning became more common in the seventeenth century, including such poems as 'On the death of... Robert Payler', 'At the death of... Perigrene Payler', and 'Upon the Sight of my abortive Birth' by Mary Carey; 'Epitaph. On her son H. P.' and 'On the death of my first and dearest childe' by Katherine Philips, printed in *Kissing the Rod: An Anthology of 17th Century Women's Verse*, ed. Germaine Greer *et al.* (London: Virago P, 1988), 155–61, 195–7. See also Anne Bradstreet's elegies, including 'In Memory of Elizabeth Bradstreet', 'In Memory of Anne Bradstreet', and 'In Memory of Mrs. Mercy Bradstreet', in *The Works of Anne Bradstreet*, ed. Jeannine Hensley (Cambridge, Mass.: Harvard UP, 1967), 235–8.

for Pembroke in 'The Ruines of Time'.[3] In his dedication of 'The Ruines', Spenser noted his own previous failure to celebrate Sidney, confessing that many friends 'which might much prevaile with me, and indeede commaund me' have 'sought to revive' Sidney and his 'noble house...by upbraiding me: for that I have not shewed anie thankefull remembrance towards him or any of them' (sig. A3ᵛ). 'Thankefull remembrance' would be particularly appropriate for a patron and does not necessarily imply friendship. S. K. Heninger observes that 'although the opportunity for acquaintance existed' when Spenser was in service at Leicester House from October 1579 until April 1580, 'it can be only a surmise that Sidney and Spenser actually met'.[4] The few extant contemporary records, which may have been coloured by a desire to increase Spenser's reputation by connecting him with the illustrious Sidney, provide inconclusive evidence. One such reference is a commendatory sonnet by 'W. L.' (probably William Lisle) printed with the 1590 edition of *The Faerie Queene*, which actually claims only Sidney's knowledge of Spenser's poetry: 'But *Sydney* heard him sing, and knew his voice.'[5] Another is Gabriel Harvey's published correspondence with Spenser, asserting the existence of an Areopagus, a literary coterie comprised of Sidney, Spenser, Dyer, Greville, Harvey himself, and perhaps some others; the existence of some loose association is confirmed by Daniel Rogers, but Harvey is probably exaggerating both his own and Spenser's connection with Sidney. As Jon Quitslund argues, the public, rather than private, character of the letters places 'their evidentiary value in doubt'. They should not be read as simple biographical fact, for the persona here is analogous to the 'textual figures of Immerito and Colin Clout'.[6] Even less reliable is an anonymous 'Life of Mr.

---

[3] *The Shepheardes Calender... Entitled to the Noble and Vertuous Gentleman most worthy of all titles both of learning and of chevalrie M. Philip Sidney* (1579); 'To the right Noble and beautifull Ladie, the La. Marie Countesse of Pembrooke', 'The Ruines of Time', in Spenser *Complaints*, sig. A3ʳ⁻ᵛ.

[4] S. K. Heninger, Jr., *Sidney and Spenser: The Poet as Maker* (University Park: Pennsylvania State UP, 1989), 10.

[5] W. L., 'When stout *Achilles* heard of *Helens* rape', rpt. *Spenser: Poetical Works*, 410.

[6] 'Spenser–Harvey Correspondence', rpt. *Spenser: Poetical Works*, 609–32; Jon Quitslund, 'Questionable Evidence in the *Letters* of 1580 between Gabriel Harvey and Edmund Spenser', in *Spenser's Life and the Subject of Biography*, ed. Judith H. Anderson, Donald Cheney, and David A. Richardson (Amherst: U of Massachusetts P, 1996), 81. The extensive debate about the literary coterie, which 'existed, if at all, for only a short time', is summarized by Reavley Gair, 'Areopagus', in *The Spenser Encyclopedia*, ed. A. C. Hamilton *et al.* (Toronto: U of Toronto P, 1990), 55.

Edmond Spenser' printed in the 1679 folio edition of his works, which claimed that Spenser showed Sidney Canto 9 of Book I of *The Faerie Queene*. Sidney was so impressed as he read that he told his servant to give Spenser first fifty, then one hundred, and then two hundred pounds. Thereafter, Sidney 'became not only his Patron, but his Friend too; entred him at Court, and obtain'd of the *Queen* the Grant of a Pention to him as *Poet Laureat*'.[7] A similar apocryphal story was (somewhat inaccurately) summarized by Aubrey, who also concluded that 'there was a great friendship between them'.[8] Despite these appealing legends, there is no conclusive evidence that Sidney ever met Spenser. Heninger, pointing to the social gulf between the two men, doubts that there was 'ever a personal exchange' between them; even if they did meet at Leicester House, 'after his departure from London in July 1580 [to Ireland, to serve under Arthur, Lord Grey of Wilton] Spenser was of negligible consequence in Sidney's busy life'.[9]

Whether or not they were personally acquainted, Sidney called *The Shepheardes Calender* 'worthy the reading' in his *Defence of Poetry*.[10] Spenser did praise Sidney in the dedication of 'The Ruines of Time' to the Countess of Pembroke as 'the hope of all learned men, and the Patron of my young Muses', and some transference of patronage is implied in his dedication to Sidney's sister, 'to whome I acknowledge my selfe bounden, by manie singular favours and great graces' (sigs. A3–4). In a dedicatory sonnet attached to *The Faerie Queene*, he once again praises Sidney, 'that most Heroicke spirit', as his first patron and appeals to Pembroke as Sir Philip's sister ('For his, and for your owne especial sake, | Vouchsafe from him this token in good worth to take'), claiming to see 'His goodly image living evermore, | In the divine resemblaunce of your face'.[11] In *Colin Clouts Come Home Againe* he likewise praises her as '*Urania*, sister unto *Astrofell*'; and it has been surmised that Spenser may have repaid

---

[7] 'A Summary of the Life of Mr. Edmond Spenser', in *The Works of that Famous English Poet, Mr. Edmond Spenser... Whereunto is added, an Account of his Life* (1679), Wing 54965, sig. A1[r–v]. T. Birch expands the biography and summarizes this tale in the 1751 edition.

[8] Aubrey, *Brief Lives*, 279.

[9] Heninger, *Sidney and Spenser*, 14–15. There is no documentary evidence for the tradition that Spenser served under Sir Henry Sidney in Ireland, but Spenser's avatar, Irenius, in the *Vewe of Ireland* does claim to have witnessed the execution of Murrough O'Brien at Limerick in July 1577, during Sidney's term of office.

[10] Sidney, *Miscellaneous Prose*, 112.

[11] 'To the right honourable and most vertuous Lady, the Countesse of Penbroke,' in Spenser, *Faerie Queene*, sig. Qq4[v], quoting from the BL copy, C.12.h.17.

her generosity, not only by writing poems praising her and her brother, but also by helping her revise and publish what may have been her earliest extant work, 'The Dolefull Lay of Clorinda'.

Astrophel is comprised of seven elegies: Spenser's title poem, 'The Dolefull Lay of Clorinda', two poems by Lodowick Bryskett, and three poems reprinted, with errors, from *The Phoenix Nest*. After 'Astrophel', the poems are presented 'in order lov'd him best', beginning with his sister, then Bryskett, and proceeding with reprinted poems by Matthew Roydon, Walter Ralegh, and an anonymous poem by Edward Dyer (or possibly Fulke Greville). Although the earliest verse had celebrated Sidney primarily as a military and religious figure, rather than as a writer, these laments also celebrate him as a poet, using the names Sidney had used for himself, Astrophel and Philisides.[12]

Lodowick Bryskett's elegy, 'A pastorall Aeglogue upon the death of Sir Phillip Sidney Knight', suggests that this poem was written specifically for *Astrophel* and that the volume was a joint project. In this dialogue between Colin, Spenser's usual self-designation, and Lycon (Lodowick Bryskett, under an anagram of Colin), Lycon invites the immortal Philisides to look down from heaven on their composition of these elegies:

> Behold my selfe with *Colin*, gentle swaine
> (Whose lerned *Muse* thou cherisht most whyleare)
> Where we thy name recording, seeke to ease
> The inward torment and tormenting paine,
> That thy departure to us both hath bred. (sig. H4^{r-v})

These lines apparently describe the compilation of this volume as an act of mourning, and, together with embedded Spenserian phrases, suggest collaboration with Spenser.[13] Bryskett, Spenser's friend and

---

[12] On the celebration of Sidney as poet, see Michael O'Connell, ' "Astrophel": Spenser's Double Elegy', *SEL* 11 (1971), 27–35. Raphael Falco says Spenser criticizes Astrophil for sacrificing 'his poetic gifts for a delusion of active heroism': *Conceived Presences: Literary Genealogy in Renaissance England* (Amherst: U of Massachusetts P, 1994), 118, 123. Lisa Klein argues that Spenser himself 'expresses despair at the failure of the humanist poetics that he and Sidney embraced, namely, the belief that poetry enabled virtuous action': 'Spenser's *Astrophel* and the Sidney Legend', *Sidney Newsletter and Journal* 12 (1993), 43. See also Theodore L. Steinberg, 'Spenser, Sidney and the Myth of Astrophel', *Spenser Studies* 11 (1990), 187–201.

[13] Frederick B. Tromly, 'Lodowick Bryskett's Elegies on Sidney in Spenser's *Astrophel* Volume', *RES* ns 37 (1986), 384–8. Katherine Duncan-Jones also suggests that Bryskett collaborated with Spenser: 'Astrophel', *Spenser Encyclopedia*, 74.

for at least five years his immediate superior in Ireland, was long associated with the Sidneys. He had served in Ireland under Sir Henry and had accompanied Sir Philip on his European tour in 1572–5. (Bryskett alludes to that tour in 'A pastorall Aeglogue', sig. H2^v.) Because he lived for a time as a member of Sir Henry's household, he would have known Pembroke since her childhood. He may even have been the 'Mr. Lodwicke' listed in the accounts as the 'Skolemaster' for Pembroke's younger sister Ambrosia.[14] For Bryskett to join with Spenser and Pembroke in order to commemorate Sidney and present the elegies to his widow would have been most appropriate. Perhaps both Bryskett and the countess gave Spenser 'The mourning Muse of Thestylis' and 'The Dolefull Lay of Clorinda', written years before, to incorporate into this memorial, along with poems reprinted from *The Phoenix Nest*, which had also been written long before their publication in 1593.[15] Bryskett then wrote 'A pastorall Aeglogue' for the occasion, probably with Spenser's help. While we do not have external evidence that it was Pembroke who asked Spenser to write his 'Astrophel', we do know that she had requested works on earlier occasions from other writers, including Samuel Daniel and even Philip Sidney, because they say so.[16] She would have been likely to request, and to reward, such praise of her brother, as other poets indicate in their dedications to her. (See p. 27.) And Spenser does say in his dedication of 'The Ruines of Time' that his commemoration of her relatives 'speciallie concerneth' Pembroke.

Such collaborative work would not be unprecedented for Pembroke or for Bryskett. In his *Discourse of Civill Life* (1606) Bryskett also records a literary dialogue with Spenser; he there subordinates his muse to Spenser's, as he does in 'A pastorall Aeglogue', where he says 'my rude rhymes, ill with thy verses frame' (sig. H2^v). Spenser's elegy does appear to be written as an introduction, and he certainly does supply verses that set up a pastoral framework for the other elegies, thus producing an unusually coherent volume. Five of the seven

[14] De L'Isle MS U1475 A54 (2).

[15] Roydon's elegy was mentioned by Thomas Nashe in 1589, and Ralegh's comparison of Sidney to Scipio and Petrarch is mentioned by Sir John Harington in 1591. See Esplin (Ph.D. diss.), 239.

[16] See Sidney's dedication of the 1593 *Arcadia*, sig. A3, and Samuel Daniel's 1594 dedication of *Cleopatra* in *Delia & Cleopatra*, sig. H5^v. An anonymous writer in the Arundel manuscript apparently also dedicated a work, now missing, to the countess, saying the countess 'unto me this woorke did first assigne', printed in the *Arundel Harington MS*, I. 258, item 228.

poems are pastoral, most celebrate Sidney as a writer, and all stress the theme of envy, as in '*Astrophill* by envie slaine' (sig. K1^v). Most striking are the parallels among the poems that appear to have been written or revised for *Astrophel*: 'Astrophel', 'The Dolefull Lay', 'The mourning Muse of Thestylis', and 'A pastorall Aeglogue'. All of them use flower imagery as they sing a 'dolefull plaint' (sig. E4), 'a dolefull lay' (sig. F4^v), 'dolefull notes' (sig. G3), or a 'dolefull ryme' (sig. H3^v). All three poems mention Sidney's 'mery' verses and love poems (sig. E4^v-F1, sig. G1^v, sig. H4). In addition, phrasing in the 'Dolefull Lay' frequently matches that of Bryskett's poems. The 'Lay' describes the 'widow state' of the fields (sig. G1^v), while the 'Aeglogue' describes the 'widow world' (sig. H4). Clorinda's sequence of 'woods, hills and rivers' which 'now are desolate' parallels Bryskett's hills, dales, and woods (sig. G1^v and sig. H4). Both describe nymphs wearing cypress garlands (sig. G1^v and sig. H3^v). Both describe Sidney as a flower, one which is 'untimely cropt' according to Clorinda and 'pluct untimely' according to Bryskett (sig. G1^v and sig. G3). Sidney is described as a 'happie spirit' by Clorinda and a 'happie sprite' by Bryskett (sig. G2^v and sig. H4), one who is now in 'everlasting blis' (sig. G2^v and sig. G4). Both 'The Dolefull Lay' and the 'Aeglogue' conclude with an appeal to Sidney to give his approval to their songs of mourning. Occasionally, the 'Lay' echoes phrases from subsequent poems, such as 'worlds delight' (sig. G2 and sig. K3^v). Although the ideas are conventional, the similarities in phrasing between these poems, as well as the parallels between 'Astrophel' and the 'Lay' noted below, suggest co-operative effort.

The physical appearance of its first publication may also lend support to the thesis that Pembroke and Bryskett worked with Spenser to prepare *Astrophel* as a commemorative volume that would include a selection of works written by his friends. First of all, the volume is set up in such a way that it distinguishes between Spenser's 'Astrophel' and the 'Lay', in contrast to the presentation of the words of Sidney's beloved 'Stella'. Spenser describes Astrophel's courtship of Stella and her mourning after his death (sig. F1^v-4). Bryskett incorporates a fictionalized lament by 'Stella' into 'The mourning Muse' without even a break in the line: '[she] piteously gan say, My true and faithfull pheere' (sig. G4^v). In contrast, the treatment of Clorinda's 'Lay' precisely matches the treatment of the other poems in *Astrophel*. Spenser uses the same verb for his own activity in transcribing Clorinda ('In sort as she it sung, I will rehearse') as of the poems from *The Phoenix Nest* ('The which I here in order will rehearse'). 'Rehearse' does not, for Spenser, mean 'compose', but rather 'recite', its standard sixteenth-century usage.

The two stanzas immediately following 'Astrophel' provide a general introduction to elegies by a variety of authors, concluding:

> And every one did make exceeding mone,
> With inward anguish and great griefe opprest:
> And every one did weep and waile, and mone,
> And meanes deviz'd to shew his sorrow best.
> That from that houre since first on grassie greene,
> Shepheards kept sheep, was not like mourning seen.   (sig. F4)

The running title, 'Colin clouts | come home againe', continues through 'Colin Clout' and through Spenser's 'Astrophel', but stops immediately after these stanzas, producing an opening with just half a running title, 'Colin clout' (sig. F4^V–G1). Signature F4^V lacks the catch-phrase that marks continuations elsewhere in the volume.[17] A separate stanza introducing the 'Lay' is printed at the top of the page; the remainder of the page is left blank, except for a double border which matches the title page, so it reads as follows:

> But first his sister that *Clorinda* hight,
> The gentlest shepheardesse that lives this day:
> And most resembling both in shape and spright
> Her brother deare, began this dolefull lay.
> Which least I marre the sweetnesse of the vearse,
> In sort as she it sung, I will rehearse.   (sig. F4^V)

Nowhere else in the volume is there so much white space. On a new gathering (sig. G1), a large ornamental initial begins the 'Lay', matching the ornamental initial that begins 'Astrophel'. The border frames the top and bottom of each page of the 'Lay', but ceases at the end of that poem on signature G2^V. Except that the 'Lay' is not given a separate title, it is difficult to imagine what else the printer could have done to set off 'The Dolefull Lay' from 'Astrophel' while retaining them in the same volume.

[17] Sig. H4^V, which completes the poems by Bryskett, is the only other page without a catch-phrase. An elaborate design using the letter 'A', matching the opening of the volume, separates Bryskett's 'Aeglogue' from *The Phoenix Nest* poems, which begin on a new gathering with a border and a large initial 'A'. 'The Dolefull Lay' is similarly separated from 'Astrophel', beginning on a new gathering with the same borders and the large initial 'A'. Note that none of these devices was used to set off Alcyon's complaint in Spenser's *Daphnaïda. An Elegie upon the death of the noble and vertuous Douglas Howard* (1591), *STC* 23079.

On the page facing the conclusion of 'The Lay', the subsequent elegies are given an introduction. The first stanza introduces the work of Lodowick Bryskett, under the name of Thestylis:

> Which when she ended had, another swaine . . .
> Hight *Thestylis*, began his mournfull tourne,
> And made the *Muses* in his song to mourne.   (sig. G3)

In the following stanza, immediately prior to 'The mourning Muse', the rest of the elegies are given a general introduction:

> And after him full many other moe,
> As everie one in order lov'd him best,
> Gan dight themselves t'expresse their inward woe,
> With dolefull layes unto the time addrest,
> The which I here in order will rehearse,
> As fittest flowres to deck his mournfull hearse.

No further editorial comments are given for the second poem by Bryskett or for the poems reprinted from *The Phoenix Nest*. Like Spenser's 'Astrophel', Bryskett's poems are printed without borders, but the end of his work is marked by his initials and an elaborate design repeated from the opening of 'Astrophel' (sig. H4^v). The elegies reprinted from *The Phoenix Next* then appear with the same border used for 'The Dolefull Lay'.[18]

Except for the use of the border, the handling of 'The Dolefull Lay of Clorinda' exactly parallels that of the succeeding poem, 'The mourning Muse of Thestylis'. Spenser calls the Countess of Pembroke 'Clorinda' as he calls Bryskett 'Thestylis'. Because Bryskett's first elegy, 'The mourning Muse of Thestylis', was recorded for publication by John Wolfe in the *Stationers' Register* on 22 August 1587, his authorship is beyond question. The second poem, signed 'L. B.', although not known to be elsewhere registered or printed, has also been generally accepted as his. Pembroke's authorship of 'The Dolefull Lay' was similarly accepted without much question until Frances Young's 1912 biography.[19] In that same year, Ernest de Selincourt suggested that if she wrote it, 'she had studied to some purpose the

---

[18] On the layout as an argument for Pembroke's authorship, see Walter G. Freidrich, 'The Astrophel Elegies: A Critical Edition' (Johns Hopkins University, Ph.D. diss., 1934), 21–5, and Sidney, Mary. *Triumph*, 57.

[19] Young, *Mary Sidney*, 134–5, who notes that 'The Dolefull Lay' was 'probably but not certainly written by Lady Pembroke'. See, for example, H.T.R., 'Mary Sidney and Her Writings', *Gentlemen's Magazine* 24 (1845), 365.

peculiarly Spenserian effects of rhythm and melody', so that: 'It is more natural...to believe that Spenser wrote it in her name'.[20] Charles Osgood later made a stronger statement, claiming that Spenser 'means to deceive as many of his own generation and succeeding ones as he can' by writing a poem 'below the quality of even the poet's most perfunctory verse' and attributing it to the countess.[21] Such a conclusion completely ignores the social context. Spenser would be most unlikely to insult a patron by writing an inferior piece in his own style and attributing it to her, particularly when she was already celebrated as a writer for her published translations and for her *Psalmes*, then circulating in manuscript. (See pp. 21 ff.) Because Pembroke was not hesitant to counter what she saw as mistreatment of her brother's works, such as the 1590 edition of *The Countesse of Pembrokes Arcadia* or the corrupt 1591 edition of *Astrophil and Stella*, it is unlikely that she would have appreciated liberties being taken with her own literary reputation.

Since Selincourt suggested Spenser as author of the 'Lay', the ensuing debate has been ostensibly textual, yet it often assumes that an Elizabethan woman would not have had the education or the rhetorical skill to write a poem in a Spenserian mode. Herbert David Rix, for example, suggests that in order for her to write the 'Lay' she would have needed 'a rhetorical training similar to Spenser's'.[22] Although he notes that her *Antonius* uses many of the same rhetorical figures that appear in the 'Lay', such as anaphora, allegory, personification, questions, and forms of repetition, Rix nevertheless concludes that she would not have studied 'the special discipline' necessary to have written the 'Lay'. Yet close examination of her other works, particularly the *Psalmes*, indicates that Pembroke did

---

[20] *Spenser: Poetical Works*, p. xxxv. In addition to critics mentioned below, those who accept Spenser's authorship include Esplin (Ph.D. diss.), 237–40; Michael O'Connell, *SEL* (1971), 27–35; Brennan, *Literary Patronage*, 61–2. Those who accept Pembroke's authorship include Waller, in his edition of her works (Sidney, Mary. *Triumph*, 54–9), and *Mary Sidney*, 89–95; Lamb (Ph.D. diss.), 26; Beilin, *Redeeming Eve*, 337; Buxton, *Sidney*, 173; Hannay, *Philip's Phoenix*, 63–8; and Klein, *Sidney Newsletter and Journal* (1993), 43. William Oram agrees that the work represents some type of collaboration with Spenser: *The Yale Edition of the Shorter Poems of Edmund Spenser* (New Haven: Yale UP, 1989), 565. Jonathan Goldberg concludes that 'there is no reason not to believe, as I do, that the countess wrote the *Lay of Clorinda*', but the matter is not susceptible to proof, *Sodometries: Renaissance Texts/Modern Sexualities* (Stanford, Calif: Stanford UP, 1992), 101.

[21] Charles W. Osgood, 'The Doleful Lay of Clorinda', *MLN* 35 (1920), 95–6.

[22] Herbert David Rix, 'Spenser's Rhetoric and the "Doleful Lay"', *MLN* 53 (1938), 265.

indeed have extensive knowledge of the standard rhetorical tropes and was certainly capable of writing a relatively simple poem like 'The Dolefull Lay'. In fact, the poem employs a wide range of techniques characteristic of her style. (See pp. 65 ff.) The poem is structured around rhetorical questions (as in 1–7, 13, 17–18, 31–2, 43–4). There is frequent alliteration, particularly in the noun and accompanying adjective, as 'vaine vowes' (90) and 'fairest flowre' (28), insistently repeated as 'faire a flowre' (32), and 'faire flowre' (38). The poem also uses alliterative phrases like 'waile their widow state' (27), 'Death the devourer of all worlds delight' (49), and 'weep, and waile, and wear our eies' (95). The author employs rhetorical repetition, although some of the figures are awkwardly handled, such as the apparent attempt at polyptoton in 'love-layes'/'layes of love' (43–4). Repetition is more mechanical than in her later works, such as the simple epizeuxis in 'happie, happie spirit' (91), or the parallel questions, 'To heavens? ah they alas' and 'To men? ah they alas' (7, 13), the repetition of 'flowre, which them adornd' in lines 38 and 39, the use of shadow and shade in lines 58–60, or the epizeuxis in the refrain:

> Great losse to all that ever him did see,
> Great losse to all, but greatest losse to me. (35–6)

The poem parallels some of the wording in *The Triumph of Death*, such as the phrase 'Angelick delight', used to describe Astrophil in heaven (76), and to describe Laura's voice, 'Angell-lyke delight' (*Triumph*, 1. 150). As 'The Dolefull Lay' asks 'What cruell hand...Hath cropt the stalke which bore so faire a flowre?' (31–2), so Death 'cropt the flower, of all this world most faire' (*Triumph*, 1. 115).

Certainly there are significant similarities in style and technique between 'Astrophel' and 'The Dolefull Lay', as numerous critics have noted, including archaic diction, repeated words and phrases, rhyme scheme, and the use of colons.[23] None of these similarities disproves her authorship; because the style and phrasing of 'The Dolefull

---

[23] G. W. Pigman, in *Grief and English Renaissance Elegy* (Cambridge: Cambridge UP, 1985), 152, makes a numerological argument against Pembroke's authorship, noting that 'Astrophel' has exactly twice as many lines as 'The Dolefull Lay'. The 108 lines of 'The Dolefull Lay' match the number of Penelope's suitors in *The Odyssey* and the number of sonnets in *Astrophil and Stella*. The editions of *Astrophil and Stella* published before *Astrophel*, however, actually contained 107 sonnets. Pembroke had the manuscript with 108 sonnets, suggesting that the numerological parallel was established by the countess herself, as Anne Prescott notes in her review of Pigman, *Spenser Newsletter* 16 (1985), 63. Either way, the argument turns on whether the two stanzas introducing 'The Dolefull Lay' are counted as part of 'Astrophel' itself.

Lay' are echoed in her subsequent works such similarities might better be explained as the result of co-operation between Spenser and the countess.

Even though Charles Osgood demonstrates that the diction of 'The Dolefull Lay' is similar to Spenser's, the very wording that Osgood uses to disprove Pembroke's authorship is quite characteristic of her style.[24] For example, 'Ay me' does occur frequently in Spenser, but also appears in Pembroke's *Antonius*, 460; and in Psalms 88. 61; 109. 7; 119L. 9; and 143. 17. Similarly, the use of 'annoy' as a rhyme word, presented as typically Spenserian, is ubiquitous. The 'joy'/'annoy' rhyme is used by Bryskett (sig. G4ᵛ) and closes *Astrophil and Stella*. It is also one of Pembroke's most frequent rhymes, as in *Triumph*, 2. 37/39 and 118/120, 'Astrea', 31/2, Psalm 46. 9/11, and 'Even now', 86/8. Pembroke also uses 'deface' as a rhyme word in Psalms 69. 19, 73. 58, 103. 10, 104. 69, 137. 28, and 146. 6 and as a pun in Psalm 83. 50. The phrase 'untimely all defac't' in the first draft of 'Angell Spirit' (31) combines 'defaced' with 'untimely', another of Osgood's test words. The verb 'unfold' is equally characteristic of her style, and appears in such places as Psalms 64. 35; 78. 131; and 81. 3. 'Doubled' is also a characteristic Pembrokian form which occurs in her other works, such as *Antonius*, 622 and 815. Other constructions mentioned by Osgood as typically Spenserian also occur in Pembroke's later works. The stressed verb with subsequent commentary that appears in 'The Dolefull Lay' ('Was *Astrophel*; that was, we all may rew') (30), also appears in 'Even now that Care', 'Who better might (O might ah word of woe)' (23) and in 'Angell Spirit', 'Yet here behold, (oh wert thou to behold!)' (22). (The usage was not peculiarly Spenserian; it also appears in the anonymous final elegy in *Astrophel*, 'He was (wo worth that word) to ech well thinking minde' (sig. K3ᵛ).) The *abbabcc* rhyme, used in both 'Astrophel' and the 'Lay', is also used in Psalm 59. Like Spenser and like her brother Philip, Pembroke frequently uses hyphenated compound words, as 'world-dwellers' (Ps. 49. 1), 'life-holding' (Ps. 55. 71), 'quarrel-pickers' (Ps 72. 12), and 'short-glorious' (*Triumph*, 1. 103). Oxymorons are also as characteristic of her style as of Spenser's, including 'gladly sadd, and richly poore' (Ps. 69. 71). More recently Steven May has suggested that the archaic phrasing in 'The Dolefull Lay' is Spenserian. While phrasing such as 'Ne fearing salvage beasts' (88) may be more characteristic of

[24] Osgood, *MLN* (1920), 90–6.

Spenser than of Pembroke's mature works, she occasionally does include archaisms in her early poems.[25] The early draft of Psalm 69, for example, includes the phrase, 'Ne from Thy Servant hide Thy helpfull face'.[26] Pembroke also uses terms such as 'dole' and 'drent' (94) in the *Psalmes*, as in 'bitter dole' (Ps. 77. 13), 'dole and dread' (Ps. 78. 147), and 'all drent, all dead, not one left of the Crue' (Ps. 106. 31). 'Sith' for since, used in the 'Lay' (as 26 and 38), occurs repeatedly in the *Psalmes* (as 68. 74, 69. 59, and 102. 34). Further-more, in 'A pastorall Aeglogue' Bryskett uses similar phrasing, 'Ne can each others sorrow yet appease' (sig. H4v). He employs other archaisms in both of his elegies, such as 'yrent' (sig. G3), 'eke' (*pas-sim*), 'yodest' (sig. H3^v), and 'yquenched' (sig. H3^v).

There are also allusions to Spenser's work in 'The Dolefull Lay', such as the phrase 'The woods, the hills, the rivers shall resound' (23) that echoes the refrain of 'Epithalamion', or the reference to gar-lands of cypress and elder (41–2) that echo *The Shepheardes Calender*, 'November', 145–7. The description of the immortal spirit of Sidney as a babe in a garden may also allude to the Garden of Adonis in *The Faerie Queene*, III. vi. As Adonis lives in 'eternall blis', 'everlasting joy' and 'Ne feareth he henceforth that foe of his...that wilde Bore' (III. vi. 47–9), so Sidney lives in 'everlasting blis' (85), 'Ne dreading harme from any foes of his, | Ne fearing salvage beasts more crueltie' (87–8).

Examination of Pembroke's work indicates that the diction, style, and phrasing of 'The Dolefull Lay' do not mandate Spenserian authorship, but they do indicate Spenserian influence. Spenser's statement that he presented Clorinda's words without emendation, 'In sort as she it sung' lest he should 'marre the sweetnesse of the vearse', does not rule out earlier collaboration. Like many writers, Pembroke habitually shared her works in progress with other poets. We have already noted that she had originally sent an elegy, possibly this one, to Wotton. Equally indicative is that her early draft of 'To the Angell Spirit of Sir Phillip Sidney' (q.v.) was found among Samuel Daniel's papers, probably because she gave it to him. Her letters to Tobie Matthew, if authentic, also demonstrate that she continued to

[25] May correctly notes that such archaic phrasing is not present in Pembroke's 'Astrea', a pastoral work that might reasonably be expected to use such diction: *Courtier Poets*, 345. But other words mentioned by May, such as 'drent', 'dole', and 'reft', occur even in the Pen-shurst MS (Pss. 77. 13; 78. 147; 106. 31; and 143. 18).

[26] MS *B* Ps. 69. 52.

exchange manuscripts with friends throughout her life. (See Correspondence: Printed Letters.)

Writing in 1916, Percy Long concluded that the similarities in rhyme scheme and punctuation 'admit of the interpretation that Spenser in writing *Astrophel* conformed to the style of Lady Pembroke's *Lay*', and, because of Spenser's reference in 'The Ruines', it is clear that 'the *Lay* preceded *Astrophel* in composition'. Yet he is reluctant to credit her with the poem, for if she wrote it, then she 'has come measurably nearer imitating Spenser' than have Shelley and Keats, an achievement that he believes is unlikely, because he does not seem to know of her other work.[27] Comparison to her *Psalmes* suggests that 'The Dolefull Lay' may have been an early effort, one certainly inferior to her mature works. If Pembroke did work with Spenser on the revision of her earliest poem, 'The Dolefull Lay' would then indicate, as Dennis Kay suggests, that Pembroke was indeed 'the first of the Spenserian poets'.[28] She later did use Spenser as a model, as she used Sidney and other English and Continental authors. (See p. 65.)

Through *Astrophel*, 'Spenser invented Spenserian poetry', giving a sense of poetic community and continuity to those who celebrated Sidney as a poet.[29] The Countess of Pembroke was included in this community of poets. As 'sister unto Astrophell' she encouraged praise of her fallen brother. As Clorinda, she may have found her own poetic voice by singing 'The Dolefull Lay'. In both of these efforts, Spenser certainly claimed to have aided this 'most Honourable and bountifull Ladie'.

[27] Percy Long, 'Spenseriana: *The Lay of Clorinda*', *MLN* 31 (1916), 80–2.
[28] Kay, *Melodious Tears*, 53.
[29] Ibid. 65–6.

[The Dolefull Lay of Clorinda]

AY me, to whom shall I my case complaine,
That may compassion my impatient griefe?
Or where shall I unfold my inward paine,
That my enriven heart may find reliefe?
  Shall I unto the heavenly powres it show?   5
  Or unto earthly men that dwell below?

To heavens? ah they alas the authors were,
And workers of my unremedied wo:
For they foresee what to us happens here,
And they foresaw, yet suffred this be so.   10
  From them comes good, from them comes also il,
  That which they made, who can them warne to spill.

To men? ah they alas like wretched bee,
And subject to the heavens ordinance:
Bound to abide what ever they decree.   15
Their best redresse, is their best sufferance.
  How then can they like wretched comfort mee,
  The which no lesse, need comforted to bee?

Then to my selfe will I my sorrow mourne,
Sith none alive like sorrowfull remaines: 20
And to my selfe my plaints shall back retourne,
To pay their usury with doubled paines.
  The woods, the hills, the rivers shall resound
  The mournfull accent of my sorrowes ground.

Woods, hills and rivers, now are desolate,   25
Sith he is gone the which them all did grace:
And all the fields do waile their widow state,
Sith death their fairest flowre did late deface.

'The Dolefull Lay of Clorinda'
*Copy-text: 1595. 1611 and 1617 are cited in the notes; spelling and punctuation variants are
selectively cited.*
5-6 *not indented in 1595*   17 they∧] ~, *1611, 1617*   wretched∧] wretched, *1611, 1617;*
wetched∧ *1595*   22 doubled] double *1611, 1617*

The fairest flowre in field that ever grew,
30 Was *Astrophel*; that was, we all may rew.

What cruell hand of cursed foe unknowne,
Hath cropt the stalke which bore so faire a flowre?
Untimely cropt, before it well were growne,
And cleane defaced in untimely howre.
35 Great losse to all that ever him did see,
Great losse to all, but greatest losse to mee.

Breake now your gyrlonds, O ye shepheards lasses,
Sith the faire flowre, which them adornd, is gon:
The flowre, which them adornd, is gone to ashes,
40 Never againe let lasse put gyrlond on.
In stead of gyrlond, weare sad Cypres nowe,
And bitter Elder, broken from the bowe.

Ne ever sing the love-layes which he made,
Who ever made such layes of love as hee?
45 Ne ever read the riddles, which he sayd
Unto your selves, to make you mery glee.
Your mery glee is now laid all abed,
Your mery maker now alasse is dead.

Death the devourer of all worlds delight,
50 Hath robbed you and reft fro me my joy:
Both you and me, and all the world he quight
Hath robd of joyance, and left sad annoy.
Joy of the world, and shepheards pride was hee,
Shepheards hope never like againe to see.

55 Oh death that hast us of such riches reft,
Tell us at least, what hast thou with it done?
What is become of him whose flowre here left
Is but the shadow of his likenesse gone.
Scarse like the shadow of that which he was,
60 Nought like, but that he like a shade did pas.

But that immortall spirit, which was deckt
With all the dowries of celestiall grace:
By soveraine choyce from th'hevenly quires select,
And lineally deriv'd from Angels race,

35 Great] *1611, 1617*; Creat *1595*   did see] *1611, 1617*; see *1595*

O what is now of it become aread.   65
Ay me, can so divine a thing be dead?

Ah no: it is not dead, ne can it die,
But lives for aie, in blisfull Paradise:
Where like a new-borne babe it soft doth lie,
In bed of lillies wrapt in tender wise,   70
  And compast all about with roses sweet,
  And daintie violets from head to feet.

There thousand birds all of celestiall brood,
To him do sweetly caroll day and night:
And with straunge notes, of him well understood,   75
Lull him a sleep in Angelick delight;
  Whilest in sweet dreame to him presented bee
  Immortall beauties, which no eye may see.

But he them sees and takes exceeding pleasure
Of their divine aspects, appearing plaine,   80
And kindling love in him above all measure,
Sweet love still joyous, never feeling paine.
  For what so goodly forme he there doth see,
  He may enjoy from jealous rancor free.

There liveth he in everlasting blis,   85
Sweet spirit never fearing more to die:
Ne dreading harme from any foes of his,
Ne fearing salvage beasts more crueltie.
  Whilest we here wretches waile his private lack,
  And with vaine vowes do often call him back.   90

But live thou there still happie, happie spirit,
And give us leave thee here thus to lament:
Not thee that doest thy heavens joy inherit,
But our owne selves that here in dole are drent.
  Thus do we weep and waile, and wear our eies,   95
  Mourning in others, our owne miseries.

---

67 not] nor *1617*   70 wise.] ~, *1611, 1617*   76 a sleep] asleepe *1611,*
1617 Angelick] Angel-like *1611, 1617*   77 Whilest] Whilst *1611, 1617*
88 salvage] savage *1611, 1617*   89 Whilest] Whilst *1611, 1617*   93 doest] doost
1611, 1617

TRANSLATIONS

Antonius

Literary Context

The Countess of Pembroke's translation of Robert Garnier's *Marc Antoine* was the first dramatization of the story of Antony and Cleopatra in England, but in the sixteenth century it had been treated in Italy by Count Giulio Landi, *La Vita di Cleopatra* (Venice, 1551), Giambattista Giraldi Cinthio, *Cleopatra tragedia* (*c*.1542, performed for the court of Duke Ercole II d'Este; pub. 1583), Cesare de' Caesari, *Cleopatra* (Venice, 1552), and Celso Pistorelli, *Marc' Antonio e Cleopatra* (Verona, 1576). There is no evidence that Garnier used these Italian dramas. (The Countess of Pembroke, with her interest in Italian literature, was more likely to be familiar with them than with the Spanish *Marco Antonio y Cleopatra* (*c*.1582) by Diego López de Castro.) Garnier did use Étienne Jodelle's *Cléopâtre captive*, the first French tragedy (performed in Reims before King Henry II on 1 January 1552/3; pub. 1574). Garnier's Act 4 has numerous similiarities with Jodelle's Act 2, particularly in the dialogue between Caesar and Agrippa. These works, and later tragedies on the theme by Samuel Daniel and Samuel Brandon (see pp. 41 ff.), follow the model of Seneca's historical tragedy *Octavia*. Written in five acts separated by choruses, they dramatize the final section of Plutarch's *Life of Antony*. Most of these tragedies, including Garnier's, introduce a philosopher, include debate on moral issues, avoid dramatic action or interaction between the major characters, and are comprised of 'rhetorical set pieces'. None the less, they allow more scope for the exploration of human dignity than does Seneca. Their protagonists tend to be held responsible for their actions, rather than simply blaming fate, and they usually repent for the harm they have caused others.[1]

[1] Mary Morrison, 'Some Aspects of the Treatment of the Theme of Antony and Cleopatra in Tragedies of the Sixteenth Century', *JES* 4 (1974), 113–25. See also J. Leeds Barroll, *Shakespearean Tragedy: Genre, Tradition, and Change in Antony and Cleopatra* (Washington: The Folger Shakespeare Library, 1984), 35–6; John Max Patrick, who includes non-dramatic works on Cleopatra in 'The Cleopatra Theme in World Literature up to 1700', in *The Undoing of Babel: Watson Kirkconnell: The Man and His Work*, ed. J. R. C. Perkin (Toronto: McClelland and Stewart, 1975), 64–76; H. B. Charlton, *The Senecan Tradition in Renaissance Tragedy* (Manchester: Manchester UP, 1946), pp. xx–xxii.

In his prose 'Argument' Robert Garnier mentions as his sources Plutarch's *Life of Antony* and Dio Cassius' *Roman History*, Book 51. Additional details were taken from Appian's *Civil Wars* and from Josephus' *The Antiquities of the Jews*. Hill and Morrison note parallels from Horace, Catullus, Tibullus, Lucan, Ariosto, Ronsard, Virgil, and, of course, Seneca.[2] Although Pembroke was likely to have known most of these sources, such knowledge would have been unnecessary for her line-by-line translation. In her 'Argument' she mentions only Plutarch, which she used primarily in Sir Thomas North's 1579 English translation of *Plutarch's Lives of the Noble Grecians and Romanes*, the work that was also the basis for Shakespeare's Roman history plays.[3] (See p. 150.)

The story of Antony and Cleopatra was familiar not only from classical sources and Renaissance drama, but also from its recurrence as a medieval *exemplum*. Sometimes Cleopatra is celebrated because she died for love, more often she is castigated as the seductress who destroyed Antony, but she is given prominence by writers such as Boccaccio, Dante, Lydgate, and Chaucer. As Marilyn Williamson establishes, the Italian writers stress 'the imperial power struggle', while the English present lovers who have thrown away an empire.[4] Pembroke, who translated at least one of Petrarch's *Trionfi*, would have particularly noted the appearance of Cleopatra conquering Julius Caesar in *The Triumph of Love* and her appearance with Helen of Troy and Zenobia in *The Triumph of Fame*. Cleopatra is included in many paintings and tapestries based on the *Trionfi*, and her suicide by asps was frequently portrayed in medieval and Renaissance art, including works by Agostino Veneziano, Domenico del Barbiere, and Michelangelo.[5]

---

[2] Robert Garnier, *Two Tragedies: Hippolyte and Marc Antoine*, ed. Christine M. Hill and Mary G. Morrison (London: Athlone P, 1975), 172–6.

[3] North translated Jacques Amyot's French translation of Plutarch, *Les Vies des Hommes* (1559); whether Pembroke also consulted Amyot, or even Plutarch in Greek and/or Latin, as well as North's translation, is difficult to ascertain. On Shakespeare's use of North's Plutarch, see particularly *Antony and Cleopatra*, ed. David Bevington (Cambridge: Cambridge UP, 1990), 2–9.

[4] Marilyn Williamson, 'Antony and Cleopatra in the Late Middle Ages and Early Renaissance', *Michigan Academician* 5 (1972), 151. See also her *Infinite Variety: Antony and Cleopatra in Renaissance Drama and Earlier Tradition* (Mystic, Conn.: Lawrence Verry, 1974); Barbara J. Bono, *Literary Transvaluation: From Vergilian Epic to Shakespearean Tragicomedy* (Berkeley: U of California P, 1984); Lucy Hughes-Hallett, *Cleopatra: Histories, Dreams and Distortions* (New York: Harper and Row, 1990).

[5] Jean Guillaume, 'Cleopatra Nova Pandora', *Gazette des Beaux-Arts* 80 (1972), 184–94; Morrison, *JES* (1974), 115–16.

Senecan drama, often called 'closet drama', was not intended for staging at a public theatre like the Globe. Although *Marc Antoine* was successfully acted in France, the staging was probably analogous to the presentation of classical drama at the universities, without sets or costumes.[6] The humanists who followed a Senecan model deliberately downplayed narrative to emphasize rhetoric and didacticism, a combination that proved enormously popular in the sixteenth century. In France, for example, well over 200 such tragedies were written before 1640. When Pembroke translated Garnier in 1590, he was a celebrated writer in the avant-garde of the French theatre and a member of the Pléiade.

Sixteenth-century neo-Senecan drama carefully observes the unities of time, place, and action in five acts divided by the meditations of the chorus. Long soliloquies, alternating with dialogues between a protagonist and a minor character, keep the focus on moral issues. As in classical Greek drama, the playwright's primary function is to interpret the meaning of a familiar narrative—to the characters through soliloquy and to society through the meditations of the chorus. Any violent action is carefully kept off stage and related by a messenger. In *Antonius* we hear of the battle of Actium from Caesar (1402–11, 1481–1501), for example, and of Antony's death from Dircetus (1562–8, 1603–94). Other conventions include restriction to a small cast of characters, commencement of the action *in medias res*, and the inclusion of *sententiae*, or proverbial statements, as marked by roman type in Pembroke's translation (the main text of the first edition, 1592, is italic).[7]

In such a context, the extended soliloquies would take on dramatic impact. The revival of these classical models helped to move the English stage from an emphasis on action toward an emphasis on character; Shakespeare notably combined the renewed interest in soliloquy, so evident in *Antonius*, with action. In neo-Senecan drama psychological probing is done in a highly stylized manner, focusing on universal passions (usually love and/or ambition) with heavy reliance on mythological references. The Furies may be evoked, as they are in *Antonius*, to represent the evil passions that lead to war, parricide,

---

[6] Coburn Freer, 'Mary Sidney: Countess of Pembroke', in *Women Writers*, 486; Gillian Jondorf, *French Renaissance Tragedy: The Dramatic Word* (Cambridge: Cambridge UP, 1990), ch. 7; John Holyoake, *A Critical Study of the Tragedies of Robert Garnier (1545–90)* (New York: Peter Lang, 1987), 27–30, 199–234.

[7] On the structure of the play, see Holyoake, *Critical Study*, 195–7.

incest, or sacrilege.[8] Antony, for example, says that it was Maegaera who enchained him; and the fire that consumed him was not Cupid's fire but 'some furies torch', the torch that made Orestes mad with rage (54–63). Philostratus also attributes the downfall of Egypt to the Furies (241) as a symbol of the wrath of the gods.

Senecan drama makes use of three structural forms to emphasize moral issues: the chorus, the rhetor (or semi-professional speaker), and formal debates. The chorus, as in Greek drama, serves to emphasize the unities of time and place, to create a mood, to reflect on the 'moral, ethical, religious, or political implications of the action', to represent public opinion, and to provide a mythic or cosmic context for the action.[9] Less familiar to twentieth-century readers is the rhetor, whom Garnier portrays as Philostrate, described by Plutarch as an eloquent sophist. The rhetor is exactly that, a rhetorician. Garnier gives Philostrate no interaction whatever with other characters; his role is simply to make one long speech emphasizing the destruction caused by the love of Antony and Cleopatra. If the lovers were seen on their own terms, they might appear to exemplify the world well lost for love. Philostrate's role is to counter this romanticism by emphasizing the cost of their love to the people of Egypt—and even to the Roman soldiers. Furthermore, Philostrate inserts the history of Antony and Cleopatra into the mythic context of classical tragedy and epic, from the actions of the cursed House of Atreus to the Trojan war.

Formal debates, often in the form of stichomythia, also emphasize moral issues. In *Antonius*, Garnier includes such well-worn topoi as fate versus free will (474–529), clemency versus severity (1511–48), and whether or not suicide is justified (550–659). Conflict may arise between idea systems as much as between characters, a technique used effectively by Philip Sidney in the confrontation between Cecropia and Pamela in Book III of the *New Arcadia* (355–63). *Antonius* includes similar conflicts, such as the debate between Cleopatra, who accepts personal responsibility for her actions, and her servant Charmion, who blames it on Fate (459–529).

Antonius was appropriately translated and published with *A Discourse of Life and Death*, for both works are grounded in a Stoic ideal, emphasizing reason over emotion and public duty over private

[8] Donald J. Stone, *French Humanist Tragedy: A Reassessment* (Manchester: Manchester UP, 1974), 108.
[9] Jondorf, *French Renaissance Tragedy*, 67.

relationships. Advocating detachment from the external world, Stoicism saw pleasure and materialism as corrupting elements, a philosophy evident in both works. Read with *A Discourse*, *Antonius* 'becomes a play illustrating the worldly life against which de Mornay inveighs'.[10] Both works have the same 'ending end' of producing 'virtuous action' that Sidney praises in his *Defence*.[11] But whereas *A Discourse* is a philosophical work that sets out Senecan and biblical precepts, *Antonius* is poetry, in Sidney's sense of fiction, despite its basis in Plutarch's history. *A Discourse* gives 'but a wordish description' (85), baldly setting out precepts, but Antony and Cleopatra make 'notable images' of virtues and vices (81). *A Discourse* tells us that ambition and passions may destroy us; *Antonius* presents us with a 'speaking picture' (80). Like the drama *Gorboduc*, so praised by Sidney, *Antonius* 'is full of stately speeches and well-sounding phrases, climbing to the height of Seneca's style, and as full of notable morality, which it doth most delightfully teach, and so obtain the very end of poesy' (113). Sidney would no doubt view *Antonius* as the superior drama, for it is not 'faulty both in place and time' like *Gorboduc* (113).

Antonius is also connected, at least tangentially, with the *ars moriendi* tradition, for the protagonists are brought on stage after all has been lost through 'one disordred act at *Actium*' (1125). All that they can do is to decide whether to await Octavius' decree or to end their own lives. Because the drama praises their self-inflicted deaths as heroic, it is inherently more Senecan and less Christian than *A Discourse*, which emphatically rejects suicide. Garnier attempts to finesse the problem by leaving the ending ambiguous; it is not entirely clear that Cleopatra has applied the asps. Because Cleopatra does not quite die at the end of the play, Daniel wrote a continuation in *Cleopatra*, focusing on her final hours. (See p. 41.) That play, like Shakespeare's, emphasizes that her sins are atoned for by her death, for she dies like a queen, as even Caesar must admit. Making a good death was a form of heroism open even to women, one that validates 'passive endurance rather than heroic action'.[12]

Plutarch focuses on the great ones themselves, but Garnier dramatizes the story to include the consequences of their actions on the

---

[10] Beilin, *Redeeming Eve*, 128.

[11] Sidney, *Miscellaneous Prose*, 83.

[12] Lamb, 'The Countess of Pembroke and the Art of Dying', in *Women in the Middle Ages*, 213. See also Lamb, *Gender*, 115–41, and Lewalski, *Writing Women*, 191–3.

people. Pembroke emphasizes this theme by opening the 'Argument' with the enslavement of the Romans: 'After the overthrowe of *Brutus* and *Cassius*, the libertie of *Rome* being now utterly oppressed'. Having destroyed the liberty of Rome, Antony returns to Cleopatra, where his actions will cause the enslavement of Egypt. In *Marc Antoine* there are three levels of commentary, according to social class, although the great ones do retain centre stage. In the five acts of the drama Antony and Cleopatra are each given two acts to meditate on their actions, with the fourth act given to Caesar. Garnier has the philosopher Philostrate speak for Egypt at the beginning of Act 2 and incorporates into the drama five choruses that give the view of the people, 'first Egiptians, and after Romane Souldiors', as Pembroke states.

The play has a rising movement as the great ones attempt to avoid blame for their actions, a central section which demonstrates the consequences of their actions for others, and a falling movement wherein Cleopatra, at least, accepts her responsibility for the destruction of Egypt. Antony opens the play by blaming first the 'cruell Heav'ns' (1) for his downfall, and then Cleopatra, who 'only hast me vanquisht' (34). Admitting that he has turned from his pursuit of Mars to that of Venus, Antony complains that his reason was entrapped 'as the fatted swine in filthy mire' after he had drunk from the poison of Cleopatra's cup (1166). Cleopatra accepts the blame for Antony's destruction from the outset: 'I am sole cause: I did it, only I' (455). But not until Act 5 does she realize the full extent of the damage she has done, not only to Antony, but also to the innocent:

> Alas! of mine the plague and poison I
> The crowne have lost my ancestors me left,
> This Realme I have to straungers subject made,
> And robd my children of their heritage.   (1825–8)

Egypt's view is presented most forcefully through the philosopher Philostratus, the aristocrat who can foresee ruin. Plutarch says that Antony's passion for Cleopatra was enflamed. Garnier reifies that image, making the flames of passion the destructive force of the drama—a metaphor which Philostratus says has become reality for the Egyptians: 'Love, playing love, which men say kindles not | But in soft harts, hath ashes made our townes' (285–6). Like comets 'flaming through the scat'red clouds | With fiery beames' (305–6), so the love of Antony and Cleopatra has brought destruction to the people, even as Paris's love for Helen brought the destruction of Troy.

In addition to the perspectives of the rulers and the aristocracy, Garnier gives the people their own voice in the choruses. As literary critics have long acknowledged, the countess's most dramatic poetry appears in her reworking of these choruses.[13] (See p. 147.) After Antony's opening soliloquy, attempting to avoid responsibility for his actions, the chorus of Egyptian people argues about free will and predestination. The philosophical debate is ironic, for their fate has been determined by their rulers; for themselves they can foresee only destruction. In Act 2 the chorus speaks twice. After Philostratus warns that their ruler's pleasure will destroy the realm, the chorus responds by singing of the cleansing powers of lamentation; completely helpless before the actions of their rulers, they find that lamentation is all that is left for them. Then, after Cleopatra admits her responsibility for Antony's fall, the chorus gives a moving lament for Egypt, 'O swete fertile land' of the Nile, which will be enslaved by the Roman Tiber as a consequence of their queen's love for Antony (751). Like the Psalmist, the chorus can find comfort in meditations on revenge and mutability, for someday Rome will also be destroyed by 'the pittie-wanting fire' which will turn it 'to humble ashes', even as Troy was destroyed (844–6). After Antony determines to commit suicide, the chorus meditates on the benefits of death, in a Senecan passage not unlike the sentiments of *A Discourse*. In Act 4, the chorus, now of Roman soldiers, mourns the cost of civil war. Because their rulers fight against each other, 'Heaps of us scattred lie, | Making the straunger plaines | Fatt with our bleeding raines' (1750–2). As in his other tragedies, Garnier had stressed the cost of war for people on both sides of the conflict. Here, even the conquering Roman legions long for peace. There is no chorus in Act 5; Egypt has been conquered, so the focus returns to Cleopatra as she contemplates the full consequences of her actions.

Character is developed through soliloquies and through dialogue with attendants, rather than through action. The character of Antony, whose god was acknowledged to be Bacchus, the god of wine and revelry, is self-revealed in the opening soliloquy:

> Thy vertue dead: thy glory made alive
> So ofte by martiall deeds is gone in smoke:
> Since then the *Baies* so well thy forehead knewe

---

[13] See, for example, Freer, 'Mary Sidney: Countess of Pembroke', in *Women Writers*, 486–9, and *The Poetics of Jacobean Drama* (Baltimore: The Johns Hopkins UP, 1981), 206–8.

> To Venus mirtles yeelded have their place:
> Trumpets to pipes: field tents to courtly bowers:
> Launces and Pikes to daunces and to feastes. (66–71)

Attributing his downfall to Cleopatra, Antony sees himself as 'A slave ... unto her feeble face' (17) and concludes that he is 'scarse maister of thy selfe | Late maister of so many nations' (130–1). He describes Cleopatra as a 'faire Sorceres' despoiling reason by her 'poisned cuppes' (83), a reference to Circe made more explicit in Act 3, wherein he accuses her of entrapping his reason (1166–72). Antony, who believed himself descended from Hercules, compares himself to Hercules 'Spinning at distaffe... in maides attire', as his unused arms hang on the wall (1233–7). Cleopatra is not presented merely as an enchantress, however. That is Antony's perspective. She is also presented as a concerned mother (1828–95) and even as a faithful wife who vows to prove her love by death (1967–2024), although there is considerable ambiguity in the moral judgement of Cleopatra.[14]

Garnier's *Marc Antoine*, with its primary focus on the character of Cleopatra, may have appealed to the countess as a political statement on the dangers of a ruler's submission to passion and the cost of civil war, or as a meditation on the female heroism of dying well, or as the portrait of a strong woman as queen, as wife, and as mother. Perhaps even more important to Pembroke, as Victor Skretkowicz suggests, was Cleopatra's renowned verbal skill and particularly her knowledge of languages.[15] Although 'Nought lives so faire' (717) as she, her voice and her knowledge of languages are emphasized over her beauty, which is nothing compared to 'th'e'nchaunting skilles | Of her cælestiall Sp'rite, hir training speache', whether she sings 'Or hearing sceptred kings embassadors | Answer to eache in his owne language make' (727–32). Certainly this queen, as a powerful rhetorician in each of her many languages, would be an appropriate model for a woman translator.

---

[14] Tina Krontiris, *Oppositional Voices: Women as Writers and Translators of Literature in the English Renaissance* (London and New York: Routledge, 1992), 69–73; Howard B. Norland, 'Englishing Garnier: Mary Sidney's *Antonie* and Daniels' *Cleopatra*', in *Tudor Theatre: Emotion in the Theatre* (Collection Theta 3. Bern: Peter Lang, 1996), 161–9; May, *Courtier Poets*, 168–9; and Eve Sanders, *Inscribing Selves: Gender and Literacy in English Public Theatre* (Cambridge: Cambridge UP, forthcoming).

[15] Victor Skretkowicz, ' "Minced Words": Mary Sidney's *Antonius* and English Philhellenism' (forthcoming).

Fidelity to Originals

Pembroke was a scholarly translator, taking care always to consult the most authoritative texts. For *Antonius*, she used the 1585 French text, known to have been substantially revised by the author, who was still living when she began her translation. For example, she follows the 1585 edition in omitting detailed passages included in Robert Garnier's 1578 edition at lines 458, 498, 1558, 1570, 1663, and 1743.[1] (See 'Transmission and Authority of Texts'.)

Her skilful translation places her, Victor Skretkowicz argues, 'at the forefront of reformers of English dramatic rhetoric and style; and indeed, of English literary style in a much broader sense'.[2] In the deliberate simplicity of her phrasing, she follows the Plutarchan model rather than the ornate style of the Greek romances used by her brother Philip in his *Arcadia*. Pembroke chose to render the drama in blank verse, demonstrating the power and flexibility of the form for drama in the same year as Marlowe's *Tamburlaine* was printed.[3] She thereby translates Garnier's alexandrines (duodecasyllabic lines), the most common metre in French, into iambic pentameter, the most natural line in English. Whereas Garnier had used rhyming couplets, alternating masculine and feminine rhymes, in the body of the drama Pembroke normally uses rhyme only for emphasis, as at the close of paragraphs, as well as for stichomythia and *sententiae*. Her choruses are rendered in a freer translation than the rest of the drama. She nevertheless retains Garnier's rhyme scheme in two of the choruses and demonstrates technical virtuosity by distilling most of the choruses into the shorter lines of iambic trimeter. (See 'Table of Verse Forms'.)

Although the Countess of Pembroke is usually an accurate translator, faithful to her original in style and mood, her 'Argument' for *Antonius* is not a translation. A discussion of the tale of Antony and Cleopatra taken as much from Plutarch as from Garnier, it occasion-

---

[1] *M. Antoine, tragedie, par Rob. Garnier…A Paris*, Par Mamert Patisson, au logis de Rob. Estienne (1578); *Les tragedies de Robert Garnier conseiller du roy…A Paris*, Par Mamert Patisson…chez Robert Estienne (1585).

[2] Victor Skretkowicz, '"Minced Words": Mary Sidney's *Antonius* and English Philhellenism' (forthcoming).

[3] Buxton, *Sidney*, 199. Cerasano and Wynne-Davies, who characterize Pembroke's translation as 'remarkably free', suggest that she was 'determined to undermine the traditional neo-Senecan language with the more contemporary blank verse': *Renaissance Drama by Women: Texts and Documents*, ed. S. P. Cerasano and Marion Wynne-Davies (London and New York: Routledge, 1996), 15, 17.

ally echoes the phrasing of Sir Thomas North's 1579 translation of Plutarch's *The Lives of the Noble Grecians and Romanes*. For example, both North and the countess explain the marriage of Antony and Octavia as an effort to create 'amitie' between Antony and Octavius; both say that Antony was not master of himself; both refer to the engines Antony unfortunately had left behind when he attacked the walls of Phraate; both describe the pitiful sight as Cleopatra 'trussed' up Antony into the monument. She probably also consulted Amyot's French translation of Plutarch, the immediate source for both Garnier and North, since she occasionally echoes the French, '*cordes*' as in Amyot, for example, instead of 'ropes' as in North.

The countess gives more background for the story of Antony and Cleopatra than Garnier does, perhaps expecting an English audience to be less familiar with this story that had been frequently dramatized in France and in Italy. In her adaptation of the 'Argument' she omits minor characters, such as Fulvia and Eros, to focus on the actions and motivations of Antony and Cleopatra. In her opening sentence, the countess translates two phrases of Garnier, omitting insignificant details to insert the crucial information that the Empire was divided between Octavius Caesar and Antony. She also condenses the explanation of Antony's marriage to Octavia, omits mention of his previous marriage to Fulvia to avoid confusion, and gives a brief explanation of his campaign against the Parthians, summarizing Plutarch. Her second sentence outlines the history of his former dalliance with Cleopatra, summarizing as 'exquisite delightes and sumptuous pleasures' the details that are so vivid in Plutarch, and echoing North's descriptions of 'The wonderfull sumptuousnes of Cleopatra...going unto Antonius' (sig. NNNN5, marginal note), or 'Cleopatraes sumptuousnes and finenesse' (sig. NNNN5ᵛ). In condensing this passage she omits Garnier's phrase '*la singuliere beauté de Cleopatre, Roine d'Egypte, arrivee en Cilice en royale magnificence*', replacing it with the identification, '*Cleopatra* Queene of Aegipt'.[4] Pembroke adds an account of Antony's return to Alexandria, not mentioned by Garnier, and omits reference to '*l'amour de ceste Royne*' that had made '*si profondes breches en son coeur*'. Her next phrase is almost a translation: '*César print occasion*

---

[4] See Witherspoon, *Garnier*, 86. Kim Hall argues that Pembroke's omission of this description of Cleopatra's beauty may be racially motivated: *Things of Darkness: Economies of Race and Gender in Early Modern England* (Ithaca, NY: Cornell UP, 1995), 184. Cleopatra, however, is later described as having hair of 'flaming golde' (724) and skin the colour of 'marble' (740).

de s'offenser et de luy faire guerre' becomes 'This occasion *Octavius* tooke of taking armes against him'. She then returns to summary for the account of the battle at Actium, omitting much of Garnier's detail and adding the conclusion that he left to Octavius 'the greatest victorye which in any Sea Battell hath beene heard off', thereby again providing historical information for the English reader. Both Pembroke and Garnier mention Antony's retreat to Alexandria, but the countess adds from Plutarch the detail that Caesar's siege began 'the next spring'. Pembroke's statement that '*Antony* finding all that he trusted to faile him' echoes Garnier, '*se voyant abandonné de ses gens*', but she has omitted the earlier statement that gave Garnier's phrase its resonance: Antony is described at the battle of Actium as '*abandonnant ses gens*'. The countess omits Garnier's description of Cleopatra's feelings ('*sa fureur et désespoir*') as she retires to her monument. Both say that she sent Antony word that she was dead, but the countess omits the account, present in both Plutarch and Garnier, that Antony first attempted suicide by commanding his servant Eros to kill him; instead, Eros kills himself and falls at his master's feet. Both Garnier and the countess include Antony's deadly self-inflicted wound, the messenger who brought Antony to Cleopatra, and her efforts to hoist up the dying Antony through a window, but the countess adds an explanation of her motivation for not opening the door, deduced from Cleopatra's later efforts to avoid capture: 'least she should be made a prisoner to the *Romaines*, and carried in *Cæsars* triumph'. In her final sentence she translates Garnier's attribution to Plutarch, but she omits the final reference to 'Dion' (Dio Cassius' *Roman History*), a work less familiar to her audience.

For the list of actors Pembroke gives Latin names for the characters and omits or changes the epithets used to describe them—Lucilius and Agrippa are not distinguished as friends of Antony or Caesar, Dircetus becomes a messenger instead of an archer, and the '*femmes d'honneur*' become merely '*Cleopatras* women'. She alters the presentation of 'The Actors' for Acts 1–3 (Garnier's first column) from order of appearance to order of importance, thereby listing Cleopatra directly after Antony. Her listing for Acts 4–5 matches the order of Garnier except that she omits reference to the Chorus, given by Garnier as two separate groups, the Egyptians and the Soldiers of Caesar. Instead, she mentions in her 'Argument' that the chorus changes persons, 'first Egiptians, and after Romane Souldiors'. Her wording may suggest that the entire cast would read the choruses together, so that no additional cast members would be needed. Her addition of the phrase 'The Stage supposed Alexandria' in her 'Argument' might be taken to indicate that she envisioned stage production, but she probably used the term 'Stage' metaphorically. (See *Antonius*: 'Literary Context'.)

Some debt to North is found in the text as well. For example, 'So pittifull a sight was never sene' (1651) echoes North, 'they never saw so pitiefull a sight' (sig. PPPP5ᵛ), more closely than Garnier, '*Jamais rien si piteux au monde ne fut veu*' (1634), although she retains the passive construction of Garnier. There are many other verbal parallels. For example, both describe Cleopatra's 'stooping' head as she pulls Antony into the tomb (1662; North sig. PPPP5ᵛ), and both describe Caesar's desire to have Cleopatra beautify his triumph (1727; North sig. PPPP6). Occasionally Pembroke will incorporate a detail from another of the *Lives*. For example, her description of the Parthians' ability to shoot arrows backwards as they ride, 'back-shooting *Parthians*' (467), comes from Plutarch's *Life of Crassus* (sig. FFF2), not from Garnier, who simply calls them archers.

Her line-by-line translation is generally so literal that it could 'constitute a reliable crib for Garnier's French', as Freer observes.[5] Like her prose translation, her *Antonius* retains most of the original rhetorical devices, including frequent parallelism (as in 2–3, 100–1, 540–4, 1173–6). She normally retains Garnier's repetition, as 'Dead, dead' (1567), or 'Die will I straight now, now streight will I die' (1993), but sometimes she adds repetition, as 'hardlie, hardlie' (1493). Sometimes she even retains the French rhyme words, as 'paine' and 'inhumaine' (558–9) or '*Benignitie*' and '*Severitie*' (1535–6).

There are, however, a few changes in the text. Most significantly, she adds lines at 1103–4, and the printer omits a line between 1424 and 1425: '*Maint trait de foudre aigu desserra sur Typhé*'. She occasionally transposes lines, particularly in the freer choruses, as at 161–2 and 215–16. Other alterations are minor, such as omitting the implication of flattery in Garnier, '*les blandices*', translating it simply as 'the woords' (102). Sometimes she adds a metaphor to her original, as the ship metaphor (1001) and the thirst metaphor (1022). More often, she expands a metaphor, such as Fortune's wheel (1136). Occasionally she will add clarification, as 'whose hand' (496), or omit a phrase, like '*au pied*' (503; Garnier, 496) or '*taut il est outrageux*' (1108; Garnier, 997).

---

[5] Coburn Freer, 'Mary Sidney: Countess of Pembroke', in *Women Writers*, 486–7. On her translation, see Sidney, Mary. *Antonie*, ed. Luce, 41–7; Buxton, *Sidney*, 199; and Brennan, *Literary Patronage*, 67.

Although she makes fewer alterations in the poetry than in her prose translation, she does add an occasional adjective, like 'frowning' (570), 'dolefull' (665), or the three epithets in line 1043, or the phrase 'Mother Earth' (1418). She also uses compounds, as 'Father-like' (764), 'Skie-coullor'd' (800), or 'hoary-headed' (1677). Occasionally, she adds her typical word play, as the alliterated oxymoron 'coward courage' for '*courage mal*' (76). She frequently replaces an epithet with a name or vice versa. She omits several proper names given in Garnier, such as Salmoneus (Garnier, 248), Philomel (Garnier, 328–38), Niobe (Garnier, 363), Cinyras (Garnier, 371), and Omphale (Garnier, 1216–31). '*L'Acheron*' becomes the 'joyles lake' (548) , '*destins*' become the 'fatall Sisters' (41), and Hercules becomes '*Alcides* bloud' (1075). Rarely she will add proper names, as '*Clotho*', the fate (670); '*Romulus*' (1458) where Garnier had used the more obscure epithet 'Quirin'; or '*Titan*' (202) or '*Phœbus*' (753) for '*le soleil*'. The names Jove and Jupiter are used interchangeably, as the metre requires (as in 1466).

She also makes a few small changes in characterization. For example, Garnier emphasizes Cleopatra's marriage to Antony when she calls him '*mon espous*'; Pembroke has simply 'He' (595), yet we cannot draw large conclusions from that omission because a few lines later she emphasizes Cleopatra's wifely role when she uses the phrase 'widdowe tombe' (629) in place of Garnier's '*un tombeau solitaire*'. She omits the adjective '*Argolique*' (from Argos), which emphasized the Grecian, as well as Egyptian, identity of the goddess Isis (277), associated with Cleopatra. She also omits Cleopatra's determination to follow Antony even to Hell, '*aux Enfers pallissans*' (Garnier, 650), perhaps for theological reasons. In the closing line, she avoids the nonheroic connotations of Garnier's final word, '*vomissant*', as Cleopatra kisses the corpse Antony and prays that her 'soule may flowe' to him as she dies.

Despite the fidelity of her translation to her original, Pembroke uses metre, rhyme, and her characteristic rhetorical devices—parallelism, figures of repetition, compound words, expansion of metaphors, alliteration, and word play—to achieve a distinctive style of English verse.[6]

[6] As in her *Discourse*, there are changes in type and punctuation. In the 1592 *Antonius*, roman type is used for the *sententiae* where the French edition uses double inverted commas. Through much of the first chorus the French edition also uses double inverted commas, which are (wisely) ignored in the English edition.

Antonius

The Argument

After the overthrowe of *Brutus* and *Cassius*, the libertie of *Rome* being now utterly oppressed, and the Empire setled in the hands of *Octavius Cæsar* and *Marcus Antonius*, (who for knitting a straiter bonde of amitie betweene them, had taken to wife *Octavia* the sister of *Cæsar*)
5 *Antonius* undertooke a journey against the Parthians, with intent to regaine on them the honor wonne by them from the Romains, at the discomfiture and slaughter of *Crassus*. But comming in his journey into Siria, the places renewed in his remembrance the long intermitted love of *Cleopatra* Queene of Aegipt: who before time had
10 both in Cilicia and at Alexandria, entertained him with all the exquisite delightes and sumptuous pleasures, which a great Prince and voluptuous Lover could to the uttermost desire. Whereupon omitting his enterprice, he made his returne to Alexandria, againe falling to his former loves, without any regard of his vertuous wife *Octavia*, by
15 whom nevertheles he had excellent Children. This occasion *Octavius* tooke of taking armes against him: and preparing a mighty fleet, encountred him at Actium, who also had assembled to that place a great number of Gallies of his own, besides 60. which *Cleopatra* brought with her from Aegipt. But at the very beginning of the battell
20 *Cleopatra* with all her Gallies betooke her to flight, which *Antony* seeing could not but follow; by his departure leaving to *Octavius* the greatest victorye which in any Sea Battell hath beene heard off. Which he not negligent to pursue, followes them the next spring, and besiedgeth them within Alexandria, where *Antony* finding all
25 that he trusted to faile him, beginneth to growe jealouse and to suspect *Cleopatra*. She thereupon enclosed her selfe with two of her women in a monument she had before caused to be built, thence sends him woord she was dead: which he beleeving for truth, gave himselfe with his S+Swoord a deadly wound: but died not untill a mes-
30 senger came from *Cleopatra* to have him brought to her to the tombe. Which she not daring to open least she should be made a prisoner to

the *Romaines*, and carried in *Cæsars* triumph, cast downe a corde from
an high window, by the which (her women helping her) she trussed
up *Antonius* halfe dead, and so got him into the monument. The
Stage supposed Alexandria: the Chorus, first Egiptians, and after   35
Romane Souldiors. The Historie to be read at large in *Plutarch* in
the life of *Antonius*.

The Actors.

Antonius.
Cleopatra.   40
Eras and ⎤
Charmion.⎦ *Cleopatras* women.
Philostratus a Philosopher.
Lucilius.
Diomede Secretary to *Cleopatra*.   45
Octavius Cæsar.
Agrippa.
Euphron, teacher of *Cleopatras* children.
Children of *Cleopatra*.
Dircetus the Messenger.   50

[Act. 1.]

Antonius.

Since cruell Heav'ns against me obstinate,
Since all mishappes of the round engin doo
Conspire my harme: since men, since powers divine,
Aire, earth, and Sea are all injurious: 5
And that my Queene her self, in whome I liv'd,
The Idoll of my hart, doth me pursue;
It's meete I dye. For her have I forgone
My Country, *Cæsar* unto warre provok'd
(For just revenge of Sisters wrong my wife,   10
Who mov'de my Queene (ay me!) to jealousie)
For love of her, in her allurements caught
Abandon'd life, I honor have despisde,

Disdain'd my freends, and of statelye Rome
15   Despoilde the Empire of her best attire,
Contemn'd that power that made me so much fear'd,
A slave become unto her feeble face.
    O cruell, traitres, woman most unkinde,
Thou dost, forsworne, my love and life betraie:
20   And giv'st me up to ragefull enemie,
Which soone (ô foole!) will plague thy perjurye.
    Yelded *Pelusium* on this Countries shore,
Yelded thou hast my Shippes and men of warre,
That nought remaines (so destitute am I)
25   But these same armes which on my back I weare.
Thou should'st have had them too, and me unarm'de
Yeelded to *Cæsar* naked of defence.
Which while I beare let *Cæsar* never thinke
Triumph of me shall his proud chariot grace
30   Not think with me his glory to adorne,
On me alive to use his victorie.
    Thou only *Cleopatra* triumph hast,
Thou only hast my freedome servile made,
Thou only hast me vanquisht: not by force
35   (For forste I cannot be) but by sweete baites
Of thy eyes graces, which did gaine so fast
upon my libertie, that nought remain'd.
None els hencefoorth, but thou my dearest Queene,
Shall glorie in commaunding *Antonie*.
40   Have *Cæsar* fortune and the Gods his freends,
To him have Jove and fatall sisters given
The Scepter of the earth: he never shall
Subject my life to his obedience.
But when that Death, my glad refuge, shall have
45   Bounded the course of my unstedfast life,
And frosen corps under a marble colde
Within tombes bosome widdowe of my soule:
Then at his will let him it subject make:
Then what he will let *Cæsar* doo with me:
50   Make me limme after limme be rent: make me
My buriall take in sides of *Thracian* wolfe.

Poore *Antonie*! alas what was the day,
The daies of losse that gained thee thy love!
Wretch *Antony*! since then *Mægæra* pale
With Snakie haires enchain'd thy miserie.   55
The fire thee burnt was never *Cupids* fire
(For Cupid beares not such a mortall brand)
It was some furies torch, *Orestes* torche,
which sometimes burnt his mother-murdering soule
(When wandring madde, rage boiling in his bloud,   60
He fled his fault which folow'd as he fled)
kindled within his bones by shadow pale
Of mother slaine return'd from Stygian lake.

    Antony, poore *Antony*! since that daie
Thy olde good hap did farre from thee retire.   65
Thy vertue dead: thy glory made alive
So ofte by martiall deeds is gone in smoke:
Since then the *Baies* so well thy forehead knewe
To Venus mirtles yeelded have their place:
Trumpets to pipes: field tents to courtly bowers: 70
Launces and Pikes to daunces and to feastes.
Since then, ô wretch! in stead of bloudy warres
Thou shouldst have made upon the Parthian Kings
For Romain honor filde by *Crassus* foile,
Thou threw'st thy Curiace off, and fearfull healme,   75
With coward courage unto *Ægipts* Queene
In haste to runne, about her necke to hang
Languishing in her armes thy Idoll made:
In summe given up to *Cleopatras* eies.
Thou breakest at length from thence, as one encharm'd   80
Breakes from th'enchaunter that him strongly helde.
For thy first reason (spoyling of their force
the poisned cuppes of thy faire Sorceres)
Recur'd thy sprite: and then on every side
Thou mad'st againe the earth with Souldiours swarme.   85
All Asia hidde: Euphrates bankes do tremble
To see at once so many Romanes there
Breath horror, rage, and with a threatning eie

54 then] *om. 1595*   59 which] Which *1595*   84 sprite] sperit *1595*
87 Romanes] *1595*; Komanes *1592*

In mighty squadrons crosse his swelling streames.
90 Nought seene but horse, and fier sparkling armes:
Nought heard but hideous noise of muttring troupes.
The *Parth*, the *Mede*, abandoning their goods
Hide them for feare in hilles of *Hircanie*,
Redoubting thee. Then willing to besiege
95 The great *Phraate* head of *Media*,
Thou campedst at her walles with vaine assault,
Thy engins fit (mishap!) not thither brought.

So long thou stai'st, so long thou doost thee rest,
So long thy love with such things nourished
100 Reframes, reformes it selfe and stealingly
Retakes his force and rebecomes more great.
For of thy Queene the lookes, the grace, the woords,
Sweetenes, alurements, amorous delights,
Entred againe thy soule, and day and night,
105 In watch, in sleepe, her Image follow'd thee:
Not dreaming but of her, repenting still
That thou for warre hadst such a Goddes left.

Thou car'st no more for *Parth*, nor *Parthian* bow,
Sallies, assaults, encounters, shocks, alarmes,
110 For diches, rampiers, wards, entrenched grounds:
Thy only care is sight of *Nilus* streames,
Sight of that face whose guilefull semblant doth
(Wandring in thee) infect thy tainted hart.
Her absence thee besottes: each hower, each hower
115 Of staie, to thee impatient seemes an age.
Enough of conquest, praise thou deem'st enough,
If soone enough the bristled fieldes thou see
Of fruitfull *Ægipt*, and the stranger floud
Thy Queenes faire eyes (another *Pharos*) lights.
120 Returned loe, dishonoured, despisde,
In wanton love a woman thee misleades
Sunke in foule sinke: meane while respecting nought
Thy wife *Octavia* and her tender babes,
Of whom the long contempt against thee whets
125 The sword of *Cæsar* now thy Lord become.

Lost thy great Empire, all those goodly townes
Reverenc'd thy name as rebells now thee leave:
Rise against thee, and to the ensignes flocke

Of conqu'ring *Cæsar*, who enwalles thee round
Cag'd in thy holde, scarse maister of thy selfe,   130
Late maister of so many nations.
    Yet, yet, which is of grief extreamest grief,
Which is yet of mischiefe highest mischiefe,
It's *Cleopatra* alas! alas, it's she,
It's she augments the torment of thy paine,   135
Betraies thy love, thy life (alas!) betraies,
Cæsar to please, whose grace she seekes to gaine:
With thought her Crowne to save, and fortune make
Onely thy foe which common ought have beene.
    If her I alwaies lov'd, and the first flame   140
Of her heart-killing love shall burne me last:
Justly complaine I she disloyall is,
Nor constant is, even as I constant am,
To comfort my mishap, despising me
No more, then when the heavens favour'd me.   145
    But ah! by nature women wav'ring are,
Each moment changing and rechanging mindes.
Unwise, who blinde in them, thinkes loyaltie
Ever to finde in beauties company.

           Chorus.   150

    The boyling tempest still
      Makes not Sea waters fome:
      Nor still the Northern blast
      Disquiets quiet streames:
      Nor who his chest to fill   155
      Sayles to the morning beames,
      On waves winde tosseth fast
      Still kepes his Ship from home.
    Nor *Jove* still downe doth cast
      Inflam'd with bloudie ire   160
      On man, on tree, on hill,
      His darts of thundring fire:
      Nor still the heat doth last
      On face of parched plaine:

---

136 (alas!)] ∧~!) *1592; 1595*   152 ff. *initial letters not capitalized in 152–4, 156–8, 160–6,*
168–74, 217–22, 224–30, 232–8 in 1595

165   Nor wrinkled colde doth still
            On frozen furrowes raigne.
        But still as long as we
            In this low world remaine,
            Mishapps our dayly mates
170   Our lives do entertaine:
            And woes which beare no dates
            Still pearch upon our heads,
            None go, but streight will be
            Some greater in their Steads.
175   Nature made us not free
            When first she made us live:
            When we began to be,
            To be began our woe:
            Which growing evermore
180   As dying life dooth growe,
            Do more and more us greeve,
            And tire us more and more.
        No stay in fading states,
            For more to height they retch,
185   Their fellow miseries
            The more to height do stretch.
            They clinge even to the crowne,
            And threatning furious wise
            From tirannizing pates
190   Do often pull it downe.
        In vaine on waves untride
            to shunne them go we should
            To *Scythes* and *Massagetes*
            Who neare the Pole reside:
195   In vaine to boiling sandes
            Which *Phœbus* battry beates,
            For with us still they would
            Cut seas and compasse landes.
        The darknes no more sure
200   To joyne with heavy night:
            The light which guildes the dayes
            To follow *Titan* pure:

192 to] To *1595*   193-4 *not indented in* 1595

No more the shadow light
The body to ensue:
Then wretchednes alwaies   205
Us wretches to pursue.
O blest who never breath'd,
Or whome with pittie mov'de,
Death from his cradle reav'de,
And swadled in his grave: 210
And blessed also he
(As curse may blessing have)
Who low and living free
No princes charge hath prov'de.
By stealing sacred fire   215
Prometheus then unwise,
Provoking Gods to ire,
The heape of ills did sturre,
And sicknes pale and colde
Our ende which onward spurre,   220
To plague our hands too bolde
To filch the wealth of Skies.
In heavens hate since then
Of ill with ill enchain'd
We race of mortall men   225
full fraught our breasts have borne:
And thousand thousand woes
Our heav'nly soules now thorne,
Which free before from those
No earthly passion pain'd.   230
Warre and warres bitter cheare
Now long time with us staie,
And feare of hated foe
Still still encreaseth sore:
Our harmes worse dayly growe,   235
Lesse yesterdaye they were
Then now, and will be more
To morowe then to daye.

212 (As] (~ *1595*;)~ *1592*   230 No∧] ~! *1592*; no! *1595*

Act. 2.

240　　　　　　　　*Philostratus.*

What horrible furie, what cruell rage,
O *Ægipt* so extremely thee torments?
Hast thou the Gods so angred by thy fault?
Hast thou against them some such crime conceiv'd,
245　　That their engrained hand lift up in threats
They should desire in thy hart bloud to bathe?
And that their burning wrath which nought can quench
Should pittiles on us still lighten downe?
　　We are not hew'n out of the monst'rous masse
250　　Of *Giantes* those, which heavens wrack conspir'd:
Ixions race, false prater of his loves:
Nor yet of him who fained lightnings found:
Nor cruell *Tantalus*, nor bloudie *Atreus*,
Whose cursed banquet for *Thyestes* plague
255　　Made the beholding Sunne for horrour turne
His backe, and backward from his course returne:
And hastning his wing-footed horses race
Plunge him in sea for shame to hide his face:
While sulleine night upon the wondring world
260　　For mid-daies light her starrie mantle cast,
　　But what we be, what ever wickednes
By us is done, Alas! with what more plagues,
More eager torments could the Gods declare
To heaven and earth that us they hatefull holde?
265　　With Souldiors, strangers, horrible in armes
Our land is hidde, our people drown'd in teares.
But terror here and horror, nought is seene:
And present death prizing our life each hower.
Hard at our ports and at our porches waites
270　　Our conquering foe: harts faile us, hopes are dead:
Our Queene laments: and this great Emperour
Sometime (would now they did) whom worlds did feare,
Abandoned, betraid, now mindes no more
But from his evils by hast'ned death to passe.

260 cast,] ~. *1595*

Come you poore people tir'de with ceasles plaints   275
With teares and sighes make mournfull sacrifice
On *Isis* altars: not our selves to save,
But soften *Cæsar* and him piteous make
To us, his pray: that so his lenitie
May change our death into captivitie.   280
    Strange are the evils the fates on us have brought,
O but alas! how farre more strange the cause!
Love, love (alas, who ever would have thought?)
Hath lost this Realme inflamed with his fire.
Love, playing love, which men say kindles not   285
But in soft harts, hath ashes made our townes.
And his sweet shafts, with whose shot none are kill'd,
Which ulcer not, with deaths our lands have fill'd,
    Such was the bloudie, murdring, hellish love
Possest thy hart faire false guest *Priams* Sonne,   290
Fi'ring a brand which after made to burne
The *Trojan* towers by *Græcians* ruinate.
By this love, *Priam*, *Hector*, *Troilus*,
Memnon, *Deiphobus*, *Glaucus*, thousands mo,
Whome redd *Scamanders* armor clogged streames   295
Roll'd into Seas, before their dates are dead.
So plaguie he, so many tempests raiseth,
So murdring he, so many Cities raiseth,
When insolent, blinde, lawles, orderles,
With madd delights our sence he entertaines.   300
    All knowing Gods our wracks did us foretell
By signes in earth, by signes in starry Sphæres:
Which should have mov'd us, had not destinie
With too strong hand warped our miserie.
The *Comets* flaming through the scat'red clouds   305
With fiery beames, most like unbroaded haires:
The fearefull dragon whistling at the bankes,
And holie *Apis* ceaseles bellowing
(As never erst) and shedding endles teares:
Bloud raining downe from heav'n in unknow'n showers: 310
Our Gods darke faces overcast with woe,
And dead mens Ghosts appearing in the night.

291 Fi'ring] Firing *1595*   294 *Deiphobus*] *Deiphæbus 1595*

Yea even this night while all the Cittie stoode
Opprest with terror, horror, servile feare,
315   Deepe silence over all: the sounds were heard
Of diverse songs, and divers instruments,
Within the voide of aire: and howling noise,
Such as madde *Bacchus* priests in *Bacchus* feasts
On *Nisa* make: and (seem'd) the company,
320   Our Cittie lost, went to the enemie.
        So we forsaken both of Gods and men,
So are we in the mercy of our foes:
And we hencefoorth obedient must become
To lawes of them who have us overcome.

325   *Chorus.*

Lament we our mishaps,
        Drowne we with teares our woe:
For Lamentable happes
Lamented easie growe:
330   And much lesse torment bring
                Then when they first did spring.
We want that wofull song,
        Wherwith wood-musiques Queene
Doth ease her woes, among,
335   fresh springtimes bushes greene,
                On pleasant branche alone
                Renewing auntient mone.
We want that monefull sounde,
        That pratling *Progne* makes
340   On fieldes of *Thracian* ground,
        Or streames of *Thracian* lakes:
                To empt her brest of paine
                For *Itys* by her slaine.
Though *Halcyons* doo still,
345   Bewailing *Ceyx* lot,
        The Seas with plainings fill
        Which his dead limmes have got,

---

330 ff. *initial letters not capitalized in* 330–1, 333–4, 336–7, 339–43, 345–9, 351–5, 357–61, 363–7, 369–73, 375–9, 381, 383–5, 387–9; *single indentation of* 330–1, 336–7, 342–3, 348–9, 354–5, 360–1, 366–7, 372–3, 378–9, 384–5 *in 1595*

Not ever other grave
Then tombe of waves to have:
And though the birde in death   350
That most *Meander* loves
So swetely sighes his breath
When death his fury proves,
As almost softs his heart,
And almost blunts his dart: 355
Yet all the plaints of those,
Nor all their tearfull larmes,
Cannot content our woes,
Nor serve to waile the harmes,
In soule which we, poore we,   360
To feele enforced be.
Nor they of *Phœbus* bredd
In teares can doo so well,
They for their brother shedd,
Who into *Padus* fell,   365
Rash guide of chariot cleare
Surveiour of the yeare.
Nor she whom heav'nly powers
To weping rocke did turne,
Whose teares distill in showers,   370
And shew she yet doth mourne,
Where with his toppe to Skies
Mount *Sipylus* doth rise.
Nor weping drops which flowe
From barke of wounded tree,   375
That *Myrrhas* shame do showe
With ours compar'd may be,
To quench her loving fire
Who durst embrace her sire.
Nor all the howlings made   380
On *Cybels* sacred hill
By Eunukes of her trade,
Who *Atys*, *Atys* still
With doubled cries resound,
Which *Echo* makes rebound.   385

376 do] doth *1595*

Our plaints no limits stay,
  Nor more then doo our woes:
Both infinitely straie
And neither measure knowes.
390   *In measure let them plaine:*
    Who measur'd griefes sustaine.

Cleopatra. Eras. Charmion. Diomede.

Cleopatra.

That I have thee betraid, deare *Antonie*,
395   My life, my soule, my Sunne? I had such thought?
That I have thee betraide my Lord, my King?
That I would breake my vowed faith to thee?
Leave thee? deceive thee? yeelde thee to the rage
Of mightie foe? I ever had that hart?
400   Rather sharpe lightning lighten on my head:
Rather may I to deepest mischiefe fall:
Rather the opened earth devower me:
Rather fierce *Tigers* feed them on my flesh:
Rather, ô rather let our *Nilus* send,
405   To swallow me quicke, some weeping *Crocodile*.
    And didst thou then suppose my royall hart
Had hatcht, thee to ensnare, a faithles love?
And changing minde, as Fortune changed cheare,
I would weake thee, to winne the stronger, loose?
410   O wretch! ô caitive! ô too cruell happe!
And did not I sufficient losse sustaine
Loosing my Realme, loosing my liberty,
My tender of-spring, and the joyfull light
Of beamy Sunne, and yet, yet loosing more
415   Thee *Antony* my care, if I loose not
What yet remain'd? thy love alas! thy love,
More deare then Scepter, children, freedome, light.
    So ready I to row in *Charons* barge,
Shall leese the joy of dying in thy love:
420   So the sole comfort of my miserie
To have one tombe with thee is me bereft.

So I in shady plaines shall plaine alone,
Not (as I hop'd) companion of thy mone,
O height of griefe! *Eras.* why with continuall cries
Your griefull harmes doo you exasperate?   425
Torment your selfe with murthering complaints?
Straine your weake breast so oft, so vehemently?
Water with teares this faire alablaster?
With sorrowes sting so many beauties wound?
Come of so many Kings want you the hart   430
Bravely, stoutly, this tempest to resist?
Cl. My ev'lls are wholy unsupportable,
No humain force can them withstand, but death.
Eras. To him that strives nought is impossible.
Cl. In striving lyes no hope of my mishapps.   435
Eras. All things do yeelde to force of lovely face.
Cl. My face too lovely caus'd my wretched case.
My face hath so entrap'd, so cast us downe,
That for his conquest *Cæsar* may it thanke,
Causing that *Antony* one army lost   440
The other wholy did to *Cæsar* yeld.
For not induring (so his amorouse sprite
Was with my beautie fir'de) my shamefull flight,
Soone as he saw from ranke wherin he stoode
In hottest fight, my Gallies making saile: 445
Forgetfull of his charge (as if his soule
Unto his Ladies soule had bene enchain'd)
He left his men, who so couragiouslie
Did leave their lives to gaine him victorie.
And carelesse both of fame and armies losse   450
My oared Gallies follow'd with his Ships
Companion of my flight, by this base parte
Blasting his former flourishing renowne.
Eras. Are you therefore cause of his overthrowe?
Cl. I am sole cause: I did it, only I.   455
Er, Feare of a woman troubled so his sprite?
Cl. Fire of his love was by my feare enflam'd.
Er. And should he then to warre have ledd a Queene?
Cl. Alas! this was not his offence, but mine.

460 *Antony* (ay me! who else so brave a chiefe!)
Would not I should have taken Seas with him:
But would have left me fearfull woman farre
From common hazard of the doubtfull warre.
    O that I had belev'd! now, now of *Rome*
465 All the great Empire at our beck should bende.
All should obey, the vagabonding *Scythes*,
The feared *Germains*, back-shooting *Parthians*,
Wandring *Numidians*, *Brittons* farre remoov'd,
And tawny nations scorched with the Sunne.
470 But I car'd not: so was my soule possest,
(To my great harme) with burning jealousie:
Fearing least in my absence *Antony*
Should leaving me retake *Octavia*.
Char. Such was the rigour of your destinie.
475 *Cl.* Such was my errour and obstinacie.
Ch. But since Gods would not, could you doe withall?
Cl. Alwaies from Gods good happs, not harms, do fall.
Ch. And have they not all power on mens affaires?
Cl. They never bow so lowe, as worldly cares.
480 But leave to mortall men to be dispos'd
Freelie on earth what ever mortall is.
If we therin sometimes some faultes commit,
We may them not to their high majesties,
But to our selves impute; whose passions
485 Plunge us each day in all afflictions.
Wherwith when we our soules do thorned feele,
Flatt'ring our selves we say they dest'nies are:
That Gods would have it so, and that our care
Could not empeach but that it must be so.
490 *Char.* Things here belowe are in the heav'ns begot,
Before they be in this our wordle borne:
And never can our weaknes turne awry
The stailes course of powerfull destenie.
Nought here force, reason, humaine providence,
495 Holie devotion, noble bloud prevailes:
And Jove himselfe whose hand doth heavens rule,
Who both to Gods and men as King commaunds,
Who earth (our firme support) with plenty stores,
Moves aire and sea with twinckling of his eie,

Who all can doe, yet never can undoe   500
What once hath been by their hard lawes decreed.
   When *Trojan* walles, great *Neptunes* workmanship,
Environ'd were with *Greekes*, and Fortunes whele
Doubtfull ten yeares now to the campe did turne,
And now againe towards the towne return'd: 505
How many times did force and fury swell
In *Hectors* veines egging him to the spoile
Of conquer'd foes, which at his blowes did flie,
As fearfull shepe at feared wolves approche:
To save (in vaine: for why? it would not be)   510
Pore walles of *Troie* from adversaries rage,
Who died them in bloud, and cast to ground
Heap'd them with bloudie burning carcases.
   No, Madame, thinke, that if the ancient crowne
Of your progenitors that *Nilus* rul'd,   515
Force take from you; the Gods have will'd it so,
To whome oft times Princes are odiouse.
They have to every thing an end ordain'd;
All worldly greatnes by them bounded is;
Some sooner, later some, as they think best: 520
None their decree is able to infringe.
But, which is more, to us disastred men
Which subject are in all things to their will,
Their will is hidd: not while we live, we know
How, or how long we must in life remaine.   525
Yet must we not for that feede on dispaire,
And make us wretched ere we wretched bee:
But alwaies hope the best, even to the last,
That from our selves the mischief may not growe.
   Then, Madame, helpe your selfe, leave of in time   530
Antonies wracke, lest it your wracke procure:
Retire you from him, save frrom wrathfull rage
Of angry *Cæsar* both your Realme and you.
You see him lost, so as your amitie
Unto his evills can yelde no more reliefe.   535
You see him ruin'd, so as your support
No more hencefourth can him with comfort raise.
With-draw you from the storme: persist not still
To loose your selfe: this royall diademe

540 Regaine of *Cæsar*. *Cl*. Soner shining light
Shall leave the daie, and darknes leave the night:
Sooner moist currents of tempestuous seas
Shall wave in heaven, and the nightlie troopes
Of starres shall shine within the foming waves,
545 Then I thee, *Antonie*, Leave in depe distres.
I am with thee, be it thy worthy soule
Lodge in thy brest, or from that lodging parte
Crossing the joyles lake to take hir place
In place prepared for men Demy-gods.
550 Live, if thee please, if life be lothsome die:
Dead and alive, *Antonie*, thou shalt see
Thy princesse follow thee, folow, and lament,
Thy wrack, no lesse her owne then was thy weale.
Char. What helps his wrack this ever-lasting love?
555 *Cl*. Help, or help not, such must, such ought I prove.
Char. Ill done to loose your selfe, and to no ende.
Cl. How ill thinke you to follow such a frende?
Char. But this your love nought mitigates his paine.
Cl. Without this love I should be inhumaine.
560 *Char*. Inhumaine he, who his owne death pursues.
Cl. Not inhumaine who miseries eschues.
Ch. Live for your sonnes. *Cl*. Nay for their father die.
Cha. Hardhearted mother! *Cl*. Wife kindhearted I.
Ch. Then will you them deprive of royall right?
565 *Cl*. Do I deprive them? no, it's dest'nies might.
Ch. Do you not them deprive of heritage,
That give them up to adversaries handes,
A man forsaken fearing to forsake,
Whome such huge numbers hold environned?
570 T'abandon one gainst whome the frowning world
Banded with *Cæsar* makes conspiring warre.
Cl. The lesse ought I to leave him left of all.
A frend in most distresse should most assist.
If that when *Antonie* great and glorious
575 His legions led to drinke *Euphrates* streames,
So many Kings in traine redoubting him;
In triumph rais'd as high as highest heavn,

566 them] them *1595*; them not *1592*   572 left] lest *1592, 1595*

Lord-like disposing as him pleased best,
The wealth of *Greece*, the wealth of *Asia*:
In that faire fortune had I him exchaung'd   580
For *Cæsar*, then, men would have counted me
Faithles, unconstant, light: but now the storme,
And blustring tempest driving on his face,
Readie to drowne, *Alas*! what would they saie?
What would himselfe in *Plutos* mansion saie?   585
If I, whome alwaies more then life he lov'de,
If I, who am his heart, who was his hope,
Leave him, forsake him (and perhaps in vaine)
Weakly to please who him hath overthrowne?
Not light, unconstant, faithlesse should I be,   590
But vile, forsworne, of treachrous crueltie.
Ch. Crueltie to shunne, you selfe-cruell are.
Cl. Selfe-cruell him from crueltie to spare.
Ch, Our first affection to our self is due.
Cl. He is my selfe. *Ch*. Next it extendes unto   595
Our children, frends, and to our countrie soile.
And you for some respect of wivelie love,
(Albee scarce wivelie) loose your native land,
Your children, frends, and (which is more) your life,
With so strong charmes doth love bewitch our witts: 600
So fast in us this fire once kindled flames.
Yet if his harme by yours redresse might have,
Cl. With mine it may be clos'de in darksome grave.
Ch. And that, as *Alcest* to hir selfe unkinde,
You might exempt him from the lawes of death.   605
But he is sure to die: and now his sworde
Alreadie moisted is in his warme bloude,
Helples for any succour you can bring
Against deaths stinge, which he must shortlie feele.

    Then let your love be like the love of olde 610
Which *Carian* Queene did nourish in hir heart
Of hir Mausolus: builde for him a tombe
Whose statelinesse a wonder new may make.
Let him, let him have sumtuouse funeralles:
Let grave thereon the horror of his fights: 615

Let earth be buri'd with unburied heaps.
Frame ther *Pharsaly*, and discoulour'd stream's
Of depe *Enipeus*: frame the grassie plaine,
Which lodg'd his campe at siege of *Mutina*.
620   Make all his combats, and couragiouse acts:
And yearly plaies to his praise institute:
Honor his memorie: with doubled care
Breed and bring up the children of you both
In *Cæsars* grace: who as a noble Prince
625   Will leave them Lords of this most gloriouse realme.
Cl. What shame were that? ah Gods! what infamie?
With *Antonie* in his good happs to share,
And overlive him dead: deeming enough
To shed some teares upon a widdowe tombe?
630   The after-livers justly might report
That I him onlie for his empire lov'd,
And high estate: and that in hard estate
I for another did him lewdlie leave?
Like to those birds wafted with wandring wings
635   From foraine lands in spring-time here arrive:
And live with us so long as Somers heate,
And their foode lasts, then seke another soile.
And as we see with ceaslesse fluttering
Flocking of seelly flies a brownish cloud
640   To vintag'd wine yet working in the tonne,
Not parting thence while they swete liquor taste:
After, as smoke, all vanish in the aire,
And of the swarme not one so much appeare.
Eras. By this sharp death what profit can you winne?
645   *Cl.* I neither gaine, nor profit seke therin.
Er. What praise shall you of after-ages gett?
Cl. Nor praise, nor glory in my cares are sett.
Er. What other end ought you respect, then this?
Cl. My only ende my onely dutie is.
650   *Er.* your dutie must upon some good be founded.
Cl. On vertue it, the onlie good, is grounded.
Er. What is that *vertue*? *Cl.* That which us beseemes.
Er. Outrage our selves? who that beseeming deemes?

632 high estate] *1595*; high st ate *[defective long s] 1592*   650 your] Your *1595*

Cl. Finish I will my sorowes dieng thus.
Er. Minish you will your glories doing thus.   655
Cl. Good frends I praie you seeke not to revoke
My fix'd intent of folowing *Antonie*.
I will die. I will die: must not his life,
His life and death by mine be folowed?
    Meane while, deare sisters, live: and while you live,   660
Doe often honor to our loved Tombes.
Straw them with flowrs: and sometimes happelie
The tender thought of *Antonie* your Lorde
And me poore soule to teares shall you invite,
And our true loves your dolefull voice commend.   665
Ch. And thinke you Madame, we from you will part?
Thinke you alone to feele deaths ougly darte?
Thinke you to leave us? and that the same sunne
Shall see at once you dead, and us alive?
Weele die with you: and *Clotho* pittilesse   670
Shall us with you in hellish boate imbarque.
Cl. Ah live, I praie you: this disastred woe
Which racks my heart, alone to me belonges:
My lott longs not to you: servants to be
No shame, no harme to you, as is to me.   675
    Live sisters, live, and seing his suspect
Hath causlesse me in sea of sorowes drown'd,
And that I can not live, if so I would,
Nor yet would leave this life, if so I could,
Without, his love: procure me, *Diomed*,   680
That gainst poore me he be no more incensd.
Wrest out of his conceit that harmfull doubt,
That since his wracke he hath of me conceiv'd
Though wrong conceiv'd: witnesse you reverent Gods,
Barking *Anubis*, *Apis* bellowing.   685
Tell him, my soule burning, impatient,
Forlorne with love of him, for certaine seale
Of her true loialtie my corpse hath left,
T'encrease of dead the number numberlesse.
    Go then, and if as yet he me bewaile,   690
If yet for me his heart one sigh fourth breathe

Blest shall I be: and farre with more content
Depart this world, where so I me torment.
Meane season us let this sadd tombe enclose,
695   Attending here till death conclude our woes.
Diom. I will obey your will. *Cl.* So the desert
The Gods repay of thy true faithfull heart.

Diomed.

        And is't not pittie, Gods, ah Gods of heav'n!
700   To see from love such hatefull frutes to spring?
And is't not pittie that this firebrand so
Laies waste the trophes of *Philippi* fieldes?
Where are those swete allurements, those swete lookes,
Which Gods themselves right hart-sicke would have made?
705   What doth that beautie, rarest guift of heav'n,
Wonder of earth? Alas! what doe those eies?
And that swete voice all *Asia* understoode,
And sunburnt *Afrike* wide in deserts spred?
Is their force dead? have they no further power?
710   Can not by them *Octavius* be supriz'd?
Alas! if *Jove* in middst of all his ire,
With thunderbolt in hand some land to plague,
Had cast his eies on my Queene, out of hande
His plaguing bolte had falne out of his hande:
715   Fire of his wrathe into vaine smoke should turne,
And other fire within his brest should burne.
        Nought lives so faire. Nature by such a worke
Her selfe, should seme, in workmanship hath past.
She is all heav'nlie: never any man
720   But seing hir was ravish'd with her sight.
The Allablaster covering of hir face,
The corall coullor hir two lipps engraines,
Her beamie eies, two Sunnes of this our world,
Of hir faire haire the fine and flaming golde,
725   Her brave streight stature, and hir winning partes
Are nothing else but fiers, fetters, dartes.
        Yet this is nothing th'e'nchaunting skilles
Of her cælestiall Sp'rite, hir training speache,

727 th'e'nchaunting] th'enchaunting *1595*

Her grace, hir Majestie, and forcing voice,
Whither she it with fingers speach consorte,   730
Or hearing sceptred kings embassadors
Answer to eache in his owne language make.
    Yet now at nede she aides hir not at all
With all these beauties, so hir sorowe stings.
Darkned with woe hir only studie is   735
To wepe, to sigh, to seke for lonelines.
Careles of all, hir haire disordred hangs:
Hir charming eies whence murthring looks did flie,
Now rivers grown', whose wellspring anguish is,
Do trickling wash the marble of hir face.   740
Hir faire discover'd brest with sobbing swolne
Selfe cruell she still martireth with blowes,
    Alas! It's our ill happ, for if hir teares
She would convert into hir loving charmes,
To make a conquest of the conqueror,   745
(As well shee might, would she hir force imploie)
She should us saftie from these ills procure,
Hir crowne to hir, and to hir race assure.
Unhappy he, in whome selfe-succour lies,
Yet self-forsaken wanting succour dies.   750

Chorus.

O swete fertile land, wherin
  Phœbus did with breath inspire
  Man who men did first begin,
  Formed first of *Nilus* mire.   755
  Whence of *Artes* the eldest kindes,
  Earthes most heavenly ornament,
  Were as from their fountaine sent,
  To enlight our mistie mindes.
  Whose grosse sprite from endles time,   760
  As in darkned prison pente,
  Never did to knowledg clime.

---

733 she] it *1595*   754 ff. *initial letters not capitalized in 754–62, 764–73, 775–84,*
786–95, 797–806, 808–13, 815–17, 819–21, 823–8, 830–9, 841–50, 852–61, 863–71 in 1595

Wher the *Nile*, our father good,
    Father-like doth never misse
765 Yearely us to bring such food,
    As to life required is:
    Visiting each yeare this plaine,
    And with fatt slime cov'ring it,
    Which his seaven mouthes do spitt,
770 As the season comes againe.
    Making therby greatest growe
    Busie reapers joyfull paine,
    When his flouds do highest flowe.
Wandring Prince of rivers thou,
775 Honor of the *Æthiops* lande,
    Of a Lord and master now
    Thou a slave in awe must stand.
    Now of *Tiber* which is spred
    Lesse in force, and lesse in fame
780 Reverence thou must the name,
    Whome all other rivers dread,
    For his children swolne in pride,
    Who by conquest seeke to treade
    Round this earth on every side.
785 Now thou must begin to sende
    Tribute of thy watrie store,
    As Sea pathes thy stepps shall bende,
    Yearely presents more and more.
    Thy fatt skumme, our frutefull corne,
790 Pill'd from hence with theevish hands
    All uncloth'd shall leave our lands
    Into foraine Countrie borne.
    Which puft up with such a pray
    Shall therby the praise adorne
795 Of that scepter *Rome* doth sway.
Nought thee helps thy hornes to hide
    Farre from hence in unknowne grounds,
    That thy waters wander wide,
    Yearely breaking bankes, and bounds.
800 And that thy Skie-coullor'd brookes
    Through a hundred peoples passe,

Drawing plots for trees and grasse
With a thousand turn's and crookes.
Whome all weary of their way
Thy throats which in widenesse passe　　805
Powre into their Mother Sea.
Noght so happie haplesse life
"In this worlde as freedome findes:
"Nought wherin more sparkes are rife
"To inflame couragious mindes.　　810
"But if force must us enforce
"Nedes a yoke to undergoe,
"Under foraine yoke to goe
"Still it proves a bondage worse.
"And doubled subjection　　815
"See we shall, and feele, and knowe
"Subject to a stranger growne.
From hence forward for a King,
　whose first being from this place
Should his brest by nature bring　　820
Care of Countrie to embrace,
We at surly face must quake
Of some *Romaine* madly bent:
Who, our terrour to augment,
His *Proconsuls* axe will shake.　　825
Driving with our Kings from hence
Our establish'd goverment,
Justice sworde, and Lawes defence.
Nothing worldly of such might
But more mightie *Destinie*,　　830
By swift *Times* unbridled flight,
Makes in ende his ende to see.
Every thing *Time* overthrowes,
Nought to ende doth stedfast staie:
His great sithe mowes all away　　835
As the stalke of tender rose.
Onlie Immortalitie
Of the Heav'ns doth it oppose
Gainst his powerfull *Deitie*.

---

822 *not indented in 1595*　　　838 Heav'ns] heavens *1595*

840
　　One daie there will come a daie
　　　　Which shall quaile thy fortunes flower,
　　　　And thee ruinde low shall laie
　　　　In some barbarous Princes power.
　　　　When the pittie-wanting fire
845
　　　　Shall, O *Rome*, thy beauties burne,
　　　　And to humble ashes turne
　　　　Thy proud wealth, and rich attire,
　　　　Those guilt roofes which turretwise,
　　　　Justly making Envie mourne,
850
　　　　Threaten now to pearce Skies.
　　As thy forces fill each land
　　　　Harvests making here and there,
　　　　Reaping all with ravening hand
　　　　They finde growing any where:
855
　　　　From each land so to thy fall
　　　　Multitudes repaire shall make,
　　　　From the common spoile to take
　　　　What to each mans share maie fall.
　　　　Fingred all thou shalt beholde:
860
　　　　No jote left for tokens sake
　　　　That thou wert so great of olde.
　　Like unto the auncient *Troie*
　　　　Whence deriv'de thy founders be,
　　　　Conqu'ring foe shall thee enjoie,
865
　　　　And a burning praie in thee.
　　　　For within this turning ball
　　　　This we see, and see each daie:
　　　　All things fixed ends do staie,
　　　　Ends to first beginnings fall.
870
　　　　And that nought, how strong or strange,
　　　　Chaungles doth endure alwaie,
　　　　But endureth fatall change.

[Act. 3.]

M. Antonius. Lucilius.

M. Ant.

Lucil, sole comfort of my bitter case,   875
The only trust, the only hope I have,
In last despaire: Ah! is not this the daie
That death should me of life and love bereave?
What waite I for that have no refuge left,
But am sole remnant of my fortune left?   880
All leave me, flie me: none, no not of them
Which of my greatnes greatest good receiv'd,
Stands with my fall: they seeme as now asham'de
That heretofore they did me ought regarde:
They draw them back, shewing they folow'd me,   885
Not to partake my harm's, but coozen me.
Lu. In this our world nothing is stedfast found,
In vaine he hopes, who here his hopes doth ground.
Ant. Yet nought afflicts me, nothing killes me so,
As that I so my *Cleopatra* see   890
Practize with *Cæsar*, and to him transport
My flame, her love, more deare then life to me.
Lu. Beleeve it not: Too high a heart she beares,
Too Princelie thoughts. *Ant.* Too wise a head she weare
Too much enflam'd with greatnes, evermore   895
Gaping for our great Empires goverment.
Lu. So long time you her constant love have tri'de.
Ant. But still with me good fortune did abide.
Lu. Her changed love what token makes you know?
An. Pelusium lost, and *Actian* overthrow,   900
Both by her fraud: my well appointed fleet,
And trustie Souldiors in my quarell arm'd,
Whom she, false she, instede of my defence,
Came to persuade, to yelde them to my foe:
Such honor *Thyre* done, such welcome given,   905
Their long close talkes I neither knew, nor would,
And treacherouse wrong *Alexas* hath me done,

875 *Lucil,*] ~. *1595*   897 *Lu.*] *1595*; *Li. 1592*

Witnes too well her perjur'd love to me.
But you O Gods (if any faith regarde)
910   With sharpe revenge her faithles change reward.
Lu. The dole she made upon our overthrow,
Her Realme given up for refuge to our men,
Her poore attire when she devoutly kept
The solemne day of her nativitie,
915   Againe the cost, and prodigall expence
Shew'd when she did your birth day celebrate,
Do plaine enough her heart unfained prove,
Equally toucht, you loving, as you love.
Ant. Well; be her love to me or false, or true,
920   Once in my soule a cureles wound I feele.
I love, nay burne in fire of her love:
Each day, each night her Image haunts my minde,
Her selfe my dreames: and still I tired am,
And still I am with burning pincers nipt.
925   Extreame my harme: yet sweeter to my sence
Then boiling Torch of jealouse torments fire:
This grief, nay rage, in me such sturre doth kepe,
And thornes me still, both when I wake and slepe.
     Take *Cæsar* conquest, take my goods, take he
930   Th'onor to be Lord of the earth alone,
My Sonnes, my life bent headlong to mishapps:
Nor force, so not my *Cleopatra* take.
So foolish I, I can not her forget,
Though better were I banisht her my thought.
935   Like to the sicke, whose throte the feavers fire
Hath vehemently with thirstie drouth enflam'd,
Drinkes still, albee the drinke he still desires
Be nothing else but fewell to his flame:
He can not rule himselfe: his health's respect
940   Yeldeth to his distempred stomackes heate.
Lu. Leave of this love, that thus renewes your woe.
Ant. I do my best, but ah! can not do so.
Lu. Thinke how you have so brave a captaine bene,
And now are by this vaine affection falne.
945   *Ant.* The ceasles thought of my felicitie
Plunges me more in this adversitie.

For nothing so a man in ill torments,
As who to him his good state represents.
This makes my rack, my anguish, and my woe
Equall unto the hellish passions growe,   950
When I to minde my happie puisance call
Which erst I had by warlike conquest wonne,
And that good fortune which me never left,
Which hard disastre now hath me bereft.

   With terror tremble all the world I made   955
At my sole worde, as Rushes in the streames
At waters will: I conquer'd Italie,
I conquer'd *Rome*, that Nations so redoubt.
I bare (meane while besieging *Mutina*)
Two Consuls armies for my ruine brought,   960
Bath'd in their bloud, by their deaths witnessing
My force and skill in matters Martiall.

   To wreake thy unkle, unkinde *Cæsar*, I
With bloud of enemies the bankes embru'd
Of stain'd *Enipeus*, hindering his course   965
Stopped with heapes of piled carcases:
When *Cassius* and *Brutus* ill betide
Marcht against us, by us twise put to flight,
But by my sole conduct: for all the time
Cæsar heart-sicke with feare and feaver laie.   970
Who knowes it not? and how by every one
Fame of the fact was giv'n to me alone.

   There sprang the love, the never changing love,
Wherin my hart hath since to yours bene bound:
There was it, my *Lucil*, you *Brutus* sav'de,   975
And for your *Brutus Antonie* you found.
Better my happ in gaining such a frende,
Then in subduing such an enemie.
Now former vertue dead doth me forsake,
Fortune engulfes me in extreame distresse: 980
She turnes from me her smiling countenance,
Casting on me mishapp upon mishapp,
Left and betraide of thousand thousand frends,
Once of my sute, but you *Lucil* are left,

965 hindering] hindring *1595*

985   Remaining to me stedfast as a tower
       In holy love, in spite of fortunes blastes.
       But if of any God my voice be heard,
       And be not vainely scatt'red in the heav'ns,
       Such goodnes shall not glorilesse be loste,
990   But comming ages still therof shall boste.
       Lu. Men in their frendship ever should be one,
       And never ought with fickle Fortune shake,
       Which still removes, nor will, nor knowes the way,
       Her rowling bowle in one sure state to staie.
995   Wherfore we ought as borrow'd things receive
       The goods light she lends us to pay againe:
       Not holde them sure, nor on them builde our hopes
       As one such goods as cannot faile, and fall:
       But thinke againe, nothing is dureable,
1000   Vertue except, our never failing hoste:
       So bearing saile when favouring windes do blowe,
       As frowning Tempests may us least dismaie
       When they on us do fall: not over-glad
       With good estate, nor over-griev'd with bad.
1005   Resist mishap. *Ant.* Alas! it is too stronge.
       Mishappes oft times are by some comfort borne:
       But these, ay me! whose weights oppresse my hart,
       Too heavie lie, no hope can them relieve.
       There rests no more, but that with cruell blade
1010   For lingring death a hastie waie be made.
       Lu. Cæsar, as heire unto his Fathers state:
       So will his Fathers goodnes imitate,
       To youwarde: whome he know's allied in bloud,
       Allied in mariage, ruling equallie
1015   Th'Empire with him, and with him making warre
       Have purg'd the earth of *Cæsars* murtherers.
       You into portions parted have the world
       Even like coheir's their heritages parte:
       And now with one accord so many yeares
1020   In quiet peace doth have your charges rul'd.
       Ant. Bloud and alliance nothing do prevaile
       To coole the thirst of hote ambitious breasts:

998 one] on *1595*

The sonne his Father hardly can endure,
Brother his brother, in one common Realme.
So fervent this desier to commaund: 1025
Such jealousie it kindleth in our hearts.
Sooner will men permit another should
Love her they love, then weare the Crowne they weare.
All lawes it breakes, turns all things upsidedowne:
Amitie, kindred, nought so holie is   1030
But it defiles. A monarchie to gaine
None cares which way, so he maie it obtaine.
Lu. Suppose he Monarch be and that this world
No more acknowledg sundrie Emperours.
That *Rome* him onelie feare, and that he joyne   1035
The East with west, and both at once do rule:
Why should he not permitt you peaceablie
Discharg'd of charge and Empires dignitie,
Private to live reading *Philosophie*,
In learned *Greece*, *Spaine*, *Asia*, anie lande?   1040
Ant. Never will he his Empire thinke assur'de
While in this world *Marke Antonie* shall live.
Sleeples Suspicion, Pale distrust, colde feare
Alwaies to princes companie do beare
Bred of Reports: reports which night and day   1045
Perpetuall guests from Court go not away.
Lu. He hath not slaine your brother *Lucius*,
Nor shortned hath the age of *Lepidus*,
Albeit both into his hands were falne,
And he with wrath against them both enflam'd.   1050
Yet one, as Lord in quiet rest doth beare
The greatest sway in great *Iberia*:
The other with his gentle Prince retaines
Of highest Priest the sacred dignitie.
Ant. He feares not them, their feeble force he knowes. 1055
Lu. He feares no vanquisht overfill'd with woes.
Ant. Fortune may chaunge againe, *L.* A down-cast foe
Can hardlie rise, which once is brought so lowe.
Ant. All that I can, is done: for last assay
(When all means fail'd) I to entreatie fell,   1060

(Ah coward creature!) whence againe repulst
Of combate I unto him proffer made:
Though he in prime, and I by feeble age
Mightily weakned both in force and skill.

1065 Yet could not he his coward heart advaunce
Baselie affraid to trie so praisefull chaunce.
This makes me plaine, makes me my selfe accuse,
Fortune in this hir spitefull force doth use
'Gainst my gray hayres: in this unhappie I

1070 Repine at heav'ns in my happes pittiles.
A man, a woman both in might and minde,
In *Marses* schole who never lesson learn'd,
Should me repulse, chafe, overthrow, destroie,
Me of such fame, bring to so lowe an ebbe?

1075 *Alcides* bloud, who from my infancie
With happie prowesse crowned have my praise.
Witnesse thou *Gaule* unus'd to servile yoke,
Thou valiant *Spaine*, you fields of *Thessalie*
With millions of mourning cries bewail'd,

1080 Twise watred now with bloude of *Italie*.
Lu. witnesse may *Afrique*, and of conquer'd world
All fower quarters witnesses may be.
For in what part of earth inhabited,
Hungrie of praise have you not ensignes spredd?

1085 *An.* Thou know'st rich *Ægypt* (*Ægypt* of my deeds
Faire and foule subject) *Ægypt* ah! thou know'st
How I behav'd me fighting for thy kinge,
When I regainde him his rebellious Realme:
Against his foes in battaile shewing force,

1090 And after fight in victorie remorse.
    Yet if to bring my glorie to the ground,
Fortune had made me overthrowne by one
Of greater force, of better skill then I;
One of those Captaines feared so of olde,

1095 *Camill, Marcellus*, worthy *Scipio*,
This late great *Cæsar*, honor of our state,
Or that great *Pompei* aged growne in armes;
That after harvest of a world of men

1072 *Marses*] *Mars his* 1595

Made in a hundred battailes, fights, assaults,
My bodie thorow pearst with push of pike 1100
Had vomited my bloud, in bloud my life,
In midd'st of millions felowes in my fall:
The lesse hir wrong, the lesse should be my woe:
Nor she should paine, nor I complaine me so.

No, no, wheras I should have died in armes, 1105
And vanquisht oft new armies should have arm'd,
New battailes given, and rather lost with me
All this whole world submitted unto me:
A man who never saw enlaced pikes
With bristled pointes against his stomake bent, 1110
Who feares the field, and hides him cowardly
Dead at the verie noise the souldiors make.

His vertue, fraude, deceit, malicious guile,
His armes the arts that false *Ulisses* us'de,
Knowne at Modena, wher the *Consuls* both 1115
Death-wounded were, and wounded by his men
To gett their armie, warre with it to make
Against his faith, against his countrie soile.
Of *Lepidus*, which to his succours came,
To honor whome he was by dutie bounde; 1120
The Empire he usurpt: corrupting first
With baites and bribes the most part of his men.
Yet me hath overcome, and made his pray,
And state of *Rome*, with me hath overcome.

Strange! one disordred act at *Actium* 1125
The earth subdu'de, my glorie hath obscur'd.
For since, as one whome heavens wrath attaints,
With furie caught, and more then furious
Vex'd with my evills, I never more had care
My armies lost, or lost name to repaire: 1130
I did no more resist. *Lu.* All warres affaires,
But battailes most, daily have their successe
Now good, now ill: and though that fortune have
Great force and power in every wordlie thing,
Rule all, do all, have all things fast enchaind 1135
Unto the circle of hir turning wheele:

1103 should be] should *1592, 1595*

Yet seemes it more then any practise else
She doth frequent *Bellonas* bloudie trade:
And that hir favour, wavering as the wind,
1140 Hir greatest power therin doth oftnest shewe.
Whence growes, we dailie see, who in their youth
Gatt honor ther, do loose it in their age,
Vanquisht by some lesse warlike then themselves:
Whome yet a meaner man shall overthrowe.
1145 Hir use is not to lende us still her hande,
But sometimes headlong back againe to throwe,
When by hir favor she hath us extolld
Unto the topp of highest happines.
Ant. well ought I curse within my grieved soule,
1150 Lamenting daie and night, this sencelesse love,
Whereby my faire entising foe entrap'd
My hedelesse *Reason*, could no more escape.
It was not fortunes ever chaunging face,
It was not Dest'nies chaungles violence
1155 *Forg'd my mishap. Alas! who doth not know*
They make, nor marre, nor any thing can doe.
Fortune, which men so feare, adore, detest,
Is but a chaunce whose cause unknow'n doth rest.
Although oft times the cause is well perceiv'd,
1160 *But not th'effect the same that was conceiv'd.*
Pleasure, nought else, the plague of this our life,
Our life which still a thousand plagues pursue,
Alone hath me this strange disastre spunne,
Falne from a souldior to a Chamberer,
1165 Careles of vertue, careles of all praise.
Nay, as the fatted swine in filthy mire
With glutted heart I wallow'd in delights,
All thoughts of honor troden under foote.
So I me lost: for finding this swete cupp
1170 Pleasing my tast, unwise I drunke my fill,
And through the swetenes of that poisons power
By stepps I drave my former witts astraie.
I made my frends, offended me forsake,
I holpe my foes against my selfe to rise.

1138 *Bellonas*] *1595*; *Ballonas 1592*

I robd my subjects, and for followers 1175
I saw my selfe besett with flatterers.
Mine idle armes faire wrought with spiders worke,
My scattred men without their ensignes strai'd:
Cæsar meane while who never would have dar'de
To cope with me, me sodainlie despis'de, 1180
Tooke hart to fight, and hop'de for victorie
On one so gone, who glorie had forgone.
Lu. Enchaunting pleasure, *Venus* swete delights
Weaken our bodies, over-cloud our sprights,
Trouble our reason, from our harts out chase 1185
All holie vertues lodging in their place.
Like as the cunning fisher takes the fishe
By traitor baite wherby the hooke is hidde:
So *Pleasure* serves to vice in steede of foode
To baite our soules theron too licourishe. 1190
This poison deadlie is alike to all,
But on great kings doth greatest outrage worke,
Taking the Roiall scepters from their hands,
Thenceforward to be by some straunger borne:
While that their people charg'd with heavy loades 1195
Their flatt'rers pill, and suck their mary drie,
Not ru'lde but left to great men as a pray,
While this fonde Prince himselfe in pleasur's drowns:
Who heares nought, sees nought, doth nought of a king,
Seming himselfe against himselfe conspirde. 1200
Then equall Justice wandreth banished,
And in hir seat sitts greedie Tyrannie.
Confus'd disorder troubleth all estates,
Crimes without feare and outrages are done.
Then mutinous *Rebellion* shewes hir face, 1205
Now hid with this, and now with that pretence,
Provoking enimies, which on each side
Enter at ease, and make them Lords of all.
The hurtfull workes of pleasure here behold.
An. The wolfe is not so hurtfull to the folde, 1210
Frost to the grapes, to ripened fruits the raine:
As pleasure is to Princes full of paine.
Lu. Ther nedes no proofe, but by th' *Assirian* kinge,
On whome that Monster woefull wrack did bring.

1215 *An.* Ther nedes no proofe, but by unhappie I,
Who lost my empire, honor, life therby.
Lu. Yet hath this ill so much the greater force,
As scarcelie anie do against it stand:
No, not the Demy-gods the olde world knew,
1220 Who all subdu'de, could *Pleasures* power subdue.
     Great *Hercules*, *Hercules* one that was
Wonder of earth and heav'n, matchles in might,
Who *Anteus*, *Lycus*, *Geryon* overcame,
Who drew from hell the triple-headed dogg,
1225 Who *Hydra* kill'd, vanquishd *Achelous*,
Who heavens weight on his strong shoulders bare:
Did he not under *Pleasures* burthen bow?
Did he not Captive to this passion yelde,
When by his Captive, so he was enflam'de,
1230 As now your selfe in *Cleopatra* burne?
Slept in hir lapp, hir bosome kist and kiste,
With base unsemelie service bought her love,
Spinning at distaffe, and with sinewy hand
Winding on spindles threde, in maides attire?
1235 His conqu'ring clubbe at rest on wal did hang:
His bow unstringd he bent not as he us'de:
Upon his shafts the weaving spiders spunne:
And his hard cloake the freating mothes did pierce.
The monsters free and fearles all the time
1240 Throughout the world the people did torment,
And more and more encreasing daie by day
Scorn'd his weake heart become a mistresse plaie.
An. In onelie this like *Hercules* am I,
In this I prove me of his lignage right:
1245 In this himselfe, his deedes I shew in this,
In this, nought else, my ancestor he is.
     But goe we: die I must, and with brave ende
Conclusion make of all foregoing harmes:
Die, die I must: I must a noble death,
1250 A glorious death unto my succor call:
I must deface the shame of time abus'd,
I must adorne the wanton loves I us'de

1222 heav'n] heaven *1595*

With some couragiouse act: that my last daie
By mine owne hand my spotts may wash away.
   Come deare *Lucill*: alas: why wepe you thus!   1255
This mortall lot is common to us all.
We must all die, each doth in homage owe
Unto that God that shar'd the Realmes belowe.
Ah sigh no more: alas: appeace your woes,
For by your griefe my griefe more eager growes.   1260

Chorus.

   Alas, with what tormenting fire.
   Us martireth this blinde desire
     To staie our life from flieng!
   How ceasleslie our minds doth rack,   1265
   How heavie lies upon our back
     This dastard feare of dieng!
Death rather healthfull succor gives,
Death rather all mishapps relieves
     That life upon us throweth: 1270
   And ever to us doth unclose
   The doore, wherby from curelesse woes
     Our wearie soule out goeth.
   What Goddesse else more milde then shee
   To burie all our paine can be,   1275
     What remedie more pleasing?
   Our pained hearts when dolor stings,
   And nothing rest, or respite brings,
     What help have we more easing?
Hope which to us doth comfort give,   1280
   And doth our fainting hearts revive,
     Hath not such force in anguish:
   For promising a vaine reliefe
   She oft us failes in midst of griefe,
     And helples letts us languish.   1285
   But Death who call on her at nede
   Doth never with vaine semblant feed,
     But when them sorow paineth,

So riddes their soules of all distresse
1290   Whose heavie weight did them oppresse,
        That not one griefe remaineth.
Who feareles and with courage bolde
Can *Acherons* black face beholde,
        Which muddie water beareth:
1295   And crossing over, in the way
Is not amaz'd at Perruque gray
        Olde rustie *Charon* weareth:
Who voide of dread can looke upon
The dreadfull shades that rome alone,
1300   On bankes where sound no voices:
Whom with her fire-brands and her Snakes
No whit afraide *Alecto* makes,
        Nor triple-barking noyses:
Who freely can himselfe dispose
1305   Of that last hower which all must close,
        And leave this life at pleasure:
This noble freedome more esteemes,
And in his hart more precious deemes,
        Then Crowne and kingly treasure.
1310   The waves which *Boreas* blasts turmoile
And cause with foaming furie boile,
        Make not his heart to tremble:
Nor brutish broile, when with strong head
A rebell people madly ledde
1315   Against their Lords assemble:
Nor fearfull face of Tirant wood,
Who breaths but threats, and drinks but bloud,
        No, nor the hand which thunder,
The hand of *Jove* which thunder beares,
1320   And ribbs of rocks in sunder teares,
        Teares mountains sides in sunder:
Nor bloudie *Marses* butchering bands,
Whose lightnings desert laie the lands
        whome dustie cloudes do cover:
1325   From of whose armour sun-beames flie,
And under them make quaking lie
        The plaines wheron they hover:

Nor yet the cruell murth'ring blade
Warme in the moistie bowells made
   of people pell mell dieng   1330
In some great Cittie put to sack
By savage Tirant brought to wrack,
   At his colde mercie lieng.
How abject him, how base think I,
Who wanting courage can not dye   1335
   When need him therto calleth?
From whom the dagger drawne to kill
The curelesse griefes that vexe him still
   For feare and faintnes falleth?
O *Antonie* with thy deare mate   1340
Both in misfortunes fortunate!
   Whose thoughts to death aspiring
Shall you protect frrom victors rage,
Who on each side doth you encage,
   To triumph much desiring.   1345
That *Cæsar* may you not offend
Nought else but Death can you defend,
   which his weake force derideth,
And all in this round earth contain,
Powr'les on them whom once enchaind   1350
   Avernus prison hideth:
Where great *Psammetiques* ghost doth rest,
Not with infernall paine possest,
   But in swete fields detained:
And olde *Amasis* soule likewise,   1355
And all our famous *Ptolemies*
   That whilome on us raigned.

1330 of] Of *1595*   1348 which] Which *1595*   1356 *Ptolemies*] Ptolomies *1595*

Act. 4.

Cæsar. Agrippa. Dircetus
1360   the Messenger.

Cæsar.

You ever-living Gods which all things holde
Within the power of your celestiall hands,
By whom heate, colde, the thunder, and the winde,
1365   The properties of enterchaunging mon'ths
Their course and being have; which do set downe
Of Empires by your destinied decree
The force, age, time, and subject to no chaunge
Chaunge all, reserving nothing in one state:
1370   You have advaunst, as high as thundring heav'n
The *Romains* greatnes by *Bellonas* might:
Mastring the world with fearfull violence,
Making the world widow of libertie.
Yet at this daie this proud exalted *Rome*
1375   Despoil'd, captiv'd, at one mans will doth bende:
Her Empire mine, her life is in my hand,
As Monarch I both world and *Rome* commaund;
Do all, can all; fourth my commaund'ment cast
Like thundring fire from one to other Pole
1380   Equall to Jove: bestowing by my worde
Happes and mishappes, as Fortunes King and Lord.
   No Towne there is, but up my Image settes,
But sacrifice to me doth dayly make:
Whither where *Phœbus* joyne his morning steedes,
1385   Or where the night them weary entertaines,
Or where the heat the *Garamants* doth scorche,
Or where colde from *Boreas* breast is blowne:
All *Cæsar* do both awe and honor beare,
And crowned Kings his verie name do feare.
1390   *Antonie* knowes it well, for whom not one
Of all the Princes all this earth do rule,

1359 *Dircetus*ʌ] ~. *1595*   1378 fourth] foorth *1595*   1389 do] doth *1595*
1391 all this] *1595*; allthis *1592*

Armes against me: for all redoubt the power
Which heav'nly powers on earth have made me beare.
　　Antonie, he poore man with fire enflam'de
A womans beauties kindled in his heart,　　　　　　　　1395
Rose against me, who longer could not beare
My sisters wrong he did so ill entreat:
Seing her left while that his leud delights
Her husband with his *Cleopatra* tooke
In *Alexandrie*, where both nights and daies　　　　　　1400
Their time they pass'd in nought but loves and plaies.
　　All *Asias* forces into one he drewe,
And forth he sett upon the azur'd waves
A thousand and a thousand Shipps, which fill'd
With Souldiors, pikes, with targets, arrowes, darts,　　1405
Made *Neptune* quake, and all the watrie troupes
Of *Glauques*, and *Tritons* lodg'd at *Actium*.
But mightie Gods, who still the force withstand
Of him, who causles doth another wrong,
In lesse then moments space redus'd to nought　　　　1410
All that proud power by Sea or land he brought.
Agr. Presumptuouse pride of high and hawtie sprite,
Voluptuouse care of fonde and foolish love,
Have justly wrought his wrack: who thought he helde
(By overweening) Fortune in his hand.　　　　　　　　1415
Of us he made no count, but as to play,
So fearles came our forces to assay.
　　So sometimes fell to Sonnes of Mother Earth,
Which crawl'd to heav'n warre on the Gods to make,
Olymp on *Pelion*, *Ossa* on *Olymp*,　　　　　　　　1420
Pindus on *Ossa* loading by degrees:
That at hand strokes with mightie clubbes they might
On mossie rocks the Gods make tumble downe:
When mightie *Jove* with burning anger chaf'd,
Disbraind with him *Gyges* and *Briareus*,　　　　　　　1425
Blunting his darts upon their brused bones.
For no one thing the Gods can lesse abide
In dedes of men, then Arrogance and Pride.

1392 all redoubt] *1595*; allredoubt *1592*　　　1393 Which] which *1595*　　　1399 *Cleo-*
patra] *Cleopatre 1595*　　　1400 *Alexandrie*] *Alexandria 1595*　　　1419 Gods] God
1595　　　1422 they] the *1595*

And still the proud, which too much takes in hand,
1430   *Shall fowlest fall, where best he thinks to stand.*
Cæs. Right as some Pallace, or some stately tower,
Which over-lookes the neighbour buildings round
In scorning wise, and to the Starres up growes,
Which in short time his owne weight overthrowes.
1435   What monstrous pride, nay what impietie
Incenst him onward to the Gods disgrace?
When his two children, *Cleopatras* bratts,
To *Phœbe* and her brother he compar'd,
Latonas race, causing them to be call'd
1440   The Sunne and Moone? Is not this folie right?
And is not this the Gods to make his foes?
And is not this himself to worke his woes?
Agr. In like proud sort he caus'd his head to leese
The Jewish king *Antigonus*, to have
1445   His Realme for balme, that *Cleopatra* lov'd,
As though on him he had some treason prov'd.
Cæs. Lydia to her, and *Siria* he gave,
Cyprus of golde, *Arabia* rich of smelles:
And to his children more *Cilicia*,
1450   *Parth's*, *Medes*, *Armenia*, *Phænicia*:
The kings of kings proclaiming them to be,
By his owne worde, as by a sound decree.
Agr. What? Robbing his owne countrie of her due
Triumph'd he not in *Alexandria*,
1455   Of *Artabasus* the *Armenian* King,
Who yelded on his perjur'd word to him?
Cæs. Nay, never *Rome* more injuries receiv'd,
Since thou, ô *Romulus*, by flight of birds
with happy hand the *Romain* walles did'st build,
1460   Then *Antonies* fond loves to it hath done.
Nor ever warre more holie, nor more just,
Nor undertaken with more hard constraint,
Then is this warre: which were it not, our state
Within small time all dignitie should loose:
1465   Though I lament (thou Sunne my witnes art,
And thou great *Jove*) that it so deadly proves:

That *Romain* bloud should in such plentie flowe,
Watring the fields and pastures where we goe.
What *Carthage* in olde hatred obstinate,
What *Gaule* still barking at our rising state, 1470
What rebell *Samnite*, what fierce *Pyrrhus* power,
What cruell *Mithridate*, what *Parth* hath wrought
Such woe to *Rome*? whose common wealth he had,
(Had he bene victor) into *Egipt* brought.
Agr. Surely the Gods, which have this Cittie built 1475
Stedfast to stand as long as time endures,
Which kepe the Capitoll, of us take care,
And care will take of those shall after come,
Have made you victor, that you might redresse
Their honor growne by passed mischieves lesse. 1480
Cæs. The seelie man when all the Greekish Sea
His fleete had hidd, in hope me sure to drowne,
Me battaile gave: where fortune, in my stede,
Repulsing him his forces disaraied.
Him selfe tooke flight, soone as his love he saw 1485
All wanne through feare with full sailes flie away.
His men, though lost, whome none did now direct,
With courage fought fast grappled shipp with shipp,
Charging, resisting, as their oares would serve,
With darts, with swords, with Pikes, and fierie flames. 1490
So that the darkned night her starrie vaile
Upon the bloudie sea had over-spred,
Whilst yet they held: and hardlie, hardlie then
They fell to flieng on the wavie plaine.
All full of Souldiors overwhelm'd with waves: 1495
The aire throughout with cries and grones did sound:
The Sea did blush with bloud: the neighbor shores
Groned, so they with shipwracks pestred were,
And floting bodies left for pleasing foode
To birds, and beasts, and fishes of the sea. 1500
You know it well *Agrippa*. *Ag.* Mete it was
The *Romain* Empire so should ruled be,
As heav'n is rul'd: which turning over us,
All under things by his example turnes.

1494 plaine.] ~, *1595*

1505 Now as of heav'n one onely Lord we know:
One onely Lord should rule this earth below.
When one self pow're is common made to two,
Their duties they nor suffer will, nor doe.
In quarell still, in doubt, in hate, in feare;
1510 *Meane while the people all the smart do beare.*
Cæs. Then to the ende none, while my daies endure,
Seeking to raise himselfe may succours finde,
We must with bloud marke this our victorie,
For just example to all memorie.
1515 Murther we must, untill not one we leave,
Which may hereafter us of rest bereave.
Ag. Marke it with murthers? who of that can like?
Cæ. Murthers must use, who doth assurance seeke.
Ag. Assurance call you enemies to make?
1520 *Cæs.* I make no such, but such away I take.
Ag. Nothing so much as rigour doth displease.
Cæs. Nothing so much doth make me live at ease.
Ag. What ease to him that feared is of all?
Cæ. Feared to be, and see his foes to fall.
1525 *Ag.* Commonly feare doth brede and nourish hate.
Cæ. Hate without pow'r, comes comonly too late.
Ag. A feared Prince hath oft his death desir'd.
Cæ. A Prince not fear'd hath oft his wrong conspir'de.
Ag. No guard so sure, no forte so strong doth prove,
1530 No such defence, as is the peoples love.
Cæs. Nought more unsure more weak, more like the winde,
Then *Peoples* favor still to chaunge enclinde.
Ag. Good Gods! what love to gracious Prince men beare!
Cæs. What honor to the Prince that is severe!
1535 *Ag.* Nought more divine then is *Benignitie.*
Cæ. Nought likes the *Gods* as doth *Severitie.*
Ag. Gods all forgive. *Cæ.* On faults they paines do laie.
Ag. And give their goods. *Cæ.* Oft times they take away.
Ag. They wreake them not, ô *Cæsar*, at each time
1540 That by our sinnes they are to wrathe provok'd.
Neither must you (beleve, I humblie praie)
Your victorie with crueltie defile.

1517 who] Who *1595*

The Gods it gave, it must not be abus'd,
But to the good of all men mildlie us'd,
And they be thank'd: that having giv'n you grace   1545
To raigne alone, and rule this earthlie masse,
They may hence-forward hold it still in rest,
All scattred power united in one brest.
Cæ. But what is he, that breathles comes so fast,
Approching us, and going in such hast?   1550
Ag. He semes affraid: and under his arme I
(But much I erre) a bloudie sworde espie.
Cæs. I long to understand what it may be.
Ag. He hither comes: it's best we stay and see.
Dirce. What good God now my voice will reenforce,   1555
That tell I may to rocks, and hilles, and woods,
To waves of sea, which dash upon the shore,
To earth, to heav'n, the woefull newes I bring?
Ag. What sodaine chaunce thee towards us hath brought?
Dir. A lamentable chance. O wrath of heav'ns!   1560
O Gods too pittiles! *Cæs.* What monstrous happ
Wilt thou recount? *Dir.* Alas too hard mishapp!
When I but dreame of what mine eies beheld,
My hart doth freeze, my limmes do quivering quake,
I senceles stand, my brest with tempest tost   1565
Killes in my throte my wordes, ere fully borne.
Dead, dead he is: be sure of what I say,
This murthering sword hath made the man away.
Cæs. Alas my heart doth cleave, pittie me rackes,
My breast doth pant to heare this dolefull tale.   1570
Is *Antonie* then dead? To death, alas!
I am the cause despaire him so compelld.
But souldiour of his death the maner showe,
And how he did this living light forgoe.
Dir. When *Antonie* no hope remaining saw   1575
How warre he might, or how agreement make,
Saw him betraid by all his men of warre
In every fight as well by sea, as lande;
That not content to yeld them to their foes
They also came against himselfe to fight: 1580
Alone in Court he gan himself torment,
Accuse the Queene, himselfe of hir lament,

Call'd hir untrue and traytresse, as who sought
To yeld him up she could no more defend:
1585   That in the harmes which for hir sake he bare,
As in his blisfull state, she might not share.

But she againe, who much his furie fear'd,
Gatt to the Tombes, darke horrors dwelling place:
Made lock the doores, and pull the hearses downe.
1590   Then fell shee wretched, with hir selfe to fight.
A thousand plaints, a thousand sobbes she cast
From hir weake brest which to the bones was torne.
Of women hir the most unhappie call'd,
Who by hir love, hir woefull love, had lost
1595   Hir realme, hir life, and more, the love of him,
Who while he was, was all hir woes support.
But that she faultles was she did invoke
For witnes heav'n, and aire, and earth, and sea.
Then sent him worde, she was no more alive,
1600   But lay inclosed dead within hir Tombe.
This he beleev'd; and fell to sigh and grone,
And crost his armes, then thus began to mone.
Cæs. Poore hopeles man! *Dir.* What dost thou more attend—
Ah *Antonie*! why dost thou death deferre:
1605   Since *Fortune* thy professed enimie,
Hath made to die, who only made thee live?
Sone as with sighes he had these words upclos'd,
His armor he unlaste, and cast it of,
Then all disarm'd he thus againe did say:
1610   My Queene, my heart, the grief that now I feele,
Is not that I your eies, my Sunne, do loose,
For soone againe one Tombe shal us conjoyne:
I grieve, whom men so valorouse did deeme,
Should now, then you, of lesser valor seeme.
1615   So said, forthwith he *Eros* to him call'd,
Eros his man; summond him on his faith
To kill him at his nede. He tooke the sworde,
And at that instant stab'd therwith his breast,
And ending life fell dead before his fete.
1620   O *Eros* thankes (quoth *Antonie*) for this

1608 of] off *1595*

Most noble acte, who pow'rles me to kill,
On thee hast done, what I on mee should doe.
   Of speaking thus he scarce had made an ende,
And taken up the bloudie sword from ground,
But he his bodie piers'd; and of redd bloud   1625
A gushing fountaine all the chamber fill'd.
He staggred at the blowe, his face grew pale,
And on a couche all feeble downe he fell,
Swounding with anguish: deadly cold him tooke,
As if his soule had then his lodging left.   1630
But he reviv'd, and marking all our eies
Bathed in teares, and how our breasts we beatt
For pittie, anguish, and for bitter griefe,
To see him plong'd in extreame wretchednes:
He prai'd us all to haste his lingr'ing death: 1635
But no man willing, each himselfe withdrew.
Then fell he new to crie and vexe himselfe,
Untill a man from *Cleopatra* came,
Who said from hir he had commaundement
To bring him to hir to the monument.   1640
   The poore soule at these words even rapt with Joy
Knowing she liv'd, prai'd us him to convey
Unto his Ladie. Then upon our armes
We bare him to the Tombe, but entred not.
For she, who feared captive to be made,   1645
And that she should to *Rome* in triumph goe,
Kept close the gate: but from a window high
Cast downe a corde, wherin he was impackt.
Then by hir womens helpe the corps she rais'd,
And by strong armes into hir windowe drew.   1650
   So pittifull a sight was never sene.
Little and little *Antonie* was pull'd,
Now breathing death: his beard was all unkempt,
His face and brest all bathed in his bloud.
So hideous yet, and dieng as he was,   1655
His eies half-clos'd uppon the Queene he cast:
Held up his hands, and holpe himself to raise,
But still with weakenes back his bodie fell.

1629 Swounding] Sounding *1595*   1649 helpe] help *1595*; helpt *1592*

The miserable ladie with moist eies,
1660   With haire which careles on hir forhead hong,
With brest which blowes had bloudilie benumb'd,
With stooping head, and bodie down-ward bent,
Enlast hir in the corde, and with all force
This life-dead man couragiously uprais'de.
1665   The bloud with paine into hir face did flowe,
Hir sinewes stiff, her selfe did breathles growe.
      The people which beneath in flocks beheld,
Assisted her with gesture, speech, desire:
Cri'de and incourag'd her, and in their soules
1670   Did sweate, and labor, no white lesse then shee.
Who never tir'd in labor, held so long
Helpt by hir women, and hir constant heart,
That *Antonie* was drawne into the tombe,
And ther (I thinke) of dead augments the summe.
1675   The Cittie all to teares and sighes is turn'd,
To plaints and outcries horrible to heare:
Men, women, children, hoary-headed age
Do all pell mell in house and strete lament,
Scratching their faces, tearing of their haire,
1680   Wringing their hands, and martyring their brests.
Extreame their dole: and greater misery
In sacked townes can hardlie ever be.
Not if the fire had scal'de the highest towers:
That all things were of force and murther full;
1685   That in the streets the bloud in rivers stream'd;
The sonne his sire saw in his bosome slaine,
The sire his sonne: the husband reft of breath
In his wives armes, who furious runnes to death.
      Now my brest wounded with their piteouse plaints
1690   I left their towne, and tooke with me this sworde,
Which I tooke up at what time *Antonie*
Was from his chamber caried to the tombe:
And brought it you, to make his death more plaine,
And that therby my words may credite gaine.
1695   *Cæs.* Ah Gods what cruell happ! poore *Antonie*,
Alas hast thou this sword so long time borne

Against thy foe, that in the ende it should
Of thee his Lord the cursed murthr'er be?
O Death how I bewaile thee! we (alas!)
So many warres have ended, brothers, frends,   1700
Companions, coozens, equalls in estate:
And must it now to kill thee be my fate?
Ag. Why trouble you your selfe with bootles griefe?
For *Antonie* why spend you teares in vaine?
Why darken you with dole your victorie?   1705
Me seemes your self your glorie do envie.
Enter the towne, give thankes unto the Gods.
Cæs. I cannot but his tearefull chaunce lament,
Although not I, but his owne pride the cause,
And unchaste love of this *Ægyptian*.   1710
Agr, But best we sought into the tombe to gett,
Lest shee consume in this amazed case
So much rich treasure, with which happelie
Despaire in death may make hir feed the fire:
Suffring the flames hir Jewells to deface,   1715
You to defraud, hir funerall to grace.
Sende then to hir, and let some meane be us'd
With some devise so holde hir still alive,
Some faire large promises: and let them marke
Whither they may by some fine conning slight   1720
Enter the tombes. *Cæsar*. Let *Proculeius* goe,
And fede with hope hir soule disconsolate.
Assure hir so, that we may wholie gett
Into our hands hir treasure and hir selfe.
For this of all things most I doe desire   1725
To kepe hir safe untill our going hence:
That by hir presence beautified may be
The glorious triumph *Rome* prepares for me.

Chorus of Romaine
Souldiors.   1730

Shall ever civile bate
    gnaw and devour our state?

1711 *Agr*,] ~. *1595*   1720 conning] cunning *1595*

Shall never we this blade,
Our bloud hath bloudie made,
1735   Lay downe? these armes downe lay
As robes we weare alway?
But as from age to age,
So passe from rage to rage?
Our hands shall we not rest
1740   To bath in our owne brest?
And shall thick in each land
Our wretched trophees stand,
To tell posteritie,
What madd Impietie
1745   Our stonie stomakes ledd
Against the place us bredd?
Then still must heaven view
The plagues that us pursue:
And every where descrie
1750   Heaps of us scattred lie,
Making the straunger plaines
Fatt with our bleeding raines,
Proud that on them their grave
So manie legions have.
1755   And with our fleshes still
Neptune his fishes fill
And dronke with bloud from blue
The sea take blushing hue:
As juice of *Tyrian* shell,
1760   When clarified well
To wolle of finest fields
A purple glosse it yelds.
But since the rule of *Rome*
To one mans hand is come,
1765   Who governes without mate
Hir now united state,
Late jointlie rulde by three
Envieng mutuallie,

1733 ff. *initial letters not capitalized in 1733–8, 1740–6, 1748–54, 1757–62, 1764–70, 1772–8, 1780–4, 1786, 1789–92, 1794, 1796–802, 1804–6, 1808–10, in 1595* 1752 *not indented in 1595*

Whose triple yoke much woe
  On *Latines* necks did throwe: 1770
I hope the cause of jarre,
  And of this bloudie warre,
  And deadlie discord gone
  By what we last have done:
  Our banks shall cherish now   1775
  The branchie pale-hew'd bow
  Of *Olive*, *Pallas* praise,
  In stede of barraine bayes.
And that his temple dore,
  Which bloudie *Mars* before   1780
  Held open, now at last
  Olde *Janus* shall make fast:
  And rust the sword consume,
  And spoild of waving plume,
  The useles morion shall   1785
  On crooke hang by the wall.
At least if warre returne
  It shall not here sojourne,
  To kill us with those armes
  Were forg'd for others harmes: 1790
  But have their pointes addrest,
  Against the *Germains* brest,
  The *Parthians* fayned flight,
  The *Biscaines* martiall might.
Olde Memorie doth there   1795
  Painted on forhead weare
  Our Fathers praise: thence torne
  Our triumphes baies have worne:
  Therby our matchles *Rome*
  Whilome of Shepeheards come   1800
  Rais'd to this greatnes stands,
  The Queene of forraine lands.
Which now even seemes to face
  The heav'ns, her glories place:
  Nought resting under Skies   1805
  That dares affront her eies.
  So that she needes but feare
  The weapons *Jove* doth beare,

Who angrie at one blowe
1810   May her quite overthrowe.

Act. 5.

Cleopatra. Euphron. Children of Cleopatra.
Charmion. Eras.

Cleop.

1815   O cruell Fortune! ô accursed lott!
O plaguy love! ô most detested brand!
O wretched joyes! ô beauties miserable!
O deadlie state! ô deadly roialtie!
O hatefull life! ô Queene most lamentable!
1820   O *Antonie* by my fault buriable!
O hellish worke of heav'n! alas! the wrath
Of all the Gods at once on us is falne.
Unhappie Queene! ô would I in this world
The wandring light of day had never sene?
1825   Alas! of mine the plague and poison I
The crowne have lost my ancestors me left,
This Realme I have to straungers subject made,
And robd my children of their heritage.
        Yet this is nought (alas!) unto the price
1830   Of you deare husband, whome my snares entrap'd:
Of you, whom I have plagu'd, whom I have made
With bloudie hand a guest of mouldie Tombe:
Of you, whome I destroid, of you, deare Lord,
Whome I of Empire, honor, life have spoil'd.
1835   O hurtfull woman! and can I yet live,
Yet longer live in this Ghost-haunted tombe?
Can I yet breathe! can yet in such annoy,
Yet can my Soule within this bodie dwell?
O Sisters you that spinne the thredes of death!
1840   O *Styx*! ô *Phlegethon*! you brookes of hell!
O Impes of *Night*! *Euph.* Live for your childrens sake:
Let not your death of kingdome them deprive.

Alas what shall they do? who will have care?
Who will preserve this royall race of yours?
Who pittie take? even now me seemes I see   1845
These little soules to servile bondage falne,
And borne in triumph. *Cl.* Ah most miserable!
Euph. Their tender armes with cursed corde fast bound
At their weake backs. *Cl.* Ah Gods what pittie more!
Euph. Their seelie necks to ground with weaknesse bend.   1850
Cl. Never on us, good Gods, such mischiefe sende.
Euph. And pointed at with fingers as they go.
Cl. Rather a thousand deaths. *Euph.* Lastly his knife
Some cruell caytive in their bloud embrue.
Cl. Ah my heart breaks. By shadie bankes of hell,   1855
By fieldes wheron the lonely Ghosts do treade,
By my soule, and the soule of *Antonie*
I you beseche, *Euphron*, of them have care.
Be their good Father, let your wisedome lett
That they fall not into this Tyrants handes.   1860
Rather conduct them where their freezed locks
Black *Æthiopes* to neighbour Sunne do shewe;
On wavie *Ocean* at the waters will;
On barraine cliffes of snowie *Caucasus*;
To Tigers swift, to Lions, and to Beares,   1865
And rather, rather unto every coaste,
To ev'rie land and sea: for nought I feare
As rage of him, whose thirst no bloud can quench.
    Adieu deare children, children deare adieu:
Good *Isis* you to place of safetie guide,   1870
Farre from our foes, where you your lives may leade
In free estate devoid of servile dread.
    Remember not, my children, you were borne
Of such a Princelie race: remember not
So manie brave Kings which have *Egipt* rul'de   1875
In right descent your ancestors have bene:
That this great *Antonie* your Father was,
Hercules bloud, and more then he in praise.
For your high courage such remembrance will,
Seing your fall with burning rages fill.   1880

1850 *Euph.*] *1595*; *Eph. 1592*

Who knowes if that your hands false *Destinie*
The Scepters promis'd of imperiouse *Rome*,
In stede of them shall crooked shepehookes beare,
Needles or forkes, or guide the carte, or plough?
1885 Ah learne t'endure: your birth and high estate
Forget, my babes, and bend to force of fate.
  Farwell, my babes, farwell, my hart is clos'de
With pitie and paine, my self with death enclos'de,
My breath doth faile. Farwell for evermore,
1890 Your Sire and me you shall see never more.
Farwell swete care, farwell. *Chil*. Madame Adieu.
Cl. Ah this voice killes me. Ah good Gods! I swounde.
I can no more, I die. *Eras*. Madame, alas!
And will you yeld to woe? Ah speake to us.
1895 *Eup*. Come children. *Chil*. We come. *Eup*. Follow we our chaunce.
The Gods shall guide us. *Char*. O too cruell lott!
O too hard chaunce! Sister what shall we do,
What shall we do, alas! if murthring darte
Of death arrive while that in slumbring swound
1900 Half dead she lie with anguish overgone?
Er. Her face is frozen. *Ch*. Madame for Gods love
Leave us not thus: bidd us yet first farwell.
Alas! wepe over *Antonie*: Let not
His bodie be without due rites entomb'de.
1905 *Cl*. Ah, ah. *Char*. Madame. *Cle*. Ay me! *Ch*. How fainte she is?
Cl. My Sisters, holde me up. How wretched I,
How cursed am! and was ther ever one
By Fortunes hate into more dolours throwne?
  Ah, weeping *Niobe*, although thy hart
1910 Beholdes it selfe enwrap'd in causefull woe
For thy dead children, that a sencelesse rocke
With griefe become, on *Sipylus* thou stand'st
In endles teares: yet didst thou never feele
The weights of griefe that on my heart do lie.
1915 Thy Children thou, mine I poore soule have lost,
And lost their Father, more then them I waile,
Lost this faire realme; yet me the heavens wrathe
Into a Stone not yet transformed hath.

Phaetons sisters, daughters of the Sunne,
Which waile your brother falne into the streames   1920
Of stately *Po*: the Gods upon the bankes
Your bodies to banke-loving Alders turn'd.
For me, I sigh, I ceasles wepe, and waile,
And heaven pittiles laughes at my woe,
Revives, renewes it still: and in the ende   1925
(Oh crueltie!) doth death for comfort lende.
    Die *Cleopatra* then, no longer stay
From *Antonie*, who thee at *Styx* attends:
Goe joine thy Ghost with his, and sobbe no more
Without his love within these tombes enclos'd.   1930
Eras. Alas! yet let us wepe, lest sodaine death
From him our teares, and those last duties take
Unto his tombe we owe. *Ch.* Ah let us wepe
While moisture lasts, then die before his feete.
Cl. who furnish will mine eies with streaming teares   1935
My boiling anguish worthilie to waile,
Waile thee *Antonie*, *Antonie* my heart?
Alas, how much I weeping liquor want!
Yet have mine eies quite drawne their Conduits drie
By long beweeping my disastred harmes.   1940
Now reason is that from my side they sucke
First vitall moisture, then the vitall bloud.
Then let the bloud from my sad eies out flowe,
And smoking yet with thine in mixture growe.
Moist it, and heate it newe, and never stopp,   1945
All watring thee, while yet remaines one dropp.
Cha. Antonie take our teares: this is the last
Of all the duties we to thee can yelde,
Before we die. *Er.* These sacred obsequies
Take *Antony*, and take them in good parte.   1950
Cl. O Goddesse thou whom *Cyprus* doth adore,
Venus of *Paphos*, bent to worke us harme
For olde *Julus* broode, if thou take care
Of *Cæsar*, why of us tak'st thou no care?
Antonie did descend, as well as he,   1955
From thine owne Sonne by long enchained line:

1935 who] Who *1595*

And might have rul'd by one and self same fate,
True *Trojan* bloud, the statelie *Romain* state.
　　Antonie, poore *Antonie*, my deare soule,
1960　Now but a blocke, the bootie of a tombe,
Thy life, thy heate is lost, thy coullor gone,
And hideous palenes on thy face hath seaz'd.
Thy eies, two Sunnes, the lodging place of love,
Which yet for tents to warlike *Mars* did serve,
1965　Lock'd up in lidds (as faire daies cherefull light
Which darknesse flies) do winking hide in night.
　　Antonie by our true loves I thee beseche,
And by our hearts swete sparks have sett on fire,
Our holy mariage, and the tender ruthe
1970　Of our deare babes, knot of our amitie:
My dolefull voice thy eare let entertaine,
And take me with thee to the hellish plaine,
Thy wife, thy frend: heare *Antonie*, ô heare
My sobbing sighes, if here thou be, or there.
1975　　　Lived thus long, the winged race of yeares
Ended I have as *Destinie* decreed,
Flourish'd and raign'd, and taken just revenge
Of him who me both hated and despisde.
Happie, alas too happie! if of *Rome*
1980　Only the fleete had hither never come.
And now of me an Image great shall goe
Under the earth to bury there my woe.
What say I? where am I? ô *Cleopatra*,
Poore *Cleopatra*, griefe thy reason reaves.
1985　No, no, most happie in this happles case,
To die with thee, and dieng thee embrace:
By bodie joynde with thine, my mouth with thine,
My mouth, whose moisture burning sighes have dried:
To be in one selfe tombe, and one selfe chest,
1990　And wrapt with thee in one selfe sheete to rest.
　　The sharpest torment in my heart I feele
Is that I staie from thee, my heart, this while.
Die will I straight now, now streight will I die,
And streight with thee a wandring shade will be,
1995　Under the *Cypres* trees thou haunt'st alone,
Where brookes of hell do falling seeme to mone.

But yet I stay, and yet thee overlive,
That ere I die due rites I may thee give.
   A thousand sobbes I from my brest will teare,
With thousand plaints thy funeralles adorne: 2000
My haire shall serve for thy oblations,
My boiling teares for thy effusions,
Mine eies thy fire: for out of them the flame
(Which burnt thy heart on me enamour'd) came.
   Wepe my companions, wepe, and from your eies   2005
Raine downe on him of teares a brinish streame.
Mine can no more, consumed by the coales
Which from my breast, as from a furnace, rise.
Martir your breasts with multiplied blowes,
With violent hands teare of your hanging haire,   2010
Outrage your face: alas! why should we seeke
(Since now we die) our beawties more to kepe?
   I spent in teares, not able more to spende,
But kisse him now, what rests me more to doe?
Then lett me kisse you, you faire eies, my light,   2015
Front seate of honor, face most fierce, most faire!
O neck, ô armes, ô hands, ô breast where death
(Oh mischief) comes to choake up vitall breath.
A thousand kisses, thousand thousand more
Let you my mouth for honors farewell give: 2020
That in this office weake my limmes may growe,
Fainting on you, and fourth my soule may flowe.

At Ramsburie. 26. of November.
1590.

2016 fierce] firce *1595*   *Colophon in 1595*: *Printed at London by P.S.* for William Ponsonby. 1595.

A Discourse of Life and Death

Literary Context

The *Excellent discours de la vie et de la mort* (1576) was written by Philippe de Mornay, seigneur du Plessis-Marly, a friend and political ally of Sir Philip Sidney. Both young men had been in Paris during the St Bartholomew's Day Massacre of Protestants in August 1572 and both had been rescued by the English ambassador, Sir Francis Walsingham, as was their mentor Hubert Languet. According to the memoirs later written by Mornay's wife, Charlotte d'Arbaleste, Sidney and Walsingham were his 'chief friends in England'.[1] When Mornay came to England with his family in 1577 and 1578, seeking Queen Elizabeth's help for the Huguenots, he visited Sidney; Mornay also asked Sidney to serve as godfather for his daughter Elizabeth, born in England in June 1578. Although there are no extant records of a friendship between the Mornays and the Herbert family, it is possible that they were at least acquainted, since Sidney was so frequently a guest at Wilton and Baynards Castle during this period while they were attempting to win the queen's support for the Huguenot cause.[2] Like Sidney, Mornay strongly opposed Elizabeth's projected marriage to the Catholic duc d'Anjou. After Mornay had discussed the marriage with Elizabeth privately, he returned to France so hurriedly that he left his family behind in England.[3] Sidney later boldly set out Protestant objections to the marriage in 'A Letter written . . . to Queen Elizabeth, touching her marriage with Monsieur'.

Their friendship went beyond this political alliance. Mornay's affection for Sidney is indicated by two letters to Walsingham after Sir Philip's death: Greville cites the 'love between plessis and h[im] besyds other affinities in ther courses' as a reason to prevent the pub-

[1] *Mémoires de Charlotte Arbaleste, sur la vie de Duplessis-Mornay son mari*, printed in *Mémoires et Correspondance de Duplessis-Mornay, tome premier* (Paris: Treutter et Würtz, 1824), 117. These *Mémoires* are translated into English by Lucy Crump, *A Huguenot Family in the XVI Century: The Memoirs of Philippe de Mornay, Sieur du Plessis Marly, Written by his Wife* (London: Routledge, 1926), 169. On Mornay's later relations with Alençon, see 182.

[2] Henry of Navarre's secretary, Ségur (who came to Sidney with a letter of recommendation from Mornay), definitely visited Wilton. See Roger Howell, *Sir Philip Sidney the Shepherd Knight* (London: Hutchinson, 1968), 103–4.

[3] *Mémoires de Charlotte Arbaleste*, 120; Sidney, *Miscellaneous Prose*, 33–57.

lication of Golding's 'mercenary book' purporting to include Sidney's translation of Mornay's *De la vérité de la religion chrestienne*;[4] and when Mornay himself heard of Sidney's death, he wrote, 'I have had troubles and labours enough in these sad days but none that touched me to the heart so nearly.'[5]

Mornay, renowned in Protestant circles as a theologian, a political theorist, and a soldier, was important enough that his works were translated into most European languages. For example, Sidney himself 'did M. du Plessis the honour to translate into English his book on the "Truth of the Christian Religion"', as Madame de Mornay wrote.[6] Sidney's friend François Perrot de Méssières translated *De la vérité de la religion chrestienne* into Italian, *Della veritate della religione christiana* (pub. 1612).[7] Mornay's *Traicté de l'église* (1581) was also 'translated into every language', as Madame de Mornay reported, including John Feilde's English translation, *A treatise of the church*

---

[4] PRO SP 12/195/33, printed in Sidney, *Poems*, 530. *A Worke concerning the Trewnesse of the Christian Religion... Begunne to be translated into English by Sir Philip Sidney Knight, and at his request finished by Arthur Golding* (1587), STC 18149. It is not possible to determine how much (if any) of this translation as printed in 1587 was by Sidney. In his dedication to the Earl of Leicester Golding claimed:

> This honorable gentleman being delighted with the excellencie of this present work, began to put the same into our language for the benefite of this his native Countrie, and had proceeded certeyne Chapters therein, untill that intending a higher kind of service [i.e. military involvements]... it was his pleasure to commit the performance of this piece of service... unto my charge; declaring unto me how it was his meaning, that the same being accomplished should bee dedicated unto your Honour. (sigs. *3ᵛ–4ʳ)

Madame de Mornay confirmed this claim, stating that Sidney did her husband: '*cest honneur quelques temps apres de traduire en anglois son oeuvre de la Verité de la Religion chrestienne*' (*Mémoires de Charlotte Arbaleste*, 117–18). Sidney's involvement in the project was still being claimed in the 1604 and 1617 editions of the *Trewnesse*, both of which were prefaced by an address to Prince Henry ('him that first began to turne it into our tongue, that valiant knight of happie memorie, Syr *Phillip Sidney*', STC 18152, sig. A3ᵛ). See Sidney, *Miscellaneous Prose*, 155–7 and *A Woorke Concerning the Trewnesse of the Christian Religion*, ed. F. J. Sypher (New York, 1976), pp. xi–xv. On Sidney's translations, see also Anne Lake Prescott, *French Poets and the English Renaissance: Studies in Time and Transformation* (New Haven: Yale UP, 1978), 17 and 178.

[5] Cited in *Mémoires de Charlotte Arbaleste*, trans. Crump, 33.

[6] Ibid., 169.

[7] Sidney's extensive correspondence with Languet has been published: *The Correspondence of Sir Philip Sidney and Hubert Languet*, ed. Steuart A. Pears (London: William Pickering, 1845; rpt. Farnborough: Gregg International Publishers, 1971); on Perrot's connection with Sidney, see Martha Winburn England, 'Sir Philip Sidney and François Perrot de Méssières: Their Verse Versions of the Psalms', *Bulletin of New York Public Library* 75 (1971), 30–54, 101–10. On translations of Mornay's works, see Raoul Patry, *Philippe du Plessis-Mornay: Un Huguenot Homme d'État (1549–1633)* (Paris: Librairie Fischbacher, 1933), 300.

(1579) and Lucas de Heere's Dutch translation, *Tractaet van de Ker-cke*, completed in 1580.[8] For Pembroke to translate Mornay's *Excel-lent discours de la vie et de la mort* in 1590 was thus a continuation of the same effort to disseminate his works throughout the international Protestant community. Perhaps it was completed in anticipation of Mornay's return to England on New Year's Day 1592, when, as his wife records, he 'had the great pleasure of meeting his old friends once again'.[9] Because Mornay maintained his connections with the Sidneys, corresponding with Robert Sidney even thirty years later, those 'old friends' probably included the Sidney family, possibly even the countess herself.[10]

Although Mornay assumes that his reader is a man active in public service, it was at his wife's request that he wrote the *Discours* and translated excerpts from Seneca, and he dedicated the work to his sister.[11] The topic of the *Discours* was particularly appropriate for these women, who lived amidst the turmoil of civil war. It may well have been of consolation to Pembroke as well, who had lost her 3-year-old daughter in 1584, and her father, mother, and brother in 1586. The writings of Seneca, ubiquitous in the Renaissance, were apparently comforting to women, including both the Protestant Countess of Cumberland, portrayed with a bible and a copy of Seneca, and the Catholic Elizabeth Tanfield Cary, Viscountess Falkland, who translated excerpts from Seneca.[12] The virtues that he advocated, such as withdrawal from the illusory goods of this world, cultivation of inner virtue, and endurance of suffering, were virtues appropriate to private life and therefore open to women, who were barred from most forms of public service.[13]

---

[8] *Mémoires de Charlotte Arbaleste*, trans. Crump, 170.

[9] Ibid., 271.

[10] Philippe de Mornay to Robert Sidney, Earl of Leicester, 21 Nov. 1621, De L'Isle MS U1475 C28. Mornay was requesting Sidney's help in gaining safe passage for two of his family from Holland to England.

[11] *Mémoires de Charlotte Arbaleste*, trans. Crump, 145. The dedication to '*Madamoiselle du Plessis*' says that it contains writing which was first composed '*en faveur de vous*' (sig. A2).

[12] An English translation of Seneca is depicted in the portrait of Margaret, Countess of Cumberland, along with a bible and her own alchemical work, in the Clifford 'Great Picture', commissioned by Anne Clifford and probably executed by Jan van Belcamp. The translation of Seneca's epistles by Elizabeth Cary is mentioned in the anonymous life written by one of her daughters, either Anne or Lucy, both Benedictine nuns. Cary, *Mariam*, ed. Weller and Ferguson, 186. See Lewalski, *Writing Women*, 180.

[13] Mary Ellen Lamb, 'The Countess of Pembroke and the Art of Dying', in *Women in the Middle Ages*, 212–13. She argues that an ideal of female heroism was developed in Pembroke's translations, *Antonius* and *The Triumph of Death*.

Mornay's *Discours* is associated with the *ars moriendi* tradition, the meditations on the art of dying that derived from the early fifteenth-century volume of that title, comprised of eleven woodcuts on the death of Moriens, each with a single page of text, so that the ideas could be made available even to those with little or no literacy.[14] The emphasis on making a good death, notable in medieval hagiography, had been translated into Protestant terms by John Foxe in his *Actes and Monuments*. The Sidneys purchased a copy of 'two books of Martirs' (the two volumes familiarly known as *Foxe's Book of Martyrs*) when Mary Sidney was a child, so she was undoubtedly familiar with those tales of heroic death, particularly that of her aunt Lady Jane Grey.[15] Martyrdom was the most obvious way to make a good Christian death, but all were taught to demonstrate their faith by meeting death with resolution and cheerfulness, instructing family and friends in Christian doctrine even with the last breath. Edmund Molyneux described the death of Pembroke's mother, Lady Sidney, as a model for his readers: her 'godlie speeches' to those who came to visit her deathbed admonished them 'to repentance and amende-ment of life'. She 'left the world most confidentlie', he recorded, and went 'to God (no doubt) most glboriouslie'.[16] As we have seen, the death of Pembroke's brother Philip was also described as exemplary by such writers as Fulke Greville and George Gifford, who recorded in formulaic terms 'the most special things whereby he declared his unfeigned faith, and special work of grace, which gave proof that his end was undoubtedly happy'.[17]

Rather than contribute to this deathbed hagiography of her relatives, Pembroke chose to translate a work that dealt with the problem of death as a philosophical and theological issue. In this decision she followed the sixteenth-century shift in focus from depicting the deathbed scene like the original *Ars Moriendi* to instructing readers on the art of living as well as the art of dying. Mornay devotes barely

---

[14] Nancy Lee Beaty, *The Craft of Dying: A Study in the Literary Tradition of the Ars Moriendi in England* (New Haven: Yale UP, 1970), ch. 1.

[15] Sidney accounts for 1573, De L'Isle MS U1475 A4/5. The second, expanded edition of Foxe had been published in 1570 in two volumes. John Foxe, *Actes and Monuments of these latter and perillous dayes touching the matters of the Church* (London, 1570), *STC* 11223.

[16] Edward Molyneux's account was published in Raphael Holinshed, *Chronicles of England, Scotland, and Ireland* (1586; rpt. New York: AMS Press, 1965), IV. 879.

[17] Fulke Greville, *A Dedication to Sir Philip Sidney*, in Greville, *Prose Works*, 3–135; George Gifford, claimed by Thomas Zouch as the author of 'The Manner of Sir Philip Sidney's Death', included in Sidney, *Miscellaneous Prose*, 166–72.

twenty lines to the actual deathbed scene (sig. D4^{r-v}); his focus is demonstrated by his concluding motto, '*Mourir pour vivre, et vivre pour mourir*' (sig. E3^v). The emphasis is similar in such works as Erasmus' *De morte declamatio* (*c.*1517) and *De praeparatione ad mortem* (1534), Thomas Lupset's *The Waye of Dyenge Well* (1534), Thomas More's *A Dialoge of Comfort against Tribulacion* (1534, pub. 1553), Innocenzo Ringhiere's *Dialoghi della vita e della morte* (1550), and Thomas Becon's *The Sycke Mannes Salve* (*c.*1561). Like Mornay's *Discours*, such works typically blend classical and Christian ideas.

Mornay addresses an audience that might find his reliance on the classics problematic. The '*Advertissement au Lecteur*' (the prefatory material is not translated by Pembroke) explains the inclusion of Seneca and justifies the use of the word '*Fortune*' as traditional: phenomena that we do not understand are discussed '*selon le langage des payens à ce titre de Fortune*'. Explaining that works by Seneca are appended after the *Discours*, the '*Advertissement*' admits that he wrote '*seulement avec son jugement naturel*' of his knowledge and experience '*de la vanité de l'homme*' and had not attained those ideas '*pour foy*'. Yet we can learn from his words (sig. A1^v). There is no attempt here to justify the use of Seneca by the legends of his conversion to Christianity or his friendship and correspondence with St Paul. That correspondence, mentioned by Jerome in the fourth century (*De viris illustribus* 12), had been exposed as spurious by the Italian humanists.[18] The tradition that Seneca was acquainted with Paul, although unsubstantiated and improbable, is not entirely impossible, since Paul was brought before Seneca's brother Junius Gallio [Novatus], the proconsul in Achaea. According to Acts 18: 12–17, Gallio refused to hear the complaints of the Jews on religious matters and 'drave them from the judgement seat' because he 'cared nothing for those things'. More surprisingly, there is no attempt to justify the use of Seneca by citing Christian authorities who had mentioned Seneca with some approval, such as Tertullian (*De anima* 20) or Augustine (*De civ. dei* VI). Nor does the '*Advertissement*' mention that John Calvin had written a commentary on his '*De clementia*'.[19]

Mornay's contribution to the *ars moriendi* tradition is almost a baptized form of Stoicism. Greek Stoic philosophy as founded by Zeno

---

[18] *Epistolae Senecae ad Paulum et Pauli Ad Senecam [Quae Vocantur]*, ed. Claude W. Barlow (Horn, Austria: Ferdinand Berger for the American Academy in Rome, 1938), 1–7.

[19] *Calvin's Commentary on Seneca's De Clementia*, ed. Ford Lewis Battles and André Malan Hugo (Renaissance Society of America: Leiden: E. J. Brill, 1969).

and systematized by Chrysippus had been mediated through the late Stoa, particularly Epictetus, Marcus Aurelius, and Seneca, who is Mornay's immediate source. The Stoic emphasis on virtue, on the need to subjugate passion to reason, on the necessity of detachment from the vagaries of Fortune, and on the beneficence of death is pervasive in the essay. Like Seneca, Mornay meditates on the fickleness of Fortune, on the ways in which men prostitute themselves for riches, on the folly of those seeking advancement, and on the fact that 'A man is as wretched as he has convinced himself that he is' (*Epistulae morales* LXXVIII).[20] Like Seneca, Mornay concludes that there is true freedom once we have escaped the fear of death (*Ep.* LXXVIII). Mornay's list of the 'common and ordinarie sufferings' (647–53) is drawn not only from experience but also from a similar list in '*De consolatione ad Polybium*' (IV).[21]

Mornay's theme is stated in a series of questions, as rendered by Pembroke: 'Now what good, I pray you, is there in life, that we should so much pursue it? or what evill is there in death, that we should so much eschue it? Nay what evill is there not in life? and what good is there not in death?' (43–6) As the reader would expect from the title, the first section of the essay is devoted to life and the second to death. The section on life is developed by the familiar trope of the ages of man, here precisely following Seneca's *Epistulae morales* (particularly LXX and XLIX) in the progression from infancy (49–57), to childhood (57–73), to a youth tempted by pleasure (73–129), to a manhood subject to the temptations of avarice (129–214) and ambition (215–465), followed inexorably by the trials of old age (605–63).[22] A digression explains that there is no way to fly from the temptations of the world, for even in the desert we encounter ourselves (466–604). The rest of Mornay's essay explains why we should not fear death, but welcome it as our entrance into true life (676–961).

---

[20] *Seneca ad Lucilium Epistulae Morales*, trans. Richard M. Gummere (Cambridge, Mass.: Harvard UP, 1967), II. 189.

[21] *Seneca: Moral Essays*, trans. John W. Basore (Cambridge, Mass.: Harvard UP, 1936), II. 366.

[22] The organizational structure is set out in a prefatory 'Ode', sig. A5–8; Pembroke neither translates the prefatory material in Mornay nor supplies her own.

Nobilis, Thomas Moffet's life of Philip Sidney, written for Pembroke's son William Herbert, also uses the traditional ages as an organizational principle, indicating in the margins the various stages of Sidney's life, *pueritia* (f. 7), *adolescentia* (f. 9), and so on. Huntington Library MS HM 1337. For Renaissance variations on this theme, see John Burrow, *The Ages of Man: A Study in Medieval Writing and Thought* (Oxford: Clarendon P, 1986).

Many of the ideas in the *Discours* are derived directly from the excerpts Mornay translated for this volume from the *Epistulae morales* and the Moral Essays, including '*De tranquillitate animi*', '*De brevitate vitae*', '*De consolatione ad Polybium*', and '*De providentia*'. For example, Mornay develops his major themes of avarice and ambition from passages he translates from '*De brevitate vitae*' (sig. G2) and '*De consolatione ad Polybium*' (sig. G6), concluding that even those such as Augustus who have conquered vast lands long only for rest (sig. G3^v). Ideas developed from these excerpts of the *Epistulae* include: each age is the death of the previous one (sig. E4); we should not fear death because it is certain (sig. E6); if you compare the span of our life to infinity, we are all equally young or old at death (sig. F4); a longer life is a longer death (sig. F5^v); man's body is but an inn which he must leave suddenly (sig. F8); and, perhaps most important, to die well is to die willingly (sig. E8^v).

Mornay's debt to Seneca extends even to metaphors, such as the comparison of life to a candle (*Ep.* LIV), to a journey (*Ep.* LXXVII and CVII), and to a military mission (*Ep.* CVII). Similarly, his memorable comparison of the fetters of the courtier and the prisoner, one of gold and one of iron, echoes Seneca's '*De tranquillitate animi* ', wherein Fortune binds some with a golden chain and others with a chain of a baser metal. Even small details echo Seneca, such as the example chosen to demonstrate our fear of pain, bleeding to relieve a headache (*Ep.* LXX). Yet Mornay does adapt his Senecan material; when he cites Augustus to illustrate the trials of a ruler as Seneca did, for example, he adds not only the traditional classical examples, but also Solomon and the Holy Roman Emperor Charles V (370–97). His illustrations include figures from Greek mythology, such as Penelope (10), Hercules (74), the Cimmerians (347), Sinon (546), and the Danaids (856–8). Other allusions demonstrate not only his knowledge of classical and contemporary history (370–415), but also his interest in geometry and astronomy (315–20), New World exploration (148), and contemporary medicine (175–82), as well as less academic topics such as children's games (194), lion keepers (243), clothing (268–72), mountain-climbing (332–7), poultry (786–92), spectacles (792–4), creditors (851–3), and, with all too much contemporary relevance, the plague (475–9, 481–90, 516–20).

Mornay also develops ideas from other classical sources, particularly Plato's *Phaedo*. Mornay's topos of the body as a 'loathsome prison' (646) from which only death can deliver us (778–9, 899–901) is less Stoic than Platonic, derived from the *Phaedo*, as mediated through the medieval *de contemptu mundi* tradition; the presentation here is similar to that of Petrarch's *Trionfo della Morte* (2. 34–5). The separation of the soul from the body as a release from fetters also comes from the *Phaedo*. In the *Discours*, Mornay develops the Platonic idea that life itself is a prison: the child is imprisoned by his subjection to a schoolmaster (64); the youth is imprisoned by his passions (97); the mature man is imprisoned by avarice (160) or by ambition (284, 303–12). Yet Mornay's use of the familiar trope of life as a voyage (669–71, 712, 936–7), present in Plato's *Phaedo*, more precisely follows Seneca's '*De consolatione ad Polybium*' in the emphasis on death as a haven after life's voyage.[23] The navigation metaphor, pervasive in the *Discours*, is echoed even in Mornay's prefatory '*Sonet pour Madamoiselle du Plessis*' and in the anonymous sonnet '*A L'Autheur*', which concludes:

> Et si la mort nous est le repos et le port
> Auquel nous aspirons: heureuse est donc la vie
> Qui monstre le chemin à une heureuse mort. (sig. A4ᵛ)

The metaphor is even more pronounced in the prefatory '*Ode*', which describes the world as '*une mèr orageuse*' that offers no harbour from tempest except death (sig. A5).

It would be difficult to overstate Mornay's debt to Seneca, and yet he is never specifically named in the *Discours*. The authority most frequently named is Solomon. This appeal to Hebrew Wisdom literature is appropriate, for the Book of Proverbs and particularly the Book of Ecclesiastes, both attributed in the Renaissance to Solomon and so titled in the Geneva Bible, sit companionably beside the *contemptus mundi* of Stoicism. 'Vanity of vanities, saith the Preacher . . . all is vanity' (Eccles. 1: 2) and Seneca agrees that life can be futile (*Ep.* XXIV). 'There is no new thing under the sunne' (Eccles. 1: 9), says Solomon, and Seneca agrees that the natural cycle continues, 'I see nothing new' (*Ep.* XXIV). 'There is none end in making manie bokes', says the prophet (Eccles. 12: 12), and Seneca agrees that the thirst for knowledge is a form of intemperance (*Ep.* LXXXVIII). Solomon rejects pleasure as meaningless, ambition as futile, and riches as transitory (Eccles. 2), and Seneca agrees (*Ep.* XVI, '*De*

---

[23] Seneca uses the metaphor frequently, as in '*De brevitate vitae*' VIII and *Ep.* LXX and CXXX. The trope of life as a voyage was ubiquitous in the Renaissance, as throughout the works of Edmund Spenser, particularly in *The Faerie Queene*, where the ship image is invoked repeatedly (see, for example, I. iii. 31–2 and III. iv. 8–10).

brevitate vitae' II-III). Wisdom gives life, says Solomon (Eccles. 7: 14), and Seneca agrees that only philosophers truly live ('*De brevitate vitae*' XIV). Mornay's combination of these two sources is most obvious when he establishes the limits of philosophy by quotations from both Socrates (577–8) and Solomon (598–601). But even Solomon must be baptized. Mornay quotes from Ecclesiastes 7: 1, 'Better, saith *Salomon*, is the day of death, then the day of birth', but supplies a Christian interpretation, 'and why? because it is not to us a last day, but the dawning of an everlasting day' (762–4). And yet Mornay's phrase echoes not only Christian doctrine but also the words of Seneca, 'That day, which you fear as being the end of all things, is the birthday of your eternity' (*Ep*. CII).

Stoic and biblical ideas are tightly interwoven throughout the *Discours*. For example, the dangers of avarice and ambition, stressed in '*De brevitate vitae*' II and XX, are illustrated in Mornay's treatise by the temptation of Christ (140–2, 511–12); the search for pastoral *otium*, discussed in Seneca's '*De otio*', is illustrated by the story of Lot's escape from Sodom (485–8); the longing after luxuries, castigated by Seneca in '*De brevitate vitae*' XII, is illustrated by the Israelites' remembrance of 'the garlike and onions of *Egipt*' during their wandering in the wilderness (539); and the problem of dying young, illustrated in the *Epistulae morales* with the metaphor of games (XCIII), is here illustrated by Jesus' parable about labourers in a vineyard (865–9).

Mornay, however, makes a clear distinction between the philosophy of Seneca and Christian doctrine. The seam between the two shows most clearly in his summary: 'In summe, even he that thinketh death simply to be the ende of man, ought not to feare it . . . But unto us brought up in a more holy schoole, death is a farre other thing' (751–6). Lest we miss the contrast, Mornay continues, 'neither neede we as the Pagans of consolations against death' (756–7). The phrase echoes the title of '*De consolatione ad Polybium*', one of the primary sources for Mornay's *Discours*, even as it deprecates that essay. Mornay's comments parallel St Paul's words to the Thessalonians, 'I wolde not, brethren, have you ignorant concerning them which are a slepe, that ye sorowe not even as other which have no hope' (1 Thess. 4: 13). For the Christian, Mornay says, death is 'not the end of life, but the end of death, and the beginning of life' (760–1).

Another major disjuncture between the two systems of thought occurs in the discussion of suicide. For Seneca, suicide provided an

honourable death, if life became insupportable ('*De providentia*' II).
Those who prohibit suicide, he claims, are 'shutting off the path to
freedom' (*Ep.* LXX). He frequently describes the nobility of Cato's
death, for example, but he also praises slaves who have committed suicide rather than be demeaned, and considers the propriety of suicide
as a release from disease or old age (see particularly *Epistulae morales*
XXIV, LXX, LXXVII, and CIV; '*De providentia*'). Mornay signals
his departure from this Roman attitude in his *refutatio*: 'By this reckoning, you will tell me death is a thing to be wished for: and to passe
from so much evill, to so much good, a man shoulde as it seemeth cast
away his life' (916–18). We should 'cast the world out of us', he
admonishes, but 'to cast our selves out of the world is in no sort permitted us' (922–3). 'We', he makes clear, are those who are Christian
and therefore have a different view than the Stoics. Seneca said that
'the brave and wise man should not beat a hasty retreat from life; he
should make a becoming exit' (*Ep.* XXIV). That is, suicide should not
be undertaken rashly but it is permissible. Developing the military
metaphor used by Seneca and sanctioned by Ephesians 6, Mornay
rephrases Seneca to forbid suicide: 'The Christian ought willingly to
depart out of this life but not cowardly to runne away' (923–5). He
must continue to fight until he is recalled by 'the grand Captaine'
(927).

Although Mornay fought for the Protestant cause with his pen and
with his sword, his *Discours* is surprisingly non-sectarian; there is no
reference to the doctrines of election, of the priesthood of all believers,
of the perseverance of saints; God's grace is specifically mentioned only
once (494), and salvation by faith rather than works is assumed rather
than stated. He does not discuss appropriate prayers for the dying, or
liturgy for burial, nor does he attack prayers for the dead. Unlike the
Calvinist Becon in *The Sycke Mannes Salve*, he includes no anti-Catho-
lic diatribes; he even mentions with apparent approval the 'Monkish
solitarines' of Charles V (396). Intended for '*toutes personnes, honnestes
et craignans Dieu*', as Mornay says in his dedication (sig. A2ᵛ), the *Discours* assumes that the reader is destined for eternal life, not damnation, and thereby sidesteps the doctrine of predestination.

Mornay addresses primarily an affluent, educated Protestant audience, men who are active in public service in the military or at court.
He explicitly omits from discussion those who are too poor to receive
a formal education (60–1), those who are foolish or unhappy 'in the
conceit of the world' (136), those who have fallen from power (367–

70), or those who fail as courtiers (419–26). Paradoxically, by carefully excluding the poor, the uneducated, and the unfortunate from his discussion, he demonstrates an awareness of their plight; if life is difficult, even under the best of circumstances, how much more untenable must it be for the poor? Even after limiting his discussion to those who are more privileged, Mornay assumes that sufferings such as 'losse of friendes and parents, banishments, exiles, disgraces, and such others' are 'common and ordinarie' (648–9) to his readers, many of whom were persecuted for their faith. People living under such conditions might well welcome the death that would end their sufferings and usher them into God's eternal rest and joy.

Much of Mornay's attention is devoted not to death, however glorious, but to the trials of court life. Into the passage on 'perfit age' (130) he slips a lengthy discussion of avarice and ambition (one third of the total essay), the two sins most likely to beset a courtier, 'promising if wee will adore them, perfect contentment of the goods and honors of this world' (138–40). So alluring are they, Mornay says, that only 'the true children of the Lord' will 'cast not themselves headlong from the top of the pinnacle' (140–2), as Satan tempted Jesus to do. To gain wealth, the avaricious man gives his life. No quantity of riches will suffice, nor can he ever find contentment, for his life is consumed with the fear of losing the goods he has amassed. Mornay applies the Petrarchan descriptions of the lover's 'burning ardour' and 'trembling colde' to the passions of the covetous (155–6). Giving neither 'any pleasure or contentment', the search for riches consumes the lives of most men (214).

Mornay's emphasis is clear in the space devoted to each temptation of manhood: less than 100 lines concern the dangers of avarice, but almost 300 concern the dangers of ambition, the besetting sin of court life. The soldier may spend his life on the battleground, losing an arm or leg, or even life itself 'at the pleasure of a Prince' who values a bit of his neighbour's land more than 'the lives of a hundred thousand such as he' (233–5). The courtier gives up his integrity to serve a prince, who delights in raising someone to great heights, only 'to cast him downe at an instant' (250–1). Mornay's metaphor of the courtier as 'the Lions keeper' vividly describes the relationship with the Prince: 'by long patience' he may have 'made a fierce Lion familiar', yet he never offers him meat 'but with pulling backe his hand, alwayes in feare least he should catch him' (243–5). But ambitious courtiers blind themselves to their true position, assuming that they are honoured when they are merely being exploited by their superiors, used by their inferiors, and plotted against by their equals. To others they may appear happy, at least when they are in favour, but they are consumed with desire to climb higher. Like the avaricious, the ambitious can never be satisfied: 'Thou thinkest them very high, and they thinke themselves very lowe' (286–7). Like Seneca, Mornay concludes that 'true greatnes consist[s] in contempt of those vaine greatnesses, whereunto they are slaves' (321–2).

Drawing on Senecan *sententiae*, classical *exempla*, and pastoral traditions, Mornay argues that even those born to high place would gladly exchange a crown for rest, and that the poor countryman sleeps more soundly than they. Yet even conquerors such as Alexander may be consumed with ambition. Using phrases from the Psalms to comment on this Senecan *exemplum*, Mornay says that even if they subdue all the kingdoms of earth, they will not be content, but will quarrel with God and 'indevour to treade under foote his kingdome', not realizing that God 'laughing at their vaine purposes . . . thunderstriketh all this presumption' (410–13), a reference to Psalm 2. 4.

In bitter disillusionment with the court, equalling that of Raphael Hythloday in Thomas More's *Utopia* (Book I), Mornay concludes that there is no place for a good man at court. If you 'do ill' then God and your conscience are your enemies; if you 'do well' then great men are your enemies. Pleasing God brings only destruction at court (439–47). Some might say that they intend 'to serve the publique', or to guide others by their good example, but they are deluding others, or even themselves (471–4).

Retirement from public life into a life of contemplation might promise some contentment, as it apparently did for Seneca, but Mornay finds that path blocked by the 'civill warre' between reason and passion in our sinful natures (499). Although he here avoids the doctrinal term, he apparently agrees with Calvin that original sin casts its shadow over our life. With Solomon, he concludes that all knowledge is 'but vanitie and vexation of minde' (565–6) and that 'the beginning and end of wisedome is the feare of God' (598–9), a wisdom that the world takes for folly. With Seneca he says that knowledge does not necessarily lead to wisdom or to self-knowledge (566–88). The only way to 'make the worlde die in us', Mornay concludes, is 'by dieng our selves' (513–14).

Having found in life no satisfaction, he turns to death. Drawing on Platonic and Senecan ideas of the body as imprisonment, he develops a metaphor of flight made more memorable in Pembroke's translation (789–92). The passage echoes Plato and Seneca; Mornay then adds a reference to Paul's letters to the Corinthians, that the body 'shal no more be subject to corruption' (801–2; cf. 1 Cor. 15: 52). We say that we believe, Mornay says; if we do believe, there is nothing to fear in life or in death. We must *'Die to live / Live to die'* (962–3).

Fidelity to Originals

The Countess of Pembroke is, on the whole, a lively and accurate translator. In her rendition of Philippe de Mornay's *Excellent discours de la vie et de la mort* she usually gives a literal word-for-word translation of the first edition, published by Jean Durant in 1576; she does, however, make some alterations in the text (described below) and she occasionally follows slight changes in wording from a later edition or from a corrected copy. (See 'Transmission and Authority of Texts'.)

The fidelity of translation is apparent in her retention of stylistic elements, such as Mornay's characteristic repetition and parallelism. She renders *'avec une tourmente d'esprit, avec une agitation d'entendement, et une pensee flottante et irresolve'* (sig. D4), as 'a tormented spirite, a troubled minde, a wavering and irresolute thought' (699–700), for example, and renders *'Par feu, par glaive, par faim, par maladie, dedans trois ans, dedans trois jours, dedans trois heures'* (sig. E2) as 'By fire, by sworde, by famine, by sickenesse: within three yeeres, within three dayes, within three houres' (902–4). She also retains and smooths the sequencing of *'tous les jours, à toutes heures, et à tous momens'* (sig. D5), rendering it as 'every day, every houre, every moment' (731–2). Mornay's complex series of parallel constructions followed by two metaphorical restatements (sig. B4) is also precisely rendered in 115–19. Occasionally she adapts the text to correct faulty parallelism, as when she changes *'cent fois'* to 'a thousand disgraces' to match the thousands in the rest of the sentence (241). Similarly, she adds the phrase 'at the ende of our labour' to match 'at the sight of our land' and 'at the approch of our happie mansion' (19–21); adds the adjective 'lothsome' to 'disdaine', paralleling the construction 'unsavery after taste' (87); and adds 'of reason' to make 'Logique of reason' match 'Arte of reason' (567–8). Because Mornay's sequence of obstacles encountered on life's journey is non-parallel in that some of the nouns lack modifiers (*'par roides montagnes, et par precipices, par deserts, et par brigandages'* (sig. B1^v)), she describes life as 'a weary jorney... over high mountaynes, steepe rockes, and theevish deserts' (13–15), rendering '*precipices*' as noun plus modifier and combining the two final nouns as another modified noun, 'theevish deserts'.[1]

Mornay's most important rhetorical device is his involvement of the reader in the text by structuring the work almost as a classical epistle. Unlike Seneca's *Epistulae morales*, Mornay's *Discours* is not addressed to a specific person. (The dedication and sonnet to his sister (sig. A2–3^v) do not constitute the text as a personal letter, since the presumed reader is addressed as male, '*mon ami*', sig. B8^v.) Nevertheless, the text employs the first person frequently, as in the phrase '*Je diray plus*' (sig. C6^v), and addresses the reader familiarly as '*tu*'. Mornay also includes the reader in the argument by his use of the first person plural, '*Nous ne voulons point enquerir ceux*' (sig. C3) as in Pembroke's 'We will not aske them' (367–8). The reader and Mornay are also portrayed as consulting authorities together, as in '*Enquerons un Empereur Auguste*' (sig. C3), rendered 'Aske we the Emperour Augustus' (381).

Pembroke heightens that effect by several small changes. She recasts the opening phrase in the first person, 'It seemes to mee strange', for '*c'est un cas estrange*' (sig. B1), making it seem more like a familiar letter. When she adds 'But you will say' (277) to Mornay's text, she anticipates the reader's response and sets up the refutation that in the next sentence begins 'True, if...' (279). Her added 'No, no' intensifies the *refutatio*, 'Let them never tell me, they apprehend the paine' (820–1), as does her added 'Nay' in 892. Such direct address parallels Mornay's use of colloquial phrases like '*Mais, direz-vous*' (sig. C2), rendered 'say you' (339), and '*Or bien, me direz-vous*' (sig. C4^v) rendered, 'Well now, you will say' (430–1). She adds other markers to the argument, as 'it seemes at first sight' that the rich are content. The phrase alerts the reader to expect the 'But' that shifts the argument (228).

Pembroke's translation procedures may be constrasted with those of the only previous English translator, Edward Aggas. Aggas, who traded as a bookseller in St Paul's Churchyard, London, between 1576 and 1625, was both a stationer and a translator from the French of literary, historical, and political works. His translation of Mornay's *Discours*, which appeared under the title *The Defence of Death* in 1576, was his first recorded publication; and in 1588 he also published a

---

[1] Sidney, Mary. *Discourse*, ed. Bornstein, 74.

translation of Mornay's *A Letter Written by a French Catholike Gentle-man.*[2] Although it might reasonably be assumed that Aggas was usually motivated more by profit than literary considerations, it is clear from his output that he was a fast-working and competent trans-lator from the French. While there can be no absolute certainty over the exact number of his translations, the range of those identified is impressive, including, between 1581 and 1588, royal edicts and polit-ical tracts relating to the affairs of King Henri III and King Henri IV (*STC* 12508, 13091.5, 13100, 13108, 13109) and works by Edmond de L'Allouette (*STC* 15137), Pierre Erondelle (*STC* 10512), François de La Noue (*STC* 15215), and Jean Taffin (*STC* 23652).[3]

Pembroke's translation is slightly more concise than the original, and considerably more concise than that by Aggas. As we have seen, Pembroke's few expansions typically supply guideposts to lead the reader through the argument, or amplify metaphors. Unlike Aggas, she does not add padding, like 'to the end' (sig. A4^v) or 'Finally, in a few words to rehearse' (sig. C2^v). Nor does she add 'do' to the verb form, as Aggas does frequently, as 'doo abandon', 'doo refrain', and 'doo so stick' on a single page, for example (sig. D8^v). Whereas Aggas signals two parts of an argument by the phrases 'Thus in few words on the one side' and 'On the other side', Pembroke simply repeats 'Loe' (119 and 124). She does not use frequent doublets for single terms as Aggas does; for example, her phrase 'fetter himselfe as it were in stockes' (117–18) condenses Aggas's doubled phrasing, 'to binde and in manner commit his person to the stocks and tor-

---

[2] Edward Aggas, *The Defence of Death* (1576), *STC* 18136, sig. A5. Two copies of this translation (at the British Library and Lambeth Palace) bear the date 1577, *STC* 18137. *A Letter Written by a French Catholike Gentleman, to the Maisters at Sorbonne. Concerning the late victories obtained by the King of Navarre* (1588), *STC* 18144. It is possible, although not certain, that Aggas himself had translated *A Letter*. The work had been entered by him in the *Stationers' Register* on 3 February 1588 and he may have been prompted into this ven-ture by the success in the previous year of Golding's translation of Mornay's *Trewnesse*, which was published by his regular business partner, Thomas Cadman. (Aggas and Cadman appear to have collaborated in the publication of *STC* 13100, 15125, and 18487. They also shared an interest in the works of George Whetstone, *STC* 25346 and 25349.)

[3] Aggas had also originally entered in the *Stationers' Register* on 20 October 1595 the rights to John Florio's translation of Michel de Montaigne's *The Essayes or Morall, Politike and Militarie Discourses* (1603), *STC* 18041, which were transferred to Edward Blount on 4 June 1600. Similarly, he had entered on 10 July 1590 the rights to Sir William Jones's trans-lation of Justus Lipsius' *Six Bookes of Politickes or Civil Doctrine* (1594), *STC* 15701, later published by William Ponsonby, who had published two years earlier the Countess of Pem-broke's translations of Mornay's *A Discourse of Life and Death* and Garnier's *Antonius* (1592), *STC* 18138. A finding-list of works entered, published, and/or translated by Aggas is included in *A Short-Title Catalogue*, III. 2.

ments' (sig. A8ᵛ). She also employs more economical sentence construction. For example, when Aggas writes 'The sting of death it self shall be killed, for all this sting is nothing but feare' (sig. E2ᵛ), she uses a relative clause to reduce repetition, 'the sting of Death it selfe shall bee dead, which is nothing else but Feare' (891–2).

She occasionally tightens Mornay's wording. Sometimes she omits superfluous introductory phrases, like '*en un mot*' (sig. B3) or '*en somme*' (sig. B4). Sometimes she employs a single word to replace a modifying phrase or clause, for example, as when 'painefully swimme' (118–19) renders '*nager... avec travail et peine*' (sig. B4), or 'trembling colde' (156) renders '*en frisson et tremblement*' (sig. B5), or, more strikingly, 'false spectacles' (792–3) renders '*de lunettes qui nous trompent*' (sig. D7) and 'unwares' (606) renders '*sans que nous y ayons pris garde*' (sig. D1ᵛ). Several times she omits a word or phrase. She omits '*qui ne guerit d'aucun mal*', a phrase that contributes little to the description of riches (169), thereby emphasizing Mornay's sequence, '*qui n'a ne force ne vertu... plus inutile et plus vile*' (sig. B5ᵛ). She omits '*en nostre mauvaise complexion*' (sig. C7), rendering only the first part of the phrase 'we have sucked the bad aire' (517–18), and she omits the somewhat redundant '*qui y ont mis le pied*' (114; sig. B4). Like Aggas, she omits the phrase '*en pouppe*' or stern wind (932; sig. E3). She occasionally omits such brief modifying phrases as '*de pied ferme*' (955; sig. E3ᵛ) and '*s'en remuoit point*' (424; sig. C4ᵛ). She also omits thieves from the list of trials of the covetous man (144; sig. B5). More significantly, she omits two entire sentences: at line 318, '*Rebas-en la base, tu verras que ce n'est comme rien*' (sig. C1ᵛ); and at line 511, '*Tous deux, à dire vray, se forgent un enfer voirement en ce monde*' (sig. C4ᵛ). Another omission is not condensation, but apparently an attempt to avoid an unpleasant topic, the kidney stones that plagued her father and her husband. Each time her text reads '*gravelles*' the word is replaced by a general phrase, 'and such like diseases' (616) and 'any disease whatsoever' (823). She, like Aggas, also omits the final 'Amen', perhaps deeming it inappropriate.

Although most earlier studies have concluded that her reliance on Aggas was minimal, some of her text exactly matches his, except for slight variations in spelling.[4] Dozens of parallel phrases could be

---

[4] Sidney, Mary. *Discourse*, ed. Bornstein, 8–16, 73–97; Paul Joseph Jackson, 'An Elizabethan Translator: The Countess of Pembroke with Particular Attention to her *Discourse of Life and Death*' (University of Washington, Ph.D. diss., 1940), 104–19; Sidney, Mary. *Antonie*, ed. Luce, 20–30.

cited, such as 'either he gives them over to a hangman, or himselfe breakes their neckes' (207–8; sig. B3^v), 'the flesh against the spirite, passion against reason, earth against heaven' (500–1; sig. C5^v) 'one evill can not bee cured but by an other' (693–4; sig. D4), 'I wil say more' (892; sig. E2^v). Such phrases are usually so close to the French that it is difficult to tell whether she is deliberately following Aggas in any particular case, yet there are enough such cases to indicate that she had read Aggas with care, whether or not she worked with his text before her. Pembroke, however, rarely follows Aggas blindly. For example, both translations read, 'Please the people [and] you please a beast' (444; sig. C3^v). As usual, the matching phrase is so close to the French ('*Complaisez au peuple, vous plaisez à une beste*', sig. C5) that it is difficult to tell if Pembroke was quoting Aggas. As frequently happens in her text, that quoted phrase is immediately followed by another that differs not only in wording but also in interpretation. Whereas Aggas says 'in pleasing of whome you shall displease your self', Pembroke says 'and pleasing such, ought to be displeasing to your selfe', translating Mornay's '*devez desplaire*' (sig. C5) more accurately. Similarly, Pembroke's words 'Thou art covetous in desiring, and prodigall in spending' exactly match Aggas's (859–60; Aggas sig. E1^v); the sentence is a literal translation of Mornay, '*Tu es avare à la desirere, et prodigue à la despendre*' (sig. E1). But Pembroke's apparent quotation is immediately followed by a differing interpretation of Mornay. '*Tu plains la Cour*' is rendered by Aggas, 'thou complainest of the Court' in the sense of lamenting or missing it (sig. E1^v). In contrast, Pembroke renders the phrase 'findest fault with the Court' (860–1), thereby replacing nostalgia with criticism and reinforcing earlier comments on the court and courtiers (particularly 215–430). She often more accurately reflects the sense of the original than Aggas, as when she retains Mornay's wry description of humanity, '*animaux, qu'on teint estre raisonnables*' (sig. C5^v), as 'creatures supposed reasonable' (463), in contrast to Aggas's less cautious phrase, 'reasonable creatures' (sig. C3^v). Nevertheless, on at least two occasions she does agree with Aggas's mistranslation. She follows him in mistranslating '*le medecin*' (physician) as 'medicine', which would be '*la medecine*' (28; sig. A5^v). Aggas also mistranslates '*et non se laissant trainer à la necessité de son destin*' (sig. E1^v) as 'and not to permit our selves to be haled after the necessitie of our destinie' (sig. E2). Pembroke's version is similar, 'and not suffering us to be drawen by the necessitie of destenie' (882–3). Whereas Mornay in this passage equates God and destiny, Aggas and Pembroke separate them, so that one may follow God rather than being drawn by destiny.

The differences between her work and that of Aggas can be illustrated by their translations of Mornay's explanation of the soul's departure from the body:

Ce corps tel qu'il est maintenant n'est que l'escorce et la coque de l'esprit. Et faut par necessité qu'elle se rompe si nous en voulons esclorre, si nous voulons vrayment vivre, si nous voulons voir le jour. Nous avons bien, ce nous semble, quelque vie, et quelque sentiment. Mais nous sommes tous accroupis, nous ne pouvons estendre nos ailes, tant s'en faut, que nous puissions prendre nostre vol verse le ciel, tant que ceste masse terrestre soit ostee de dessus nous. (sig. D6ᵛ–7)

Aggas's translation is fairly accurate but wordy and pedestrian:

This body such as it is, is no other then a bark or shel over the spirit, and therfore must of necessitie flee a sunder when we come to our departure, if we will perfectly live or cleerly behold, the day. We have as we thinck some life, and some feeling: but we are altogether impotent, we can not stretch out our winges, neither can we take our flight into Heaven, until this earthly masse of flesh be taken from us. (sig. D7)

Pembroke retains some of his wording, such as the words 'barke' and 'shell', and the phrase, 'stretch out our wings', but her verbs 'broken' and 'hatched' amplify the metaphor absent from Aggas's phrase, 'when we come to our departure'. She retains Mornay's parallel 'if' clauses, supplies alliteration, and plays with the word 'burthen', producing a far more lively passage:

This body such as now it is, is but the barke and shell of the soule: which must necessarily be broken, if we will be hatched: if we wil indeed live and see the light. We have it semes, some life, and some sence in us: but are so croked and contracted, that we cannot so much as stretch out our wings, much lesse take our flight towards heaven, untill we be disburthened of this earthlie burthen. (786–92)

Such concern for rhetorical effect is pervasive in Pembroke's translation. She chooses the more colourful phrase, 'burning ardour' (155) instead of 'painful heat and travail' (sig. B2), for example, or describes gold as the 'vile excrement of the earth' (218) instead of 'vile dirt' (sig. B4). She also makes the biblical allusions more obvious by quoting the language of the Geneva Bible. Aggas's phrase 'vanitie and travaile of minde' (sig. C7ᵛ) becomes 'vanitie and vexation' (565), quoting the Genevan version of Ecclesiastes 1: 14 and thereby making Mornay's allusion more obvious to an English reader; similarly, the 'rootes and onions of Egypt' (sig. C6ᵛ) becomes the biblical 'garlike and onions of Egipt' (539). Aggas apparently does not catch the Senecan reference in Mornay's '*la consolation contre la mort*' (sig. D6); his 'comforte against death' (sig. D6) obscures the Senecan title emphasized in Pembroke's more accurate 'consolations against death' (756–7).

Pembroke makes some adaptations to her audience. Sometimes she omits an explanation which ought to be clear to her readers. '*La deesse Isis*' becomes simply '*Isis*' (274), for example. Her use of the term 'barber' reflects current English medical practice; although Mornay has the barber as both dentist and surgeon, Pembroke has the barber pulling teeth but not performing surgery, since the medical work of barbers had been restricted to dentistry since the time of Henry VIII (29–36). Similarly, she renders Mornay's '*yeux...couverts d'une taye*' (sig. D7) as 'eyes but overgrowen with pearles' (793), a common English description of cataracts, and replaces Mornay's '*fausse faim*' (sig. B5ᵛ) with 'dogs hunger' (178), the colloquial term for bulimy or an insatiable appetite.

Most of her alterations complete the idea or emphasize the metaphor in her original. She also completes the comparison of the reader to a creditor by retaining 'Thou' (851–2) instead of switching to third person as does Mornay (sig. D8ᵛ). She adds the word 'death' to clarify '*la fin de nos miseres*' (sig. B2), rendering it 'death, the end of our miseries' (38). She also expands '*La souffrance se beura parmi l'esperance*' (sig. E1ᵛ) to read, 'the sufferance of ill, swallowed in the confidence of good' (890–1), thereby emphasizing the biblical echo 'swallow' and connecting it to the next phrase, 'the sting of Death': both come from 1 Cor. 15: 54–5, 'Death is swallowed up into victorie. O death, where is thy sting! ô grave where is thy victorie!'

Occasionally she chooses not to render the French idiom exactly, particularly when it is inappropriate in English. For example, Pembroke eliminates the literal reference to spitting in Mornay's '*craché au visage*' (sig. B7ᵛ), rendering it as 'disgraces' (241), and omits the literal reference to sticking out the tongue in Mornay's '*ne les salvent qu'en tirent la langue*' (sig. B8), rendering it 'never but with scorne do so much as salute them' (257). She replaces the numerical thousands with 'infinite' at 813–14, which is the sense of the French '*mille*' here (sig. D7ᵛ). Yet sometimes she is overly literal, thereby rendering a phrase in obscure or awkward English, as 'is no reason' (843) for '*il n'y point de raison*' (sig. D8ᵛ), or 'payne of the teeth' (29–30) for

'*mal de dents*' (sig. B1ᵛ), and particularly the long awkward sentence in
552–7. She also misses one idiom in making it 'bad pay-maisters'
rather than debtors who fear the day of payment (621–2), since
'*paye*' does usually mean paymaster, but not in the idiom '*mauvaise
paye*' (sig. D2). She, perhaps following Aggas (sig. E1), must have
interpreted the phrase as a paymaster who was embezzling, and so
feared to be caught when he had to pay out those funds.

Errors or mistranslations in the countess's work are minimal, and
often may be deliberate, such as when she follows Aggas in removing
the mouse from the chamber of the rich (297), or in listing the musi-
cian's 'voyces, and soundes, and times' (572–3) for the perceived
redundancy of '*les voix, les sons et les tons*' (sig. C8ᵛ). She renders '*la
vie et la veuê*' (sig. D7) as 'life and light' (796) apparently to retain
the alliteration in Mornay's phrase, and describes the image of Hecate
as 'ougly, terrible, and hideous' (682), rather than '*triste, have et
hydeuse*' (sig. D3ᵛ), since sorrow would not be as visible as ugliness
in the paintings Mornay is describing. She emends '*douleur*' (sig.
B3ᵛ), probably a printer's error for '*douceur*', to 'sweetness' in the
phrase 'the sweetnes thereof be as an infusion of wormewood' (93–
4), thereby continuing the pattern of contrast from Mornay's preceding phrase. She also replaces a transition, '*voire plus*' (sig. D3), with
the more idiomatic 'yea, sooner then hee' (658), changes '*presens*'
(sig. C4ᵛ) to 'pleasures' as the ambushes of the devil (428), and
makes a few other small changes, as in the order of presentation.
She reverses the terms praise and thank (868), as does Aggas (sig.
E1ᵛ), but unlike Aggas, she also reverses court and palace (453), and
even entire sentences (717–19). She also shows the young man study-
ing before playing (61–2) as did English schoolboys, and switches the
order of the physician and the historian (577–83).

Pembroke, or more likely her printer, John Windet, takes considerable liberties with paragraphing and punctuation.[5] The 1592 edition
typically ignores Mornay's paragraph divisions, supplying others;
later editions have yet other paragraphing, particularly toward the
end. Pembroke or her printer also alters the punctuation, most often

---

[5] Windet also printed for William Ponsonby Sidney's *Arcadia* (1590 and 1593 editions),
STC 22539, 22540; Richard Harvey, *The Lambe of God and his Enemies* (1590), *STC* 12915;
Sir Walter Ralegh, *A Report of the Truth of the Fight . . . Betwixt the Revenge, and an Armada*
(1591), *STC* 20651; Adam Hill, *The Defence of the Article* (1592), *STC* 13466, and Philippe
de Mornay, *Fowre Bookes, of the Institution, Use and Doctrine of the Sacrament* (1598), *STC*
18142. See Michael G. Brennan, 'William Ponsonby: Elizabethan Stationer', *Analytical and
Enumerative Bibliography* 7 (1984 for 1983), 91–110.

employing colons and semicolons to combine short sentences (as in 510, 525, 615, 799, 829, and 904). Sometimes this produces elegant periodic sentences that seem Baconian in style (as in 101–5). More rarely, a longer sentence is separated (as in 721). Despite these minor changes in wording, order, and punctuation, however, Pembroke produces a remarkably faithful translation.

A Discourse of Life and Death,
Written in French by *Ph. Mornay.*
Sieur du Plessis Marly.

It seemes to mee strange, and a thing much to be marveiled, that the
laborer to repose himselfe hasteneth as it were the course of the
Sunne: that the Mariner rowes with all force to attayne the porte,
and with a joyfull crye salutes the descryed land: that the traveiler is
never quiet nor content till he be at the ende of his voyage: and that   5
wee in the meane while tied in this world to a perpetuall taske, tossed
with continuall tempest, tyred with a rough and combersome way,
cannot yet see the ende of our labour but with griefe, nor behold
our porte but with teares, nor approch our home and quiet abode
but with horrour and trembling. This life is but a *Penelopes* web,   10
wherein we are always doing and undoing: a sea open to all windes,
which sometime within, sometime without never cease to torment us:
a weary jorney through extreame heates, and coldes, over high mountaynes, steepe rockes, and theevish deserts. And so we terme it in
weaving at this web, in rowing at this oare, in passing this miserable   15
way. Yet loe when death comes to ende our worke, when she stretch-
eth out her armes to pull us into the porte, when after so many dangerous passages, and lothsome lodgings she would conduct us to our
true home and resting place: in steede of rejoycing at the ende of our
labour, of taking comfort at the sight of our land, of singing at the   20
approch of our happie mansion, we would faine, (who would beleeve
it?) retake our worke in hand, we would againe hoise saile to the
winde, and willinglie undertake our journey anew. No more then
remember we our paines, our shipwracks and dangers are forgotten:
we feare no more the travailes nor the theeves. Contrarywise, we   25
apprehende death as an extreame payne, we doubt it as a rocke, we
flye it as a theefe. We doe as litle children, who all the day complayne,

A Discourse of Life and Death
Copy-text: *1592. 1600, 1606, and 1608 (when it diverges substantively from 1606) are cited in
the notes; 1607 is not cited because it is a reissue of 1606. Spelling and punctuation variants are
selectively cited; turned characters (three instances of* i, *three of* u, *two of* n, *two of* s, *and one of* ?
*in 1592) are silently corrected; added paragraphing in 1606–8 is ignored; press variants are dis-
cussed elsewhere.*

2 it] is *1606*   3 to attayne] t'attain *1606*   4 traveiler] traveller *1600, 1606*

and when the medicine is brought them, are no longer sicke: as they
who all the weeke long runne up and downe the streetes with payne of
30 the teeth, and seeing the Barber comming to pull them out, feele no
more payne: as those tender and delicate bodyes, who in a pricking
pleurisie complaine, crie out, and cannot stay for a Surgion, and
when they see him whetting his Launcet to cut the throate of the disease, pull in their armes, and hide them in the bed, as, if he were come
35 to kill them. We feare more the cure then the disease, the surgion then
the paine, the stroke then the impostume. We have more sence of the
medicins bitternes soone gone, then of a bitter languishing long continued: more feeling of death the end of our miseries, then the endlesse misery of our life. And whence proceedeth this folly and
40 simplicitie? we neyther knowe life, nor death. We feare that we
ought to hope for, and wish for that we ought to feare. We call life a
continuall death: and death the issue of a living death, and the
entrance of a never dying life. Now what good, I pray you, is there
in life, that we should so much pursue it? or what evill is there in
45 death, that we should so much eschue it? Nay what evill is there not
in life? and what good is there not in death? Consider all the periods of
this life. We enter it in teares, we passe it in sweate, we ende it in
sorow. Great and litle, ritch and poore, not one in the whole world,
that can pleade immunitie from this condition. Man in this point
50 worse then all other creatures, is borne unable to support himselfe:
neither receyving in his first yeeres any pleasure, nor giving to others
but annoy and displeasure, and before the age of discretion passing
infinite dangers. Only herein lesse unhappy then in other ages, that
he hath no sence nor apprehension of his unhappines. Now is there
55 any so weake minded, that if it were graunted him to live alwayes a
childe, would make accompt of such a life? So then it is evident that
not simplie to live is a good, but well and happilie to live. But proceede. Growes he? with him growe his travailes. Scarcely is he come
out of his nurses hands, scarcely knowes he what it is to play, but he
60 falleth into the subjection of some Schoolemaister: I speake but of
those which are best and most precisely brought up. Studies he? it
is ever with repining. Playes he? never but with feare. This whole
age while he is under the charge of an other, is unto him but as a
prison. He only thinks, and only aspires to that time when freed
65 from the mastership of another, he may become maister of himselfe:

58 travailes] travelles *1606*   59 he] *om. 1600, 1606*

pushing onward (as much as in him lies) his age with his shoulder,
that soone he may enjoy his hoped libertie. In short, he desires nothing more then the ende of this base age, and the beginning of his
youth. And what else I pray you is the beginning of youth, but the
death of infancy? the beginning of manhood, but the death of   70
youth? the beginning of to morow, but the death of to day? In this
sort then desires he his death, and judgeth his life miserable: and so
cannot be reputed in any happines or contentment. Behold him
now, according to his wish, at libertie: in that age, wherein *Hercules*
had the choise, to take the way of vertue or of vice, reason or passion 75
for his guide, and of these two must take one. His passion entertains
him with a thousand delights, prepares for him a thousand baites,
presents him with a thousand worldly pleasures to surprize him:
and fewe there are that are not beguiled. But at the reconings ende
what pleasures are they? pleasures full of vice which hold him still 80
in a restles feaver: pleasures subject to repentance, like sweete meates
of hard disgestion: pleasures bought with paine and perill, spent and
past in a moment, and followed with a long and lothsome remorse of
conscience. And this is the very nature (if they be well examined) of
all the pleasures of this world. There is in none so much sweetenes, 85
but there is more bitternes: none so pleasant to the mouth, but leaves
an unsavery after taste and lothsome disdaine: none (which is worse)
so moderated but hath his corosive, and caries his punishment in it
selfe. I will not heere speake of the displeasures confessed by all, as
quarells, debates, woundes, murthers, banishments, sicknes, perils, 90
whereinto sometimes the incontinencie, sometimes the insolencie of
this ill guided age conductes him. But if those that seeme pleasures,
be nothing else but displeasures: if the sweetnes thereof be as an infusion of wormewood: it is plaine enough what the displeasure is they
feele, and how great the bitternes that they taste. Behold in summe 95
the life of a yong man, who rid of the government of his parents
and maisters, abandons himselfe to all libertie or rather bondage of
his passion: which right like an uncleane spirit possessing him, casts
him now into the water, now into the fire: sometimes caries him cleane
over a rocke, and sometime flings him headlong to the bottome. 100
Now if he take and followe reason for his guide, beholde on the
other part wonderfull difficulties: he must resolve to fight in every

82 disgestion] digestion *1606*   90 perils] peril *1606*   97 and maisters] *om.*
1606   to] to to *1600*

part of the field: at every step to be in conflict, and at handstrokes, as
having his enemy in front, in flanke, and on the reareward, never leav-
105 ing to assaile him. And what enemy? all that can delight him, all that
he sees neere, or farre off: briefly the greatest enemy of the world, the
world it selfe. But which is worse, a thousand treacherous and dangerous intelligences among his owne forces, and his passion within himselfe desperate: which in that age growne to the highest, awaits but
110 time, houre, and occasion to surprize him, and cast him into all
viciousnes. God only and none other, can make him choose this
way: God only can hold him in it to the ende: God only can make
him victorious in all his combats. And well we see how fewe they
are that enter into it, and of those fewe, how many that retire againe.
115 Follow the one way, or follow the other, he must either subject himselfe to a tyrannicall passion, or undertake a weery and continuall
combate, willingly cast himselfe to destruction, or fetter himselfe as
it were in stockes, easily sincke with the course of the water, or painefully swimme against the streame. Loe here the young man, who in
120 his youth hath drunke his full draught of the worlds vaine and deceivable pleasures, overtaken by them with such a dull heavines, and
astonishment, as drunkards the morow after a feast: either so out of
taste, that he will no more, or so glutted, that he can no more: not
able without griefe to speake, or thinke of them. Loe him that stoutly
125 hath made resistance: he feeles himselfe so weery, and with this continuall conflict so brused and broken, that either he is upon the point
to yeeld himselfe, or content to dye, and so acquit himselfe. And this
is all the good, all the contentment of this florishing age, by children
so earnestlie desired, and by old folkes so hartely lamented. Now com-
130 meth that which is called perfit age, in the which men have no other
thoughts, but to purchase themselves wisedome and rest. Perfit in
deede, but herein only perfit, that all imperfections of humane nature,
hidden before under the simplicitie of childhood, or the lightnes of
youth, appeere at this age in their perfection. We speake of none in
135 this place but such as are esteemed the wisest, and most happie in
the conceit of the world. We played as you have seene in feare: our
short pleasures were attended on with long repentance. Behold, now
present themselves to us avarice, and ambition, promising if wee will
adore them, perfect contentment of the goods and honors of this
140 world. And surely there are none, but the true children of the Lord,

135 this] th's *1600* (*a light impression of a dot is all that appears of the* i)

who by the faire illusions of the one or the other cast not themselves
headlong from the top of the pinnacle. But in the ende, what is all this
contentment? The covetous man makes a thousand voiages by sea and
by lande: runnes a thousand fortunes: escapes a thousand shipwrackes
in perpetuall feare and travell: and many times he either looseth his   145
time, or gaineth nothing but sicknesses, goutes, and oppilations for
the time to come. In the purchase of this goodly repose, he bestoweth
his true rest: and to gaine wealth looseth his life. Suppose he hath
gained in good quantitie: that he hath spoiled the whole East of
pearles, and drawen dry all the mines of the West: will he therefore   150
be setled in quiet? can he say that he is content? All charges and jour-
neys past, by his passed paines he heapeth up but future disquietnes
both of minde and body: from one travell falling into another, never
ending, but changing his miseries. He desired to have them, and
now feares to loose them: he got them with burning ardour, and pos-   155
sesseth in trembling colde: he adventured among theeves to seeke
them, and having found them, theeves and robbers on all sides,
runne mainely on him: he laboured to dig them out of the earth, and
now is enforced to redig, and rehide them. Finally comming from
all his voiages he comes into a prison: and for an ende of his bodely   160
travels, is taken with endlesse travails of the minde. And what at
length hath this poore soule attained after so many miseries? This
Devill of covetise by his illusions, and enchantments, beares him in
hand that he hath some rare and singuler thing: and so it fareth
with him, as with those seely creatures, whome the Devill seduceth   165
under couler of releeving their povertie, who finde their hands full
of leaves, supposing to finde them full of crownes. He possesseth or
rather is possessed by a thing, wherein is neither force nor vertue:
more unprofitable, and more base, then the least hearbe of the earth.
Yet hath he heaped togither this vile excrement, and so brutish is   170
growne, as therewith to crowne his head, which naturally he should
tread under his feete. But howsoever it be, is he therewith content?
Nay contrarywise lesse now, then ever. We commend most those
drinks that breede an alteration, and soonest extinguish thyrst: and
those meates, which in least quantitie do longest resist hunger. Now   175
hereof the more a man drinkes, the more he is a thirst, the more he
eates, the more an hungred: It is a dropsie, (and as they tearme it)
the dogs hunger: sooner may he burst then be satisfied. And which

161 travails] travels *1606*   165 seely] sillie *1600*; silly *1606*

is worse, so strange in some is this thyrst, that it maketh them dig the
pits, and painefully drawe the water, and after will not suffer them to
drinke. In the middest of a river they are dry with thirst: and on a
heape of corne cry out of famine: they have goodes and dare not use
them: they have joyes it seemes, and do not enjoy them: they neither
have for themselves, nor for another: but of all they have, they have
nothing: and yet have want of all they have not. Let us then returne
to that, that the attaining of all these deceivable goods is nothing
else but weerines of body, and the possession for the most part, but
weerines of the minde: which certenly is so much the greater, as is
more sensible, more subtile, and more tender the soule then the
body. But the heape of all misery is when they come to loose them:
when either shipwracke, or sacking, or invasion, or fire, or such like
calamities, to which these fraile things are subject, doth take and
cary them from them. Then fall they to cry, to weepe, and to torment
themselves, as little children that have lost their play-game, which
notwithstanding is nothing worth. One cannot perswade them, that
mortall men have any other good in this world, but that which is mortall. They are in their owne conceits not only spoyled, but altogither
flayed. And for asmuch as in these vaine things they have fixed all
their hope, having lost them, they fall into despaire, out of the
which commonly they cannot be withdrawen. And which is more,
all that they have not gained according to the accompts they made,
they esteeme lost: all that which turnes them not to great and extraordinary profit, they accompt as damage: whereby we see some fall into
such despaire, as they cast away themselves. In short, the recompence
that Covetise yeelds those that have served it all their life, is oftentimes like that of the Devill: whereof the ende is, that after a small
time having gratified his disciples, either he gives them over to a hangman, or himselfe breakes their neckes. I will not heere discourse of the
wickednes and mischiefes whereunto the covetous men subject themselves to attaine to these goodes, whereby their conscience is filled
with a perpetuall remorse, which never leaves them in quiet: sufficeth
that in this over vehement exercise, which busieth and abuseth the
greatest part of the world, the body is slaine, the minde is weakened,
the soule is lost without any pleasure or contentment.

Come we to ambition, which by a greedines of honor fondly holdeth occupied the greatest persons. Thinke we there to finde more?

198 flayed] slayed *1606*   215 honor] ho- nor *1592 (line break)*

nay rather lesse. As the one deceiveth us, geving us for all our travaile,
but a vile excrement of the earth: so the other repayes us, but with
smoke and winde: the rewards of this being as vaine, as those of that
were grosse. Both in the one and the other, we fall into a bottomles   220
pit; but into this the fall by so much the more dangerous, as at the
first shewe, the water is more pleasant and cleare. Of those that geve
themselves to courte ambition, some are great about Princes, others
commanders of Armies: both sorts according to their degree, you
see saluted, reverenced, and adored of those that are under them.   225
You see them appareled in purple, in scarlet, and in cloth of gould:
it seemes at first sight there is no contentment in the world but theirs.
But men knowe not how heavy an ounce of that vaine honor weighes,
what those reverences cost them, and how dearely they pay for an ell
of those rich stuffes: who knewe them well, would never buy them at   230
the price. The one hath attained to this degree, after a long and painefull service hazarding his life upon every occasion, with losse ofttimes
of a legge or an arme, and that at the pleasure of a Prince, that more
regards a hundred perches of ground on his neighbours frontiers, then
the lives of a hundred thousand such as he: unfortunate to serve who   235
loves him not: and foolish to thinke himselfe in honor with him, that
makes so litle reckening to loose him for a thing of no worth. Others
growe up by flattering a Prince, and long submitting their toongs and
hands to say and doe without difference whatsoever they will have
them: whereunto a good minde can never commaund it selfe. They   240
shall have indured a thousand injuries, received a thousand disgraces,
and as neere as they seeme about the Prince, they are nevertheles
alwayes as the Lions keeper, who by long patience, a thousand feed-
ings and a thousand clawings hath made a fierce Lion familiar, yet
geves him never meate, but with pulling backe his hand, alwayes in   245
feare least he should catch him: and if once in a yere he bites him,
he sets it so close, that he is paid for a long time after. Such is the
ende of all princes favorites. When a Prince after long breathings
hath raised a man to great height, he makes it his pastime, at what
time he seemes to be at the top of his travaile, to cast him downe at   250
an instant: when he hath filled him with all wealth, he wrings him
after as a sponge: loving none but himself, and thinking every one
made, but to serve, and please him. These blinde courtiers make
themselves beleeve, that they have freends, and many that honor

240 a] a a *1606*   250 travaile] travell *1600, 1606*

255 them: never considering that as they make semblance to love, and
honor every body, so others do by them. Their superiors disdaine
them, and never but with scorne do so much as salute them. Their
inferiors salute them because they have neede of them (I meane of
their fortune, of their foode, of their apparell, not of their person)
260 and for their equalls betweene whome commonly frendship consistes,
they envy each other, accuse each other, crosse each other; continually
greeved either at their owne harme, or at others good. Nowe what
greater hell is there, what greater torment, then envie? which in
truth is nought else but a feaver *Hectique* of the minde: so they are
265 utterly frustrate of all frendship, ever judged by the wisest the chiefe
and soveraigne good among men. Will you see it more clearely? Let
but fortune turne her backe, every man turnes from them: let her
frowne, every man lookes aside on them: let them once be disroabed
of their triumphall garment, no body will any more knowe them.
270 Againe, let there be apparelled in it the most unworthie, and infamous
whatsoever: even he without difficultie by vertue of his robe, shall
inherit all the honours the other had done him. In the meane time
they are puffed up, and growe proude, as the Asse which caried the
image of *Isis* was for the honors done to the Goddesse, and regard
275 not that it is the fortune they carry which is honored, not themselves,
on whome as on Asses, many times she will be caried. But you will
say: At least so long as that fortune endured, they were at ease, and
had their contentment, and who hath three or foure or more yeeres
of happy time, hath not bin all his life unhappie. True, if this be to
280 be at ease continually to feare to be cast downe from that degree,
whereunto they are raised: and dayly to desire with great travaile to
clime yet higher. Those (my friend) whome thou takest so well at
their ease, because thou seest them but without, are within farre
otherwise. They are faire built prisons, full within of deepe ditches,
285 and dungeons: full of darkenes, serpents and torments. Thou suppos-
est them lodged at large, and they thinke their lodgings straite. Thou
thinkest them very high, and they thinke themselves very lowe. Now
as sicke is he, and many times more sicke, who thinkes himselfe so,
then who in deed is. Suppose them to be Kings: if they thinke them-
290 selves slaves, they are no better: for what are we but by opinion? you
see them well followed and attended: and even those whome they have
chosen for their guard, they distrust. Alone or in company ever they

281 travaile] travell *1600, 1606*

are in feare. Alone they looke behinde them: in company they have an
eye on every side of them. They drinke in gould and silver; but in
those, not in earth or glasse is poison prepared and dronke. They 295
have their beds soft and well made: when they lay them to sleepe
you shall not heare a mouse stur in the chamber: not so much as a
flie shall come neere their faces. Yet nevertheles, where the countrey-
man sleepes at the fall of a great river, at the noise of a market, having
no other bed but the earth, nor covering but the heavens, these in the 300
middest of all this silence and delicacie, do nothing but turne from
side to side, it seemes still that they heare some body, there rest it
selfe is without rest. Lastly, will you knowe what the diversitie is
betwene the most hardly intreated prisoners and them? both are
inchained, both loaden with fetters, but that the one hath them of 305
iron, the other of gould, and that the one is tied but by the body,
the other by the mind. The prisoner drawes his fetters after him,
the courtier weareth his upon him. The prisoners minde sometimes
comforts the paine of his body, and sings in the midst of his miseries:
the courtier tormented in minde weerieth incessantly his body, and 310
can never give it rest. And as for the contentment you imagine they
have, you are therein yet more deceived. You judge and esteeme
them great, because they are raised high: but as fondly, as who should
judge a dwarfe great, for being set on a tower, or on the top of a moun-
taine. You measure (so good a Geometrician you are) the image with 315
his base, which were convenient, to knowe his true height, to be measured by it selfe: whereas you regard not the height of the image, but
the height of the place it stands upon. You deeme them great (if in this
earth there can be greatnes, which in respect of the whole heavens is
but a point.) But could you enter into their mindes, you would judge, 320
that neither they are great, true greatnes consisting in contempt of
those vaine greatnesses, whereunto they are slaves: nor seeme unto
themselves so, seeing dayly they are aspiring higher, and never
where they would be. Some one sets downe a bound in his minde.
Could I attaine to such a degree, loe, I were content: I would then 325
rest my selfe. Hath he attained it? he geves himselfe not so much as
a breathing: he would yet ascend higher. That which is beneath he
counts a toy: it is in his opinion but one step. He reputes himselfe
lowe, because there is some one higher, in stead of reputing himselfe
high, because there are a million lower. And so high he climes at last, 330

that either his breath failes him by the way, or he slides from the top
to the bottome. Or if he get up by all his travaile, it is but as to finde
himselfe on the top of the Alpes: not above the cloudes, windes and
stormes: but rather at the devotion of lightnings, and tempests, and
335 whatsoever else horrible, and dangerous is engendred, and conceived
in the aire: which most commonly taketh pleasure to thunderbolt and
dash into pouder that proude height of theirs. It may be herein you
will agree with me, by reason of the examples wherewith both histories, and mens memories are full. But say you, such at least
340 whome nature hath sent into the world with crownes on their heads,
and scepters in their hands: such as from their birth she hath set in
that height, as they neede take no paine to ascend: seeme without con-
troversie exempt from all these injuries, and by consequence may call
themselves happie. It may be in deed they feele lesse such incommod-
345 ities, having bene borne, bred and brought up among them: as one
borne neere the downfalls of *Nilus* becomes deafe to the sound: in
prison, laments not the want of libertie: among the *Cimmerians* in perpetuall night, wisheth not for day: on the top of the Alpes, thinks not
straunge of the mistes, the tempests, the snowes, and the stormes. Yet
350 free doubtles they are not when the lightening often blasteth a flowre
of their crownes, or breakes their scepter in their handes: when a drift
of snowe overwhelmes them: when a miste of heavines, and griefe
continually blindeth their wit, and understanding. Crowned they are
in deede, but with a crowne of thornes. They beare a scepter: but it is
355 of a reede, more then any thing in the world pliable, and obedient to
all windes: it being so far off that such a crowne can cure the maigrims
of the minde, and such a scepter keepe off and fray away the griefes
and cares which hover about them: that it is contrariwise the crowne
that brings them, and the scepter which from all partes attracts them.
360 O crowne, said the Persian Monarch, who knewe howe heavy thou sit-
test on the head, would not vouchsafe to take thee up, though he
found thee in his way. This Prince it seemed gave fortune to the
whole world, distributed unto men haps and mishaps at his pleasure:
could in show make every man content: himselfe in the meane while
365 freely confessing, that in the whole world, which he held in his hand
there was nothing but griefe, and unhappines. And what will all the
rest tell us, if they list to utter what they found? We will not aske
them who have concluded a miserable life with a dishonorable

---

332 travaile] travell *1600*; travel *1606*   358 hover] ho- ver *1592 (line break)*
368 dishonorable] dishorable *1606*

death: who have beheld their kingdomes buried before them, and have
in great misery long overlived their greatnes. Not of *Dionyse* of *Sicill*, 370
more content with a handfull of twigs to whip little children of *Corinth*
in a schoole, then with the scepter, wherewith he had beaten all *Sicill*:
nor of *Sylla*, who having robbed the whole state of *Rome*, which had
before robbed the whole world, never found meanes of rest in himselfe, but by robbing himselfe of his owne estate, with incredible 375
hazard both of his power and authoritie. But demaund we the opinion
of King *Salomon*, a man indued with singuler gifts of God, rich and
welthie of all things: who sought for treasure from the Iles. He will
teach us by a booke of purpose, that having tried all the felicities of
the earth, he found nothing but vanitie, travaile, and vexation of 380
spirit. Aske we the Emperour *Augustus*, who peaceably possessed the
whole world. He will bewaile his life past, and among infinite toiles
wish for the rest of the meanest man of the earth: accounting that
day most happy, when he might unloade himselfe of this insupportable greatnes to live quietly among the least. Of *Tiberius* his successor, 385
he will confesse unto us, that he holdes the Empire as a wolfe by the
eares, and that (if without danger of biting he might) he would gladly
let it goe: complayning on fortune for lifting him so high, and then
taking away the ladder, that he could not come downe agayne. Of *Dioclesian*, a Prince of so great wisedome and vertue in the opinion of the 390
world: he will preferre his voluntary banishment at *Salona*, before all
the Romaine Empire. Finally, the Emperour Charles the fifth,
esteemed by our age the most happy that hath lived these many
ages: he will curse his conquestes, his victories, his triumphes: and
not be ashamed to confesse that farre more good in comparison he 395
hath felt in one day of his Monkish solitarines, then in all his triumphant life. Now shall we thinke those happie in this imaginate greatnes,
who themselves thinke themselves unhappie? seeking their happines
in lessening themselves, and not finding in the world one place to
rest this greatnes, or one bed quietly to sleepe in? Happie is he only 400
who in minde lives contented: and he most of all unhappie, whome
nothing he can have can content. Then miserable *Pyrrhus* King of
Albanie, who would winne all the world, to winne (as he sayd) rest:
and went so farre to seeke that which was so neere him. But more
miserable *Alexander*, that being borne King of a great Realme, and 405
Conqueror almost of the earth, sought for more worlds to satisfye

380 travaile] travell *1600, 1606*   393 the most] most *1606*

his foolish ambition, within three dayes content, with sixe foote of
grounde. To conclude, are they borne on the highest Alpes? they
seeke to scale heaven. Have they subdued all the Kings of the earth?
410 they have quarels to pleade with God, and indevour to treade under
foote his kingdome. They have no end nor limit, till God laughing at
their vaine purposes, when they thinke themselves at the last step,
thunderstriketh all this presumption, breaking in shivers their scepters in their hands, and oftentimes intrapping them in their owne
415 crownes. At a word, whatsoever happines can be in that ambition promiseth, is but suffering much ill, to get ill. Men thinke by dayly clim-
ing higher to plucke themselves out of this ill, and the height
whereunto they so painefully aspire, is the height of misery it selfe.
I speake not heere of the wretchednes of them, who all their life
420 have held out their cap to receive the almes of court fortune, and
can get nothing, often with incredible heart griefe, seeing some by
lesse paines taken have riches fall into their hands: of them, who jus-
tling one an other to have it, loose it, and cast it into the hands of a
third: Of those, who holding it in their hands to hold it faster, have
425 lost it through their fingers. Such by all men are esteemed unhappie,
and are indeed so, because they judge themselves so. It sufficieth that
all these liberalities which the Devill casteth us as out at a windowe,
are but baites: all these pleasures but embushes: and that he doth
but make his sport of us, who strive one with another for such things,
430 as most unhappie is he, that hath best hap to finde them. Well now,
you will say, the Covetouse in all his goodes, hath no good: the Ambitious at the best he can be, is but ill. But may there not be some, who
supplying the place of Justice, or being neere about a Prince, may
without following such unbrideled passions, pleasantly enjoy their
435 goodes, joyning honor with rest and contentment of minde? Surely
in former ages (there yet remayning among men some sparkes of sin-
ceritie) in some sort it might be so: but being of that composition they
nowe are, I see not how it may be in any sorte. For deale you in
affayres of estate in these times, either you shall do well, or you
440 shall do ill. If ill, you have God for your enemy, and your owne conscience for a perpetually tormenting executioner. If well, you have
men for your enemies, and of men the greatest: whose envie and mal-
ice will spie you out, and whose crueltie and tyrannie will evermore
threaten you. Please the people you please a beast: and pleasing
445 such, ought to be displeasing to your selfe. Please your selfe, you displease God: please him, you incurr a thousand dangers in the world,

with purchase of a thousand displeasures. Whereof it growes, that if you could heare the talke of the wisest and least discontent of this kinde of men, whether they speake advisedly, or their words passe them by force of truth, one would gladly change garment with his tenaunt: an other preacheth how goodly an estate it is to have nothing: a third complaining that his braines are broken with the noise of Courte or Pallace, hath no other thought, but as soone as he may to retire himself thence. So that you shall not see any but is displeased with his owne calling, and envieth that of an other: readie neverthelesse to repent him, if a man should take him at his word. None but is weerie of the bussinesses whereunto his age is subject, and wisheth not to be elder, to free himselfe of them: albeit otherwise hee keepeth of olde age as much as in him lyeth.

What must we then doe in so great a contrarietie and confusion of mindes? Must wee to fynde true humanitie, flye the societie of men, and hide us in forrestes among wilde beastes? to avoyde these unrulie passions, eschue the assemblye of creatures supposed reasonable? to plucke us out of the evills of the world, sequester our selves from the world? Coulde wee in so dooing live at rest, it were something.

But alas! men cannot take heerein what parte they woulde: and even they which do, finde not there all the rest they sought for. Some would gladly doo, but shame of the world recalls them. Fooles to be ashamed of what in their heartes they condemne: and more fooles to be advised by the greatest enemye they can or ought to have. Others are borne in hande that they ought to serve the publique, not marking that who counsell them serve only themselves: and that the more parte would not much seeke the publique, but that they founde their owne particular. Some are told, that by their good example they may amende others: and consider not that a hundred sound men, even Phisitions themselves, may sooner catch the plague in an infected towne, then one be healed: that it is but to tempt God, to enter therein: that against so contagious an aire there is no preservative, but in getting farre from it. Finally, that as litle as the freshe waters falling into the sea, can take from it his saltnes: so little can one *Lot* or two, or three, reforme a court of *Sodome.* And as concerning the wisest, who no lesse carefull for their soules, then bodies, seeke to bring them into a sound and wholesome ayre, farre from the infection of wickednes: and who led by the hande of some Angell of God, retire

450

455

460

465

470

475

480

459 of olde] off old *1600, 1606*

485 themselves in season, as *Lot* into some little village of *Segor*, out of the
corruption of the world, into some countrie place from the infected
townes, there quietlie employing the tyme in some knowledge and
serious contemplation: I willinglie yeeld they are in a place of lesse
daunger, yet because they carie the danger in themselves not absolute-
490 lie exempt from danger. They flie the court, and a court folowes them
on all sides: they endevoure to escape the world, and the world pursues them to death. Hardly in this world can they finde a place where
the world findes them not: so gredelie it seekes to murther them. And
if by some speciall grace of God they seeme for a while free from these
495 daungers, they have some povertie that troubles them, some domestic-
all debate that torments them, or some familiar spirit that tempts
them: brieflie the world dayly in some sorte or other makes it selfe
felt of them. But the worst is, when we are out of these externall
warres and troubles, we finde greater civill warre within our selves:
500 the flesh against the spirite, passion against reason, earth against heav-
en, the worlde within us fighting for the world, evermore so lodged in
the botome of our owne hearts, that on no side we can flie from it. I
will say more: he makes profession to flie the worlde, who seekes
thereby the praise of the worlde: hee faineth to runne away, who
505 according to the proverbe, By drawing backe sets himselfe forward:
he refuseth honors, that would thereby be prayed to take them: and
hides him from men to the ende they shoulde come to seeke him.
So the world often harbours in disguised attire among them that flie
the world. This is an abuse. But follow wee the company of men,
510 the worlde hath his court among them: seeke we the Deserts, it hath
there his dennes and places of resorte, and in the Desert it selfe temp-
teth Christ Jesus. Retire wee our selves into our selves, we find it there
as uncleane as any where. Wee can not make the worlde die in us, but
by dieng our selves. We are in the world, and the worlde in us, and to
515 seperate us from the worlde, wee must seperate us from our selves.
Nowe this seperation is called Death. Wee are, wee thinke, come
out of the contagious citie, but wee are not advised that we have
sucked the bad aire, that wee carry the plague with us, that we so participate with it, that through rockes, through desarts, through moun-
520 taines, it ever accompanieth us. Having avoyded the contagion of
others, yet we have it in our selves. We have withdrawen us out of

488 willinglie] willinly *1606*   499 greater] great *1606*   513 die] dye *1600*,
1606   514 dieng] dying *1600*, *1606*

men: but notwithdrawen man out of us. The tempestuous sea torments us: we are grieved at the heart, and desirous to vomit: and to
be discharged thereof, we remove out of one ship into another, from
a greater to a lesse: we promise our selves rest in vaine: they being 525
always the same winds that blow, the same waves that swel, the
same humors that are stirred. To al no other port, no other mean of
tranquilitie but only death. We were sicke in a chamber neere the
street, or neere the market: we caused our selves to be carried into
some backer closet, where the noise was not so great. But though 530
there the noise was lesse: yet was the feaver there neverthelesse: and
thereby lost nothing of his heate. Change bedde, chamber, house,
country, againe and againe: we shall every where finde the same
unrest, because every where we finde our selves: and seek not so
much to be others, as to be other wheres. We folow solitarines, to 535
flie carefulnes. We retire us (so say we) from the wicked: but cary
with us our avarice, our ambition, our riotousnes, all our corrupt
affections: which breed in us 1000. remorses, and 1000. times each
day bring to our remembrance the garlike and onions of *Egipt*. Daily
they passe the Ferry with us: so that both on this side, and beyond the 540
water, we are in continual combat. Now could we cassere this company, which eats and gnaws our mind, doubtles we should be at
rest, not in solitarines onely, but even in the thicket of men. For the
life of man upon earth is but a continual warfare. Are we delivered
from externall practizes? Wee are to take heed of internall espials. 545
Are the Greekes gone away? We have a *Sinon* within, that wil betray
them the place. Wee must ever be waking, having an eie to the watch,
and weapons in our hands, if wee will not every houre be surprised,
and given up to the wil of our enimies. And how at last can we escape?
Not by the woodes, by the rivers, nor by the mountaines: not by 550
throwing our selves into a presse, not by thrusting our selves into a
hole. One only meane there is, which is death: which in ende seperat-
ing our spirite from our flesh, the pure and clean part of our soule
from the uncleane, which within us evermore bandeth it selfe for
the worlde, appeaseth by this seperation that, which conjoyned in 555
one and the same person coulde not, without utter choaking of the
spirit, but be in perpetuall contention.

And as touching the contentment that may be in the exercises of the
wisest men in their solitarinesse, as reading divine or prophane

---

550 by the mountaines] mountains *1606*　　　552 in] in the *1606*

560 Bookes, with all other knowledges and learnings: I hold well that it is
indeed a far other thing, then are those madde huntings, which make
savage a multitude of men possessed with these or the like diseases
of the minde. Yet must they all abide the judgement pronounced by
the wisest among the wise, *Salomon*, that all this neverthelesse applied
565 to mans naturall disposition, is to him but vanitie and vexation of
minde. Some are ever learning to correct their speach, and never
thinke of correcting their life. Others dispute in their Logique of reason, and the Arte of reason: and loose thereby many times their naturall reason. One learnes by Arithmetike to divide to the smallest
570 fractions, and hath not skill to part one shilling with his brother.
Another by Geometry can measure fields, and townes, and countries:
but can not measure himselfe. The Musitian can accord his voyces,
and soundes, and times togither: having nothing in his heart but dis-
cordes, nor one passion in his soule in good tune. The Astrologer
575 lookes up on high, and falles in the next ditch: fore-knowes the future,
and forgoes the present: hath often his eie on the heavens, his heart
long before buried in the earth. The Philosopher discourseth of the
nature of all other things: and knowes not himselfe. The Historian
can tell of the warres of *Thebes* and of *Troy*: but what is doone in
580 his owne house can tell nothing. The Lawyer will make lawes for all
the world, and not one for himselfe. The Physition will cure others,
and be blinde in his owne disease: finde the least alteration in his
pulse, and not marke the burning feavers of his minde. Lastlie, the
Divine will spend the greatest parte of his time in disputing of faith
585 and cares not to heare of charity: wil talke of God, and not regard to
succor men. These knowledges bring on the mind an endlesse labour,
but no contentment: for the more one knowes, the more he would
know.

They pacify not the debates a man feeles in himselfe, they cure not
590 the diseases of his minde. They make him learned, but they make not
him good: cunning, but not wise. I say more. The more a man
knowes, the more knowes he that he knowes not: the fuller the
minde is, the emptier it findes it selfe: forasmuch as whatsoever a
man can knowe of any science in this worlde is but the least part of
595 what he is ignorant: all his knowledge consisting in knowing his ignorance, al his perfection in noting his imperfections, which who best

565 to mans] *1600, 1606*; to to mans *1592*   581 for himselfe] from himselfe
1606   595 in knowing] n knowing *1606*

knowes and notes, is in truth among men the most wise, and perfect.
In short we must conclude with *Salomon*, that the beginning and end
of wisedome is the feare of God: that this wisedome neverthelesse is
taken of the world for meere folly, and persecuted by the world as a   600
deadly enemy: and that as who feareth God, ought to feare no evill,
for that all his evils are converted to his good: so neither ought he
to hope for good in the worlde, having there the devil his professed
enemy, whom the Scripture termeth Prince of the world.

But with what exercise soever we passe the time, behold old age   605
unwares to us coms upon us: which whether we thrust our selves
into the prease of men, or hide us somewhere out of the way, never
failes to find us out. Every man makes accompt in that age to rest himselfe of all his travailes without further care, but to keepe himselfe at
ease and in health. And see contrariwise in this age, there is nothing   610
but an after taste of all the fore going evils: and most commonly a
plentifull harvest of all such vices as in the whole course of their
life, hath held and possessed them. There you have the unabilitie
and weakenesse of infancie, and (which is worse) many times accompanied with authoritie: there you are payed for the excesse and riot-   615
ousnes of youth, with gowts, palsies, and such like diseases, which
take from you limme after limme with extreame paine and torment.
There you are recompenced for the travailes of mind, the watchings
and cares of manhoode, with losse of sight, losse of hearing, and all
the sences one after another, except onely the sence of paine. Not   620
one parte in us but death takes in gage to be assured of us, as of bad
pay-maisters, which infinitely feare their dayes of payment. Nothing
in us which will not by and by bee dead: and neverthelesse our vices
yet live in us, and not onely live, but in despite of nature daily growe
yoong againe. The covetous man hath one foote in his grave, and is yet   625
burieng his money: meaning belike to finde it againe another day. The
ambitious in his will ordaineth unprofitable pompes for his funeralles,
making his vice to live and triumph after his death. The riotous no
longer able to daunce on his feete, daunceth with his shoulders, all
vices having lefte him, and hee not yet able to leave them. The childe   630
wisheth for youth: and this man laments it. The yong man liveth in
hope of the future, and this feeles the evill present, laments the false
pleasures past, and sees for the time to come nothing to hope for.
More foolish then the childe, in bewailing the time he cannot recall,

613 unabilitie] unhabilitie *1600*; unhability *1606*   618 There] There also *1606*
travailes] rravels *1606*; travels *1608*   623 which will] that will *1606*

635 and not remembring the evill hee had therein: and more wretched
then the yongman, in that after a wretched life not able, but wretch-
edly to die, he sees on all sides but matter of dispaire. As for him, who
from his youth hath undertaken to combate against the flesh, and
against the world: who hath taken so great paines to mortifie himselfe
640 and leave the worlde before his time: who besides those ordinarie
evilles findes himselfe vexed with this great and incurable disease of
olde age, and feeles notwithstanding his flesh howe weake soever,
stronger oftentimes then his spirite: what good I pray can hee have
but onlie herein: that hee sees his death at hand, that hee sees his com-
645 bate finished, that he sees himselfe readie to departe by death out of
this loathsome prison, wherein all his life time hee hath beene racked
and tormented? I will not heere speake of the infinite evilles wherewith men in all ages are annoyed, as losse of friendes and parents, banishments, exiles, disgraces, and such others, common and ordinarie in
650 the world: one complayning of loosing his children, an other of having
them: one making sorrow for his wifes death, an other for her life, one
finding faulte, that hee is too high in Courte, an other, that hee is not
high enough. The worlde is so full of evilles, that to write them all,
woulde require an other worlde as great as it selfe. Sufficeth, that if
655 the most happie in mens opinions doe counterpoize his happs with
his mishaps, he shall judge himselfe unhappy: and hee judge him
happy, who had he beene set three dayes in his place, would give it
over to him that came next: yea, sooner then hee, who shall consider
in all the goodes that ever hee hath had the evilles hee hath endured to
660 get them, and having them to retaine and keepe them (I speake of the
pleasures that may be kept, and not of those that wither in a moment)
wil judge of himselfe, and by himselfe, that the keeping it selfe of the
greatest felicitie in this worlde, is full of unhappinesse and infelicitie.
Conclude then, that Childhoode is but a foolish simplicitie, Youth, a
665 vaine heate, Manhoode, a painefull carefulnesse, and Olde-age, a noy-
some languishing: that our playes are but teares, our pleasures, fevers
of the minde, our goodes, rackes, and torments, our honors, heavy
vanities, our rest, unrest: that passing from age to age is but passing
from evill to evill, and from the lesse unto the greater: and that
670 alwayes it is but one wave driving on an other, untill we be arrived
at the Haven of death. Conclude I say, that life is but a wishing for
the future, and a bewailing of the past: a loathing of what wee have

653 them] of *1606*

tasted, and a longing for that wee have not tasted, a vaine memorie
of the state past, and a doubtfull expectation of the state to come:
finally, that in all our life there is nothing certaine, nothing assured,   675
but the certaintie and uncertaintie of death. Behold, now comes
Death unto us: Behold her, whose approch we so much feare. We
are now to consider whether she be such as wee are made beleeve:
and whether we ought so greatly to flie her, as commonly wee do.
Wee are afraide of her: but like little children of a vizarde, or of the   680
Images of *Hecate*. Wee have her in horror: but because wee conceive
her not such as she is, but ougly, terrible, and hideous: such as it pleas-
eth the Painters to represent unto us on a wall. Wee flie before her:
but it is because foretaken with such vaine imaginations, wee give not
our selves leisure to marke her. But staie wee, stande wee stedfast,   685
looke wee her in the face: wee shall finde her quite other then shee
is painted us: and altogether of other countenaunce then our miserable
life. Death makes an ende of this life. This life is a perpetuall misery
and tempest: Death then is the issue of our miseries and entraunce of
the porte where wee shall ride in safetie from all windes. And shoulde   690
wee feare that which withdraweth us from misery, or which drawes us
into our Haven? Yea but you will say, it is a payne to die. Admit it bee:
so is there in curing of a wounde. Such is the worlde, that one evill can
not bee cured but by an other, to heale a contusion, must bee made an
incision. You will say, there is difficultie in the passage: So is there no   695
Haven, no Porte, whereinto the entraunce is not straite and combersome. No good thing is to be bought in this worlde with other then the
coyne of labour and paine. The entraunce indeede is hard, if our
selves make it harde, comming thither with a tormented spirite, a
troubled minde, a wavering and irresolute thought. But bring wee   700
quietnesse of mind, constancie, and full resolution, wee shall not
finde anie daunger or difficultie at all. Yet what is the paine that
death brings us? Nay, what can shee doe with those paines wee
feele? Wee accuse her of all the evilles wee abide in ending our life,
and consider not howe manie more greevous woundes or sickenesses   705
wee have endured without death: or howe many more vehement
paines wee have suffered in this life, in the which wee called even
her to our succour. All the paines our life yeeldes us at the last
houre wee impute to Death: not marking that life begunne and continued in all sortes of paine, must also necessarily ende in paine.   710

679 greatly] grealy *1600*   680 vizarde] vizor *1606*   705 greevous woundes or
sickenesses] woundes or grievous sicknesses *1606*

Not marking (I saie) that it is the remainder of our life, not death, that tormenteth us: the ende of our navigation that paines us, not the Haven wee are to enter: which is nothing else but a safegarde against all windes. Wee complayne of Death, where wee shoulde complayne
715 of life: as if one havyng beene long sicke, and beginning to bee well, shoulde accuse his health of his last paynes, and not the reliques of his disease. Tell mee, what is it else to bee dead, but to bee no more living in the worlde? Absolutelie and simplie not to bee in the worlde, is it anie payne? Did wee then feele any paine, when as yet wee were not?
720 Have wee ever more resemblaunce of Death, then when wee sleepe? Or ever more rest then at that time? Now if this be no paine, why accuse we Death of the paines our life gives us at our departure? Unlesse also we wil fondly accuse the time when as yet we were not, of the paines we felt at our birth? If the comming in be with teares,
725 is it wonder that such be the going out? If the beginning of our being, be the beginning of our paine, is it marvell that such be the ending? But if our not being in times past hath bene without payne, and all this be- ing contrarywise full of paine: whome should we by reason accuse of the last paines, the not being to come, or the remnant of this present
730 being? We thinke we dye not, but when we yeeld up our last gaspe. But if we marke well, we dye every day, every houre, every moment. We apprehend death as a thing unusuall to us: and yet have nothing so common in us. Our living is but continuall dyeng: looke how much we live, we dye: how much we encrease, our life decreases. We
735 enter not a step into life, but we enter a step into death. Who hath lived a third part of his yeares, hath a third part of himselfe dead. Who halfe his yeares, is already half dead. Of our life, all the time past is dead, the present lives and dies at once, and the future likewise shall dye. The past is no more, the future is not yet, the present is, and
740 no more is. Briefely, this whole life is but a death: it is as a candle lighted in our bodies: in one the winde makes it melt away, in an other blowes it cleane out, many times ere it be halfe burned: in others it endureth to the ende. Howsoever it be, looke how much it shineth, so much it burneth: her shining is her burning: her light a vanishing
745 smoke: her last fire, hir last wike, and her last drop of moisture. So is it in the life of man, life and death in man is all one. If we call the last breath death, so must we all the rest: all proceeding from one place, and all in one manner. One only difference there is betweene this

744 light] lighte is *1606*

life, and that we call death: that during the one, we have alwayes
wherof to dye: and after the other, there remaineth only wherof to   750
live. In summe, even he that thinketh death simply to be the ende
of man, ought not to feare it: in asmuch as who desireth to live longer,
desireth to die longer: and who feareth soone to die, feareth (to speake
properlie) lest he may not longer die.

But unto us brought up in a more holy schoole, death is a farre   755
other thing: neither neede we as the Pagans of consolations against
death: but that death serve us, as a consolation against all sorts of
affliction: so that we must not only strengthen our selves, as they,
not to feare it, but accustome ourselves to hope for it. For unto us it
is not a departing from pain and evil, but an accesse unto all good: not   760
the end of life, but the end of death, and the beginning of life. Better,
saith *Salomon*, is the day of death, then the day of birth, and why?
because it is not to us a last day, but the dawning of an everlasting
day. No more shall we have in that glorious light, either sorow for
the past, or expectation of the future: for all shall be there present   765
unto us, and that present shall never more passe. No more shal we
powre out our selves in vaine and painfull pleasures: for we shal be
filled with true and substantiall pleasures. No more shal we paine
our selves in heaping togither these exhalations of the earth: for the
heavens shall be ours, and this masse of earth, which ever drawes us   770
towards the earth, shalbe buried in the earth. No more shal we over-
wearie our selves with mounting from degree to degree, and from
honor to honor: for we shall highlie be raysed above all heights of
the world; and from on high laugh at the folly of all those we once
admired, who fight together for a point, and as litle children for   775
lesse then an apple. No more to be brief shal we have combates in
our selves: for our flesh shall be dead, and our spirit in full life: our
passion buried, and our reason in perfect libertie. Our soule delivered
out of this foule and filthie prison, where, by long continuing it is grow-
en into an habite of crookednes, shall againe draw her owne breath,   780
recognize her ancient dwelling, and againe remember her former glory
and dignity. This flesh my frend which thou feelest, this body which
thou touchest is not man: Man is from heaven: heaven is his countrie
and his aire. That he is in his body, is but by way of exile and confinement. Man in deed is soule and spirit: Man is rather of celestiall and   785
divine qualitie, wherin is nothing grosse nor materiall. This body such

750 wherof] wheref *1606*   752 live longer] live long *1600, 1606*

as now it is, is but the barke and shell of the soule: which must necessarily be broken, if we will be hatched: if we wil indeed live and see the
light. We have it semes, some life, and some sence in us: but are so
790 croked and contracted, that we cannot so much as stretch out our
wings, much lesse take our flight towards heaven, untill we be disburthened of this earthlie burthen. We looke, but through false spectacles: we have eyes but overgrowen with pearles: we thinke we see,
but it is in a dreame, wherin we see nothing but deceit. All that we
795 have, and all that we know is but abuse and vanitie. Death only can
restore us both life and light: and we thinke (so blockish we are)
that she comes to robbe us of them. We say we are Christians: that
we beleeve after this mortall, a life immortall: that death is but a
separation of the body and soule: and that the soule returnes to his
800 happie abode, there to joy in God, who only is all good: that at the
last day it shall againe take the body, which shal no more be subject
to corruption. With these goodly discourses we fill all our bookes:
and in the meane while, when it comes to the point, the very name
of death as the horriblest thing in the world makes us quake and trem-
805 ble. If we beleve as we speak, what is that we feare? to be happy? to be
at our ease? to be more content in a moment, then we might be in the
longest mortal life that might be? or must not we of force confesse,
that we beleve it but in part? that all we have is but words? that all
our discourses, as of these hardie trencher knights, are but vaunting
810 and vanitie? Some you shall see, that wil say: I know well that I
passe out of this life into a better: I make no doubt of it: only I feare
the midway step, that I am to step over. Weak harted creatures! they
wil kill themselves to get their miserable living: suffer infinite paines,
and infinite wounds at another mans pleasure: passe infinit deaths
815 without dying, for things of nought, for things that perish, and perchance make them perish with them. But when they have but one
pace to passe to be at rest, not for a day, but for ever: not an indifferent
rest, but such as mans minde cannot comprehende: they tremble,
their harts faile them, they are affrayde: and yet the ground of their
820 harme is nothing but feare. Let them never tell me, they apprehend
the paine: it is but an abuse: a purpose to conceale the litle faith
they have. No, no, they would rather languish of the goute, the scia-
tica, any disease whatsoever: then dye one sweete death with the least
paine possible: rather pininglie dye limme after limme, outliving as it

813 infinite paines] infinitie paines *1600*   817 pace] pase *1606*

were, all their sences, motions, and actions, then speedily dye, imme- 825
diatly to live for ever. Let them tell me no more that they would in
this world learne to live: for every one is thereunto sufficiently
instructed in himselfe, and not one but is cunning in the trade. Nay
rather they should learne in this world to dye: and once to dye well,
dye dayly in themselves: so prepared, as if the ende of every dayes 830
worke, were the ende of our life. Now contrarywise there is nothing
to their eares more offensive, then to heare of death. Senselesse people! we abandon our life to the ordinarie hazards of warre, for seaven
franks pay: are formost in an assault, for a litle bootie: goe into places,
whence there is no hope of returning, with danger many times both of 835
bodies and soules. But to free us from all hazards, to winne things
inestimable, to enter an eternall life, we faint in the passage of one
pace, wherein is no difficultie, but in opinion: yea we so faint, that
were it not of force we must passe, and that God in despite of us
will doe us a good turne, hardly should we finde in all the world 840
one, how unhappy or wretched soever, that would ever passe. Another
will say, had I lived till 50. or 60. yeares, I should have bin contented:
I should not have cared to live longer: but to dye so yong is no reason.
I should have knowen the world before I had left it. Simple soule! in
this world there is neither young nor olde. The longest age in compar- 845
ison of all that is past, or all that is to come, is nothing: and when thou
hast lived to the age thou now desirest, all the past will be nothing:
thou wilt still gape, for that is to come. The past will yeeld thee but
sorrowe, the future but expectation, the present no contentment. As
ready thou wilt then be to redemaund longer respite, as before. 850
Thou fliest thy creditor from moneth to moneth, and time to time,
as readie to pay the last daye, as the first: thou seekest but to be
acquitted. Thou hast tasted all which the world esteemeth pleasures:
not one of them is new unto thee. By drinking oftener, thou shalt be
never awhit the more satisfyed: for the body thou cariest, like the 855
bored paile of *Danaus* daughters, will never be full. Thou mayst
sooner weare it out, then weary thy selfe with using, or rather abusing
it. Thou cravest long life to cast it away, to spend it on worthles
delights, to mispend it on vanities. Thou art covetous in desiring,
and prodigall in spending. Say not thou findest fault with the 860
Court, or the Pallace: but that thou desirest longer to serve the common wealth, to serve thy countrie, to serve God. He that set thee on

838 pace] pase *1606*

worke knowes untill what day, and what houre, thou shouldest be at
it: he well knowes how to direct his worke. Should he leave thee there
865 longer, perchance thou wouldest marre all. But if he will pay thee lib-
erally for thy labour, as much for halfe a dayes worke, as for a whole:
as much for having wrought till noone, as for having borne all the
heate of the day: art thou not so much the more to thanke and prayse
him? but if thou examine thine owne conscience, thou lamentest not
870 the cause of the widdow, and the orphan, which thou hast left
depending in judgement: not the dutie of a sonne, of a father, or of
a frend, which thou pretendest thou wouldest performe: not the
ambassage for the common wealth, which thou wert even ready to
undertake: not the service thou desirest to doe unto God, who knowes
875 much better howe to serve himselfe of thee, then thou of thy selfe. It is
thy houses and gardens thou lamentest, thy imperfect plottes and purposes, thy life (as thou thinkest) imperfect: which by no dayes, nor
yeares, nor ages, might be perfected: and yet thy selfe mightst perfect
in a moment, couldest thou but thinke in good earnest, that where it
880 ende it skilles not, so that it end well.

Now to end well this life, is onely to ende it willingly: following
with full consent the will and direction of God, and not suffering us
to be drawen by the necessitie of destenie. To end it willingly, we
must hope, and not feare death. To hope for it, we must certainely
885 looke after this life, for a better life. To looke for that, wee must
feare God: whome whoso well feareth, feareth indeede nothing in
this worlde, and hopes for all things in the other. To one well resolved
in these points death can be but sweete and agreeable: knowing that
through it hee is to enter into a place of all joyes. The griefe that
890 may be therein shall bee allaied with sweetnes: the sufferance of ill,
swallowed in the confidence of good: the sting of Death it selfe shall
bee dead, which is nothing else but Feare. Nay, I wil say more, not
onely all the evilles conceived in death shall be to him nothing: but
he shall even scorne all the mishappes men redoubt in this life, and
895 laugh at all these terrors. For I pray what can he feare, whose death
is his hope? Thinke we to banish him his country? He knows he
hath a country other-where, whence wee cannot banish him: and
that all these countries are but Innes, out of which he must part at
the wil of his hoste. To put him in prison? a more straite prison he
900 cannot have, then his owne body, more filthy, more darke, more full
of rackes and torments. To kill him and take him out of the worlde?
that is it he hopes for: that is it with all his heart he aspires unto. By

fire, by sworde, by famine, by sickenesse: within three yeeres, within three dayes, within three houres, all is one to him: all is one at what gate, or at what time he passe out of this miserable life. For his businesses are ever ended, his affaires are dispatched, and by what way he shall go out, by the same hee shall enter into a most happie and everlasting life. Men can threaten him but death, and death is all he promiseth himselfe: the worst they can doe, is, to make him die, and that is the best hee hopes for. The threatnings of tyrants are to him promises, the swordes of his greatest enemies drawne in his favor: forasmuch as he knowes that threatning him death, they threaten him life: and the most mortall woundes can make him but immortall. Who feares God, feares not death: and who feares it not, feares not the worst of this life.

By this reckoning, you will tell me death is a thing to be wished for: and to passe from so much evill, to so much good, a man shoulde as it seemeth cast away his life. Sure, I feare not, that for any good wee expect, we will hasten one step the faster: though the spirite aspire, the body it drawes with it, withdrawes it ever sufficiently towardes the earth. Yet is it not that I conclude. We must seeke to mortifie our flesh in us, and to cast the world out of us: but to cast our selves out of the world is in no sort permitted us. The Christian ought willingly to depart out of this life but not cowardly to runne away. The Christian is ordained by God to fight therein: and cannot leave his place without incurring reproch and infamie. But if it please the grand Captaine to recall him, let him take the retrait in good part, and with good will obey it. For hee is not borne for himselfe, but for God: of whome he holdes his life at farme, as his tenant at will, to yeeld him the profites. It is in the landlord to take it from him, not in him to surrender it, when a conceit takes him. Diest thou yong? praise God as the mariner that hath had a good winde, soone to bring him to the Porte. Diest thou olde? praise him likewise, for if thou hast had lesse winde, it may be thou hast also had lesse waves. But thinke not at thy pleasure to go faster or softer: for the winde is not in thy power, and in steede of taking the shortest way to the Haven, thou maiest happily suffer shipwracke. God calleth home from his worke, one in the morning, an other at noone, and an other at night. One he exerciseth til the first sweate, another he sunneburneth, another he rosteth and drieth throughly. But of all his he leaves

905
910
915
920
925
930
935
940

---

902 hopes] hops *1606*   918 as ^it seemeth^] (it seemeth) *1606*

not one without, but brings them all to rest, and gives them all their
hire, every one in his time. Who leaves his worke before God call him,
looses it: and who importunes him before the time, looses his reward.
We must rest us in his will, who in the middest of our troubles sets us
945 at rest.

To ende, we ought neither to hate this life for the toiles therein, for
it is slouth and cowardise: nor love it for the delights, which is follie
and vanitie: but serve us of it, to serve God in it, who after it shall
place us in true quietnesse, and replenish us with pleasures whiche
950 shall never more perish. Neyther ought we to flye death, for it is child-
ish to feare it: and in flieng from it, wee meete it. Much lesse to seeke
it, for that is temeritie: nor every one that would die, can die. As much
despaire in the one, as cowardise in the other: in neither any kinde of
magnanimitie. It is enough that we constantly and continually waite
955 for her comming, that shee may never finde us unprovided. For as
there is nothing more certaine then death, so is there nothing more
uncertaine then the houre of death,
                  knowen onlie to God, the onlie Author of life
                        and death, to whom wee all ought en-
960   devour both to live
                              and die.

                    Die to live,
                       Live to die.

                 The 13. of May 1590.
965   At Wilton.

---

941 not one without, but brings them] *om.* 1600 *(Bodleian, British Library, Newberry), 1606*

The Triumph of Death

Literary Context

Interest in Italian culture and literature was widespread in Tudor England. Roger Ascham, for example, praises Elizabeth's 'perfit readines, in *Latin, Italian, French* and *Spanish*', but because knowledge of those languages was fairly common, he emphasizes, as more unusual, that 'she readeth here now at Windsore more Greek every day, than some Prebendarie of this Church doth read *Latin* in a whole weeke'.[1] Torn between his love for Italian literature and his hatred for 'Papists', Ascham satirizes Italianate Englishmen and yet praises the Italian language, 'which next the Greeke and Latin tonge, I like and love above all other'.[2] Like many other educated women of her class, Pembroke had studied Italian from early childhood; the Penshurst accounts of 1572–3 include payment of 'Mistress Maria, the Italian', probably an Italian tutor for the Sidney children.[3] Her youthful readings no doubt included selections from Petrarch, for he was included with Dante and Boccaccio in the triumvirate of the greatest Italian poets, as in Sidney's *Defence*.[4]

Francesco Petrarca (1304–74) was a scholar and poet celebrated initially for his Latin works, such as his epic *Africa* on Scipio Africanus; his Roman biographies, *De viris illustribus*; and his dialogues of comfort in adversity, *De remediis utriusque fortunae*. He also wrote a series of Italian sonnets, the *Canzoniére*, to Laura, whom he first saw on 6 April 1327. In 1338, he began writing the *Trionfo d'Amore*, portraying himself as Love's captive. In the next decade he apparently completed that Triumph and the *Trionfo della Castità*, wherein Laura's Chastity triumphs over Cupid. The *Trionfo della Morte* was begun in 1348, the year that Laura died, and completed shortly there-

---

[1] Roger Ascham, *The Scholemaster* (London: John Daye, 1571), *STC* 834, copy 1, sig. H1. This copy was once in the library of Thomas Herbert, eighth Earl of Pembroke (d. 1733). For details of the acquisition of books from Wilton House by the Folger Shakespeare Library, see Brennan (D.Phil. diss.), 331–6.

[2] Ascham, *Scholemaster*, sig. H3.

[3] De L'Isle MS U1474 A33/3.

[4] Sidney, *Miscellaneous Prose*, 74. Petrarch was crowned the first modern poet laureate in Rome on 8 April 1341. On Petrarch's cultural significance, see William J. Kennedy, *Authorizing Petrarch* (Ithaca, NY: Cornell UP, 1994).

after. Petrarch continued to work on the *Trionfi* for almost thirty years, completing three more sections, *Trionfo della Fama*, *Trionfo del Tempo*, and *Trionfo della Divinità*, before his death in 1374.[5]

Petrarch's *I Trionfi* was a radically new work, but with its roots in the verbal and visual descriptions of Roman military triumphs. Petrarch himself described Scipio's Triumph in *Africa* (9. 324–402), and Pompey's Triumph in *De remediis utriusque fortunae* (1. 37).[6] Literary sources include Ovid's Triumph of Love (*Amores* 1. 2), the conflict between vices and virtues in Prudentius' *Psychomachia*, Dante's description of the pageant of Beatrice and the Church at the close of the *Purgatorio*, and Boccaccio's description of Love, Glory, Wisdom, Riches, and Fortune on a triumphal chariot in *Amorosa Visione*.[7] Petrarch's poem is comprised of six sections, each devoted to a different Triumph. Much has been written about the coherence, or lack thereof, in the narrative, but the basic sequence is clear.[8] Love triumphs over the poet, but Chastity triumphs over Love when Laura will not yield, Death appears to triumph over Chastity when Laura dies, Fame triumphs over Death as she is celebrated, Time appears to triumph over Fame, but is finally conquered by Eternity.[9] *I Trionfi* is structured as a dream vision in *terza rima*, like Dante's *Divine Comedy*. Read as a moral allegory, the work was much to the taste of its first readers. They were drawn to the extensive moralizing of a Christian/Senecan nature, such as the famous *ubi sunt* passage from the *Trionfo della Morte*. Pembroke renders the passage:

[5] Ernest Hatch Wilkins, 'On the Chronology of the Triumphs', in *Studies in the Life and Works of Petrarch* (Cambridge, Mass.: Medieval Academy of America, 1955), 254–72; *Lord Morley's Tryumphes of Fraunces Petrarcke: The First English Translation of the Trionfi*, ed. D. D. Carnicelli (Cambridge, Mass.: Harvard UP, 1971), 20–4.

[6] See Paul Colilli, 'Scipio's Triumphal Ascent in the *Africa*', in *Petrarch's Triumphs: Allegory and Spectacle*, ed. Konrad Eisenbichler and Amilcare A. Iannucci (Toronto: U of Toronto P, 1990), 147–59.

[7] On Petrarch's sources, see the first four essays in *Petrarch's Triumphs*: Amilcare A. Iannucci, 'Petrarch's Intertextual Strategies in the *Triumphs*'; Richard C. Monti, 'Petrarch's *Trionfi*, Ovid and Vergil'; Aldo S. Bernardo, 'Triumphal Poetry: Dante, Petrarch, and Boccaccio'; Sandro Sticca, 'Petrarch's *Triumphs* and its Medieval Dramatic Heritage'.

[8] See, for example, the deconstructive reading by Marguerite R. Waller, *Petrarch's Poetics and Literary History* (Amherst: U of Massachusetts P, 1980), 107–34.

[9] Carlo Calcaterra (ed.), *Trionfi* (Turin: Unione Tipografico—Editrice Torinese, 1927), pp. xiii–xv, argues that Chastity triumphs only over the body of Laura. For a discussion of the nature of Death's triumph, see Aldo S. Bernardo, *Petrarch, Laura, and the Triumphs* (Albany: SUNY Press, 1974), 119–23.

There sawe I, whom their times did happie calle,
    Popes, Emperors, and kings, but strangelie growen,
    All naked now, all needie beggers all.
where is that wealth? where are those honor's gonne?
    Scepters, and crounes, and roabe's, and purple dye?
    And costlie myters, sett with pearle and stone?
O wretch, who doest in mortall things affye:
    (yett who but doeth) and if in end they dye
    Them-selve's beguil'd, they finde but right, saie I.   (1. 79–87)

Contemporary readers would also have enjoyed the lengthy catalogues of notable images of vice and virtue, such as the procession of love's captives that concludes the first *capitolo* of the *Trionfo d'Amore*.

Both the *Trionfi* and the *Canzoniére* circulated widely in manuscript before they were first printed in 1470 by Vindelinus de Spiro.[10] The popularity of the *Trionfi* is indicated by the fact that there are at least 85 extant fourteenth- and fifteenth-century manuscripts of Petrarch's *Trionfi* alone, with another seventy-nine manuscripts that combine the *Trionfi* with the *Canzoniére*. The complexity of the textual history of the *Trionfi* may be indicated by the fact that just between 1470 and 1500 there were nine printed editions of the *Trionfi* alone and twenty-five combined editions.[11] So revered was the work that scholarly editions were printed, treating it as the equal of the Greek and Latin classics. The 1471 edition included Antonio da Tempo's 'Life of Petrarch'; in 1477 Antonio's 'Life' and his 'Commentary', the first annotations on the *Trionfi*, were published. The most influential annotated edition was that of Bernardo da Pietro Lapini da Montalcino, often called 'Illicino', whose lengthy commentaries on the *Trionfi* were first printed in 1475. His reading of the poem as an allegory of the soul's journey is echoed in virtually all interpretations of *I Trionfi* until the late sixteenth century, including Jacopo Pollio's *Sopra el triumpho di Petrarca* (1485), *Il Petrarca con l'espositione d'Alessandro Vellutello* (1525; 27 editions of Vellutello's commentary had been issued by 1585), and *Petrarcha colla spositione di Misser Giovanni Andrea Gesualdo* (Venice, 1533). Pembroke used as her original a work in this tradition (see 'Transmission and Authority of Texts'), but she

---

[10] *Canzoniére* (Venice, 1470).
[11] Ernest Hatch Wilkins, *The Making of the 'Canzoniére', and other Petrarchan Studies* (Rome: Edizioni di Storia e Letteratura, 1951), 379; see also *Lord Morley's Tryumphes*, ed. Carnicelli, 28–37.

may also have consulted Castelvetro's commentary, *Le rime del Petrarca brevemente sposte per Lodovico Castelvetro* (Venice, 1582), that interpreted the *Trionfi* as the continuation of the sonnet sequence, an interpretation encouraged by the frequent joint publication of the two works.

Equally important to the dissemination of *I Trionfi*, however, was the visual tradition, so that even those who were unlearned knew the story. The standard iconography is that of an allegorical figure (of Love, Chastity, Death, Fame, Time, or Eternity) enthroned on a chariot pulled by allegorical beasts, surrounded by a crowd of victims similar to those that Petrarch catalogues; however, the details of the illustrations usually, as Carnicelli notes, 'have virtually nothing to do with the contents of the poem'.[12] For example, Petrarch describes Death as a woman 'Black, and in black' (1. 31). Yet the woodcut illustrating the *Trionfo della Morte* in the 1544 reprinting of *Le volgari opere del Petracha con la espositione di A. Vellutello da Lucca* shows a skeleton draped with a robe and holding a scythe, standing on a low hearse pulled sedately by one ox over a field littered with corpses.[13] The 1563 Vellutello edition shows a naked skeleton riding a hearse with huge wheels drawn by oxen which trample people.[14] The 1544 Vellutello edition is more dramatically illustrated, for an undraped skeleton is balanced on one foot, driving a hearse pulled by oxen that careers wildly, crushing all in its path.[15] A 1600 edition '*di Bellissime Figure*' shows the skeleton swinging its scythe at bodies even as they are trampled by oxen; a long swath of bodies curves back in an arc toward distant mountains.[16]

In addition to the watercolours and miniatures illustrating manuscripts and woodcuts or engravings in printed editions, the pageants were depicted by thousands of art works, including paintings, drawings, tapestries, miniatures, frescos, medals, *desci da parto* or birth trays, *cassoni* or marriage chests, illustrated psalters, glass cups, majo-

[12] *Lord Morley's Tryumphes*, ed. Carnicelli, 38.

[13] The woodcut was not restricted to Vellutello editions; for example, it also illustrates *Petrarcha colla spositione di Misser G. A. Gesualdo* (Venice, 1553) and *Il Petrarcha con l'espositione di M. Gio. Andrea Gesualdo* (Venice 1581).

[14] *Il Petrarca con l'espositione di M. Alessandro Vellutello* (Venice, 1563), sig. AA1; the woodcut is frequently reprinted, as in the 1545 Vellutello edition and in the 1574 Gesualdo edition.

[15] *Le volgari opere del Petrarcha con la espositione di A. Vellutello da Lucca* (Venice, 1544). See also *Il Petrarcha con l'espositione d'Alessandro Vellutello* (Venice 1545).

[16] *Il Petrarcha di Nuova Ristampato et di bellissime figure intagliate rame adornato* (Venice, 1600).

lica dishes, and statues.[17] Vivid examples of the tradition may still be seen in England, such as the Hampton Court tapestry series on the *Trionfi* (Flemish, sixteenth century) and Luca Signorelli's painting, 'The Triumph of Chastity', at the National Gallery in London. The Victoria and Albert Museum has a particularly rich collection of works illustrating the *Trionfi*, including a series of three tapestry panels (Flemish, sixteenth century), two fifteenth-century *cassoni*, and three wooden birth trays.[18]

The first English translations of Petrarch were of individual poems from the *Canzoniére* rather than the *Trionfi*. Geoffrey Chaucer translated Sonnet 132 of the *Canzoniére* as the 'Canticus Troili' in *Troilus and Criseyde* (1. 400–20). Thomas Wyatt brought the Italian sonnet to England with his twenty-seven translations, or paraphrases, of Petrarch's *Canzoniére*; none of his poems is based on *I Trionfi*.[19] Similarly, twelve of Surrey's poems are translations or paraphrases of Petrarch's *Canzoniére*, but only one work is from the *Trionfi*— 'Suche waiwarde waies hath love', from *Trionfo d'Amore* 3. 151–87.[20] Both sets of English Petrarchan poems circulated through scribal publication before they were printed in Tottel's *Songes and Sonnettes* (1557). The English sonnet sequence, sonnets arranged to tell a coherent narrative of love, was an *imitatio* of Petrarch's *Canzoniére* that read the work as a discourse on love rather than a work of moral instruction. The genre was inaugurated in England by Philip Sidney in his *Astrophil and Stella*. After some manuscript circulation, it was published by Thomas Newman in 1591 as an unauthorized, corrupt edition of 107 sonnets with a preface by Thomas Nashe. Pembroke issued a corrected edition in the 1598 *Arcadia* that included Sonnet 37, with its identification of Stella as Penelope Devereux Rich, who 'Hath no

[17] Sara Charney, 'Artistic Representations of Petrarch's *Triumphus Famae*', in *Petrarch's Triumphs*, 223–33.

[18] *Lord Morley's Tryumphes*, ed. Carnicelli, 40–3 notes that the Hampton Court tapestries, 'The Triumph of Death over Chastity' and 'The Triumph of Fame over Death', are identical to those at the Victoria and Albert except for minor details. Carnicelli includes some of these works among his 16 illustrations; see also the illustrations in *Petrarch's Triumphs*.

[19] *Lord Morley's Tryumphes*, ed. Carnicelli, 26. For a list of Wyatt's sources, see A. K. Foxwell, *A Study of Sir Thomas Wyatt's Poems* (London: U of London P, 1911), 147–52.

[20] *Henry Howard, Earl of Surrey: Poems*, ed. Emrys Jones (Oxford: Clarendon P, 1964), (no. 13), 8–10, 112–15. William Kennedy notes (in private correspondence): 'The first complete translation of the *Canzoniére* did not appear until 1851 with Robert MacGregor's *Petrarch's Odes* (though omitting poem 105); in 1859 Thomas Campbell claimed to be the first complete translator, but actually he had assembled various translations by other hands; otherwise C. B. Cayley offers the first totally complete translation by a single hand in 1879.'

misfortune but that Rich she is'. *Astrophil and Stella* began a fashion
for sonnet sequences, two of which were written by other Sidneys.
Robert Sidney wrote, but never printed, his poems from Rosis to
Lysa, which he inscribed 'For the Countess of Pembroke'; Lady
Wroth's *Pamphilia and Amphilanthus* was published in the 1621 *Urania*.[21] Other poets associated with the Sidneys, or who sought Pembroke's patronage, also wrote sonnet sequences, including Samuel
Daniel, *Delia* (1592); Fulke Greville, *Caelica* (publ. 1633); and Barnabe Barnes, *Parthenophil and Parthenophe* (1593), which repeatedly
refers to Sidney.[22] At least 50 sonnet sequences were published in
England, many of which have entered well-deserved obscurity, such
as Richard Nugent's *Cynthia* (1604).[23]

English interest in the *Trionfi* was demonstrated more by tapestries
than by poetry in the early sixteenth century. The young Thomas
More designed tapestries for his father's house in London and composed 'Nyne Pageauntes', nine stanzas in *rhyme royal*, to accompany
them (*c*.1503). The 'Pageauntes' included four adapted from Petrarch:
Death, Fame, Time, and Eternity; the tapestry of Venus and Cupid
was, perhaps, adapted from the *Trionfo d'Amore*. Three are taken
from the proverbial Ages of Man: Childhood, Manhood, and Age.
The final tapestry depicts the Poet, who gives Latin verses interpreting
the entire series as a traditional moral allegory on the ages of man.[24]
The *Trionfi* were also portrayed in tapestries owned by Henry VIII:
11 at Westminster, 5 at Windsor, 6 'at the Lady Elizabeth Guardrobe',
and 5 at Hampton Court (of the eight panels purchased by Cardinal
Wolsey about 1522, and later acquired by Henry, three are still on dis-
play in the Great Watching Chamber).[25] In *Colin Clout* (*c*.1522), John
Skelton condemns Wolsey's purchase of the tapestry series as

---

[21]   Robert Sidney's holograph notebook is preserved as BL Add. MS 58435, and printed
in Sidney, Robert. *Poems*. See also Millicent Hay, *The Life of Robert Sidney: Earl of Leicester
(1563–1626)* (Washington: Folger Shakespeare Library, 1984); and Germaine Warkentin,
'Reading all the Signs: Robert Sidney's Lyric Book, Add. 58435' (forthcoming).

[22]   See, for example, Canzon 2 in praise of *'Astrophill's* byrth-day', Barnes, *P and P*, ed.
Doyno, 94.

[23]   See Thomas P. Roche, Jr., *Petrarch and the English Sonnet Sequences* (New York: AMS
Press, 1989).

[24]   'Venus and Cupyde' appears as the third tapestry, between 'Manhod' and 'Age'; 'Age'
is appropriately followed by 'Deth', 'Fame', 'Tyme', and 'Eternitee', as in the *Trionfi*. *The
English Works of Sir Thomas More*, ed. W. E. Campbell, 2 vols. (London: 1931), 1. 332–5.
Robert Coogan points to parallels with the illustrations of MS 5506, Bibliothèque de l'Ar-
senal: 'Petrarch's "Trionfi" and the English Renaissance', *SP* 67 (1970), 306–27, 310–12.

[25]   *Lord Morley's Tryumphes*, ed. Carnicelli, 42; W. G. Thomson, *A History of Tapestry
from the Earliest Times until the Present Day* (London, 1930), 168.

evidence of his worldly extravagance and lust. According to Skelton, the tapestries portray such titillating subjects as 'Dame Dyana naked', 'lusty Venus', Paris's 'lusty sporte and joy' with Helen, 'Naked boyes strydynge', and 'wanton wenches wynkyng'.[26]

Knowledge of the *Trionfi* was widespread even before it was translated into English. In addition to the tapestries, three printed editions of the poem are known to have been at Henry's court: a Spanish translation, *Francisco Petrarca con los seys triunfos* (1512); *Trionfi* (1512); and *Il Petrarcha con l'espositione d'Alessandro Vellutello* (1544).[27] An early literary echo appears in the personification of Fame, Time, and Eternity in the conclusion of Stephen Hawes's *The Pastime of Pleasure* (1509; first complete edition 1517).[28] So popular had the work become by 1570 that Ascham lamented that Italianate Englishmen had 'in more reverence, the triumphes of Petrarche: than the Genesis of Moses'.[29]

Despite that popularity, the entire *Trionfi* inspired fewer English translations and adaptations than did selected poems from the *Canzoniére*. There are just three fragments and two complete translations known to have been written before Pembroke's work.[30] As we have noted, the first extant translation is Surrey's 'Suche waiwarde waies hath love'. The young Princess Elizabeth translated the first 90 lines the *Trionfo della Divinità* in pedestrian quatrains; the unpublished meditation on changes of Fortune, ending with a reference to 'a youthfull hart', would have been an appropriate school exercise to be set by her Italian tutor, Giovanni Battista Castiglione.[31] Henry Parker, Lord Morley, translated the *Tryumphes of Fraunces Petrarcke*, apparently in the 1540s, but it was not published until 1554; it may have been known to Pembroke.[32] (See 'Methods of Composition

---

[26] *John Skelton: The Complete English Poems*, ed. John Scattergood (New Haven: Yale UP, 1983), 270.

[27] Ivy L. Mumford, 'Petrarchism in Early Tudor England', *Italian Studies* 19 (1964), 56–63.

[28] Stephen Hawes, *The historie of graunde Amoure and la bell Pucel, called the Pastime of pleasure* (1554), *STC* 12950, sig. Cc2ᵛ–Dd3ᵛ.

[29] Ascham, *Scholemaster*, sig. I 4.

[30] See D. G. Rees, 'Petrarch's "Trionfo della Morte" in English', *Italian Studies* 7 (1952), 82–96; Coogan, *SP* (1970), 322–3.

[31] *Arundel Harington MS*, I. 360–3 (no. 320); II. 456–60.

[32] The edition itself bears no date. Kenneth R. Bartlett suggests that the 78-year-old Morley printed this early work with a new dedication to Maltravers in 1554 as part of the effort to marry him to Elizabeth, a conspiracy which also involved William Herbert, first Earl of Pembroke: 'The Occasion of Lord Morley's Translation of the *Trionfi*: The Triumph of Chastity over Politics', in *Petrarch's Triumphs*, 325–34.

and Translation'.) She may also have known the few lines from the *ubi sunt* passage of the *Trionfo della Morte* that were translated (probably by Sidney's friend Sir Edward Dyer) in *The Prayse of Nothing* (1585), although her translation does not appear to be indebted to it.[33] She was less likely to have known the 1587–8 translation by William Fowler, Secretary to Queen Anne of Scotland, that survives in only one manuscript, which William Drummond of Hawthornden apparently corrected and subsequently donated to the University of Edinburgh in 1627.[34]

Morley's motives for making his translation were both personal and national. In dedicating the printed work to Lord Maltravers, son of the Earl of Arundel, Morley hopefully recounts the story of an unnamed courtier who presented a French translation of the *Trionfi* to Francis I 'whyche he toke so thankefully, that he gave to hym for hys paynes an hundred crounes', but explains that he received only praise when he gave the manuscript to Henry VIII, implying that he would welcome a more tangible reward from Maltravers.[35] His dedication also suggests that there was a type of international competition in producing vernacular translations of secular works, as there was for the Psalms (see 'Even now', 30; 'Angell Spirit', Variant, 8–14). Morley speaks with patriotic pride: 'I beynge an Englyshe man, myght do aswell as the Frenche man' and therefore 'dyd translate this sayde worke into our maternall toungue'. Writing at the same time as Wyatt and Surrey were introducing the Petrarchan sonnet, Morley still read Petrarch as a moral authority. He did know Petrarch's reputation for 'many a swete sonnet' written for Laura, but he commends the *Trionfi* to Maltravers not because they continue the love story, but because the understanding reader 'shall se in them comprehended al morall vertue, all Phylosophye, all storyall [*sic*] matters, and briefely manye devyne sentences theologicall secretes declared'.[36]

Pembroke certainly did not seek a monetary reward for her translation, like Morley, but she may have desired to give Petrarch to England, as she gave the Psalms. An additional motivation for trans-

[33] E. D., *The Prayse of Nothing* (1585), *STC* 7383, sig. G1. See Ralph M. Sargent, 'The Authorship of "The Prayse of Nothing"', *Transactions of the Bibliographical Society (The Library)*, 4th ser. 12 (1931), 322–31.

[34] *The Works of William Fowler*, ed. H. W. Meikle, James Craigie, and John Purves, 3 vols. (Edinburgh, 1914–40), I. 16; Coogan, *SP* (1970), 323.

[35] 'Unto the mooste towarde yonge gentle Lorde Matravers', *Lord Morley's Tryumphes*, ed. Carnicelli, 78.

[36] Ibid., 77–8.

lation is that by the time she translated the work, it had been appropriated as a Protestant text by reformers like John Bale and John Foxe. As John King demonstrates, such *psychomachia* (warfare between personifications of vices and virtues) had been adopted 'as a means of endorsing the Elizabethan settlement in religion'.[37]

Even more important was the connection of the *Trionfi* with praise of royalty. The *Trionfo d'Amore*, for example, was considered appropriate to the 1501 betrothal of Catherine of Aragon and Prince Arthur. Fame appeared in her chariot to take Henry VIII to the 1511 jousts. Fame was also featured in the pageants for Elizabeth at Bristol in 1574 and at Norwich in 1578. The nine Roman worthies, described in the second *capitolo* of the *Trionfo della Fama*, were frequently used for civic pageantry, as in the triumphal return of John of Lancaster, Duke of Bedford in 1427, and Queen Margaret's entry into Coventry in 1456. By the end of the sixteenth century they had become such a cliché that Shakespeare mocked the convention in *Love's Labour's Lost*, V. ii.[38]

The *Trionfo della Castità* was thought to be particularly appropriate for queens. For example, George Buchanan composed Latin verses based on the *Trionfo della Castità* for a masque performed for Mary Stuart at Holyrood.[39] But no queen was more celebrated for her chastity than Elizabeth, the self-styled Virgin Queen. She was frequently celebrated as the heroine of the 'Triumph of Chastity', as in her 1578 progress in Suffolk, and the far more elaborate 1581 Accession Day tilt, the *Four Foster Children of Desire*, or the 'Fortress of Perfect Beauty', in which Philip Sidney appeared.[40] The iconography of these Triumphs became exceedingly complex, as the imagery intertwined with that of the Virgin Queen (adopted from the Catholic cult of the Virgin Mary), the unattainable Petrarchan mistress of the *Canzoniére*, the goddess Astraea (see 'Astrea'), biblical figures (see

---

[37] King, *Iconography*, 118.

[38] Alexandra F. Johnston, 'English Civic Ceremony', in *Petrarch's Triumphs*, 395–402. See also Thomas Martone, 'Piero della Francesca's "Triumphs of the Duke and Duchess of Urbino"', in *Petrarch's Triumphs*, 211–22.

[39] Coogan, *SP* (1970), 321; Mary Stuart herself owned a copy of the *Trionfi*.

[40] John Nichols, *The Progresses and Public Processions of Queen Elizabeth*, 3 vols. (London: John Nichols and Sons, 1788–1821), II. 67; on the political frustration expressed through this device, see Richard McCoy, 'Sir Philip Sidney and Elizabethan Chivalry', in *Sir Philip Sidney's Achievements*, ed. M. J. B. Allen *et al.* (New York: AMS Press, 1990), 34–7, and Katherine Duncan-Jones, *Sir Philip Sidney: Courtier Poet* (New Haven: Yale UP, 1991), 194–6.

'Even now that Care'), and with various traditional symbols of virginity, like the sieve, the ermine, and the pearl.

Iconography from the *Trionfo della Castità* was also used to honour Elizabeth in paintings. For example, the 'Ermine Portrait' of Elizabeth by William Segar (1585, Hatfield House), portraying her with an ermine that wears a golden circlet, is ultimately derived from the ermine banner of Laura and her chaste companions described in *Trionfo della Castità* and *Trionfo della Morte*. Pembroke translates the passage:

> Borne in greene field, a snowie Ermiline
> Colored with topaces, sett in fine golde
> was this faire companies unfoyled signe. (1. 19–21)

Thus, translating the *Trionfi*, like paraphrasing the Psalms, could be seen as an appropriate homage to Queen Elizabeth.

In the *Arcadia* Sidney parodies the tradition in the triumph of Artesia, who appears in 'a triumphant chariot, made of carnation velvet enriched with purl and pearl' and drawn 'by four winged horses'; she is followed by attendants who carry pictures of the beauties she has conquered.[41] The *Trionfi* also inform parts of Spenser's *Faerie Queene*, particularly the triumphal procession of Lucifera (Pride) and the other six Deadly Sins in the House of Pride (Book I), the Masque of Cupid in the House of Busirane (Book III), and the procession of the Seasons in the Mutability Cantos (Book VII). Pembroke herself emphasizes the idea of the Triumph in her translation of *Antonius*, wherein both Antony and Cleopatra are motivated by their desire to escape the ignominy of appearing in Caesar's Triumph (see Argument, 31–2, 1847–68). She also introduces the image into her version of Psalm 108, portraying the nations of Gilead, Manashe, Ephraim, Moab, and Palestine as forced to take part in the Triumph of Israel. (See also Psalm 110.)

We cannot make too much of the fact that only her *Triumph of Death* survives, because our only surviving copy of the Countess of Pembroke's translation of the *Trionfo della Morte* was haphazardly preserved in a transcript of papers sent by John Harington to Lucy, Countess of Bedford. That manuscript includes just three of Pembroke's *Psalmes*, and so it may include just a portion of her Petrarch translation.[42] It is

---

[41] Sidney, *New Arcadia*, 94.

[42] The transcribed letter accompanying the manuscript, dated 29 December 1600, mentions Pembroke's Psalms as the reason for sending the manuscript, but does not mention the

thus quite possible that she translated the entire *Trionfi*. As we have seen, Moffet's instruction to rest from her labours suggests an ambitious undertaking. (See p. 15.) Nevertheless, the *Trionfo della Morte*, like Mornay's *Discours*, was part of the literature of consolation in the *ars moriendi* tradition, and may have been of some comfort to a woman who had lost father, mother, daughter, and two brothers in less than a decade.

It seems that Pembroke's decision to translate the *Trionfo* may have been influenced by a variety of factors: its value as a work of Christian/Senecan moral philosophy, its function as Protestant allegory, its use to praise Queen Elizabeth, and its place in the literature of consolation. She may also have been drawn to the portrayal of Laura as an eloquent figure, unlike the silent presence of the beloved in English Petrarchan sonnets.

Pembroke's translation presents Laura as a vibrant figure of joy and power, whose accomplishments are stressed in martial terms. She is gallant, a 'joyefull Conquéresse', who has been wise enough to defeat Love 'the mightie foe, | whose wylie stratagems the world distresse' (1. 1–6). Comparison of Pembroke's version with that of Morley shows a somewhat different interpretation of Laura's character. In Morley's translation, the women who mourn her lament the loss of 'So swete a speache, so Angelyke a voyce!' In Pembroke's translation, the ladies lament their loss of her wit, that is, her wisdom:

> The ladies saide: And now, what shall we doe?
> Never againe such grace shall blesse our sight;
> Never lyke witt, shall we from woman heare
> And voice, repleate with Angell-lyke delight. (1. 147–50).

That is, her voice is angelic, not because it is sweet, but because it is wise. Similarly, 'Petrarch' says that he misses her voice, 'which often did my heart reconsolate; | Now wiselie grave, then beawtifulie true' (2. 65–6).

The collective impact of Morley's epithets is to depict a Laura who is charming and almost girlish. She is a sweet maid, a 'fayre creature' who wears a garland (1. 49, 104). Pembroke's Laura is more regal. She speaks with authority, acts with noble courtesy, and wears a coronet. The difference in presentation is particularly striking in the passage

'The Triumph of death translated out of Italian by the Countesse of Pembrooke' which immediately follows her versions of Psalms 51, 104, and 137. (See 'Transmission and Authority of Texts'.)

where Laura meets a personified Death. Whereas Morley's Laura has not yet felt Death's 'fearefull stroke' (1. 97), Pembroke's Laura 'Didst never yett unto [Death's] scepter bowe' (1. 63). Morley's Laura passively accepts Death, saying 'Do thou unto me as thou doest to all men' (1. 113). Pembroke's Laura is the noble lady greeting even this most unwelcome guest: 'As others doe, I shall thee entretaine' (1. 72). Similarly, as Laura approaches the hour on the sixth day of April when she must die, Morley says 'thys fayre Lady...must the doubtfull passe assay' (1. 145). Pembroke, in contrast, stresses the glory of her former conquest and presents her actively preparing 'that short-glorious life hir leave to take' (1. 103). Morley's Laura is not only more passive than Pembroke's, but also less eloquent. He consistently downplays Laura's speech, as is evident even in his allocation of lines. It takes him four lines (2. 149–52) to translate a single line that Pembroke renders, 'The mother had a rodd, yett kinde is she' (2. 93). It takes him six lines to render Petrarch's tercet on his query to Laura (2. 189–94). Yet he merely summarizes Laura's final speech, giving 28 lines to Petrarch's 59—and even at that, several of Morley's lines are simply filler rather than translation. Apparently he had little interest in Laura's speech, for he implies that he finds it boring and repetitious when he adds a parenthetic statement, 'I say agayne' (2. 201). In Pembroke's translation, Laura's speech is enhanced.

This second *capitolo* of the *Trionfo della Morte* purports to retell the Petrarchan love story from Laura's viewpoint, so that Pembroke's translation could be seen as another continuation, or expansion, of her brother's work.[43] Like the *Canzoniére*, *Astrophil and Stella* depicts the man's desire controlled by the woman's reason, as when Astrophil cries, 'Thou art my Wit, and thou my Vertue art' (*Astrophil* 64). The struggle is comically presented in *Astrophil* 52, wherein 'A strife is growne betweene Vertue and Love | While each pretends that Stella must be his'. Astrophil concludes that Virtue may have Stella's soul if only 'Vertue but that body graunt' to him. He is prevented from that passionate dualism by Stella's virtue (*Astrophil* 69) and by her voice, which says only 'No, no, no, no, my Deare, let be' (*Fourth Song*, 54).

Laura also said no to Petrarch in the *Canzoniére*, but in the *Trionfo della Morte* the spirit of Laura returns to explain her constant refusal of his love. As Pembroke renders the passage:

[43] For a gendered reading of the Petrarchan sonnet in English, see Barbara L. Estrin, *Laura: Uncovering Gender and Genre in Wyatt, Donne, and Marvell* (Durham, NC: Duke UP, 1994).

> Thow saw'est what was without, not what within.
>> And as the brake the wanton steede doeth tame,
>> So this did thee from thy disorders winne.
> A thousand times wrath in my face did flame,
>> My heart meane-while with love did inlie burne,
>> But never will; my reason overcame: (2. 97–102)

Because of her wise alternation of 'kinde acceptance' and 'sharp disdaine', as his reason or his passion prevailed, Laura has saved him: 'thus farre I have thee brought | wearie, but safe, to my no litle joye' (2. 119–20). She had nothing to blame in his love, except its 'measure'. Only in that did he fail, for while she kept her feelings secret, 'Thow didst thy heart to all the world disclose' (2. 135). Their love burnt 'In equale flames', but her silence was as painful a role as his eloquence: 'But not the lesse becoms concealed woe, | Nor greater growe's it utte'red, then before' (2. 139, 145–6). Indeed, one of Pembroke's most significant omissions occurs in this passage, for, as William Kennedy observes, by omitting Petrarch's adjective *quasi*, 'almost' ('*Fur quasi equali in noi fiamme amorose*') she emphasizes the equality of their love.[44]

Pembroke's translation of the *Trionfo della Morte* thus dramatizes the same problem of passion versus reason as does *Antonius*. Laura and Cleopatra represent opposite poles of female behaviour; the chaste Laura leads her lover to God, while the passionate Cleopatra causes her lover's destruction.[45] Yet both women are eloquent and both die nobly.[46]

Both the *Triumph* and *Antonius*, like Mornay's *Discours*, give a Senecan philosophical approach to the problems of life and of death, warning of the dangers of avarice, ambition, and illicit passion, and advocating a life ruled by Reason. While *Antonius* depicts a pre-Christian world, such Stoic philosophy is baptized in the *Triumph* and the *Discourse*. The tone of the *Triumph*, however, is closest to that of the *Psalmes*, for both works go beyond resignation to adversity and mortality; in both works we see a vision of joyful, triumphant Christian faith that conquers even death.

---

[44] William Kennedy, *The Site of Petrarchism* (forthcoming).

[45] Note her appearance in the *Triumph of Fame*: 'Cleopatra, that was burnte with loves fyre, | There she was with all her hote desire', *Lord Morley's Tryumphes*, ed. Carnicelli, 139.

[46] On Laura and Cleopatra, see Beilin, *Redeeming Eve*, 128, 131–7; Lamb, *Gender*, 129–40; Gary Waller suggests that Laura's farewell 'echoes something of the Countess' own feelings for her brother', Sidney, Mary. *Triumph*, 17.

Fidelity to Originals

The Triumph of Death is the most remarkable instance of Pembroke's fidelity as a translator, a quality which distinguishes her most notably from Lord Morley. Not only does her translation have the same number of lines as in the Italian (Morley adds over 100 lines to the *Trionfo della Morte*), but it corresponds *terzina* for *terzina* to the original and even retains the *terza rima* stanza form (Morley uses couplets), a *tour de force* not attempted again in an English version until 1836.[1] Although the edition of the Italian text used by Pembroke has not been precisely identified (see 'Transmission and Authority of Texts'), it is clear that she used a text in the Aldine tradition as established by Pietro Bembo and subsequently edited probably by either Alessandro Vellutello or Giovanni Andrea Gesualdo, both of whose commentaries (influenced by Bernardo da Lapini, 'Illicino') appeared in numerous printings throughout the sixteenth century.[2] For comparison, we have used the 1528 edition printed with Vellutello's commentary by Vidali. (See 'Transmission and Authority of Texts'.)

Pembroke's literal approach to translating does not prevent her from achieving an English version that is 'smooth and eloquent' and marked by 'fluency and naturalness which verse translations so often lack'.[3] Except for a few places that are lacking in clarity (e.g. 1. 37–8, 2. 61–3, 186), the translation is mainly accurate. Rees does find among the errors two which seriously affect the meaning: *Altri* has been mistaken for a plural form (1. 52), and *havei* (a shortened form of the plural *[h]avevi*) for a first person form (2. 128–9). He might have added that another error or misinterpretation occurs in 1. 133, where *L'hora prim' era* ('It was the first hour') appears as 'one a clock it was'. A few other slips are not Pembroke's, but those of Harington's copyist. Coogan noted that two of them, 'send' (1. 25) and 'spring' (1. 120), are scribal errors for 'seem'd' and 'sing', respectively, as *pareano* and *cantai* in the Italian prove. Other instances of scribal error are

---

[1] A *terza rima* translation was published by Barbarina Wilmot, Baroness Dacre, in 1836. D. G. Rees, 'Petrarch's "Trionfo della Morte" in English', *Italian Studies* 7 (1952), 91.

[2] Mary Fowler provides descriptions of scores of fifteenth- and sixteenth-century editions now in the Kroch Library at Cornell University in *Catalogue of the Petrarch Collection Bequeathed by Willard Fiske* (London: Oxford UP, 1916). We have made a full collation of *Trionfo della Morte* in eight sixteenth-century editions of Petrarch's vernacular poems, and we have checked ten significant variants in 80 others (including all those between 1547 and 1596 at Cornell), as well as eight separate editions of the *Trionfi*.

[3] Rees, *Italian Studies* (1952), 83.

noted in the commentary (see e.g. the notes on lines 1. 102 and 2. 4, 18, 81, 130, 158, 178).[4]

A few omissions of details seem to be deliberate, although the reasons for them are not always obvious. Perhaps, as Coogan says, it was the exigencies of verse translation, particularly the retention of the Italian verse form, that led to the substitution of the general category 'Tyrrants' (2. 43) for the list of five offenders named by Petrarch: Sulla, Marius, Nero, Gaius, and Mezentius.[5] She does, however, make similar substitutions in *Antonius* and *Discourse*. The omission of the comparison of death with absinthe (2. 44–5) may reflect unfamiliarity with the Latinate term for wormwood, *assentio*.[6] The dropping of *casto letto* or 'chaste bed' (1. 146) in the description of Laura's death is more difficult to account for, although Gary Waller suggests that she may at this point have been under the influence of Morley, who also omits the phrase:

> 'Vertue,' sayde they that were present there,
> 'Excellent beutye and moost womanly chere
> Nowe is deade and gone...' (189–91)[7]

Because there is otherwise little parallel between Morley and Pembroke in these lines (and elsewhere), however, another possible explanation is simply that Pembroke omitted the words to make more room for the kind of extended balanced construction that she often writes (especially in her metrical Psalms):

> *Virtu morta è, bellezza, et cortesia,*
> *Le belle donne intorno al casto letto*
> *Triste, diceano...* (145–7)

> Vertue is dead; and dead is beawtie too,
> And dead is curtesie, in mournefull plight,
> The ladies saide...

In any case, such excision of details is rare.

While Pembroke probably knew Morley's version (see *Triumph of Death*: Literary Context), comparison of the two translations fails to show any sustained indebtedness on her part. Most obvious among the differences are those cited earlier: verse form and length. The later translator could have found little to borrow in her predecessor's

---

[4] Coogan, *SP* (1970), 324.
[5] Ibid., 324.
[6] The earliest entry for 'absinthe' in the *OED* is from 1612.
[7] Sidney, Mary. *Triumph*, 147.

halting, padded lines. What verbal correspondences there are, are likely coincidental. Of fourteen scattered parallels, all are direct translations of the Italian: e.g. 'gentle heart' (l. 29; Morley 1. 38) for *gentil core* (1. 28); 'Oh humane hopes' (l. 129; Morley, 'O humayne hope' 1. 172) for *O humane speranze*; 'to thee most deare' (2. 68; Morley, 'unto the moost dere' 2. 109) for *a te piu cara*; 'written in your eye' (2. 83; Morley, 'wrytten in your eyes' 2. 133) for *ne begliocchi scritte*. Even though Morley's translation is wordy, he often omits Petrarch's imagery, such as the light and fire imagery in the sun of Laura's face, the lightning of her eyes, and the flames of love. Sometimes he mistranslates even straightforward passages. For example, Pembroke accurately translates Laura's paradoxical statement that she has led him with 'pleasure' and 'annoye', with warm 'red' and with 'colde pale', and thus has brought him 'wearie, but safe, to my no litle joye' (2. 118–20). Morley apparently just sees random colours and turns the passage into nonsense:

> Thus with dyvers colours many mo,
> With hoote, with grene, and with golde, with white
> I kepte the alwayes styll in honest plyte.   (2. 184–6)

Morley also misses the pun on Petrarch's 'flowrie nest' in Florence (Pembroke 2. 167; Morley 2. 220).

Pembroke's usual method is to find ways to evoke the full force of the original. Thus, although she neglects to adapt Petrarch's pun on *lauro* (the laurel tree and Laura) by translating it as 'bay' (2. 18), she does characteristically seize other opportunities to amplify the text with vivid language. Early in the first chapter, when Laura is said to have defeated 'love' (as Cupid) with no other arms than her pure heart (*Non con altr'arme, che col cor pudico*), Pembroke underscores the nature of the victory by specifying just what kind of weapons Laura lacked: 'And foyl'd him, not with sword, with speare or bowe, | But with chaste heart' (7–8). At 1. 83, *le gemme* becomes 'pearle and stone' (84). At 1. 133–4, the detail of tying is added to the more general imagery of binding and freeing. At 1. 141, a general reference to Laura's untimely death is recast in nature imagery: 'hir leafe quail'd, as yett but freshlie newe'. Rees notes other instances of amplification in the form of 'vigorous verb forms', 'double epithets' (e.g. 'woe-darkned skyes' in 2. 87), and patterns of repetition, all of which the countess uses frequently in her other works.[8]

---

[8] Rees, *Italian Studies* (1952), 85–8.

An example of both the strengths and weaknesses of Pembroke's translation is her handling of Laura's answer to Petrarch's question about the fear of death:

> *Negar, disse, non posso; che l'affanno,*
> > *Che va inanzi al morir, non doglia forte:*
> > *Ma piu la tema de l'eterno danno.*
> *Ma pur che l'alma in Dio si riconforte,*
> > *E'l cor, che'n se medesmo forse è lasso;*
> > *Che altro, ch'un sospir breve è la morte?* (2. 46–51)

> I not denye (quoth she) but that the crosse
> > Preceeding death, extreemelie martireth,
> > And more the feare of that eternall losse.
> But when the panting soule in God take's breath;
> > And wearie heart affecteth heavenlie rest,
> > An unrepented syghe, not els, is death.

The elliptical phrasing of the first *terzina* is awkward (though perhaps more so to modern ears); it is the result of the need to find English equivalents of the Italian words to fit into the verse form. On the whole, however, Pembroke allows Laura to speak with greater emotional intensity than does Petrarch, who seems to be drafting a discourse rather than a speech of consolation. The substitution of the evocative 'crosse' for the more ordinary *affanno* (sorrow) is the sort of change (even if partly motivated here by the need to find a rhyme word) that readers of the countess know to expect of her. The resulting conjunction of 'crosse' and 'martireth' heightens the religious overtones of the passage. The apparent relinquishing of the probable pun in *danno* (loss and damnation) may seem at first to be a simple case of yielding to the pull of rhyme, but the softening of the phrase in English (where some ambivalence is retained) is not inappropriate in a context where Laura is acknowledging that, to a degree and in a certain sense, the love between her and Petrarch is reciprocal (see 2. 88–9, 100–1). It is the second set of lines that evokes the feeling most strongly.[9] The allusion to Psalm 42. 1 in line 49 is Pembroke's own, echoed from Philip Sidney's paraphrase:

> As the chafed hart which brayeth
> Seeking some refreshing brook,

[9] Beilin, *Redeeming Eve*, 136–7, discusses the second *terzina*: 'This terzina, an exhalation of simultaneous physical and spiritual release, heralds the concise style of many of the countess's Psalms, where a single metaphor may convey the whole history of the soul's quest for God.'

> So my soul in panting playeth,
> Thirsting on my God to look.   (1–4)

She also added the colloquial 'take's breath' (find a time for recovery, a pause) which replaces the more abstract *si riconforte* and which may be another echo of her brother's Psalm 42:

> I by day thy love shall tast,
> I by night shall singing last,
> Praying, prayers still bequeathing
> To my God that gave me breathing.   (37–40)

Earthly life we have from God, and, from the Christian perspective of the *Triumph*, after death we take breath of another life. The final line of the passage, with its continuation of the breathing metaphor, further reinforces Laura's confident view of death, not only by turning the question into an assertion, but also by replacing the neutral *un sospir breve* with the assured and resonant phrase, 'An unrepented syghe'.

The Triumph of death translated out of Italian by the Countesse of Pembrooke. the first chapter.

That gallant Ladie, gloriouslie bright,
    The statelie piller once of worthinesse,
    And now, a little dust, a naked spright:
Turn'd from hir warre's a joyefull Conqueresse:
    Hir warre's, where she had foyl'd the mightie foe,   5
    whose wylie stratagems the world distresse.
And foyl'd him, not with sword, with speare or bowe,
    But with chaste heart, faire visage, upright thought,
    wise speache, which did with honor linked goe:
And love's new plight to see strange wonders wrought   10
    with shivered bowe, chaste arrowe's, quenched flame,
    while-here som slaine, and there laye others caught.
She, and the rest, who in the glorious fame
    Of the exploit, hir chosen mates, did share,
    All in one squadronet close ranged came.   15
A few, for nature make's true glorie rare,
    But eache alone (so eache alone did shine)
    Claym'd whole Historians, whole Poete's care
Borne in greene field, a snowie Ermiline
    Colored with topaces, sett in fine golde   20
    was this faire companies unfoyled signe.
No earthlie march, but heavenly, did they hould;
    Their speaches holie were, and happie those,
    who so are borne, to be with them enroll'd.
Cleare starr's they seem'd, which did a Sunne unclose,   25
    who hyding none, yett all did beawtifie
    with Coronets deckt with violet and rose:
And as gain'd honor, filled with jollitie
    Eache gentle heart, so made they merrie cheere,
    when loe, an ensigne sad I might descrie,   30

The Triumph of Death
Copy-text: *Petyt MS 538. 43, ff. 286–9.*
the first chapter   25 seem'd] send *Petyt*

Black, and in black, a woman did appeere,
  Furie with hir, such as I scarcelie knowe
  If lyke at Phlegra with the Giants were.
Thow Dame, quoth she, that doeth so proudlie goe,
35 Standing upon thy youth, and beawties state,
  And of thy life, the limit's doest not knowe.
Loe, I am shee, so fierce, importunate,
  And deafe, and blinde, entytled oft by yow,
  yow, whom with night ere evening I amate.
40 I, to their end, the Greekish nation drewe,
  The Trojan first, the Romane afterward,
  with edge and point of this my blade I slewe.
And no Barbarian my blowe could warde,
  who stealing-on with unexpected wound,
45 Of idle thoughts have manie thousand marr'd.
And now no lesse to yow-ward am I bound,
  while life is dearest, ere to cause yow moane,
  Fortune som bitter with your sweetes compound.
To this, thow right or interrest hast none,
50 Little to me, but onelie to this spoile,
  Replide then she, who in the world was one.
This charge of woe on others will recoyle,
  I knowe, whose safetie on my life depends:
  For me, I thank who shall me hence assoile.
55 As one whose eyes som noveltie attend,
  And what it mark't not first, it spyde at last,
  New wonders with it-self, now comprehends.
So far'd the cruell, deepelie over-gast
  with doubt awhile, then spake, I knowe them now.
60 I now remember when my teethe they past.
Then with lesse frowning, and lesse darkned browe,
  But thow that lead'st this goodlie companie,
  Didst never yett unto my scepter bowe.
But on my counsell if thow wilt relye,
65 who maie inforce thee; better is by farre
  From age and ages lothsomnesse to flye.
More honored by me, then others are
  Thow shalt thee finde: and neither feare nor paine
  The passage shall of thy departure barre.

As lykes that Lord, who in the heav'n doeth raigne,   70
    And thence, this All, doeth moderatelie guide:
    As others doe, I shall thee entretaine.
So answered she, and I with-all descryde
    Of dead appeere a never-numbred summe,
    Pestring the plaine, from one to th'other side.   75
From India, Spaine, Cattay, Marocco, Coome,
    So manie Ages did together falle.
    That worlds were fill'd, and yett they wanted roome.
There sawe I, whom their times did happie calle,
    Popes, Emperors, and kings, but strangelie growen,   80
    All naked now, all needie beggers all.
where is that wealth? where are those honor's gonne?
    Scepters, and crounes, and roabe's, and purple dye?
    And costlie myters, sett with pearle and stone?
O wretch, who doest in mortall things affye: 85
    (yett who but doeth) and if in end they dye
    Them-selve's beguil'd, they finde but right, saie I.
What meane's this toyle? Oh blinde, oh more then blinde:
    yow all returne, to your greate Mother, olde,
    And hardlie leave your verie names behinde.   90
Bring me, who doeth your studies well behoulde,
    And of your cares not manifestlie vaine,
    One lett him tell me, when he all hath tolde.
So manie lands to winne, what bootes the payne?
    And on strange land's, tributes to impose,   95
    with hearts still griedie, their oune losse to gaine.
After all theise, wherin yow winning loose
    Treasure's and territories deere bought with blood;
    water, and bread hath a farre sweeter close.
And golde, and gemme gives place to glasse and wood: 100
    But leaste I should too-long degression make
    To turne to my first taske I think it good.
Now that short-glorious life hir leave to take
    Did neere unto the uttmost instant goe,
    And doubtfull stepp, at which the world doeth quake. 105
An other number then themselves did shewe
    Of Ladies, such as bodies yett did lade,
    If death could pitious be, they faine would knowe.

    76 Cattay] Gattay *Petyt*   102 taske] talke *Petyt*

And deepe they did in contemplacion wade
110   Of that colde end, presented there to view,
       which must be once, and must but once be made.
All friends and neighbors were this carefull crue,
       But death with ruthlesse hand on golden haire
       Chosen from-out those amber-tresses drewe.
115 So cropt the flower, of all this world most faire,
       To shewe upon the excellentest thing
       Hir supreame force, And for no hate she bare.
How manie dropps did flowe from brynie spring
       In who there sawe those sightfull fountaines drye,
120   For whom this heart so long did burne and sing.
For hir in midst of moane and miserie,
       Now reaping once what vertues life did sowe,
       with joye she sate retired silentlie.
In peace cryde they, right mortall Goddesse goe,
125   And so she was, but that in noe degree
       Could death entreate, hir comming to forslowe.
what confidence for others? if that she
       Could frye and freese in few nights changing cheere:
       Oh humane hopes, how fond and false yow bee.
130 And for this gentle Soule, if manie a teare
       By pittie shed, did bathe the ground and grasse,
       who sawe, doeth knowe; think thow, that doest but heare.
The sixt of Aprill, one a clock it was
       That tyde me once, and did me now untye,
135   Changing hir copie; Thus doeth fortune passe.
None so his thralle, as I my libertie;
       None so his death, as I my life doe rue,
       Staying with me, who faine from it would flye.
Due to the world, and to my yeares was due,
140   That I, as first I came, should first be gonne,
       Not hir leafe quail'd, as yett but freshlie newe.
Now for my woe, guesse not by't, what is showne,
       For I dare scarce once cast a thought there-too,
       So farre I am of, in words to make it knowne.
145 Vertue is dead; and dead is beawtie too,
       And dead is curtesie, in mournefull plight,
       The ladies saide: And now, what shall we doe?

           120 sing] spring *Petyt*

Never againe such grace shall blesse our sight;
      Never lyke witt, shall we from woman heare
      And voice, repleate with Angell-lyke delight.   150
The Soule now prest to leave that bosome deere
      Hir vertues all uniting now in one,
      There, where it past did make the heavens cleare.
And of the enemies so hardlie none,
      That once before hir shew'd his face obscure   155
      with hir assault, till death had thorough gonne.
Past plaint and feare when first they could endure
      To hould their eyes on that faire visage bent,
      And that dispaire had made them now secure.
Not as greate fyers violently spent,   160
      But in them-selves consuming, so hir flight
      Tooke that sweete spright, and past in peace content.
Right lyke unto som lamp of cleerest light,
      little and little wanting nutriture,
      Houlding to end a never-changing plight.   165
Pale? no, but whitelie; and more whitelie pure,
      Then snowe on wyndless hill, that flaking falle's:
      As one, whom labor did to rest allure.
And when that heavenlie guest those mortall walles
      Had leaft; it nought but sweetelie sleeping was   170
      In hir faire eyes: what follie dying calles
Death faire did seeme to be in hir faire face.

                Marie Sidney Coun: of Pem:

The Second Chapter of the Triumph of death.

      That night, which did the dreadfull happ ensue,
           That quite eclipst; Naie, rather did replace
           The Sunne in Skyes, and me bereave of view.
      Did sweetelie sprinkle through the ayrie space
           The Summers frost, which with Tithon's bryde   5
           Cleereth of dreame the darke-confused face.

      The Second Chapter   4 sprinkle] sprintle *Petyt*

When loe, a Ladie, lyke unto the tyde
  with Orient jewells crown'd, from thousands moe
   Crouned as she; to me, I comming spyde:
10 And first hir hand, somtime desyred so
  Reaching to me; at-once she sygh't and spake:
   whence endlesse joyes yett in my heart doe growe.
And know'st thow hir, who made thee first forsake
  The vulgar path, and ordinarie trade?
15   while hir, their marke, thy youthfull thoughts did make?
Then doune she sate, and me sitt-doune she made.
  Thought, wisedome, Meekenesse in one grace did strive,
   On pleasing bank in bay, and beeches shade.
My Goddesse, who me did, and doeth revive,
20   Can I but knowe? (I sobbing answered)
   But art thow dead? Ah speake, or yett alive?
Alive am I: And thow as yett art dead,
  And as thow art shalt so continue still
   Till by thy ending hower, thow hence be led.
25 Short is our time to live, and long our will:
  Then lett with heede, thy deedes, and speaches goe.
   Ere that approaching terme his course fullfill.
Quoth I, when this our light to end doeth growe,
  which we calle life (for thow by proofe hast tryde)
30   Is it such payne to dye? That, make me knowe.
while thow (quoth she) the vulgar make thy guide,
  And on their judgements (all obscurelie blynde)
   Doest yett relye; no blisse can thee betyde.
Of lothsom prison to eache gentle mynde
35   Death is the end: And onelie who employe
   Their cares on mudd, therin displeasure finde.
Even this my death, which yealds thee such annoye
  would make in thee farre greater gladnesse ryse,
   Couldst thow but taste least portion of my joye.
40 So spake she with devoutlie-fixed eyes
  Upon the Heavens; then did in silence foulde
   Those rosie lips, attending there replyes;
Torments, invented by the Tyrrants olde;
  Diseases, which eache parte torment and tosse,
45   Causes, that death we most bitter houlde.

    18 On pleasing] vnpleasing *Petyt*

I not denye (quoth she) but that the crosse
    Preceeding death, extreemelie martireth,
    And more the feare of that eternall losse.
But when the panting soule in God take's breath;
    And wearie heart affecteth heavenlie rest,   50
    An unrepented syghe, not els, is death.
with bodie, but with spirit readie prest,
    Now at the furthest of my living wayes,
    There sadlie-uttered sound's my eare possest.
Oh happless he; who counting times and dayes   55
    Thinks eache a thousand yeares, and live's in vayne
    No more to meete hir while on earth he stayes.
And on the water now, now on the Maine
    Onelie on hir doeth think, doeth speake, doeth write,
    And in all times one manner still retaine.   60
Heere-with, I thither cast my failing-sight,
    And soone espyde, presented to my view,
    who oft did thee restraining, me encyte.
well, I hir face, and well hir voice I knewe,
    which often did my heart reconsolate;   65
    Now wiselie grave, then beawtifulie true.
And sure, when I, was in my fairest state,
    My yeares most greene, my self to thee most deare,
    whence manie much did think, and much debate.
That life's best joye, was all most bitter cheere,   70
    Compared to that death, most myldelie sweete,
    which coms to men, but coms not everie-where.
For I, that journie past with gladder feete,
    Then he from hard exile, that homeward goes,
    (But onelie ruth of thee) without regreete.   75
For that faith's sake, time once enough did shewe,
    yett now to thee more manifestlie plaine,
    In face of him, who all doeth see and knowe.
Saie Ladie, did yow ever entretaine
    Motion or thought more lovinglie to rue   80
    (Not leving honor's-height) my tedious paine?
For those sweete wrath's, those sweete disdaine's in yow,
    In those sweete peaces written in your eye,
    Diverslie manie yeares my fanzies drewe.

      81 leving] loving *Petyt*

85   Scarce had I spoken, but in lightning wise
              Beaming, I sawe that gentle smile appeare,
              Somtimes the Sunne of my woe-darkned skyes.
        Then sighing, thus she answered: Never were
              Our hearts but one, nor never two shall be:
90   Onelie thy flame I tempred with my cheere:
        This onelie waye could save both thee and me;
              Our tender fame did this supporte require,
              The mother had a rodd, yett kinde is she.
        How oft this saide my thoughts: In love, naie fire
95   Is he: Now to provide must I beginne,
              And ill providers are feare and desire.
        Thow saw'est what was without, not what within.
              And as the brake the wanton steede doeth tame,
              So this did thee from thy disorders winne.
100   A thousand times wrath in my face did flame,
              My heart meane-while with love did inlie burne,
              But never will; my reason overcame:
        For, if woe-vanquisht once, I sawe thee mourne;
              Thy life, our honor, joyntlie to preserve,
105   Myne eyes to thee sweetelie did I turne.
        But if thy passion did from reason swarve,
              Feare in my word's, and sorrowe in my face
              Did then to thee for salutation serve.
        Theis arte's I us'd with thee; thow ran'st this race
110   With kinde acceptance; now sharp disdaine,
              Thow know'st, and hast it sung in manie a place.
        Somtimes thine eyes pregnant with tearie rayne
              I sawe, and at the sight; Behould he dyes:
              But if I help, saide I, the signes are plaine.
115   Vertue for ayde, did then with love advise:
              If spurr'd by love, thow took'st som running toye,
              So soft a bitt (quoth I) will not suffice.
        Thus glad, and sad, in pleasure, and annoye;
              what red, colde pale; thus farre I have thee brought
120   wearie, but safe, to my no litle joye.
        Then I with teares, and trembling; what it sought
              My faith hath found, whose more then equall meede
              were this; if this, for truth could passe my thought.

              97 Thow] Tho *Petyt*   104 our] or *Petyt*

Of little faith (quoth she) should this proceede,
  If false it were, or if unknowne from me;   125
  The flames withall seem'd in hir face to breede.
If lyking in myne eyes the world did see
  I saie not, now, of this, right faine I am,
  Those cheine's that tyde my heart well lyked me.
And well me lyke's (if true it be) my fame,   130
  which farre and neere by thee related goes,
  Nor in thy love could ought but measure blame.
That onelie fail'd; and while in acted woes
  Thow neede's wouldst shewe, what I could not but see.
  Thow didst thy heart to all the world disclose. 135
Hence sprang my zeale, which yett distempreth thee,
  Our concord such in everie thing beside,
  As when united love and vertue be.
In equale flames our loving hearts were tryde,
  At leaste when once thy love had notice gott. 140
  But one to shewe, the other sought to hyde.
Thow didst for mercie calle with wearie throte
  In feare and shame, I did in silence goe.
  So much desire became of little note.
But not the lesse becoms concealed woe,   145
  Nor greater growe's it utte'red, then before,
  Through fiction, Truth will neither ebbe nor flowe.
But clear'd I not the darkest mists of yore?
  when I thy words' alone did entretaine
  Singing for thee? my love dares speake no more. 150
with thee my heart, to me I did restraine
  Myne eyes; and thow thy share canst hardlie brooke
  leesing by me the lesse, the more to gayne.
Not thinking if a thousand times I tooke
  Myne eyes from thee, I manie thousands cast 155
  Myne eyes on thee; and still with pittying looke.
whose shine no clowd had ever over-cast:
  Had I not fear'd in thee those coles to fyre
  I thought would burne too-dangerouslie fast.
But to content thee more ere I retyre   160
  For end of this, I somthing will thee tell,
  Perchance agreable to thy desire:

130 fame] flame *Petyt*   139 tryde] ry *altered in Petyt*   158 fyre] fyres *Petyt*

In all things fullie blest, and pleased well,
     Onelie in this I did my-self displease;
165   Borne in too-base a toune for me to dwell:
And much I grieved, that for thy greater ease,
     At leaste, it stood not neere thy flowrie nest,
     Els farre-enough, from whence I did thee please.
So might the heart on which I onelie rest
170   Not knowing me, have fitt it-self elswhere,
     And I lesse name, lesse notice have possest.
Oh no (quoth I) for, me, the heavens third spheare
     To so high love advanc't by speciall grace,
     Changelesse to me, though chang'd thy dwelling were.
175 Be as it will, yett my greate Honor was,
     And is as yett (she saide) but thy delight
     Make's thee not mark how fast the howers doe passe.
See from hir golden bed Aurora bright
     To mortall eyes returning Sunne and daye
180   Breast-high above the Ocean bare to sight.
Shee to my sorrowe, calle's me hence awaie,
     Therfore thy words in times short limits binde,
     And saie in-brief, if more thow have to saie.
Ladie (quoth I) your words most sweetelie kinde
185   Have easie made, what ever erst I bare,
     But what is left of yow to live behinde.
Therfore to knowe this, my onelie care,
     If sloe or swift shall com our meeting-daye.
     Shee parting saide, As my conjectures are,
190 Thow without me long time on earth shalt staie.

               Marie Sydney Countesse of Pembrooke:

172 (quoth I)] *Parentheses written over commas in Petyt*   178 See] Shee *Petyt*

CORRESPONDENCE

Manuscript Letters

I. Mary Sidney Herbert, Countess of Pembroke, to Robert Dudley, Earl of Leicester.

Undated, probably 15 August 1578. Addressed 'Very good Lord and the Earle of Leycester geve these'. (The left margin of the address is worn off.) Holograph. Manuscript of the Marquess of Bath, Longleat House, Warminster. Dudley Papers II/187.

My most honorid Lord, ~~your sone~~ I perceve by your lordships leteres your ar ofendid with me for not sending you worde of your sones amendment, from agreter Siknes then I thanke god ther was cause, it shuld be reportid so, ~~for~~ indede when your ~~lordship~~ mane wase here he was not very well, as I wrote to your lordship with sume payne in his hede and I thinke a littell fitt he had with all so as I was desirus to have hime send for his fesision, ~~but~~ ᵞᵉᵗ befor he came ~~he~~ ᵐʸ ~~was~~ lord was so well as he had but littell nede of his helpe, ᵃⁿᵈ since that time [?] hath bin so ~~well~~ as I never say hime beter ~~in this~~ since I was aquaynted with hime, and I thinke that sore Siknes that is spoken of was when he was as well as he is now. truly my lord if ther had bine any such caus you shuld have hard of it by me tho I know it would have bine ~~ve~~ most unwellcome, and Nues that I ʷᵒᵘˡᵈ very unwillingly writ to your lordship, yet much rather then ~~if~~ you shuld here of it after this maner. I trust your anger will be at anend when you here how littell I ame in faute, yet gretly I most confes if your sone had bine sike in dede and I not send my lord my father word of his amendment, thus wanting time to say any more I end being not alitell glad to here your lordship is well Becehing god I may never here the contrary. Cribled in hast this fryday morning.

   Your lordships most faythfull
   loving Daughter.
   M. Pembroke

II. Mary Sidney Herbert, Countess of Pembroke, to Barbara Gamage, Lady Sidney

Dated from 'Willton this. 9. of September 1591'. The year is crossed out and '1590' written in. Inscribed 'To my beloved Sister the Lady Sidney these'. Holograph. Bound in BL Additional MS 15232.

Sister.

how yow ar guided of a Midwife I know not butt I hope well and dowt not. for a Nurce I will asuer yow for that time ^till^ it pleased God to free her from that Charge I found so good Cawse to lyke of her in evry respect as I doo not thinke yow coold have bin better furnished any way: yow shall find her most queit and most carefull, of so young a woman so littell experienced more then woold be thought and as much as ^yow^ woold wisshe and shall be nesesary, lett her be much mad of as I know she shall and as I am suer she will deserve if god send her wel and safe to yow undertaking so unusiall a travaile. and thus have yow the fortune to succeed me still. and my Nurses onely to fitt yow. God send yow a Goodly boy and I asuer my selfe she will doo her part to yowr content if the sea deliver her no worse to yow then from home she departeth. the same god send yow a blessed and a happy time I wisshe it from my hart with my blessing to my pretey Daughter my god Barbara fare well as my selfe.

Willton this .9. of September ~1591~ 1590

> Yowr most loveing
> Sister
> M. Pembroke

III. Mary Sidney Herbert, Countess of Pembroke, to Sir Edward Wotton

Undated, probably 1594. Addressed 'To my good Cosen and worthy frend Sir Edward Wotton'. Endorsed '*Copie d'une lettre de la Comtesse de Pembrooke a Sir Edouard Wootton*'. In different ink, '1594'. Scribal copy. Bacon Papers. Lambeth Palace MS 650/346.

Cossen Wotton the first message this paper shall deliver is my Best salutacion and ever welwishinge to your self from that wonted good affeccion still continued doe acknowledge yow worthy of the same regarde wherein yow are asseured to rest for suche hath bin your merit not onlie towards my self but in memory that love to him

which held yow a deere and spetial frende of his (who was to me as
yow knowe) I must and doe and ever will doe yow this right which
doome the next is that these maie redeeme a certain Idle passion
which loonge since I left in your hands onlie beinge desyrous to review
what the Image could be of those sadd tymes, I very well know
unworthy of the humour that then possest me and suche as I knowe
no reason ~~whie~~ yow should yeld me any account of, Yet yf your care
of these follies of suche a toy have chanced to keepe that which my
self have lost, my earnest desire is that I maie againe see it, that by
this bearer my honest Servant Ramsey safely seeled I maie receive
it, asseuringe yow, I will when yow will store yow with other things
better worth your keepinge, only satisfie me in this and I will make
good my worde at any tyme more I will not trouble yow with at this
present, I rest now and ever

Your frend and lovinge Cosen
M. Pembrooke

IV. Mary Sidney Herbert, Countess of Pembroke, to Julius Caesar

1 June 1596 from Wilton. Inscribed 'To my good frend Mr. Doctor Caesar'.
Endorsed '1 Junii 1596. The Countess of Pembroke. on the behalfe of a poor
servant in the Court of Requests'. Scribal hand with holograph signature. 'Sister of Sir Philip Sidney' has been added in pencil under her signature in a
later hand. Caesar Papers. BL Additional MS 12506, f. 235; inscription f.
236^{v}.

Good Mr. Caesar, understanding by this bringer my poore servant
how greatly she hath bene in hir just cause by your favorable regard
relieved and furthered, I would not omitt by hir to make you know,
that my self therin am much beholden unto you, and do with all
thankfulnesse acknowledg your curtesie. Which if it shall please you
to continue to the ending of this long and troublesome sute support-
ing (as you have done) right against oppression you shall do in respect
of the poore Complainants a charitable dede, and binde me for them
to be doublie thankfull. And so I heartily bidd you farewell. At Wilton
the first of June 1596.

Your loving frend
M. Pembroke

V. Mary Sidney Herbert, writing on behalf of Henry Herbert, Earl of Pembroke, to Robert Devereux, Earl of Essex

Undated, probably 1596. Holograph manuscript in the Robert H. Taylor Collection, Princeton University Library. Mary Sidney Herbert transcribed the letter and signed it in her usual small script under the closing; her husband then signed to the left of her name in a larger script. Trusting the discretion of 'this wise post', he did not follow his usual practice of filling the blank space on the paper with hatch marks to prevent unauthorized additions.

My Lords ernest desire to understand of yowr Lordships safe arivale at Plimoth, as allso yowr happy dispach thence, hath made retorne of this wise post to feche a better satisfaction, and by these few, for want of a secretary, to Lett yow know his thankfullnes conceved of yowr honorable and so kind passage by him, of which coold he by fitter means make better testemony, yowr Lordship, he saith, shoold therof be as fully assured as hee wishes his praiers may be effectuall for yowr most fortunate and blessed succes. my selfe beeing willing to repete the arrant. Lest the messengers naturall inclynation shoold cawse him forget it, haveing trobled yow thus may well sort my praiers with the best that ar for yow.

Yowr Lordships frend that
wishes yow all honor and safty
Pembroke and M. Pembroke

VI. Mary Sidney Herbert, Countess of Pembroke, to William Cecil, Lord Burghley

16 August 1597. Inscribed 'To the Right honorable my very good Lord the Lord Threasorer—these'. Endorsed '16 August 1597 the Countess of Pembrook by Messynger'. Holograph manuscript of the PRO SP 12/264/85.

My good Lord what retorne to make for so many Noble favors and kindnes both to my sonne and my selfe I must needs bee to seeke: but I assuer yowr Lordship what defect so ever may bee in my words is supplid in my hart, and my thankfullnes is to be conceved farr other then I can any way expres. yowr Lordships fine token is to mee of Infinight esteeme, and no less in regard of the sender then the vertu in it selfe It is indeed a cordiall and presious present. not unlyke to proove a spesiall remedy of a sadd spleene, for of lyke effect do I allredy find what so ever ^{is} of lykely succes proseeding from the cawse whence this proseeded: wherin I now may boldly promis to my selfe that hopefull comfort which but thence, I protest, I coold expect, so much to Joy in as I do. So far foorth I find my sonns best lykeing affection to and resolution to answere my desire heerein as if the late interview have mutually wrought it is suffisient: suer I am, ther needes no more to yowr assurance and satisfaction hence; wishing the same to yowr Lordship there, accompaned with as many comforts and best bleasings of health and happenes as this earth may yeeld yow. God have yow in his safe keeping acording to my hartest praiers. I rest

Yowr Lordships affectionally
assured
M. Pembroke

VII. Mary Sidney Herbert, Countess of Pembroke, to Sir Robert Cecil

August 1597. Addressed 'To my very honorable good frend Sir Robert Cecyll. these'. Endorsed 'August 1597. The Countesse of Pembrooke to my Master'. Holograph. Sealed twice with the Sidney pheon. Manuscript of the Marquess of Salisbury. Cecil Papers 55/6.

Sir   to bee silent now finding so Just Cawse to bee thankfull were a wrong to yow and an Injury to my selfe whos disposision hath ever held yow in very worthy regard and yowr owne merrit doth chaling much more then my best acknowlidgment can acquit. howbeit lett my desire and endevor supply the rest, not dowting heereafter of fitter meanes to manefest the same. Yowr great kindnes to my sonn and frendly remembrance of my selfe, no less kindly imbrased, have-ing given life to this dead paper yow may please to except as a present testemony as well of my profession as unfained wellwisshing the mynd wherof may it take effect acording to the porpos most affected (and not the least in yowr owne respect) will better approve it selfe if god so please. In the meane while and ever I wishe yow all honor and happenes, resting

Yowr frend ever and
most assured
M. Pembroke

[In the left margin, parallel to her signature, is a postscript:]

If it please yow to grace my humblest thankfullnes and Joy for the gratious mention ~~I~~ receved from her Majesty, ~~in~~ takeing knowlidg therof
in what manes may seeme fittest to yowr owne wisdome yow shall add
much to the bond allredy very great.

VIII. Mary Sidney Herbert, Countess of Pembroke, to Sir Robert Cecil

29 September 1597 from Wilton. Endorsed '29 September 97 Countesse of
Pembroke to my Master To my very honorable good frend Sir Robert Cecyll.
these'. Holograph. Sealed with Sidney pheon. Manuscript of the Marquess
of Salisbury. Cecil Papers 55/ 81. *c*.4 cm. of blank space after 'so reported',
indicated here by the paragraph.

Sir   I understand report hath bin made unto yow of sum speech
that shoold pass my Lord (not in the best part to be taken) tuching
Cramborne. My desire is yow shoold be trewly satisfied therin, and
that in regard of truth and the respect I beare yow, for otherwise I
woold be silent. I protest unto yow the report was most untrue; And
uppon myne owne knowlidg, word, and honor, do assuer yow ther
was not any word spoken at any time to which had yowr selfe bin present yow coold have taken any exception. If this may suffise yow shall
right both my Lord and yowr selfe in Conceving rightly; if not, if yow
please to make knowne the Aughter (which exceedingly I desire) it
will more manefestly appeere the wrong yow have both receved, for
he must give him selfe the lye that so reported.

I do acknowlidg what is of my part dwe for yowr kindnes to this
part of me; I hope he will deserve it, and I know my selfe will be
ever thankfull. So do I rest

> Yowr frend as wellwisshing
> as any
> M. Pembroke

Wilton this
29th September 97

IX. Mary Sidney Herbert, Countess of Pembroke, to Queen Elizabeth

Dated 1601, using the new style. Addressed 'To the Queenes most Excellent
Majesty'. Endorsed '1601, Countesse of Pembroke to her Majesty'. Holo-

graph. Sealed twice with the Sidney pheon. Manuscript of the Marquess of Salisbury. Cecil Papers 90/147. The countess leaves *c.*4 cm. of space between the salutation and the body of the letter, and *c.*4 cm. of space in the closing between 'most bound' and 'the humblest of yowr Creturs'. The signature is placed in the right-hand bottom corner, a position signifying extreme humility. There are no deletions or ink blots in this carefully written letter, unlike most of her holograph correspondence.

Most sacred Soveraigne

Pardon I humbly beceech yow this first boldnes of yowr humblest Creture, and lett it please that devine goodnes which can thus enlive and comfort my life to vouchsafe to know that not presumtion, O no, but the vehement working desire of a thankfull harte so to acknowlidg it selfe for so hygh and presious a favor receved hath guided my trembling hand to offer these worthless wordes to yowr exelent eies: wherin I woold, if any words coold, present a thankfullnes unexpresible; not onely for my selfe but for my sonn who of yowr Majestys ever Prinsly Grace yow ar pleased to take into yowr Care, to fasshen fitt to live in yowr sight, to add and supply whatsoever want or defect may be in him. for which both my lord and I doe umble our selves at yowr hyghnes feete. And for myne owne part rem^{em}bring (what is of deerest memory) how in my youngest times my selfe was grased by the same heavenly grace, the same sunn which evermore hath powre to perfit the greatest imperfection by the rarest exemple of all perfection Give me leve, humbly I beceech yowr Majesty, to unfold my Comfort, hetherto with held in the prison of my hart, and now even with teares of Joy thus to powre foorth my joyfullnes finding that unspeakable goodnes so begun in me thus continued in myne. What shoold I say or what can wordes say for me But that I, who, by a more particuler bond, was borne, and bred, more, yowr Majesty then any other Creture and do, I protest, desire to live but to serve and observe yow, do know that he partisepating of the same sprite must lykewise make that his life, his end, his sole care and desire. to which endevour I do as gladly leve him and give him as ever I was made mother of him; And acordingly am to take Comfort in him as he shall be blessed in yowr gratious sight and frame him selfe wholy to please and serve yowr most Exelent Majesty to whom all blessednes belongeth; and blessed indeed ar they that may behold yow. My pen hath now hitt uppon my parte of torment, I that doo not, and yet still doo behold yow with the humblest eies of my mynds love, and admiration. I againe, and againe in all reverent humblenes begg pardon for this fearefull boldnes, do end with my never ending praiers. Long Long may that purest light live, and shine to his ever living praise and glory who hath made yowr Majesty this worlds wonder and Inglands Bliss.

   Yowr hyghnes
             most bound

             the humblest of yowr Creturs
             M. Pembroke

X. Mary Sidney Herbert, Dowager Countess of Pembroke, to Sir Robert Cecil

3 August 1602 from Cardiff Castle. Addressed 'To the right honorable Sir Robert Cecyll. these'. Holograph. Sealed twice with Sidney pheon. Manuscript of the Marquess of Salisbury. Cecil Papers 94/106.

Sir
Not that I can make any retorne unto yow worthey of yow; but that this blanke may wittnes what I woold had I powre to expres more then words can. A mynd more then thankefull, and a thankefullnes answereable to that mynd which thus in paper forme (since otherwise it can not present the willing desire to pay the debtt it owes) doth onely apeere before yow. It may please yow to except of the dumbe shew till with that entrest dwe, better performance may folow of what belonges unto yow. This frendly favore; the honor, ~~to have~~ queit, and strengthe yow have given ᵐᵉ I well may say: ~~is~~ is of such a ~~vaile~~ ᵛᵃⁱˡᵉ in consideration of the place and condission of this people as ~~that~~ I had no reason to expect nor to hope after: so hath it coucht them all; yowr honorable address heerein, it is wonder to see the change. It might seeme strange to me to have to contest with such, in such a kind before yow. But more strange to have the matter so aprehended, so extraordnarely righted onely by yow. finding by Jhon Udales relation, indeed admiration, how in this too unworthey ocation (I protest I am owt of countnance to thinke yow shoold be once moovd in, much more knowing how farr encumbred withall) my selfe nevertheless so exceedingly grased as that the want of thos frends of myne long since lost hath bin with full effectuall care and most praise worthey merrit in your selfe to the uttermost supplied. For which, and all, it is all I can endevor to deserve, what undeservedly in so great measure received from yow: And so must yowr

owne worthey disposission, thus Nobly expresed to me ward, remaine unanswerd, unsatisfied But in it selfe; which as yowr selfe doth make yow knowne and honord acordingly. Now for this sedisious beggerly wreche whom it plead yow to bring downe under my mercy and now seemes most penetent, I must confess it were no conquest his utter ͧ ruein: and yet thinke it not fitt to take his present submission to retorne him to be disposed of acording to yowr will, if please yow in regard of his missiry to be released of his imprisonment. The other his Barbarus demeanur hath bin so odious and therein so obstenate as this hand may in no reason consent to become any meane for his release till by a more thorow feeling of his fowle offence others lykewise will be better tought by his smart. if so it may be agreable to yowr owne best Judgment to which I very willingly and most most thankfully doo submitt both my selfe and them. And wishing unto yow Eternall happenes Sease yowr further troble.

> By her whom yow have bownd ever
> more to acknowlidg the bond
> M. Pembroke

Cardiff castell this
.3. of August 1602

XI. Mary Sidney Herbert, Dowager Countess of Pembroke, to Sir Julius Caesar

4 July 1603 from Windsor. Inscribed 'To my honorable good frend Sir Julius Cesar knight. geve these'. The letter was endorsed on receipt '4. July. 1603. The Countess of Pembroke touching Mathewes examination'. Scribal hand with holograph signature. Sealed with Sidney pheon. Caesar Papers. BL Additional MS 12503, f. 150; inscription f. 153ᵛ.

Sir to make good unto his majestie, the reasons and truth, that I have apprehended, and justlie accepted against mathew. I have to their great charge, as standinge ingadged uppon myne honor, unto his highnes, mathew to bee the very author, of soe foule an indignitie offred. as also to make good to the whole worlde, I woulde not possesse his princely eares with any untruth. I have I say to their great trouble and charge, brought upp those soe sufficient, and honest men, and of good reputacion. as will directlie upon their oathes depose the truth. I have tendred them, to the Lord Wotton. whose answere is. the matter is past their handes. I will not say a strange answere unto mee. but soe farr from my expectacion, as the miracle hath brought, a strange Intelligence to mee. Soe as nowe I ame left onlie unto you. that you will for my sake, and at my earnest request, for a thorowe satissfaction of his highnes, to take these men sworne. and that by your honorable meanes, at least it may remayne upon record. Untill aptlie you may possesse, his majestie, with the truth. Soe as the sooner, you shall doe it, the sooner you shall make mee, infinitelie beholdinge unto you. as an argument of the true feeling you hold of myne honor heere in. whereof I ame but to full of. And soe restinge

> Your ever thankfull and most
> assuered frend
> M. Pembroke

> Winsor this fowerth of July 1603

XII. Mary Sidney Herbert, Dowager Countess of Pembroke, to Sir Julius Caesar

8 July 1603 from Burham. Addressed 'To my honorable good frend Sir Julius Cesar knight. master of his highnes Requestes geve these'. Endorsed on receipt '8. July. 1603. The Countess of Pembroke touching Mathewes examination'. Scribal hand with holograph signature and postscript. Sealed with Sidney pheon. Caesar Papers. BL Additional MS 12503, f. 151; inscription f. 152^v.

Sir I thanke you, for your great paynes and kindnes, in this troublesome busines of myne. the which I assure you, I will not nor cannott forgett. and nowe I ame further to pray you. to acquaint his highnes, that you find, I did nothinge maliciously against mathew which I hope is proved before you. and of the effect of that prooff, which is against him, I pray you enforme his majestie or otherwise I shall not bee righted. according to the truth and my expectacion. Thus ever restinge most thankfull unto you, I bidd you hartelie farewell.

Burnam this viiith
of July 1603

My trust is onely in yow now lett me Crave yowr thorow frendly proceeding tuching this fowle abuce that his Majesty may justly Conceve the unworthenes of that Bace Mathew so as he may not receve any Grace here, nor hold the place of a Justice in the contrey haveing so aparently transgresd therein. it is the Sister of Sir Philip Sidney who yow ar to right and who will worthely deserve the same.

Yowr affectionat

frend

M. Pembroke

XIII. Mary Sidney Herbert, Dowager Countess of Pembroke, to Sir Julius Caesar

14 July 1603. Inscribed 'To my honourable frend Sir Julious Ceasor Knight of his Majesties requests'. Endorsed on receipt '14°. July. 1603. The Countess of Pembrok to acquaint the King with the state of Mathewes cause'. Holograph. Seal missing. Caesar Papers. BL Additional MS 12503, ff. 39; inscription 40v. No salutation.

This day had that most injurious bace Comepanion prevailed had not strangers to me prevented my dishonor therein. My hope, nay my Confidence was that yow woold have fownd time to have with his Majesty to have putt this matter owt of further question by fully enforming him of the trwth of my Cawse and this phelows aprooved viloney towards me But I perceve though yow ar willing yow can gett no oportunety which is no small cross unto me. Well then must I worke otherwise what I may and to that end do post away this berear praying yow to deliver him the origenall report examanation which is under yowr hand and which is still in yowr owne hands yow haveing sent me onely the coppy that I may gett it presented to his Majesty thereby to give his hyghnes ocation to Call yow unto it Not dowting then of yowr frendly proceeding acording to yowr promis and my beleefe in yow which now is come to the tuch: faile me not I beceech yow it consernes me neerely to urge thus to be righted by yow: it is needless to tell yow againe and againe I shalbe more then thankefull. in hast I rest

Yowr frend

M. Pembroke

XIV. Mary Sidney Herbert, Dowager Countess of Pembroke, to Sir Julius Caesar

6 September 1603 from Greenwich. Addressed 'To my honourable frend Sir Julius Cesar knight his highnes Master of Requests at Micham geve these'.

Endorsed on receipt '6. Sept. 1603. The Countess of Pembroke touching the sending to her of the examination concerninge Master Mathewes'. Scribal hand with holograph signature. Caesar Papers. BL Additional MS 12503, f. 42; inscription f. 45^v.

Sir, I ame, to praye your advise, and Counsell, that you will advertize mee. whether I may not deprive one that holdeth a Benefice of mee. that hath two wyves living. And whate is my best course, for the depriving of him, being soe lewd a liver as I ame enformed hee is. for willinglie I woulde not bestowe it soe baselie. upon any of soe unhonest behaviour. Also I ame further to desyre you, to send mee, the Examinacion which you tooke, at Winsor, touching the barbarous abuse, that was donne upon my Steward, by the procurement of Edmond Mathewe. which Examinacions you were determined to deliver to the Lord President of the Marches of Wales. Good Sir, send them mee, by this bearer. for that I have occasion to have further use for the same. So Resting ever thankfull unto You, for all your former kindnesses, I bidd you farewell.

Your very assuered frend

M. Pembroke

Greenwich vi^{to}
Septembris 1603

XV. Mary Sidney Herbert, Dowager Countess of Pembroke, to Gilbert Talbot and Mary Cavendish, Earl and Countess of Shrewsbury

29 September 1604 from the Savoy. Addressed 'To the Right honorable my good Lord brother the Earle of Shrewsbury'. Endorsed 'Sept. 1604 Countess dowager Pembroke'. Holograph manuscript. Sealed with Sidney pheon. Talbot Papers M259, reclassified as Lambeth Palace Library MS 3202/259. Two ink blots, several additions above the line, one totally unsuccessful attempt to erase and replace a word, water stained on the left margin. Her signature ends with a flourish similar to slashed S, or S fermé, that she later repeated around her signature.

Noble Lord:, and Lady
Such a testemony of yowr kind favors and love to me how needless so ever ~~thu~~ tuching yowr dawghter and myne, whose fortune yow well may rest Confident in, as which will never, nor her selfe in any sort have Cawse to make any use of me, or those poore helpes that is in

me to add there unto: onely my Care and wellwisshing must ever be a part of me and never to be wanted, as that which I do acknowlidg dwe to the very worthey respect I have found in her honorable parents who hath justly hetherunto perchasd a greater intrest in me, then it may be, I shall have means to make shew of, but such it is in my unfained regard. And so woold appeere if to speake plainely, as I love to do (withowt disguise) and at that ᶯᵒʷ at first, as last, and ever ᴵ ˢᵃʸ if bace instrments (with he whom I am ᶦᶯ no sort to partisopate) stood not in the ᵐʸ way such a one monster as hath devided myne owne from me (ʰᵉ that was ʰᵉˡᵈ the deerest part of me). Such a one as beeing best knowne to me must if I live be made knowne by me, and recieve his rights from me . in the meane time not [2–3 characters in left margin faded, illegible] spleene but ᵗʳʷᵉ scorne of so falce, so curupt and ˢᵒ vile a Creture lett these words from yowr sister and frend, both in affection, remaine with yow: which time will otherwise conferme, and make even the best mynds know theire ᵒʷᶯᵉ errors by reposing trust there. And I will wisshe the best both to yow and yowrs acording to that better knowlidg which may heereafter better express me unto yow. So resting

Yowrs very affec
tionately,
Pembroke

in hast from the
Savoy this Sunday 29th
of September. 1604.

XVI. Mary Sidney Herbert, Dowager Countess of Pembroke, to Robert Cecil, Earl of Salisbury

27 July 1607 from Ditchley. Addressed 'To the Right honourable My Lord the Earle of Sallsbury. these'. Endorsed on receipt, '27. July[?] 1607 Countesse of Pembroke to my Lord'. Holograph. Sealed twice with the countess's own device, two intersecting pheons crossed with an H to form the initials MH. Manuscript of the Marquess of Salisbury. Cecil Papers 122, f. 43.

My Lord.

I was once so rude as to moove your Lordshipe for the wardshipe of Sir Jhon Gennings sunn who now as I am enformed is very lyke to bee in your guift if allredy hee bee not, I was then told you were pleased to favore mee so much as that no other shoold have the grawnt thereof;

and so, that my selfe might hope, if the father died, I was lyke enough to receve so great an inlargment of my bond unto yow. I doo now, as I did then, blush, to putt your Lordshipe in mynd that such a thinge there was: and so doo leve my selfe and the matter to your ever Noble and favorable Judgment. Wisshing yow everlasting honore and all happenes to whom I rest

Acording to my long
unfained profession
Pembroke

Ditchlye this 27ᵀᴴ of July.1607.

Printed Letters Attributed to Mary Sidney Herbert, Dowager Countess of Pembroke

I. Mary Sidney Herbert, Dowager Countess of Pembroke, to Sir Tobie Matthew

John Donne the younger published three letters said to be from the Countess of Pembroke in his edition, *A Collection of Letters made by Sir Tobie Matthew, Knight* (1660), Wing M1319, 85–92. Presenting the letters as models of epistolary style, Donne omits the dates, the inscriptions, and the signatures. He titles the first letter, '*A Letter of the late Countess of* Pembrook, *to an humble Servant of hers by way of excuse, for being so unable to make him happy*'. In order to make the letters more readable, we have supplied paragraphing. Otherwise, the spelling and punctuation are as printed by Donne.

SIR,

THE first work I have to doe, is to repair an inexcusable errour; for, my former Letter to you, was no sooner out of my hands, than I was ashamed of my ill fortune, in that I might seem to have forgotten your Other-self. I say, that I might seem; for I have witnesses enow, that I committed not the sinne, indeed. And now that I have received those idle Papers, which you are pleased not to despise for my sake, you shall know, that it contents me nothing, that restitution is now made to me, by anie other hands, than wherein I left them. I doubt not, but you believe that I would have commanded them, to wait upon you e're this, if my desires and cares could have wrought as stronglie with others, as they are, and shall ever be of force enough in themselves, when you shall be anie way concerned. But how to spur on a rustie, dull, old, torn world, to anie expedition, though it be but for the dispatch of toies: how, I say, to find out a receipt for this, were worth the knowing; and if it were once known, it would be verie well worth the buying.

It vexes me at the heart, that yet I can send you no account at all, of the other businesse. But ease me if you can, by being satisfied as well as you can, till I may give you cause to be better satisfied: yet now, as that vexes me, so is there somewhat else, which pleases me; and it is, that the two so worthie, and so well-paired Friends, can find anie thing in me, which may be worthie, to entertain anie of their most idle hours. And since you will needs be so good, you shall here have your reward. For now I will tell you somewhat, which I know, will please you; and it is this: That whereas you thought and told me, that the *Spaw* would do no bodie good; this last season, I owe too much, bothe to it, and you, to let you goe away with that errour. For if you saw me now, you would say, it had created a new creature. Therefore, let all Pictures now hide themselves; for, believe me, I am not now, as I was then.

My Translation shall be verie shortlie with you; and you shall have better matter, for your thoughts to work upon, if this mind of mine could fit it selfe with power enough for your service; but nothing shall take me from being a friend as perfect to you, as you can have anie, in the whole world.

II. Mary Sidney Herbert, Dowager Countess of Pembroke, to Sir Tobie Matthew

Introduced by Donne as '*The late Countess of* Pembroke, *expresses great favour and goodnesse to the same humble Servant of hers*'.

SIR,

I Had written before my receit of your last; but, I protest, I was so far out of all taste and temper, till I had laid about me against some who were near me, that nothing could digest with me, nor passe at all out of these hands. So I staid the former dispatch.

And now I send you inclosed this Nothing, which yet is all that I have been able to get. Within a few daies, (and yet but a few daies) which indeed had yet been fewer, but that I have been sick, [(] as I am yet not well) I shall be there, where, I hope, I may prove much more able to say somewhat of this new world to you. In the mean time, you are, and shall for ever be, sure of nothing more, than that, if (as you tell me) you be to be undone, by the infinitenesse of good-will, and by such affection, as shall never do lesse, than aspire to your contentment, in the most effectuall manner, to which, by any possibility, I may arrive and reach, you are then likelie enough to be undone indeed.

And now let me turn my self to give you more thanks, than I have words to use, for the Present of those things which I received from you, for they are all most excellent. And though my desires prove not yet so fruitfull, as I would they did; nor my self so usefull to you, as I wish I were: yet let me still receive commands from you by your Letters, for they all are extreamly welcome to me. And if herein you harken to me, you have your will by doing that, which you are pleased to say, you so much desire; for so you shall do me more favour, than by all I am worth I can merit. I send you herewith such parts of what you asked, as I have yet been able to procure; and though I cannot discreetly pray you to esteem them, yet cast your eyes kindly upon them, because they have parted from me to none but your self. And as this Copie is the first, so also is it to be the last.

I am likely enough to see the *Spaw* again, though not with that grace which you give me to bestow upon it, by that too-favourable judgment of yours, which makes me such as I am, if that be any thing. But, in what I am to your very worthie self, see you lessen me not by your own conceit, since you cannot therewith exceed, what I am indeed in my desires and purposes, to esteem highlie, and deserve perfectlie well of you. Think the best you can, and yet I will defie you for over-thinking; for I am your perfect friend beyond that, which even you have faith to believe.

III. Mary Sidney Herbert, Dowager Countess of Pembroke, to Sir Tobie Matthew

The final letter printed by Donne is titled '*The same Noble Countesse of* Pembroke *showes the impatience of her Desires, to do favour to the same humble Servant*'.

SIR,

IT was but a Dream, and that as void of true effect, as the idlest of them all use to be. For otherwise, I should not speak thus loud, nor thus far off, nor make so long a reach to you still, by the Arms of my ill-written Lines. But I thought once, that you were both nearer hand, and comming to my little Lodge, to visit me; when, soon after, I found by one of yours, that you had frustrated that hope, and designed your self towards other ends. Which put me into such a brave choler, as some of them know, who are near me, and must have a part of that humour, whether they will or no. For I can do nothing, but in earnest, though that Earnest, God knows, proves commonly as true a Nothing, as if I were in Jeast. But, it is strange, nay, monstrous, that such undertakers as there are in the world, should be able to make nothing good, by the effects. For, to doubt of their will, were not onely to make them strangely wicked, but almost even to allow my self to be mad. For, they speak as well as I would wish; and, I am sure, that which they pretend to endeavour, must needs be advantagious to themselves. I will know more, shortly; and then you shall know, what I can learn concerning our businesse. And you shall never be the owner of any care, whereof I will not have a part, either by taking it, if you will give it; or else by stealing it, if you will needs be the first to offend Justice so far, as to hide it from me.

IV. Mary Sidney Herbert, Dowager Countess of Pembroke, to 'her son'

Reference to an excerpt of a letter to 'her son', probably Philip Herbert, undated (if this were authentic, probably November 1603), printed in *Extracts from the Letters and Journals of William Cory*, ed. Francis Warre Cornish (Oxford, 1897), 168. William Cory, Greek tutor to young Lord Herbert, wrote from Wilton House on 5 August 1865:

The house (Lady Herbert said) is full of interest . . . we have a letter, never printed, from Lady Pembroke to her son, telling him to bring James I from Salisbury to see *As You Like It* 'we have the man Shakespeare with us'. She wanted to cajole the king in Raleigh's behalf—he came.

Transmission and Authority of Texts

Original Works

'A Dialogue betweene two shepheards, Thenot, and Piers in praise of Astrea'

No manuscript of 'A Dialogue' exists. It was first printed in Francis Davison's 1602 *Poetical Rapsody* (entered in the *Stationers' Register* 28 May 1602), *STC* 6373, sigs. B5^r–6^r:

A | POETICAL RAPSODY | *Containing,* | *Diverse Sonnets, Odes, Elegies, Madrigalls,* | *and other Poesies, both in Rime, and* | *Measured Verse.* | Never yet published. | *The Bee and Spider by a diverse power,* | *Sucke Hony'* [*sic*] *and Poyson from the selfe same flower.* | [ornament] | *Printed at London by V. S. for John Baily,* | *and are to be solde at his Shoppe in Chancerie lane,* | *neere to the Office of the six Clarkes.* | 1602.

Title of 'A Dialogue': [woodcut border] | *A* DIALOGUE *betweene two shepheards,* Thenot, | *and* Piers, *in praise of* ASTREA, *made by the ex-* | *cellent Lady* Mary Countesse of Pembroke, | *at the Queenes Majesties being at her house at* | Anno 15 .

Collation: 12°, A^4(−1), B–K^{12}, L^8(−1).

Contents: (A1 lacking) A2^r title page; A2^v blank; A3^r '*To the Most Noble, Hono-* | rable and Worthy Lord, William | Earle of Pem- broke, Lord Herbert of | *Caerdiffe, Marmion, and Saint* | *Quintine.*'; A3^v–A4^v '*To the Reader*'; B1^r–B4^v text; B5^r–B6^r text of 'A DIALO- GUE *betweene two shepheards,* Thenot, | *and* Piers, *in praise of* ASTREA, *made by the ex-* | *cellent Lady* Mary Countesse of Pembroke, | *at the Queenes Majesties being at her house at* | Anno 15 .' B6^v–L7^v text (L8 lacking).

Copies collated: Bodleian, Folger, Pierpont Morgan

We have used 1602 as our copy-text. Subsequent editions of 1608 (*STC* 6374), 1611 (*STC* 6375), and 1621 (*STC* 6376, titled *Davisons Poems*) correct two misprints: 'there' for 'three' in 1602 (34) and 'shine' (1611, 1621) for 'thine' (44). Such obvious corrections, which we have adopted as emendations of 1602, could have been made independently. Other minor variants in the later editions give no evidence of authorial intervention, but imply lack of it: 'Heaven' for 'Heav'n' in 1602 (8), 'in clouds' for 'enclowdes' (46), and 'to onely' (1621) for 'do only' (58). The three later editions also omit everything in the title after 'ASTREA', but retain the attribution to the countess at the end of the poem.

As Rollins notes in his edition of *A Poetical Rapsody*, Davison attributes 'A Dialogue' to 'A. W.' in a list of titles in BL MS Harl. 280, f. 102. Rollins, however, concurs with a nineteenth-century 'American anthologist', W. J. Linton, who said that the initials are probably an abbreviation of 'Anonymous Writer'.[1] He himself suggests that Davison learned the identity of the author before the anthology was printed and argues at length that (along with other evidence) the relatively large quantity and varied sources of the poems attributed to 'A. W.' in the published text support the view that the initials cannot refer to a single writer.[2] The specificity of the title and the dedication of the volume to Mary Sidney Herbert's son, William Herbert, third Earl of Pembroke, corroborate the attribution to the countess. Rollins comments further on the title: 'The blank spaces in the title should evidently be filled with *Wilton* and 99 . . . The *DNB* comments that Queen Elizabeth honoured the countess "late in 1599 . . . with a visit at Wilton. No account of the royal visit is extant".'[3] (See p. 82.)

The following is a list of minor press variants in the Bodleian (*B*), British Library (*BL*), Folger (*F*), Harvard (*Hv*), and Huntington (*Ht*) copies of the editions indicated:

4 truth,] truth∧ 1602 *(F)*
   plainly] plainely *[broken* e, *resembling* c*]* 1602 *(F)*
16 holds] hol 1608 *(Ht, B)*; ho 1608 *(Hv)*
22 minde] min 1608 *(Ht, B)*; mi 1608 *(Hv)*
29 goe,] go: 1611 *(Hv)*; g∧ 1611 *(BL)*

Dedicatory Poems from the Tixall Manuscript of the *Psalmes*: 'Even now that Care' and 'To the Angell Spirit'

The two dedicatory poems are extant in one manuscript only, the *Psalmes* manuscript owned by Dr Bent E. Juel-Jensen, our copy-text. The date 1599 (altered from 1699) appears at the end of the verses to the queen. A variant of 'Angell Spirit', found among the papers

---

[1] *A Poetical Rapsody*, ed. Hyder Rollins (Cambridge, Mass.: Harvard UP, 1931), 48, 65–6.
[2] Ibid., 60–74.
[3] Ibid., 100.

of Samuel Daniel, was wrongly attributed to him and printed in *The Whole Workes of Samuel Daniel Esquire in Poetrie* (1623), *STC* 6238, sigs. [M7ᵛ–M8ᵛ] in the second set of single capital signatures. *The Whole Workes*, the source of our copy-text for the variant, is a composite volume, the first part of which is a reprint of the *Civil Wares* of 1609 (hence, the repeated alphabet of signatures). There are no press variants in the text of the poem in the British Library, Huntington, or Trinity College (Dublin) copies. The printed version is an incomplete copy of an earlier draft, omitting the final two lines and the attribution. In this early version, there is no reference in the text to the *angel* spirit of the title; that reference was expanded in the revised lines 57–63. That the printed version is an earlier draft is also suggested by the more precise and vivid diction in Tixall, changes consistent with the countess's usual pattern of revision (see p. 74).

Disputed Work

'The Dolefull Lay of Clorinda'

There is no extant manuscript. The poem was first printed as part of Spenser's 'Astrophel' in *Colin Clouts Come home againe* (1595; entered in the *Stationers' Register* Aug. 1587), *STC* 23077, sigs. G1ʳ–G2ᵛ:

COLIN CLOUTS | Come home againe. | *By Ed. Spencer.* | [device, McKerrow, 299] | LONDON | Printed for *William Ponsonbie.* | 1595.
Collation: 4°, A–K⁴.
Contents: A1ʳ title page; A1ᵛ blank; A2ʳ⁻ᵛ TO THE RIGHT | worthy and noble Knight | Sir *Walter Raleigh*...; A3ʳ–E2ᵛ COLIN CLOUTS | come home againe.; E3ʳ ASTROPHEL... *[title page]*; E3ᵛ blank; E4ʳ–K4ʳ text; K4ᵛ blank.

Colophon: LONDON | Printed by T.C. for William Ponsonbie. | 1595.

Copies collated: Bodleian, British Library (3), Folger (4), Glasgow University, Harvard, Huntington, John Rylands, New York Public Library (2), Pierpont Morgan, Trinity College (Cambridge)

We have chosen 1595 as our copy-text. The 'Lay' also appears in copies of *Colin Clout* bound with editions of *The Faerie Queene*. A few corrections and other minor changes were introduced in the version printed in the 1611 folio edition of *The Faerie Queene* (*STC* 23077.3), but Spenser scholars generally agree in viewing all the variants in the volume as non-authorial.[4] This seems to apply as well to the 'Lay'. Such corrections of the 1595 'Lay' as the following could have been made independently: 'wretched' for 'wetched' (17), 'Great' for 'Creat' (35), and the probably conjectural 'did see' for 'see' (also in 35, an otherwise defective line). That the text in the 1617 folio of *The Faerie Queene* (*STC* 23077.7) is a reprint of 1611 is indicated by extensive correspondence in accidentals and also by the sharing of the variants in 17 and 35. Examination of more than ten copies of 1611 and 1617 shows that the complex matter of the varying dates of the folio editions is irrelevant to the text of the 'Lay'. The poem is also unaffected by the existence of revised and unrevised states of the outer forme of sheet C in copies of the 1595 *Colin Clout*, as described by W. L. Renwick.[5]

Translations

Antonius

There is no manuscript copy of the translation, which first appeared bound with *A Discourse* in 1592 (entered in the *Stationers' Register* 3 May 1592), *STC* 18138, sigs. F1ʳ–O2ᵛ:

A | Discourse of Life | *and Death.* | Written in French by *Ph.* | *Mornay.* | Antonius, | *A Tragœdie written also in French* | by *Ro. Garnier.* | Both done in English by the | *Countesse of Pembroke.* | [device, McKerrow, 282, J. Windet] | AT LONDON, | Printed for *William Ponsonby.* | 1592.

Collation: 4°, A–O⁴. H3 signed H5; L2 signed L3. E4 lacking in all copies.

Contents: A1ʳ title page; A1ᵛ blank; A2ʳ–E3ʳ text of 'A Discourse . . . .'; F1ʳ⁻ᵛ'The Argument.'; F2ʳ–O2ᵛ text of 'Antonius.'; O3ʳ–O4ᵛ blank.

Copies collated: Bodleian (lacks *A Discourse*), British Library, Folger, Huntington

The translation itself is precisely dated 'At Ramsburie. 26. of November 1590', shortly after Garnier's death on 20 September 1590. A reprint, without *A Discourse*, appeared in 1595, *STC* 11623:

---

[4] See Francis R. Johnson, *A Critical Bibliography of the Works of Edmund Spenser Printed Before 1700* (Baltimore: Johns Hopkins UP, 1933), 47–8, and Sam Meyer, 'Spenser's *Colin Clout*: The Poem and the Book', *PBSA* 56 (1962), 406–7.

[5] *Daphnaida and Other Poems*, ed. W. L. Renwick (London: 1931), 233–4. See also Meyer, 'Spenser's *Colin Clout*', 404.

THE | TRAGEDIE OF | Antonie. | *Doone into English by the* | Countesse of | *Pembroke* | [device, McKerrow, 278, Peter Short] | Imprinted at London for *William* | *Ponsonby* 1595.
Collation: 8°, A–G⁸. A2 signed A3.
Contents: A1ʳ title page; A1ᵛ blank; A3ʳ [= A2ʳ]–A3ᵛ'The Argument.'; A3ᵛ *'The Actors.'*; A4ʳ– G7ʳ text; G7ᵛ colophon; G8 blank.
Colophon: Printed at London by P. S. | for William Ponsonby. 1595.
Copies collated: Bodleian, British Library (2), Dyce, Edinburgh University, Folger, Huntington, Newberry

We have adopted 1592 as our copy-text. That 1595 was based on 1592 is indicated not only by the running title '*ANTONIUS*' (rather than 'Antonie' as on the title page), but also by common errors such the following omissions: the first parenthesis in 136, the missing period in 424, and 'be' in 1103. The second printing does correct some errors that appear in 1592, but it is not a revision. It contains new errors (e.g. 'doth' for 'do', 376, in 1592; 'God' for 'Gods', 1419; 'Sounding' for 'Swounding', 1629; and the omission of 'then' in 54 and 'leaving' in 'The Argument', 21). There are also inconsistencies in indentation and capitalization, especially in the choruses. At a few points it is marred by additional misreadings or deliberate, non-authorial alterations. One simple instance is the substitution of 'Alexandria' for '*Alexandrie*' (1400), with the result that the line becomes hypermetrical. A more complex example is in 733, where 1595 has 'it' for 'she' in 1592. The 1592 text reads, 'Yet now at nede she aides hir not at all | With all these beauties, so hir sorowe stings' (733–4), a reflexive construction, as in Garnier: '*Toutesfois au besoin elle s'aide point | De toutes ces beautez, tant le malheur la poind*'.

The variant copy of 1595 at Edinburgh University confirms the view that the later printing was based on the earlier one. This copy contains the corrections made to the inner forme of sheet C (as in other copies, but not Bodleian) and those made to both formes of sheet E. (Huntington and Dyce have the corrections in the outer forme of E; Dyce shows a partially corrected inner forme.) The outer forme of sheet A in Edinburgh, however, is uncorrected and thus retains '*Pelusuim*' on A4ᵛ (22), the misspelling (without italics) in 1592 which was corrected in other copies of 1595 and which thus establishes a link between the first and second printings of the play. (For sheet C, at least, it is possible to reconstruct the probable printing sequence: Bodleian, Huntington, Dyce, Edinburgh.)

Evidence that the countess did not supervise the printing of 1595 is mainly internal. She was a careful reader and reviser of her own work, as the abundant marginal notes in Woodforde's transcription (MS *B*) of one of her working copies of the *Psalmes* clearly shows. (See 'Relationship of the Texts of the *Psalmes*'.) Thus it is unlikely that, were she involved in preparing the 1595 edition, she would have overlooked both the substantive and the accidental errors it contains. Nor would her direct involvement have been necessary for the correction of obvious errors such as *Komanes* for *Romanes* (87).

We have reversed the fonts in 1592, where the text is printed in italic type, with most proper nouns, other key words, and most speech prefixes printed in roman (1595 consistently reverses the roman and italic types used in 1592, but also prints the argument mainly in italics). The reason for the reduction of most initial upper-case letters in the choruses in 1595 is unclear (especially since the reduction begins only after the first few lines of the first chorus). The quotation marks that appear only at the beginnings of certain lines are intended (according to usual sixteenth-century practice) to mark *sententiae*. The printing of groups of lines in different type has the same purpose. (The countess does not preserve the unusually extensive use of quotation marks at the beginnings of lines in the first chorus in the French. The excess is probably a printer's error.)

The countess used the 1585 edition of *Marc Antoine* in making her translation. Garnier extensively reworked the text of the play for this authoritative edition, mainly by excising long passages, which do not appear in the countess's translation.[6] That 1585 was her source is also indicated by the lack of numerous divergences that occur in the later editions: 'against me obstinate' vs. '*contre moy se mutine*' (2), 'my dearest Queene' vs. '*ma Roine*' (38), 'Within tombes bosome' vs. '*Couvercle d'un tombeau*' (47), and so on, including longer passages such as lines 6–13.

There are minor press variants (listed below) in the extant copies of both editions. We print an emended text based primarily on the Huntington copy of 1592, even though it preserves a small number of typographical errors which were corrected before the printing of other extant copies. We have adopted the corrections as emendations of Huntington. The Folger copy contains the unique variant, 'doth groowe'

[6] See the textual notes on lines 1558–64, 1770–1 in Robert Garnier, *Two Tragedies: Hippolyte and Marc Antoine*, ed. Christine M. Hill and Mary G. Morrison (London: Athlone P, 1975).

for 'dooth growe' (probably the corrected reading), on sig. G1^r; on G2^v Folger omits the 'o' in horrible and prints the 'o' in 'Deiphobus' slightly below the line rather than slightly above it as in the other copies. Of special interest is an anomaly in the British Library copy of 1592, which preserves duplicate leaves containing the Argument (sig. F1^r), one of them revised, the other unrevised. The leaves of the whole volume are inlaid, and the evidence of the condition of wear and discoloration suggests that *Antonius* is from a different copy of the 1592 edition than *A Discourse*. The first leaf more closely resembles the condition of the preceding leaves of *A Discourse*; the second looks more like the following leaves of *Antonius*. This copy also contains uncorrected states of sigs. F4 and G4 (the right parenthesis in 136, sig. F4^r, which is in the British Library copy but missing in the others, must have been lost during correction). Sig. I1 was inverted when the inlaid leaves were rebound so that the recto and verso are now reversed.

Press Variants in Copies of *Antonius* (1592)

Line numbers for the Argument as in Huntington copy (Ht), collated with Bodleian (B), British Library (BL), and Folger (F) copies.

The Argument (*lacking in B*)

F		*There are two copies of this leaf in BL: BL^1 is the revised state as in Ht and B, BL^2 is the unrevised state.*
F	2	*libertie*] *libertin BL^2*
	5	*The original lineation in BL^2 is different from here on.*
	7	*journey*] *jonrney BL^2*
	10	Crassus] Cassius *BL^2*
	11	*in*] *into BL^2*
	14	*delightes*] *delights BL^2*
		pleasures] *pleasure BL^2*
	16	*enterprice,*] *enterprice$_\wedge$ BL^2*
	17	*returne*] *return BL^2*
	18	*regard*] *regarde BL^2*
	21	*mighty fleet,*] *mightye fleete$_\wedge$ BL^2*
		Actium] *Actin BL^2*
	23	*own*] *owne BL^2*
	26	*follow;*] *follow, BL^2*
F^v	4	*growe*] *grow BL^2*
	13	*window*] *windowe BL^2*
	14	*(her*] *(h r BL^2*

The Text of the Play:

[F4]	121	thee] *the* BL
	125	sword] *swoord* BL
	130	Cag'd] *Cag'de* BL
		selfe,] *selfe*$_\wedge$ BL
	136	$_\wedge$alas] *(alas* BL
	139	foe$_\wedge$] *foe,* BL
		common] *comon* BL
	141	heart-killing] *killing* BL
	145	more,] *more*$_\wedge$ BL
[F4v]	156	Sayles] *Soules* BL
	158	kepes] *keepes* BL
	166	raigne] *raine* BL
	177	Steads] *Steades* BL
G	180	dooth growe] *doth groowe* F
G2	265	horrible] *h rrible* F
	294	Deiphobus [o *slightly above line]*] *Deiphobus* [o *slightly below line]* F
[G4]	377	*Not indented in* BL.
[G4^v]	397	breake] *break* BL
	401	mischiefe] *mischeefe* BL
	407	hatcht] *hatchte* BL
	409	stronger,] *stronger*$_\wedge$ BL
I^{r-v}		*Reversed in the binding and inlaying process in* BL.
K^v	959	besteging] *besieging* B, BL, F
L3 [*i.e.* L2]	1226	bar e] *bare* B, BL, F
[L3]	1301	Snakes] *There is a light impression of a second final* s *in* Ht, BL, *and* F, *but not* B.
[N4^v]	1880	fall$_\wedge$] *fall,* B, BL
	1884	Needles$_\wedge$] *Needles,* B, BL

Press Variants in Copies of *Antonie* (1595)

Based on Huntington (Ht), collated with Bodleian (B), Dyce (D), Edinburgh University (E), Folger (F), Yale (Y), and Newberry, which agrees with Ht; lemmata from 1592.

Title:		Doone ... English] *Done ... englishe* E
The Argument		
A3^v [*i.e.* A2^v]	8–9	intermitted] *intermetted* E

The Text of the Play:

A4ᵛ	22	*Pelusium*] *Pelusuim E*
C2	566	them] them not *B, D*
C3ᵛ	617	ther] their *Ht, E, F, Y*; the *B, D*
	626	infamie] infemie *B, D*
[C4ᵛ]	632	state] estate *Ht, E, F, Y*; state *B, D*
[C5ᵛ]	699	heav'n] heav'n! *B, D*
[C6]	715	of] out of *B, D*
E2	1187	cunnig] cunning *E*
[E5ᵛ]	1328	murth'ing] murthr'ing *E*
[E7]	1378	foorth] fourth *B, Y*
[E7ᵛ]	1399	*Cleopatre*] *Cleopatra D, E*
[E8]	1422	clubbes the] clubs they *D, E*

A Discourse of Life and Death

The first edition was published with *Antonius* in 1592 (entered in the *Stationers' Register* 3 May 1592), *STC* 18138, sigs. A2ʳ–E3ʳ. See the bibliographical description in the section on *Antonius*, above.

Copies collated: Bodleian (lacks *Antonius*), British Library, Emmanuel College (Cambridge) (lacks *Antonius*), Folger, Huntington, Yale (lacks *Antonius*).

The translation is precisely dated, 'The 13. of May 1590. At Wilton' (sig. E3ʳ).

We have chosen Yale as our copy-text because it contains a unique correction on sig. C2ᵛ, where the comma following 'danger' has been deleted and the phrase, 'in themselves,' (including the comma), has been shifted slightly to the left. Even though the Yale copy lacks *Antonius* (which is still mentioned on the title page), it is bound in old limp vellum or parchment and has blank endpapers containing watermarks similar to (though not identical with) several pots of the same period recorded by Briquet and Heawood. The Yale binding suggests that the Bodleian and Emmanuel College copies, which now have modern bindings, may also have originally existed apart from *Antonius* and may not have been separated from it later. (The Emmanuel College copy is bound with a diverse collection of works by other authors dating from 1597 and 1599.)

There are two minor press variants on sig. D1^r in the Folger and Huntington copies of 1592: 'iucurable' for 'incurable' in the other copies collated, and 'rio tousnes' for 'riotousnes'.

Ponsonby published another edition in 1600, *STC* 18139:

A DISCOURSE | OF LIFE AND | DEATH. | Written in French by Phil. | Mornay. | Done in English by the *Coun-* | *tesse of Pem-* *broke*. | [device, McKerrow, 164, R. Field] | AT LONDON, | Printed for William Ponsonby. | 1600.
Collation: 8°. A–E^8, F^4, G^2.
Contents: A1^r title page; A1^v blank; A2^r–G2^r text; G2^v blank.
Copies collated: Bodleian, British Library (2), Folger, Newberry, Trinity College (Dublin), Yale.

Subsequent editions were issued by H. and M. Lownes in 1606 (*STC* 18140) and 1608 (*STC* 18141.5). The 1606 edition was reissued with a reset title page, dated 1607 (*STC* 18141), to be sold with *Six Excellent Treatises* (*STC* 18155), also dated 1607. The status of 1607 as a reissue is indicated by identical typographical features throughout 1606 and 1607, such as dropped letters, broken type or imperfectly printed characters, excessive or inadequate spacing between characters, as well as exact correspondence in spelling (including abbreviations) and punctuation. None of the editions after 1592 appears to include authorial changes. On the contrary, the text deteriorates steadily from 1600 on. For example, 1600 omits 'he' in 59 ('knowes he' 1592), repeats 'to' in 97, and reduces 'longer' to 'long' in 752. These divergences from 1592 are retained in 1606 and later. A more extensive variant in some of the copies of 1600 provides evidence that the subsequent editions derive from an uncorrected copy of that edition. The Bodleian, British Library, and Newberry copies all lack 'not one without, but brings them' in 941 (sig. G1^r), as do all copies of 1606–8. The omission has been corrected in Dublin, Folger, and Yale, and the rest of the text on sheet G has been reset.

Further evidence of the dependence of the subsequent printings on 1592 is Bornstein's observation that the spelling and inflections in 1600 (as well as 1606–8) are on the whole later, closer to what became the modern standard (and less like the forms in the holograph letters), and are thus probably not authorial.[7] Typical examples are 'account'

---

[7] *The Countess of Pembroke's Translation of Philippe de Mornay's Discourse of Life and Death*, ed. Diane Bornstein (Detroit: Michigan Consortium for Medieval and Early Modern Studies, 1983), 21.

(1600) for 'accompt' (1592), 'perfect' for 'perfit', 'coulour' for 'couler', 'together' for 'togither', 'give' for 'geve', and 'weares' for 'weareth'.

Among the numerous common variants in 1606, 1607, and 1608 are omissions, which include 'and maisters' in 97, 'by the' in 550 ('by the mountaines' 1592), and 'as' in 918. As Bornstein observes (p. 21), 1607 seems to be an exact reprint of 1606, as if the only change were in the date. The text of 1608 is also clearly based on 1606–7. Whole lines are often retained letter for letter, except that the number of lines on the page is increased in 1608 from 19 to 20 with the probably intended result that the volume ends with a complete signature (through F12) rather than part of the way into a new one (1606–7 end with G4; G5–6 are blank). 1608 does correct 'n knowing' on D11ᵛ in 1606–7 to 'in knowing'. The correct reading appears also in the Illinois copy of 1607, but not in the BL copy or any of the copies of 1606 that we have seen. The unusually wide space after the 'n' when it appears alone suggests that the 'i' may have been lost during printing and that the Illinois copy is thus not 'corrected', but a surviving sheet from early in the printing of 1606.

All copies of 1606 and the Edinburgh copy of 1608 are bound with *Six Excellent Treatises of Life and Death, Collected (and published in French) by Philip Mornay, Sieur du Plessis: And now (first) Translated into English* (1607). (The Bodleian copy of 1608 is bound separately.) This volume is a translation of Mornay's *Excellens Traitez et Discours de la Vie et de la Mort* (1581) and thus contains, in addition to Pembroke's *Discourse*, the following treatises by an anonymous translator: 'Plato his *Axiocus*, a Dialogue entreating of Death',[8] 'A Discourse of Tullius Cicero's, concerning Death', 'Collections out of Seneca's Works, touching Life and Death',[9] 'A Sermon of Mortality, made by S. Cyprian', 'A Treatise of Saint Ambrose, touching the benefit and happinesse of Death', and 'Certain places of Scripture, Prayers and Meditations, concerning Life and Death'. (The Folger copy of *Six Excellent Treatises* lacks *A Discourse*.) 'The French Authors Adver-

---

[8] Another translation of *Axiochus* (*STC* 19974.6), published in 1592, has sometimes been attributed to Edmund Spenser (even though the title page reads 'Edw. Spenser'. Anthony Munday has also been given credit for the work. See *The Spenser. Encyclopedia*, ed. A. C. Hamilton (Toronto and Buffalo: U of Toronto P, 1990) sv. 'Axiochus'; and *The Axiochus of Plato, Translated by Edmund Spenser*, ed. Frederick Morgan Padelford (Baltimore: Johns Hopkins UP, 1934).

[9] The excerpts from Seneca are also printed in the 1576 edition of *Discours* and Edward Aggas includes them in his translation of the same year, *The Defence of Death* (entered in the *Stationers' Register* 1 July 1577). Pembroke apparently did not translate them.

tisement to the Reader' notes that this is a second edition, to which the selections from Cyprian and Ambrose have been added (sig. A4^r). There are separate title pages for the countess's translation and the collection of other treatises. The running title throughout, however, is *A Discourse of Life and Death*. It is likely that *A Discourse* was not originally intended to be bound with the other works. This is suggested, not only by the separate title pages, but also by the note of 'The Translator to the Reader', which makes clear that *A Discourse* is not numbered among the six other treatises:

Here knowe, that the first Discourse, mentioned in the ['French Authors'] Advertisement ensuing, is none of these sixe here set down; but another precedent to these, and formerly translated by the Countesse of Pembroke. (sig. A2^v)

The author of this note sounds as if he did not know that *A Discourse* was bound with *Six Excellent Treatises*. His words also eliminate the possibility that the unidentified translator is the countess herself. Her work has apparently been attached to the *Treatises* by someone who thought that the volume would thereby become more attractive to prospective buyers. Hence, the 1607 title page for the cancelled title page of the first issue in 1606.

Comparison with the variants recorded in Mario Richter's edition shows that the countess used the *A* state of the French text that was published in Geneva in 1576 and in a subsequent edition in 1581 by Jean Durant.[10] Bornstein (p. 4) suggests that 1576 was likely the source because Mornay may well have had a presentation copy with him when he visited Philip Sidney in England in 1578. In any case, the countess's text agrees with *A* in nearly every instance against the other editions (of which those published later than 1590 can be disregarded because the translation is dated in that year). For instance, both the *B* state (Paris: 1580, 1583, 1584, 1585) and the *C* state (La Rochelle: 1581, 1595) can be eliminated because they omit passages which the English translation retains. The countess's version also shares with *A* some unique readings, such as the phrasing and punctuation of the passage, 'He will bewaile his life past, and among infinite toiles wish for the rest of the meanest man of the earth' ('... *sa vie passée, en infinis travaux souhaitera*...') which appears thus in the other French editions: '*il regrettera sa vie, passée en infinis*

---

[10] *Il 'Discours de la vie et de la mort' di Philippe du Plessis-Mornay*, ed. Mario Richter (Milan: Editrice Vita e Pensiero, 1964).

travaux, souhaitera le repos du moindre homme de la terre.' The translation and *A* also both have 'drawen dry' ('*tari*', not the more general
'*espouisé*', 'exhausted'), 'paile' ('*seau*', rather than '*vaisseau*'), and 'vnto
thee' ('*te*', omitted in *B*, *C*).

Bornstein suggests (p. 4) that a few anomalies may indicate that the
countess used a corrected copy or that she compared her copy with a
later edition. But it is also possible that Pembroke emended her text,
in writing, for instance, 'seeing the Barber comming to pull them
[teeth] out' rather than 'coming to pull it out' ('*la vient arracher*') as
in all the pre-1590 editions except for *C*, which reads, '*les vient arracher*'. Yet another possibility is that Pembroke used an untraced edition which may have been published in London by Thomas
Vautrollier in 1577. As Richter notes,[11] Jacques-Charles Brunet
cites such a volume,[12] but he himself seems to have taken the citation
from Jean G. T. Graesse,[13] where, however, no source or location is
given. Vautrollier would have been the likely London publisher of
such a volume because he was a Huguenot immigrant who published
another work of Mornay's, *Traicte. De l'eglise* (*STC* 18156a.5), in
1578. Neither title was entered in the *Stationers' Register*. Perhaps
Graesse simply confused the *Excellent discours* with the *Traicte* (a
copy of which he could have seen in the Bodleian).

A manuscript of *A Discourse* (Sloane MS 1032, ff. 1^r–28^r) was discovered in the British Library in the late 1980s independently by Hilton Kelliher, Curator of Manuscripts, and by J. K. Moore.[14] It
diverges extensively from the printed texts, but it has no independent
textual authority because it is an unreliable transcript of 1592. Such a
relationship is suggested from the first line, which imitates the
appearance of the opening of 1592 on the page (where the first few
lines are shortened to accommodate a large ornamental capital): 'IT
Seemes to mee–' (f. 1^r). That the source is the first edition is shown
also by Sloane's agreement with it in the places where there are omissions in the later editions. The transcription itself is often careless.
Corrections have sometimes had to be added over carets (at one

[11] Ibid., 9.
[12] Jacques-Charles Brunet, *Manuel du Libraire et de l'Amateur de Livres* (Paris: Didot,
1860–5), III. 1910–11.
[13] Jean G. T. Graesse, *Trésor de Livres Rares et Precieux* (Dresden: Rudolf Kuntze, 1862),
IV. 610.
[14] J. K. Moore, *Primary Materials Relating to Copy and Print in English Books of the Sixteenth and Seventeenth Centuries*, Occasional Publication 24 (Oxford Bibliographical Society:
Oxford, 1992), 15, 39, and pl. 7.

point even the word 'teeth' is supplied above the line after 'the'), and the spelling is occasionally erratic ('loasome' for 'lothsome', 'worewood' for 'wormewood', 'Arithetike' for 'Arithmetike', among other instances). None of the initially more plausible alterations can be considered authorial revisions (if indeed they are deliberate and not simply errors). Thus, 'it is' is substituted for 'is it' (719) to make an interrogative sentence declarative even though the question mark is retained. 'Armes' replaces 'wings' (791) and thus weakens the imagery of flight in the passage. In line 829, 'he' replaces 'they', but 'themselves' is allowed to remain in 830. Similarly non-authorial substitutions are 'ymortalie' for 'immediatly' (825–6), 'there heires' for 'their eares' (832), and 'appeareth' for 'appeaseth' (555).

Kelliher notes in his description in personal correspondence that, besides altering the text (in lighter ink), 'the same hand has occasionally added words between lines and underlined phrases and sentences' and that 'the attribution after "A discourse of" in the title is added in this hand'. He adds that 'this is a cast-off copy, the letter (= sig.) "B[?]" occurring on f. 12, with, apparently, page-numbers from 2 to 18 on ff. 13b–24b, and cast-off marks occurring at corresponding places in the text'. The volume was prepared for publication in the seventeenth century, as a note on f. 28v, the final leaf, indicates: 'Jan 28, 1623° | Let this booke be printed | ⟨consistin⟩ contayning 26 pages | in 8°: | [*signed*] Tho: Worall:' and below it 'xviii° Feb 1623 | George Cole'.

The attribution after the title on f. 1ʳ, 'By T. H. Gent:' (perhaps an unidentified member of the Herbert family), is apparently conjectural. Kelliher suggests that 'the edition never in the end appeared because the publisher found it had been done already, and by whom'.

The Triumph of Death

The translation from Petrarch survives in a single manuscript in the Library of the Inner Temple, Petyt MS 538.43.14, ff. 286ʳ–289ʳ, which is our copy-text:

The Triumph of death translated out of Italian by the | Countesse of Pembrooke. the first chapter.

'The first chapter' ends on f. 287ᵛ, followed by the subscription, 'Marie Sidney Coun: of Pem:'; this is followed by a rule and the heading, 'The Second Chapter of the Triumphe of death.'; another subscription is at the bottom of f. 289ʳ at the end of the translation,

'Marie Sydney Countesse of Pembrooke:'. This portion of the Petyt volume is a copy of verses that Sir John Harington sent to his cousin, Lucy Harington, Countess of Bedford, along with a letter (f. 303ᵛ) dated 29 December 1600. The letter mentions the enclosure only of three of the countess's Psalms: 'I have sent yow heere the devine, and trulie devine translation of three of Davids psalmes, donne by that Excellent Countesse, and in Poesie the mirrois [*sic*] of our Age'. But these 'Psalmes translated by the Countesse of Pembrooke', i.e. Psalms 51, 104, and 137 (ff. 284ʳ–286ʳ), are followed immediately by *The Triumph* in the same ink and hand. (The text of the Psalms is related, but not identical, to one of the British Library manuscripts, Additional MS 12047, MS *I*, that was owned by Harington.) The letter does note the inclusion of some of Harington's own work: 'I have presumed to fill-up the emptie paper with som shallowe meditations of myne owne', apparently a reference to the 'Certaine Epigram's...composed by Sir Jhon Harryngton' on ff. 289ᵛ–290ᵛ. A miscellany of other works, written in the same hand and on similar paper, completes this section of the manuscript: 'To the right Honorable Robert Earle of Essex' ('Thow that felt'st stoutly in youths greenest houres'), two excerpts from 'Virgil: Æneid', 'The yeare about. as it was acted and plaide at Oxeford...by Doctor Gwinne', 'A foolish song upon Tobacco...[by] I: F:', 'The speache of a Prince', 'The choise of valentines....[by] Thomas Nash', 'A Dialogue betweene Constancie and Inconstancie spoken before the Queenes Majestie at Woodstock', and 'Bastards Libell of Oxeford' (ff. 291ʳ–303ʳ). Harington's letter is transcribed on the verso of the last leaf.

The complex bibliographical history of the publication of Petrarch's *Trionfi* in the sixteenth century makes identifying the countess's Italian textual source difficult.[15] Modern critical editions are not of much use for the purpose because they are based on manuscripts not later printings, which are sometimes quite different. Comparison of early printed editions, however, has led to some general conclusions. It is clear, first of all, that Pembroke used a text deriving from the edition prepared by Pietro Bembo and published by Aldus in 1501, *Le Cose Volgari di Messer Francesco Petrarcha* (sigs. [u viiʳ–u xvʳ]), and in a second edition in 1514, which became the basis of

---

[15] See, for example, Mary Fowler's *Catalogue of the Petrarch Collection Bequeathed by Willard Fiske [to Cornell University Library]* (London: Oxford UP, 1916). There are many textual omissions and insertions that differ from edition to edition in the frequent reprintings of Vellutello.

numerous later editions issued by other printers. As far as the countess's translation is concerned, the most important feature of the Aldine text is Bembo's rejection of the disputed passage of 21 lines that began the *Trionfo della Morte* in earlier editions and was retained as late as 1581 in the reprint of the 1554 Basle edition of the complete works (the first containing the Italian texts): *Quanti, gia nel'eta matura* ... The Aldine text begins, *Questa leggiadra et gloriosa donna.*

That Pembroke's translation does not otherwise agree in every detail with the 102 sixteenth-century editions we have consulted is not surprising in view of what is known about her approach to her literary activity. As she did in other cases, she must have examined more than one edition, a procedure which allowed her to select from among variant readings (disputed by the commentators) and to identify and correct misprints which occur to varying degrees in all the texts. Recognition of her eclectic method makes it easier to choose a base text for comparison and to emend that text from other editions when there is clear warrant for doing so in the translation. Primarily for the sake of convenience, then, we have chosen an early text, that of the first Vellutello edition of 1525, not only because it agrees more frequently with Pembroke's text than others, but also because it is relatively free of printing errors. Variants are cited from the first Gesualdo edition of 1533.

The similarities between the early Vellutello and Gesualdo texts are greater than the substantive differences.[16] For instance, both have the one clear variant that distinguishes them from most of the other sixteenth-century texts and associates them most clearly with the English translation. When at 2. 136, Pembroke wrote, 'Hence sprang my zeale, which yett distempreth thee', she was following an edition which read, *Quinci'l mio zelo; ond' anchor ti distempre*, rather than one with the opposite statement which substitutes *gelo*—'coldness'—for *zelo*. The early Vellutello editions have *zelo*, and so do all those of Gesualdo, who in his commentary explicitly states a preference for it.[17] Another point of correspondence among Vellutello, Gesualdo,

---

[16] The Gesualdo text is comparatively more stable than Vellutello's, which was published in many later editions without the distinctive variants discussed below.

[17] In contrast to Daniello, who (in a 1541 edition, for instance) agrees with all modern and most sixteenth-century editors in saying that *gelo*, which *significa la castità de M. L.[aura]*, is supported by the earliest texts, a claim also made by Gesualdo for *zelo*, although he acknowledges that the variant has some support. Bembo has *zelo* in 1501, but *gelo* in the second edition of 1514, which, according to Fowler, was accepted as standard by most subsequent editors and printers.

and Pembroke occurs at 1. 113–14, where the Italian texts have *treccia* (not *testa* as in most other editions) in the description of Death's plucking a hair from among Laura's 'amber-tresses', as the English translation has it.

On the other hand, Gesualdo has the standard reading *à Phlegra* (*à Flegra* in some editions) for the place name in the mythological reference in 1. 33, whereas the early Vellutello text reads, *Alphegra*. Pembroke has 'at Phlegra'. Allowing for the possibility that the spelling in the Petyt manuscript may frequently be scribal, a less substantive divergence between Vellutello and Gesualdo further associates the translation with the former. At 1. 21, the English reads, 'topaces' ('topazes'), which is closer to Vellutello's *topaci* (rare in other editions) than Gesualdo's more common *topati*.

Pembroke may have been influenced by one other distinctive edition, Lodovico Castelvetro's *Le Rime del Petrarca* (*Triompho di Morte*, sigs. [kkk 4ᵛ]–mmm 3ʳ), which was censured because of its 'heretical' commentary and which thus appeared in only one contemporary printing in 1582.[18] The influence was more interpretive than textual, however. The traditional approach to the *Trionfi*, associated in the Renaissance with the late fifteenth-century commentator, Bernardo Lapini (called Illicino), was to treat the work as an allegory of the soul. Vellutello, like Gesualdo and others before 1582, echoes this view: *VOLSE il nostro moralissimo Poeta nella sua presente divinissima opera, vari stati dell'anima rationale esprimere, iquali in sei parti dividendo*...(sig. a 2ʳ). Castelvetro, on the contrary, speaks of the work in biographical and moral terms; he views it as a record of Petrarch's repentance for his natural inclination to love and pursue fame in this world: *Da due cose fu stimolato il P.[etrarca] principalmente, da disiderio amoroso, et da vaaghezza di fama* (sig. z 2ʳ). Such an interpretation is more appropriate to the approach taken by Pembroke, who seizes the rare opportunity in her age of allowing a woman to speak of grief and love, not as an allegorical abstraction, but in her own voice.

Young printed two versions of the text of *Triumph*, one as an appendix to her biography of the countess (209–18; lines 118–41 of the first part are lacking) and the other in *PMLA* (1912), 52–75 (along with a 1903 edition of the Italian). Waller's printing of the text appears in *Triumph*, 67–79.

---

[18] Fowler, *Catalogue*, 110.

Commentary

'A Dialogue betweene two shepheards, *Thenot* and *Piers*, in praise of *Astrea*'

In each stanza of 'Astrea' Thenot sets forth a proposition that is immediately undercut by Piers. Thenot's opening statement of his desire to praise Elizabeth and his invocation to the muse is countered by Piers's admonition to speak the simple truth, as in the opening sonnet of Sidney's *Astrophil and Stella*. Such rejection of literary diction is itself traditional; Sidney rejected Petrarchan conventions, Pembroke epideictic rhetoric (Mary C. Erler, 'Davies' *Astraea* and Other Contexts of the Countess of Pembroke's "A Dialogue"', *SEL* 30 (1990), 56). Thenot appears to grow more confused as each of his seemingly self-evident statements is challenged. He makes the traditional statements that her worth is known to all and the equal of anything on earth; Piers responds that the divine Astrea is beyond comparison in this mutable world, so that metaphors become lies. When Thenot offers the traditional praises of her wisdom and virtue, Piers objects. Merely saying that wisdom and virtue 'stay in her' (21) becomes lying that will undervalue or 'staine her' (24); without her, wisdom cannot see and virtue cannot act because those qualities 'emanate from the divine' (Beilin, *Redeeming Eve*, 140.) Offering another cliché, Thenot says that her face attracts good and banishes evil; Piers says that her existence, not merely her physical presence, accomplishes this end. (A primary duty of the monarch is to reward the good and punish the evil. Cf. Psalm 101). Appealing to self-interest, Thenot suggests what many Englishmen felt at the end of the century when the succession was uncertain, that Elizabeth is their 'chiefest joy' and 'chiefest guarde against annoy' (31–2); Piers once again questions Thenot's language, for the term 'chiefest' implies the existence of other joys and other protection, whereas 'To us none else but only shee' (35). Looking for metaphors that cannot be disputed, Thenot gives two of the most overworked comparisons, that Astrea is their Spring and their Sun; Piers undercuts those comparisons because neither Spring nor daylight will last, while Elizabeth will never fade. Thenot then tries a multi-faceted comparison to trees: the 'manly Palme', usually a reference to marriage, as on Argalus's shield in the *New Arcadia*; and the 'Maiden Bay' (50). Thereby he praises Elizabeth's two bodies, as the ruling Prince married to her people, and as a lovely Virgin. Piers once again stresses mutability; the natural world cannot yield a true parallel for the divine Astrea. Reduced to complete frustration, Thenot cries, '*Piers*, of friendship tell me why, | My meaning true, my words should ly'? (55–6).

Piers's response calls into question, not only the metaphors suggested by Thenot, but the whole genre of the encomium: 'Words from conceit do only rise . . . But silence, nought can praise her' (58–60).

The *aabccb* form is used in six of Sidney's Psalms. The pattern here precisely follows that of his Psalm 32 (May, *Courtier Poets*, 177).

4 *plainly*. Piers stresses the Protestant plain style.

10 *not no*. Double negative emphasizes that accurately naming the queen is impossible.

15 *Momus*. Greek god of ridicule, banished from heaven for censure of the gods. Personification of fault-finding.

16 *Compare may thinke*. Comparison is appropriate only between like things, but Elizabeth has no equal. A radical statement of the topos of outdoing.

24 *staine*, *v*. blemish, disgrace. 'Stay in her' in line 21 must be elided to match 'staine her' here (Erler, *SEL* 30 (1990), 47).

34 *there*. Emended. A judicious correction in 1611 for the obvious error 'three' in 1602.

40 Piers explains that Astrea's spring is not a season, but 'the eternal spring of the golden age' (Yates, *Astraea*, 67).

44 *shine*. Emended. That 'thine' in 1602 is an error is clear from the context, which is in the third person here. The emendation is taken from 1608.

50 *manly Palme, Maiden Bay*. Praise of the Queen's Two Bodies, as monarch and as virgin.

58–60 *conceit*, *n*. thought; understanding or apprehension (obs.) Words cannot express the thoughts of her worth; indeed, her honour surpasses even what may be apprehended by the mind. A radical statement of the inexpressibility topos.

60 *But silence*. A pun. The primary meaning is that nothing but silence can adequately praise her, but the words are also an implied imperative to Thenot: Silence!

'Even now that Care'

This dedicatory poem begins with the self-reflexive question, Is it appropriate to interrupt the queen's work by presenting poetry (1–8)? The answer is that the poetic effort is not toil for the queen, but relaxation appropriate to her moments of comparative leisure (9–18). Therefore the 'Senders' will present the poems; the plural authorship decorously introduces mourning for Sidney, the 'richer' of the two writers (19–26). Using a clothing metaphor, Pembroke then discusses the process of composition and presentation to the queen, who is the appropriate patron for all English verse (41–50), but particularly for the Psalms, because her situation parallels that of David (51–73). The singular achievements of Elizabeth's reign include the defeat of the Armada and the paradox of a woman's rule (73–88). In the concluding stanza, Pembroke describes herself as the handmaid of the queen, presenting the poem and praying that the queen may continue her triumphal reign, as Elizabeth continues to praise God and to be praised by men.

4–5 The muse offends and the line outgoes, or overreaches, because presenting a psalter will interrupt the queen's work.

5 A typical polyptoton, here emphasizing the queen's will, or desire, to read poetry, but questioning whether she can spare the time from her responsibilities as the leader of Europe.

13 *heav'nly powrs*. Emphasizes the divine appointment of Elizabeth as ruler, one who has been given the goodness and strength to carry the burden of government (14–15).

17–18 A compliment following up lines 15–16, which states that the queen is so strong that what would be 'toile' for others is 'Exercise' for her. So even though she has heavy burdens of office, given to her by God (13–14), the countess speculates that there must be times when she is under less pressure than usual (17–18). At such a time, she might be willing to receive the 'Rimes', described here as the 'Postes of Dutie and Goodwill' (19).

18 *most*. This may be a scribal error for 'must'. Alternatively, if the scribe was working from an autograph manuscript, the word 'most' may have been written since the countess spells 'must' as 'most' in Correspondence: Manuscript Letter I ('yet gretly I most confes'). The *OED* also cites 'most' as a variant of 'must' current in the sixteenth century.

19 *these*. These lines of poetry, as posts, or messengers, of duty and goodwill urge her to offer themselves as a partial repayment of the writers' debt to Elizabeth. Cf. 33–4, where the livery robe is presented to Elizabeth like the traditional New Year's gifts.

21 *once in two*. This may imply that Pembroke worked on the *Psalmes* from the beginning, since they once had two authors, but since Philip Sidney's death only one remains. Yet the metaphor of warp and woof in 27 implies a sequential composition.

22 Emended. See textual notes.

25 Emended. See textual notes.

25–34 The composition of the *Psalmes* is compared to the creation of a garment in this traditional metaphor. Cf. 'Angell Spirit', 8–10. The *Psalmes* were given their original shape (the warp) by Sidney; Pembroke completed the weaving to dress the Hebrew words of the Psalms in English. The Sidneian *Psalmes* become a 'liverie robe' as a gift for the queen in turn to bestow as she chooses.

32 An uncomplimentary reference to unspecified earlier English Psalters. Cf. 'Angell Spirit', Variant, 10–11. See also *Psalmes*: 'Literary Context'.

38 *will...will.* Typical polyptoton. We intend to do our best, though scanted (restricted) in our 'will', in the obsolete sense of delight or joy.

40 *unwalthy.* Perhaps a scribal error for 'unwealthy', making these lines a complaint about Elizabeth's treatment of the Sidney/Herbert family. That is, except for their lack of wealth, they are not unworthy to till the fields of the queen's favour. Cf. similar complaints in the correspondence of Sir Henry Sidney, Lady Mary Sidney, and the Earls of Pembroke.

44 *woold.* The scribe may have shifted the comma from before 'woold'. The humble Lawrells grown in her shadow would repine if made into garlands for someone other than the queen.

52 *Authors state.* The estate of the author, David, i.e. kingship.

54 Typical polyptoton and chiasmus used to express Elizabeth's equality with David as a divinely appointed monarch.

63 *holy garments.* Protestants were admonished to fit the Psalms to their own condition. Pembroke, again using the clothing metaphor of 25–34, compares this process to trying on garments. They can be worn by all, but they fit perfectly only Queen Elizabeth.

70 *foes of heav'n.* Primarily Catholic Spain. Cf. 77–8.

72 *secure to lose.* Secure against loss.

75 *two hemispheres.* The British Isles and Virginia.

77–8 *windes...rocks.* Defeat of the Spanish Armada.

80 *Eagles.* Symbol of royalty. With decorous humility, Pembroke declines to soar into the realms open only to monarchs. Cf. 90.

84 *herselfe unmov'd.* The list of paradoxes includes here a reference to the queen as the Unmoved Mover or *primum mobile* of Ptolemaic astronomy.

85 *vanitie, n.* Genitival. Vanity's exile.

92 Emended. See textual notes.

93 *living Peeres.* Elizabeth had already outlived most of the European monarchs who had been her contemporaries; the prayer is that she will outlive even the few who survive.

96 *Sing what God doth.* Probably a reference to the translation of Psalm 13 attributed to Queen Elizabeth and printed by John Bale with her youthful translation, *Margaret of Angoulême. A godly medatacyon of the christen sowle* (1548), STC 17320.

'To the Angell Spirit of ... Sir Phillip Sidney'

Like 'The Dolefull Lay', this dedicatory poem for the completed Sidneian *Psalmes* laments Sidney's death, praises him, and offers consolation. Once again Sidney's apotheosis is seen; the poet, protected from envy, sings in the angelic choir. 'Angell Spirit', however, eschews the traditional pastoral elegiac motifs and the conventional invocation of Sidney as Astrophil frequently employed in the *Astrophil* poems, including 'The Dolefull Lay'. Instead, the poem develops metaphors from clothing (6, 9–11), accounting (43–5), and architecture (64–77). Sidney is also praised by graceful allusions to his own poems. For example, 'this Audit of my woe' (44) echoes 'Reason's audite' (*Astrophil and Stella* 18); 'thoughts, whence so strange passions flowe' (45) echoes 'Like those sicke folkes, in whome strange humors flowe' (*Arcadia*, III. 41); and 'such losse hath this world ought | can equall it?' (75–6) echoes 'Hath this world ought so faire as *Stella* is?' (*Astrophil and Stella* 21). (May, *Courtier Poets*, 180, n. 19.)

Although the final version retains the same poetic form as the earlier variant (seven lines of iambic pentameter, rhymed *abbabba*), the revisions are significant enough to illustrate Pembroke's writing process. See p. 74.

6 A continuation of the clothing metaphor in 'Even now', 27–34, 63–4. Cf. 'tire' or attire in line 9.

8–9 See *Psalmes*: 'Literary Context'.

12 *cælestiall Quire*. Cf. 'The Dolefull Lay', 61–4. Angel reference added to earlier version here and in 59–61.

13 *tongues*. The learned tongues (Greek, Latin, and Hebrew). The sense here is that all scholars of Hebrew admire the Psalms as written by David. Her task is to clothe those Psalms in English. See *Psalmes*: 'Literary Context'.

18 *halfe maim'd peece*. The Sidneian *Psalmes* have been wounded, even as Sidney was.

22 Cf. 'Even now', 23, also using a parenthetic reference, repeating and expanding upon the verb, to mourn Sidney's death.

26 *zeale*. Protestant terminology frequently used to describe mourning for Philip Sidney, as in 'A pastorall Aeglogue upon the death of Sir Phillip Sidney Knight', *Astrophel*, sig. H4ᵛ, and 'An Epitaph upon the right Honourable Sir Phillip Sidney knight: Lord Governor of Flushing', *Astrophel*, sig. K2.

34 Emended. See textual notes.

35–6 Striking use of enjambment across stanzas. See also textual notes.

35 *debt*. Cf. debt to Elizabeth in 'Even now', 35–6.

41–2 *there, there*. Heaven.

43–9 Pembroke, like other writers, is inadequate to praise Sidney. To this inexpressibility topos, she adds the motif that her heart's grief has stricken her dumb.

43 Note accounting metaphor, also added to Psalm 51.

45 *passions*. Usually strong emotions, particularly grief, but probably here including a self-referential statement to the dedicatory poems themselves, in the obsolete sense of literary compositions marked by deep emotion, often synonymous with 'elegy'. See Matthew Roydon, 'An Elegie, or friends passion, for his *Astrophill*', printed in *Astrophel*. In Pembroke's letter to Sir Edward Wotton she refers to her earlier elegy as 'a certain Idle passion', analogous to the self-deprecation in this reference to her poems as 'strange passions'.

46–9 Her words, and those of other poets, are not adequate to praise Sidney. Inexpressibility topos. Cf. Ps. 92. 13 'what witt can find'.

48 *short, adj.* Inadequate.

50–70 Added to earlier version.

51 *my blood should partialize.* Demonstrate partiality to her kindred.

55 *owly blinde.* Blind like the proverbial owl. The best minds, open to wisdom, see the truth of Sidney's worth, which is 'seal'd' or acknowledged in heaven. Cf. 'blindely madde', 69.

63 *Envie.* Sidney's friends and relatives believed he was slain by envy at court, which prevented the queen from giving the necessary support to the military campaign in the Netherlands. Cf. 'The Dolefull Lay', 84, and recurring references in the other *Astrophel* elegies, as in 'A pastorall Aeglogue' (sig. H3) and 'An Elegie, or friends passion, for his *Astrophill*' (sig. I4ᵛ).

64–77 Expanded from earlier version.

64–8 Cf. Hugh Sanford's statement that the 1593 edition is 'the conclusion, not the perfection of *Arcadia*', for 'Sir Philip Sidneies writings' cannot 'be perfected without Sir Philip Sidney' (sig. A4).

70 *Beyonde compare.* Topos of outdoing.

above all praise. Inexpressibility topos.

78 *To which.* To Sidney's name.

78–84 Added to earlier version. Her sorrow is compared to a wound that bleeds and festers, like Sidney's gangrenous leg. Cf. Robert Sidney's similar usage in his Sonnet 26. (Sidney, Robert. *Poems*, 45–6, 227).

81–4 A self-reflexive characterization of the poem as an artless product of love. Cf. *Astrophil and Stella* 1. Both Sidneys drew on the conventional pretence that poetry could be the spontaneous outpouring of emotion.

81 *smart, n.* Grief.

82 *sadd, adj.* Serious, grave.

84 *meanest part.* Her limitations as a writer mean that she is able to express only the least portion of her grief. Humility topos. Cf. 32–3.

85 *theise Hymnes.* The Sidneian *Psalmes.*

theise obsequies. Funeral rites. Self-reflexive reference to dedicatory poems.

91 *could I so take my leave.* The conventional wish in elegy that the mourner could join the departed was frequently employed in reference to Sidney. Cf. Spenser's 'Ruines of Time', 307–8 and 'Astrophil' (sig. F3ᵛ–4); Bryskett's 'Mourning Muse' (sig. G4ᵛ–H1). The convention is gently mocked in Thomas Moffet's *Silkewormes* (sig. D1–2), dedicated to Pembroke.

Variant: 'To the Angell Spirit of . . . Sir Phillip Sidney'

This early version, printed in the 1623 edition of *The Whole Workes of Samuel Daniel Esquire in Poetrie* (see 'Transmission and Authority of Texts'), is incomplete, lacking the final lines and attribution. Like the final version, it is composed in seven-line stanzas of iambic pentameter, rhymed *abbabba.*

10–14 Description of an international competition in vernacular Psalms translation, expressing the desire to improve upon the poetic quality of previous English Psalters.

11 *vulgar, n.* Vernacular, but perhaps also common or uneducated. A reference to previous English metrical versions of the Psalms.

22–35 Omitted in revision.

27 *Rites to aright.* To arrange properly the funeral rites.

bloud. She would not spare her blood to ensure that Sidney is properly mourned. Note that the blood becomes ink in the revision, lines 78–80.

28 For poetic inspiration Pembroke appeals to God, the author of life who parted Sidney from his earthly life.

31 *wracke of time.* May refer to Spenser's 'The Ruines of Time'.

35 *Triumph of death.* Allusion to Petrarch's poem, translated by the countess some time during the 1590s.

49–55 Substantially altered in revision, omitting catalogue of qualities. See also textual notes.

56 *controule, n.* In the obsolete sense of censure, finding fault. The line connects with the vision of Sidney in a heaven without envy in the revised version (63).

59 *rase, n.* Erasure. Obscure phrasing, subsequently emended, seems to say that her griefs know erasure, or silence, because words are inadequate to

express them. Cf. inexpressibility topos in revision 43–9, 70, and in 'Astrea', 58–60.

71–5 An incomplete stanza. The two final lines and the attribution may have been lost in Daniel's papers and are omitted from 1623 edition of his poems. Or Pembroke may have revised the poem to eliminate the partial stanza, as she did for some Psalms. (See 'Major Revisions of Psalms 1–43'.)

'The Dolefull Lay of Clorinda'

Traditional in its tripartite structure, the lay laments Sidney's death, praises him, and offers consolation. As in Bryskett's 'A pastorall Aeglogue', Sidney is portrayed as joyful in heaven; the poets mourn their 'owne miseries' (96), not his. Using iambic pentameter in an *ababcc* rhyme as in Spenser's 'Astrophel' (see 'Literary Context'), the poet makes use of such elegiac motifs as a series of questions, repetition, echo, appeals to nature, equation of flowers and verse, and the apotheosis of the deceased. A more personal note is sounded when Sidney is praised, not for military prowess, but in the private context of shared verses, referring to his 'love-layes' (43) and the riddles he wrote 'to make you mery glee' (46).

17 *wretched*. Emended. The correction in the folio texts of an obvious error in 1595.

35 Emended. *Great* is an unsurprising correction in 1611, 1617. The addition of 'did' in the later printings judiciously completes a line which is one syllable short, although there is no evidence for its authorial status.

41 *Cypres*, n. Dark conifer, symbolic of mourning. Cf. *The Shepheardes Calender*, 'November', 145, wherein nymphs change their garlands of olive for 'balefull boughes of Cypres'.

42 *Elder*, n. Shrub or low tree. Cf. *The Shepheardes Calender*, 'November', 147, wherein the muses wear 'bitter Eldre braunches seare'.

43 *love-layes*. Sidney's love poems in *Astrophil and Stella* and *Arcadia*.

48 *alasse*. Exclamation, alas. As in old French, the word here takes the gender of the speaker.

63 *By soveraine choyce . . . select*. Chosen by God.

quires, n. Choirs. Cf. description of Sidney singing with the angelic choirs in 'Angell Spirit'.

65–6 The question about death that demands a reading, or interpretation, is given an orthodox Christian answer in lines 67–96. Sidney now lives in heavenly bliss; we mourn not for him, but for ourselves.

66 *Ay me*. An exclamation characteristic of Pembroke's style. Cf. *Antonius*, 460 and 1905, and l. 1.

70–8 A representation of 'the celestial pastoral' that contrasts with the laments of 'earthly nature' in lines 1–60 (Beilin, *Redeeming Eve*, 138).

84 *jealous rancor*. A recurring theme in the *Astrophel* elegies, which repeatedly describe Sidney as slain by envy (e.g. sigs. H2, H3, K1^v, K3).

Antonius

3 *round engin*. Earth. From Lucretius, *De rerum natura*, 5. 96: *machina mundi*, 'engine of the world'.

14 *statelye*. Trisyllabic.

18 *cruell, n*. Cruel one. Used to describe a disdainful mistress in Petrarchan poetry.

traitres, n. Traitress.

22 *Pelusium*. A city at the mouth of the Nile that fell to Octavius in 30 BC; Plutarch records a rumour that it surrendered 'by *Cleopatraes* consent', North, sig. PPPP5.

30 *Not*. Perhaps a printing error for the ordinarily expected 'Nor' in this construction. Garnier has '*non*', but the construction is different.

32 *triumph*. Probably a reference to Petrarch, *Trionfo d'Amore*, which portrays Cleopatra as triumphing over Julius Caesar.

44 *glad refuge*. Cf. *Discourse*, particularly 755–802, portraying death as our safe haven.

51 *Thracian*. Thrace, located on the Black Sea adjoining Macedonia, sided with Brutus and Cassius against Antony and Octavius; it was later made a Roman province.

54 *Mægæra*. One of the three Furies. Cf. 58, 241.

58 *Orestes*. The son of Agamemnon and Clytemnestra who killed his mother to avenge his father's death at her hands. In some versions of the story, he is driven mad by the pursuing Furies.

70 The contrast between 'field tents' and 'courtly bowers' is not in Garnier.

74 *Crassus*. Marcus Licinius Crassus had been defeated and killed by the Parthians in 53 BC.

82 *their force*. The force of the 'poisned cuppes' of the 'Sorceres'. The implied comparison of Cleopatra and Circe is made clearer in 1166–72.

92 *Parth*. Inhabitant of Parthia, an empire of Western Asia south-east of the Caspian sea. According to Plutarch, Antony 'fell in love with' Cleopatra on his way to wage war against the Parthians; she eventually helped to fund that unsuccessful campaign: North, sig. NNNN5.

Mede. Inhabitant of Media, a mountainous country south-west of the Caspian Sea, adjoining Parthia.

93 *Hircanie*. A region adjacent to Media and Parthia on the Caspian Sea.

94 *Redoubting*. Dreading: a direct translation of Garnier's '*Redoutant*' and the first use recorded in the *OED*. Cf. 958; Ps. 121. 5. The countess may be deliberately ambiguous here, to imply that they were building redoubts, or fortifications, but she elsewhere translates the word as 'fearing'.

95 *Phraate*. Trisyllabic. Phraata, 'the chiefest and greatest citie the king of Media had', was one of the cities besieged by Antony during his war against the Parthians: North, sig. OOOO2.

102 *the woords*. The countess omits the implication of flattery in Garnier: '*les blandices*'.

111 *Nilus streames*. In Garnier, '*les Canopides ondes*', referring to Canopus, an Egyptian port near the mouth of the Nile.

117 *bristled*. Thickly set with standing crops.

119 *Pharos*. The pun on Pharaohs and Pharos (an island near Alexandria with a lighthouse that was one of the Seven Wonders of the ancient world) is more evident in Pembroke's translation than in Garnier: '*Phar*'.

146–9 Senecan *sentences*, or proverbs, are indicated by roman type in Pembroke's translation and by quotation marks in Garnier.

151–66 The distinctive negative construction reinforces the idea that misfortune is as inevitable as natural phenomena like storms, lightning, heat, and cold.

188 *furious wise*. In a furious manner.

189 *pates*. Heads. Derogatory.

193 *Scythes* and *Massagetes*. Warlike nomads who lived in northern sections of Europe and Asia.

202 *Titan*, i.e. the sun god Hyperion. Garnier has simply '*le Soleil*'.

203 *light, adj.* Garnier: '*L'ombre legère*'.

204 *ensue*. To follow. Suffering pursues humanity as inevitably as the shadow follows the body.

215–22 Prometheus' theft of sacred fire is responsible for the 'sicknes pale and colde' that will 'spurre' or hasten our end, death. Death, paradoxically, is both part of the curse and a blessed release from it. Cf. *Discourse* on the benefits of death, although it emphatically rejects the suicide so glorified by Plutarch (*Discourse*, 916–31).

230 *No earthly passion pain'd*. Garnier: '*franche de passions*'. The exclamation mark in 1592 and 1595 is probably a printer's misreading, perhaps of a long comma in the manuscript.

241 *furie.* Named as Mægæra in Garnier. Cf. 54.

248 *lighten.* To strike, as Jove's lightning. Cf. 400.

251 *Ixion.* Murdered his father-in-law, obtained forgiveness from Zeus, and then attempted to seduce Hera. Zeus outwitted him by forming a cloud, Nephele, to resemble Hera. She bore him the Centaurs.

252 *him who fained lightnings found.* Salmoneus, punished by Jupiter for attempting to imitate thunderbolts with burning torches.

253–6 *Tantalus.* In some accounts, Tantalus fed his sons to the gods. He was condemned to an eternity of hunger and thirst in Hades, with water and fruit tantalizingly just out of reach.

Atreus and *Thyestes.* Grandsons of Tantalus. Because Thyestes seduced his wife, Atreus served Thyestes a banquet of his own sons, whereupon Thyestes cursed the house of Atreus. The Egyptian philosopher emphasizes that Egyptians are not descended from these cursed Greeks. See Gillian Jondorf, *French Renaissance Tragedy: The Dramatic Word* (Cambridge: Cambridge UP, 1990), 59.

275–80 Philostratus prays for captivity rather than death, reversing the prayers of Antony and Cleopatra. Class distinction.

277 *Isis.* Pembroke omits Garnier's adjective '*Argolique*' (from Argos) which emphasized the Grecian, as well as Egyptian, identity of the goddess Isis.

290–6 *Priams Sonne.* Hector, leader of the Trojan forces. The first of three comparisons between Egypt and Troy, both destroyed by unlawful love. (Cf. 502–13 and 862–5.) Pembroke assumes that her readers have knowledge not only of such major figures in the *Iliad* as King Priam and his sons Hector and Troilus, but also of minor characters.

294 *Memnon.* Leader of the Ethiopian forces that fought for Troy, killed by Achilles.

Deiphobus. A younger son of Priam. According to later tradition, he married Helen after the death of Paris.

Glaucus. Leader of the Lycian allies of the Trojans.

295 *Scamander.* A river near Troy. Garnier mentions '*le roux Simoïs*', a tributary of the Scamander.

296 *before their dates are dead.* Before their appointed time to die.

308 *Apis.* Egyptian bull god.

319 *Nisa.* The birthplace of Bacchus in India. Pembroke omits Garnier's reference to the Edonides or Bacchantes, the Thracian women who followed Bacchus.

333–43 *wood-musiques Queene.* Philomel was raped by her brother-in-law, Tereus, King of Thrace, who cut out her tongue to prevent her telling of his crime. She told the tale through needlework that she sent to her sister Progne. She was eventually changed into a nightingale, and Progne into a swallow.

343 *Itys.* Son of Tereus and Progne, slain by the sisters and served to Tereus in revenge for the rape of Philomel.

344 *Halcyons.* Kingfishers. Alcyone threw herself into the sea to join her drowned husband, *Ceyx.* Both were changed into sea birds.

351 *That most Meander loves.* The swan, beloved of the river Meander, supposedly sang most sweetly just before death. Cf. Michael G. Brennan, 'The Date of the Death of Abraham Fraunce', *The Library* 6th ser., 5 (1983), 391–2.

362 *of Phœbus bredd.* The sisters of Phaethon mourned for him after he failed to control the chariot of his father, the sun-god Phoebus Apollo, and was killed by a thunderbolt from Jupiter before the chariot could set the earth on fire. They were eventually turned into alders. Cf. 1922.

365 *Padus.* The Italian river Po, called Eridan by Garnier, into which Phoebus fell. In England, the Po had become a symbol for Italian poetry. Cf. Samuel Daniel's dedication of *Cleopatra* to Pembroke: 'Wherby great SYDNEY and our SPENSER might, | With these *Po*-singers being equalled' (sig. H7).

368 *she.* Niobe, whose children were slain by Apollo, mourned until she was turned into a marble fountain on Mount Sipylus. Cf. 1909–13.

376 *Myrrhas shame.* Myrrha committed incest with her father Cinyras and was changed into a myrrh tree.

381 *Cybels sacred hill.* Mount Dindymus in Phrygia, sacred to the goddess Cybele.

383 *Atys.* A mortal beloved of Cybele, who in a frenzy castrated himself and then joined her eunuchs.

385 *Echo.* A nymph loved by Pan who was turned into a voice that could only repeat what she was told. An appropriate association with Philomel, who represents the silencing of women, is added by Pembroke. Garnier has only '*en longs cris redoublez*'.

403 *Tigers.* Cf. Antony's preference to be eaten by a Thracian wolf rather than to be taken in Caesar's triumph. Cleopatra asks for exile or death for her children rather than to be borne in Caesar's triumph, 1847–68. Cf. Argument.

406 *royall hart.* Part of appeals to blood and rank. Cf. 495.

418 *Charons barge.* Charon ferried the dead across the river Styx to Hades.

422 *in shady plaines shall plaine alone.* Complain, in a poetic sense. Another use of polyptoton.

455 *I am sole cause.* Cleopatra admits her responsibility; Antony avoids such admission until line 1152.

466–9 Scythians, Germans, Parthians, Numidians, Britons, and the desert peoples formed the periphery of the Roman empire.

467 *back-shooting Parthians.* The detail about the Parthians' ability to shoot an arrow backwards as they ride comes from Plutarch's *Life of Crassus*, not from Garnier, who simply calls them archers. Cf. also Philip Sidney's 'A Shepheard's tale' (first printed in the 1593 *Arcadia*): 'So have I heard to pierce pursuing shield | By Parents train'd the *Tartars* wilde are tought, | With shafts shott out from their back-turned bow'. Wroth uses this passage metaphorically in *Urania*, ed. Roberts, 253.

469 Pembroke follows 1585 edition in omitting detailed passages here and elsewhere (included in Garnier's 1578 edition at lines 458, 498, 1558, 1570, 1663, and 1743.)

471 Jealousy for Octavia seems a more credible motive to Garnier than politics, as in Plutarch. Pembroke translates faithfully.

490–1 *begot . . . borne.* Pembroke adds the connection of 'begot' to 'borne', so that predestination functions almost like Sir Philip Sidney's foreconceit. Events are begotten in the minds of the gods before they are born on earth.

563 *Wife.* According to Dio Cassius (*Roman History*, 50), Antony divorced Octavia and married Cleopatra in 37 BC. Charmion admits that Cleopatra's 'wivelie love' is 'scarce wivelie' in 597–8.

572 *left.* Emended. Comparison with Garnier supports the emendation of 'lest' to 'left': '*Tant moins le faut laisser que tout est contre luy*'. The scribe or printer probably mistook an 'f' for a long 's'.

585 *Plutos mansion.* Hades.

602 *have,* The comma indicates that Cleopatra interrupts, as Bullough's added dash more clearly shows.

604 *Alcest.* Alcestis, frequently used as a model for wifely love, died in place of her husband Admetus, but was rescued by Hercules.

611 *Carian Queene.* Queen Artemisia of Caria built a tomb for her husband Mausolus at Halicarnassus in 353 BC that was one of the wonders of the world. Some statues from the tomb are now in the British Museum.

617 *Pharsaly.* Pharsalus in Thessaly was the battlefield where Antony helped Caesar to defeat Pompey the Great.

618 *Enipeus.* A river near Pharsalus.

619 *Mutina.* Modena. Beseiged by Antony in 43 BC. Two consuls, Hirtius and Pansa, who opposed Antony were killed.

621 *yearly plaies.* Abraham Fraunce portrays Pembrokiana conducting such yearly commemorations for her brother Philip in *The Second Part of the Countesse of Pembrokes Ivychurch.*

670 *Clotho.* Pembroke replaces Garnier's generic '*l'impiteuse Parque*' with the proper name of the Fate who holds the distaff. (Lachesis pulls off the thread of life as it is spun and Atropos cuts it.)

702 *Philippi.* Pembroke uses the name of the city founded by Philip of Macedonia in place of Garnier's less precise 'Macedon'.

717–32 Garnier derived this blazon, spoken by Cleopatra's female servant, largely from Petrarchan tradition, including the attributes of her pale skin and blonde hair for the Grecian Ptolemy. Plutarch stressed her voice more than her appearance.

732 Cleopatra's ability to answer each ambassador in his own language, mentioned by Plutarch and Garnier, could be construed in England as praise of Queen Elizabeth.

753 *Phœbus.* Phoebus Apollo, the god of the sun and of poetry. Garnier has simply '*le soleil*'.

841 *fortunes flower.* Added by Pembroke to continue the flower imagery of 835–6.

850 *pearce.* Disyllabic.

894 *weare.* Spevack, 500, emends to 'weare[s]'.

900 *Pelusium.* Cf. 22.

Actian. Antony's defeat off Actium, a promontory on the western coast of Greece, is described in the Argument, 15–22, and by Caesar in 1481–1500.

905 *Thyre.* Thyreus, an eloquent man sent by Caesar to beguile Cleopatra, aroused Antony's jealousy: North, sig. PPPP5.

907 *Alexas.* Slain by Caesar for betraying Antony to Herod.

945–6 Adapted from Francesca's words in Dante's *Inferno*, Canto 5. The circle of the carnal lovers includes Semiramis, Helen of Troy, Achilles, Paris, Tristan, Dido, and Cleopatra herself.

959 *Mutina.* See note to 619.

965 *Enipeus.* See note to 618.

967 *Cassius and Brutus* were defeated by Antony and Octavius at Philippi in 42 BC and committed suicide.

973–6 Lucilius surrendered himself to Antony to save Brutus, thereby winning Antony's friendship.

1001 Pembroke adds the ship metaphor.

1013 *allied in bloud.* According to Plutarch, Mark Antony's mother was related to Julius Caesar and hence to Octavius, who was both Julius Caesar's grand-nephew and his adopted son.

1022 Pembroke adds the thirst metaphor.

1047 *Lucius.* Antony's wife Fulvia and his brother Lucius Antony rebelled against Octavius and were starved into surrender at Perugia.

1048 *Lepidus.* The third triumvir with Antony and Octavius was deposed in 36 BC. Cf. 1119.

1075 *Alcides bloud.* The line of Hercules, from whom Antony was supposedly descended. Cf. 1243–6 and 1877–8.

1080 *Twise watred.* The Romans fought two battles in Thessaly, at Pharsalus (48 BC) and at Philippi (42 BC).

1095 *Camill.* Marcus Furius Camillus, Roman general and statesman, defeated the Gauls.

Marcellus. Marcus Claudius Marcellus, consul and general, captured Syracuse after a siege.

Scipio. Probably Aemilianus Scipio, called Scipio Africanus Minor, consul and general, who destroyed Carthage in 146 BC. Possibly Publius Cornelius Scipio Aemilianus Africanus Major, who had driven the Carthaginians out of Spain in 210 BC.

1096 *late great Cæsar.* Julius Caesar.

1097 *Pompei.* Pompey the Great, the renowned general who married Julius Caesar's daughter, became Caesar's primary opponent in the civil war, and was murdered in Egypt. After Antony took his house in Rome, his son, Pompey, became Antony's enemy.

1103–4 Lines added by Pembroke.

1103 *should be.* Emended. The extra syllable is needed for both the sense and the metre.

1114 *false Ulisses.* The Greek hero, who devised the plan of the Trojan horse, was naturally considered traitorous by the Trojans and by the Europeans who identified themselves as descendants of Aeneas. Dante places him in the eighth circle of the *Inferno*, the place for evil counsellors. Antony argues that Octavius conquered only by guile, not by heroism in battle.

1138 *Bellona.* Personification of war. The form with 'e' occurs in 1592 at 1371.

1166–72 A comparison between Cleopatra and Circe is implied. Circe, with her poison cup, changed Ulysses' followers into swine, a story often allegorized as women destroying male reason through lust. Cf. 83. Parallels Spenser's Acrasia in *The Faerie Queene*, Book II.

1177 *idle armes faire wrought with spiders worke.* Traditional picture of the conquest of Mars by Venus.

1183 *Venus.* Added. Garnier: '*delices de Cypris*'.

1213 *Assirian kinge.* Possibly Sardanapalus, notorious for his self-indulgence; or Sennacherib, 'who led a fruitless and self-indulgent expedition against Egypt, while back in Assyria the Medes began a rebellion and won their independence'. *Renaissance Drama by Women: Texts and Documents*, ed. S. P. Cerasano and Marion Wynne-Davies (London and New York: Routledge, 1996), 184.

1221–6 The twelve labours of Hercules included the adventures listed here: killing the giant Antaeus; aiding Lycus in overcoming the Bebryces; stealing the cattle of the monster Geryon; killing the many-headed Hydra; capturing Cerberus, the watchdog of hell; marrying Deianeira after defeating her suitor, the river-god Achelous; and holding the heavens for Atlas.

1225 *Achelous.* Pronounced as four syllables.

1228–42 The story of Omphale, Queen of Maeonia in Lydia, whom Pembroke refers to only as 'his Captive' (1229). Hercules, after completing his labours, was vanquished by love for Omphale, who set him to spinning. Pembroke adds the familiar detail about dressing him 'in maides attire'. The comparison of Antony and Cleopatra to Hercules and Omphale is made in Plutarch's *Comparison of Demetrius and Antony* IV. Parallels Spenser's Radigund in *The Faerie Queene*, Book V.

1281 *our.* 'Or' is recorded as a 17th-century spelling variant in the *OED*. Its appearance here, however, may result from the compositor's having worked from a manuscript containing the abbreviation 'or', for 'our'. (See also *Triumph*, 2. 104.)

1293 *Acheron.* One of the rivers of hell.

1302 *Alecto.* One of the Furies.

1310 *Boreas.* The North Wind, called '*des Aquilons*' by Garnier.

1351 *Avernus.* A lake near the cave through which Aeneas descended to the underworld. Often used as a synonym for Hades itself.

1352, 1355 *Psammetique, Amasis.* Former kings of Egypt in the Ptolemaic line.

1407 *Glauques, and Tritons.* Sea gods.

1418–26 The Giants sought to attack the gods on Mount Olympus by piling mountains on top of each other. They were struck by Jove's thunderbolts, but could not be finally defeated without the help of a mortal, Hercules.

1424 The next line in Garnier (1407) is lacking in the translation, probably inadvertently dropped by the printer: '*Maint trait de foudre aigu desserra sur Typhé*'.

1425 *Gyges* and *Briareus*. Hundred-handed giants, the sons of Uranus and Ge. Pembroke omits Typhon, the third such giant listed by Garnier.

1437–40 According to Plutarch, Antony compared his children by Cleopatra to the son and the moon. Dio Cassius says that he named them Helios and Selene, the children of the goddess Latona. (Plutarch, XLIV, and Dio Cassius, L, ch. 24, and LI, ch. 21.)

1444 *Antigonus*. Plutarch, XLIV, identifies him as king of the Jews.

1455 *Artabasus*. The Armenian king was conquered by Antony, who angered Rome by holding an unauthorized triumph in Alexandria. (Plutarch, LXV, and Dio Cassius, XLIX, ch. 40.)

1458 *Romulus*. Legendary founder of Rome, who chose the site for the city after augury. Pembroke adds the proper name; Garnier had used the epithet '*Quirin*'.

1471 *rebell Samnite*. The mountaineers of Abruzzi fought valiantly but were finally conquered by Rome after three wars.

fierce Pyrrhus. A cousin of Alexander the Great. He was attempting to reinstate the Macedonian empire when he won his proverbial 'Pyrrhic victory' against the Romans at Asculum, losing most of his army. He reputedly said, 'One more such victory and we are undone.'

1472 *cruell Mithridate*. During his campaign against Rome, Mithridates was reputed to have ordered the massacre of some 80,000 Italian citizens living in Asia.

1501 *You know it well*. Agrippa had commanded part of the fleet at Actium.

1530 *the peoples love*. Traditional debate over clemency or severity as the best policy for a ruler is given topical resonance by Pembroke's adaptation of Queen Elizabeth's assertion that she ruled by the love of her people.

1602 *crost his armes*. Renaissance pose symbolic of mourning, also used in the love complaint.

1649 *helpe*. Emended. A noun, not a verb, is required after 'by' and 'hir womens'. A final manuscript 'e' may have been mistaken for a 't'.

1664 *life-dead*. Perhaps an error for 'half-dead'. Garnier (1647): '*demy-mort*'. Cf. 1900 (Garnier 1877), where the same phrase is translated as 'Half-dead'.

1721 *Proculeius*. Octavius's envoy. In accounts of Cinthio and Jodelle (Plutarch, CI).

1761 Pembroke omits the town of Canusium as the source of the finest wool, perhaps preferring the famous wool of Wilton.

1779–82 The doors of the temple of Janus were open in war, closed in peace. According to Dio Cassius, LI, ch. 20, the doors were closed in 29 BC for the first time in 200 years.

1794 *Biscaines.* The Cantabri, a Spanish people later conquered by Agrippa.

1839 *Sisters.* Pembroke here omits the names of the Fates, given in Garnier.

1840 *Phlegethon.* Like the more familiar Styx, a river of hell.

1883 *shepehookes.* Cleopatra evidences the traditional ambiguity inherent in pastoral, which is a fall in rank for the nobility and yet a safe retreat.

1905 *Ch.* Cleopatra has both the preceding and the subsequent speeches. Garnier (1882): '*Eras*'.

1909 *Niobe.* See note to 368.

1919 *Phaetons sisters.* See note to 362.

1921 *Po.* See note to 365.

1927 Stage directions are not supplied, but Cleopatra apparently applies the asps here. Note that they are sucking her moisture and then her blood in 1941–2.

1953 *Julus broode.* Venus, who favoured Julius Caesar and his descendants, should remember that Octavius is also related to Caesar. Cf. 1013.

1978 *Of him.* Julius Caesar had aided in her war with her brother Ptolemy. Dio Cassius, XLII, chs. 34–44.

A Discourse of Life and Death

14 *theevish deserts.* Deserts full of thieves.

15 *weaving at this web.* Pembroke adds the metaphor, developing the reference to Penelope's web above (10). Penelope, who had promised to wed one of the suitors who besieged her as soon as she finished weaving a shroud for her father-in-law, wove during the day, but unravelled her work at night.

22 *hoise saile.* Raise the sail.

30 *Barber.* Reflecting current English medical practice, Pembroke translates the word 'barbier' as 'barber' here, but as 'Surgion' in lines 32 and 35. The Barber-Surgeons, incorporated 1461, had practised both dentistry and surgery, but under Henry VIII the medical work of barbers had been restricted to dentistry.

65 *maister of himselfe.* Cf. *Antonius*, 130.

74 *Hercules.* At the age of 18, Hercules was asked to choose between two symbolic women, Pleasure and Virtue. He chose the life of virtue, with its toil and its eventual honour.

93–4 *infusion of wormewood.* Bitter medicine. Mornay, '*infusion en eau d'absinthe*'.

98 *uncleane spirit.* Cf. Mark 5: 1–20.

148 *gaine wealth.* Cf. Luke 9: 25.

149–50 Mornay alludes to the pearls brought back from Asia and the gold that the Spanish found in the New World.

170 *vile excrement.* Gold, as the excrement of the earth. Cf. 218.

178 *dogs hunger.* Bulimy, an insatiable appetite.

198 *flayed.* Skinned, as in Mornay, '*escorchez*'. Altered to 'slayed' in 1606 and subsequent editions, probably because the 'f' was misread as a long 's'. See Sidney, Mary. *Discourse,* ed. Bornstein, 82.

239 *without difference.* Without discrimination or discernment. Mornay, '*sans aucune discretion*'.

264 *feaver Hectique.* Consumption or tuberculosis.

268 *lookes aside.* Looks askance. Mornay, '*regarde de travers*'.

346 *downfalls.* Waterfalls. Mornay, '*cataractes*'.

347 *Cimmerians.* According to Homer, the sun never shone on their land, which was always covered with mist from the stream Oceanus. Odysseus met the spirits of the dead there (*Odyssey,* Book 11).

353–4 The crown of thorns, deriving from the biblical account of the mocking of Christ (Matt. 27: 29), had been adapted in Protestant iconography to symbolize the spiritual humility necessary for ideal kingship.

360 *Persian Monarch.* Xerxes I, King of Persia, whose invasion of Greece is recorded in Herodotus.

370 *Dionyse of Sicill.* Dionysius II of Syracuse, whom Dion and Plato had hoped to make the ideal 'Philosopher King', was exiled in 357 BC.

373 *Sylla.* Silius Italicus, Tiberius Catius Asconius (*c.*AD 26–*c.*101), a Roman senator whose wealth enabled him to retire from public office and devote himself to art and literature. He wrote the lengthy epic *Punica* on the Second Punic War.

377 The king's search for pleasure and riches is summarized in Ecclesiastes 2, attributed to Solomon in the Geneva Bible.

379 *booke.* Ecclesiastes.

381 *Augustus.* Gaius Octavius, the first Roman emperor, ruled Rome after his defeat of Marcus Antonius at Actium in 31 BC. Seneca discusses his search for rest, '*De brevitate vitae*', IV.

385 *Tiberius.* Tiberius Claudius Nero Caesar, son of Nero, was Roman emperor from AD 14 to 37.

389–90 *Dioclesian.* Gaius Aurelius Valerius Diocles, who changed his name to Diocletian when he became Roman emperor in AD 284. A persecutor of Christians, he abdicated in 305 and retired to his palace at Salonae.

392 *Emperour Charles the fifth.* Holy Roman Emperor (1519–56), abdicated and retired to the Spanish monastery of Yuste.

402 *Pyrrhus King of Albanie* attempted to recapture the empire of his second cousin Alexander the Great, but won the battle of Asculum in 279 BC at too great a cost—hence the expression 'Pyrrhic victory.' See *Antonius*, 1471.

405 *Alexander* the Great, who succeeded his father Philip II of Macedon in 336 BC, freed the Greeks from Persian rule and conquered most of the known world, from Greece to India.

411 *God laughing.* Cf. Ps. 2: 4.

478 *contagious an aire.* Disease was thought to be spread by foul air. Cf. Elizabeth's letter inviting young Mary Sidney to court to escape the 'unpleasant ayre' of Wales that was thought to have killed her sister Ambrosia. Elizabeth to Sir Henry Sidney, 1575, PRO SP 40/1, f. 83. Printed in Young, *Mary Sidney*, 27–8, and Hannay, *Philip's Phoenix*, 31–2.

485 Lot escapes from Sodom to the village of Zoar in *Gen.* 19: 15–23, rendered as '*Segor*' by Mornay.

511–12 The temptation of Christ in the desert is recorded in Matt. 4: 1–11; Mark 1: 13; and Luke 4: 1–13.

530 *some backer closet.* A private room in the back of the building, farther from the noise of the street.

539 Tired of eating manna in the wilderness, the Israelites missed the garlic and onions of Egypt, along with fish, cucumbers, melons, and leeks. Num. 11: 5.

546–7 After the Greeks sailed out of sight, the Greek Sinon, pretending to help the Trojans, convinced them to bring in the Trojan horse.

565 Emended. See textual notes.

vanitie and vexation. A judgement attributed to Solomon, Eccles. 1: 14.

578 *knowes not himselfe.* Cf. the maxim inscribed on the Temple of Apollo at Delphi, 'Know thyself', ascribed in Plato's *Protagoras* to the Seven Wise Men.

579 The legendary wars of Thebes, particularly as dramatized in the Oedipus cycle by Sophocles, and of Troy, particularly as presented in Homer's *Iliad* and the *Odyssey*. Seneca drew from these sources for his own tragedies.

598–9 Proverbial. Quoted in Ps. 111: 10 and in Prov. 1: 7 and 9: 10, called 'The Proverbes of Solomon' in the *Geneva Bible*.

599–600 Cf. 1 Cor. 1: 18–21, 3: 19.

604 The Devil is called the Prince of the world in John 12: 31, 14: 30, and 16: 11.

681 *Hecate*, originally a beneficent moon goddess, had become associated with night and with ghosts and witches. Three-faced statues of Hecate, traditionally placed at crossroads, could well frighten children.

692 *payne to die.* Cf. *Triumph*, 2: 30.

751 *even he.* The Stoic, contrasted with 'us brought up in a more holy schoole' (755).

756–7 *consolations against death.* Echoes the title *'De Consolatione'*, written by Seneca to console Polybius on the death of his brother.

761–4 Eccles. 7: 1.

793 *eyes but overgrowen with pearles.* Eyes covered with a milky film, cataracts.

800–2 Cf. 1 Cor. 15: 42–57.

809 *trencher knights.* Braggarts who are valiant only at the dinner table.

856 *bored paile of Danaus daughters.* Danaus was forced to marry his fifty daughters to the fifty sons of his enemy Aegyptus. All but one of Danaus' daughters obeyed his command to stab their husbands; they were punished in Hades with the never-ending task of filling leaking water jars.

865–9 Alludes to Jesus' parable of the householder who hired workers at different hours, but gave each of them a full day's wages. Matt. 20: 1–16. Cf. 939–42.

881–3 Choosing to follow God's direction rather than being forced to obey destiny. The person dies in either case, but it is better to make a good death. Cf. 826–31.

891 *sting of Death.* 1 Cor. 15: 55. 'O death, where is thy sting? ô grave where is thy victory!'

962–3 *Die to live,* | *Live to die.* Cf. Laura's words in *Triumph*, 2. 22–4.

The Triumph of Death

References are made to the following sources in this section of the commentary:

Ariani	*Triumphi*, ed. Marco Ariani (Milan: Mursia, 1988).
Calcaterra	*Trionfi*, ed. Carlo Calcaterra (Turin: Unione Tipografico-Editrice Torinese, 1927).
Gesualdo	*Il Petrarcha colla spositione di misser Giovanni Andrea Gesualdo . . . MDXXXIII* [Venice: Giovann' Antonio di Nicolini & fratelli da Sabbio, 1533].
Ramat	*Rime e Trionfi*, ed. Raffaello Ramat (Milan: Rizzoli, 1957).

Rees   D. G. Rees, 'Petrarch's "Trionfo della Morte" in
                        English', *Italian Studies* 7 (1952), 82–90.
Sidney, Mary. *Triumph* *The Triumph of Death and Other Unpublished and
                        Uncollected Poems by Mary Sidney, Countess of
                        Pembroke (1561–1621)*, ed. Gary F. Waller (Salz-
                        burg, Austria: U of Salzburg, 1977).
Vellutello   *Il Petrarcha con l'espositione d'alessandro vellutello e
                        con molte altre utilissime cose in diversi luoghi di
                        quella nuovamente da lui aggiunte...MDXXVIII*
                        [Venice: Bernardino de Vidali, 1528].
Wilkins   *The Triumphs of Petrarch*, trans. Ernest Hatch
                        Wilkins (Chicago: U of Chicago P, 1962).

The First Chapter

1–6 Laura, 'That gallant Ladie', has, in the preceding *Triumph of Chastity*,
conquered Cupid, 'the mightie foe'.

13–15 The souls of the noble company of women who, like Laura, have
attained victory over passion through chastity.

19–20 According to early commentators, the green field represents
youth. The 'snowie Ermiline' (ermine) represents purity or chastity, as
does topaz set in gold (Ariani, 235). Citing earlier precedents in Petrarch,
Ariani also proposes as an alternative that green recalls the laurel and
may represent here the 'colour' of lasting virtue (' *"colore" dell'onestà dure-
vole'*).

25 *seem'd*. Emended. The Italian text, *pareano*, shows that 'send' is a scribal
error.

unclose, 'disclose', 'reveal' (cf. Sidney, Mary. *Triumph*, 185). The Italian
reads, *in mezzo un sole*.

31 *a woman*. Death.

33 *Phlegra*. A valley of Thessaly where Jupiter struck the Giants with
thunderbolts when they were making an assault on Olympus.

37–8 The syntax is unclear in the translation. In the Italian, it is 'you' who
are 'deafe, and blinde'. Cf. Sidney, Mary. *Triumph*, 185.

50 *spoile*. The body of Laura. Death has no power over her soul.

51 *one*, unique (Italian, *una*, glossed by Ariani, 239, as *unica*).

52 Pembroke has mistaken *Altri* for a plural form: *Altri so, che n'hara piu di
me doglia*. The reference is to Petrarch (Rees, 84).

54 *assoile*, 'discharge', 'release', 'absolve'.

57 *comprehends*. An imprecise rendering of *riprende*, 'corrects oneself'.

58 *the cruell*, i.e. Death.

over-gast. Although no such compound is cited in the *OED*, 'gast' is defined as a participial adjective meaning 'terrified, afraid'. Sidney, Mary. *Triumph*, 186, glosses, 'made gloomy'.

63 Pembroke alters the image by omitting the reference to poison: *Pur non sentisti mai mio duro tosco.*

75 *Pestring*, 'crowding'. Pembroke omits the specific mention of verse and prose.

76 *Cattay*, i.e. Cathay, China: *Cattaio.* Emended. 'Gattay' is probably a scribal error. The place names represent the extreme points of the East and West (Calcaterra, 90).

Coome, i.e. 'come'.

79 *whom*, i.e. the powerful rulers of the earth (Ramat, 593).

82 Ramat notes the use here of the medieval *ubi sunt* motif.

86 The parenthesis means 'yet who does otherwise'.

89 *your greate Mother*, the earth (Ariani, 242).

91–3 i.e. perhaps 'bring me one who is serious and not vain'. Italian: *Pur de le mille un'utile fatica, | Che non sian tutte vanita palesi; | Chi'ntende a vostri studi simil* [Gesualdo: *sime'l*] *dica.*

102 *taske.* Emended. The emendation of 'talke' is supported by the Italian, *lavoro*, i.e. to tell of the death of Laura.

105 *doubtfull stepp*, i.e. of death. Doubtful because of the uncertainty of what follows death in a given case, salvation or damnation (Calcaterra, 91).

107 *lade*, 'load' or 'burden' (Sidney, Mary. *Triumph*, 186). The sense of 106–8 is that women who are still alive—whose souls are still laden with bodies—gather at Laura's deathbed.

113 *on*, i.e. 'one': *un aureo crine.* Calcaterra, 92, Ramat, 595, and Ariani, 243, cite classical precedents (e.g., *Aeneid* 4. 698–705) for this picture of the moment of death as the plucking of a single hair from Laura's head.

118–19 The mourners weep at the death of Laura, whose eyes remain dry (because of her faith in the afterlife).

120 *burne*, i.e. with love (Calcaterra, 93).

sing. Emended. The emendation is supported by the Italian, *cantai*, and by the probability that Pembroke did not intend to repeat a rhyme word.

124 *mortall Goddesse*, Laura.

125–6 Laura's mortal perfection could not prevent her death.

133 *The sixt of Aprill.* The day of Petrarch's falling in love with Laura, as well as of her death and of the current dialogue.

one a clock it was. Pembroke has misinterpreted the phrase, *L'hora prim' era* 'It was the first hour', the first hour of sunrise.

134 Pembroke adds the metaphor of tying. Petrarch was tied by love; he is set free through the death of Laura.

135 *Changing hir copie*, 'changing one's style or course of action' (*OED*). The Italian has *stile*, which in the context means about the same.

136 *libertie.* The word combines 'religious echoes of Pauline liberty with class-interest echoes of aristocratic liberty'. Cf. *Astrophil and Stella* 47 and *Pamphilia to Amphilanthus* 14. (William Kennedy, private correspondence.)

136–8 Pembroke's alteration of tense from past definite *si dolse* and *mi tolse* into the present 'doe rue' and 'faine ... would flye' emphasizes the 'developing reciprocity between Laura's and the speaker's attitudes toward moral freedom'. See William Kennedy, *The Site of Petrarchism* (forthcoming).

141 Pembroke makes the line metaphorical: 'hir' refers to Laura. The sense of 139–41 seems to be the speaker's assertion that he should have died first, not Laura, whose 'leafe' was 'quail'd' in its green freshness.

146 Pembroke omits *casto letto* 'chaste bed'.

154–6 Vellutello, sig. b, cites Augustine in commenting on *gliaversari*, i.e. 'devils or demons' (Ariani, 248: *diavoli*). Wilkins, 59, translates: 'No evil adversary ventured then | To make appearance with malignant mien | Before the task of Death was all complete'.

157 *they.* The witnesses of Laura's death.

171–2 The lack of punctuation after 171 obscures the construction of 172 as a separate clause, which is a famous line in Italian literature. Vellutello, sig. b, has a period after 171.

The Second Chapter

1 *the dreadfull happ*, i.e. the death of Laura.

3 *Sunne*, Laura.

4 *sprinkle.* Emended. Emendation of 'sprintle' in *Petyt* is supported by *spargea* in the Italian.

5 *Tithon's bryde*, Aurora, the dawn.

7 *a Ladie*, Laura, 'comming' (9) from Paradise.

18 *On pleasing bank.* Emended. That *Petyt*'s 'unpleasing' is a scribal error is proven by the Italian, *in una riva*.

beeches shade. The beech is a symbol of amorous solitude (Ariani, 260) and poetical meditation (Calcaterra, 99).

22 Laura is alive in heaven; Petrarch is dead on the earth. Gesualdo, sig. ff[5]v, Vellutello, sig. b2, *et al.* note that Laura's paradoxical assertion is both Christian and Neoplatonic.

27 *terme*, time of life. Pembroke substitutes a universal statement with moral implications for Petrarch's simple observation that he and Laura are soon to be parted by the return of day and the loss of the vision.

32 *obscurelie*. The Italian has *dura*, which Gesualdo, sig. ff[5]ᵛ, glosses as 'obstinate'. Pembroke may have thought 'obscurelie' an appropriate adverb to accompany 'blynde'.

36 *mudd*. A literal translation of *fango*, glossed by Ariani, 262, as 'earthly woes' (*delle miseri terrene*).

43 *Tyrrants*. Pembroke thus reduces to a category Petrarch's list of names: Sulla, Marius, Nero, Gaius, and Mezentius.

44–5 Pembroke omits the comparison of death to bitter absinthe (*assentio*).

46 *crosse*. In the Italian, *affanno*, 'sorrow'.

48 *that eternall losse*, damnation (Calcaterra, 101).

55–60 Laura recalls Petrarch's grief at her parting.

55 *he*, Petrarch (Ariani, 261). The Italian text has '*colui*'.

57, 59 *hir*, i.e. Laura.

60 *manner*. In the Italian, *stile* (59), glossed by Ariani, 264, and others as 'way of life', *modo di vivere*.

81 *Not leving*. Emended. The emendation of 'loving' to 'leving' is supported by the Italian, *Non lasciando vostr' alta impresa honesta*. The sense is that Petrarch's love should be within the bounds of honour.

97 *Thow*. Emended. Although emendation of 'Tho' in *Petyt* is not clearly supported by the Italian, which has a different construction, the context and especially the verb, 'saw'est', require a clear second person pronoun.

104 *our*. Emended. 'or' is probably a scribal misreading of the common abbreviation of 'our' as 'o' and a superscript 'r'. The Italian, in 105, has *nostro honore*. (See also *Antonius*, 1281.)

114 *But if*, i.e. 'unless'.

116 *som running toye*. The *OED* helps elucidate this phrase. 'Toy' can mean 'a light composition' or 'amorous sport, dallying'. 'Running' can mean 'cursory, hasty', 'volatile, flighty, giddy', or (with reference to metre or music) 'smooth, easy, or rapid character'. Laura is thus probably referring to Petrarch's too passionate or facile expressions of his love for her. The Italian, *sproni al fianco*, is an idiom, '(to have) spurs in the side (like a horse)', meaning 'very excited or impassioned'. Sidney, Mary. *Triumph*, 188, glosses: 'hastily took offence'.

119 *what*, i.e. 'hot', as in the Italian, *calda* (118).

123 i.e. if I could accept that as true.

128–9 Pembroke mistakes the shortened second person *havei* (*[h]avevi*) for a first person form (Rees, 85): *Questo mi taccio: pur quel dolce nodo | Mi piacque assai; ch'ntorno al core havei.*

130 *fame*. Emended. The emendation of the probably scribal error, 'flame', is supported by the Italian, *'l bel nome* 'fair name', glossed by Calcaterra, 106, as 'high fame' (*la bella fama*).

132 The sense is 'your love was not moderate enough'. The Italian has *Ne mai 'n tuo amor richiesi altro, che modo*, 'Never did I demand in your love anything other than moderation' (Ariani, 271, glosses *modo* as *moderazione*, 'moderation').

136 *zeale. Zelo* is the reading in at least 24 sixteenth-century editions and the one preferred by Gesualdo, sig. ff6ᵛ, who acknowledges, however, that *alcuni testi antichi hanno . . . gielo*, which (usually in the form *gelo*) is in at least 78 other sixteenth-century editions. The modern editions also have *gelo* ('frost' or 'frostiness').

139 *equale flames*. Pembroke omits Petrarch's *quasi*, 'almost'. See William Kennedy, *The Site of Petrarchism* (forthcoming).

150 *singing*. Pembroke follows Vellutello in portraying Laura singing Petrarch's words for him, 'my love dares speake no more', rather than following Gesualdo, who portrays Petrarch singing to her *'dir piu non osa il nostro amor'* or 'our love dares not say more than this'. (William Kennedy, private correspondence.)

158 *fyre*. Emended. Although *Petyt*'s 'fyres' generally corresponds with the Italian, *faville*, the rhyme in the translation at this point requires the singular. The manuscript reading is thus probably another scribal error.

164–8 Laura contrasts her humble birthplace in the vicinity of Avignon with Petrarch's Tuscany, specifically Florence ('thy flowrie nest' with a pun on 'flowery'—*fiorito* [167]—and Florence—*Firenze* (Calcaterra, 109) or *Fiorenza* (Ramat, 605)—in the Italian).

178 Emendation of 'Shee' to 'See' is supported by *vedi*.

186 Obscure; perhaps the sense is that Laura's explanation of her silent love has made easy Petrarch's former burden of love: 'But what you have left of me (i.e. not his heart, which she has?) is forced to live after you have left me behind'. William Kennedy (in private correspondence) suggests that the phrase might mean 'my memory of you', or, if it is to be read as a verb clause, 'but now what remains to console me after having lost you?'. The Italian says, fairly directly, 'It is hard for me to live without you' (*Ma'l viver senza voi m'è duro e greve*).

Correspondence
Manuscript Letters

For these holograph letters, the only words surviving in Pembroke's hand, we have attempted to present a text as close to the original as print will allow by including deletions, corrections, and additions in the text, rather than placing them in an apparatus. (On the importance of typographical features that allow editors 'to interfere as little as possible with the sound of [the writer's] voice', see *The Letters of Lady Arbella Stuart*, ed. Sara Jayne Steen. Women Writers in English 1350–1850 (New York: Oxford UP, 1994), 108n., 110; and Steen's article, 'Behind the Arras: Editing Renaissance Women's Letters', rpt. in *New Ways*, 229–38.) We have also preserved Pembroke's original spelling, punctuation, word division, and capitalization, although we have expanded abbreviations for clarity. See 'Editorial Procedure'.

I. Mary Sidney Herbert, Countess of Pembroke, to Robert Dudley, Earl of Leicester

Leicester's 'sone' is the Earl of Pembroke, as indicated by the 16-year-old countess's most significant correction. She deleted the phrase 'he was so well', and wrote 'my lord was so well', thereby referring to this 'sone' in the appropriate way for an aristocratic wife to speak of her husband; the designation had not yet become automatic. As this letter would indicate, she called her uncle Leicester 'my lord my father'. After her marriage Leicester delighted in calling his contemporary Henry Herbert, Earl of Pembroke, his son. In his will, for example, Leicester termed Pembroke his 'good Sonne in Lawe' (Probate Court Record, 11/73).

The letter, written in haste and marred by deletions and several ink blots, is dated only 'this fryday morning'. It was probably written on Friday, 15 August 1578, because of the letter from the Earl of Pembroke dated 14 August 1578 (a Thursday) and addressed to Leicester as 'My deere good Lord and fathir'. The slight sickness he had after returning from Buckstone kept him from writing sooner, 'But being I thanck God, nowe perfectly well', he sent a bearer (Philip Williams) to enquire of Leicester's 'well doing also' (Longleat House, Dudley Papers, II/185). The nineteenth-century compiler of the Dudley Papers dated the letter 1578 and bound it with the letter from Pembroke.

Leicester's man had visited when Pembroke had a trifling illness, exaggerated by rumour. Leicester had been worried about his friend and, when he received Pembroke's letter indicating that he was in good health, apparently sent a furious note back by Pembroke's messenger berating Mary Sidney Herbert because she had not sent 'worde of...[his] a mendment'. She nervously 'Cribled in hast' to beg Leicester's forgiveness as soon as she received his letter.

say. Probably a slip for 'saw'.

II. Mary Sidney Herbert, Countess of Pembroke, to Barbara Gamage, Lady Sidney

In his correspondence with his wife and with Rowland Whyte, Robert Sidney frequently mentions letters to and from his sister, but this is the Countess of Pembroke's only extant letter to her family. Demonstrating a warm affection for her sister-in-law, the countess offers her own nurse to care for Barbara while she was in Flushing, where Sir Robert Sidney was serving as Governor. The letter may also indicate that the countess had recently lost a child, perhaps to miscarriage, since the birth is not otherwise recorded. Lady Sidney bore a total of eleven children (three sons and eight daughters) between 1587 and 1602.

a Goodly boy. William Sidney, eldest son and heir of Robert Sidney, was born in Flushing on 10 November 1590. He died at the Pembrokes' London home, Baynards Castle, on 3 December 1612 and was buried at Penshurst.

my pretey Daughter. The countess's niece and namesake, Mary Sidney (later Lady Wroth), who was about 4 years old.

III. Mary Sidney Herbert, Countess of Pembroke, to Sir Edward Wotton

Sir Edward Wotton, known for his facility in French, Italian, and Spanish, went on several embassies to Scotland and to France for Queen Elizabeth.

deere and spetial frende. A close friend of Sir Philip Sidney, he had worked with Sidney in Vienna in 1574–5. Sidney had mentioned him in the opening sentence of *A Defence of Poetry*, and Queen Elizabeth sent Wotton to Scotland under Sidney's instruction in 1585. The following year, Wotton was a pallbearer at Sidney's funeral.

doome. Perhaps an error for 'doone'.

passion. An elegy, possibly the 'The Dolefull Lay of Clorinda'.

IV. Mary Sidney Herbert, Countess of Pembroke, to Julius Caesar

Julius Caesar [Adelmare], Doctor of Laws and knighted in 1603, was Master of Requests, the appropriate officer to support the countess's servant in her lawsuit. The name of the servant and the nature of the lawsuit remain unknown; this letter would be typical of the voluminous business correspondence she would be expected to conduct on behalf of friends and servants, as part of the patronage system.

V. Mary Sidney Herbert, writing on behalf of Henry Herbert, Earl of Pembroke, to Robert Devereux, Earl of Essex

This undated letter refers to one of Essex's voyages prior to Pembroke's death in January 1601: 1589, when Essex sailed with Drake to support Don Antonio of Portugal; 1591, when Essex was given command of the English forces sent to assist Henri IV against the French Catholics; June 1596, when Essex left to attack Cadiz; or August 1597, when Essex unsuccessfully attempted to attack the new Spanish armada and capture treasure vessels returning from South America. The letter probably refers to the 1596 voyage, since it appears that young William, Lord Herbert sailed with Essex and was knighted by him. (List of knights made at Cadiz, *HMC Salisbury*, XIII. 500; Hannay, *Philip's Phoenix*, 153–6, 261.) Herbert could well be the 'wise post' who delivered the letter.

Through 1596 the Pembrokes had maintained a close friendship with Essex and his wife, Frances Walsingham, widow of Sir Philip Sidney, despite the earls' ongoing struggle for ascendancy in Wales. See, for example, the postscript in Robert Sidney's letter to his wife on 8 September 1594, which implies a lengthy visit by the Pembrokes to Essex when Pembroke was sick and Lady Essex pregnant: 'My Lady of Essex grows very big. My Lord of Pembroke is now fully recovered and returned from [Essex]' (De L'Isle MS U1475 C81/ 47). In 1597, however, Pembroke and Essex quarrelled so bitterly over Norwood Park and over the appointment of favourites that they never returned to their former friendship; this enmity meant that the Herberts were not implicated in Essex's later fall, as were so many of the Welsh aristocracy.

This letter was folded three times before it was sent and bears the following inscriptions:

[Written along the fold, left margin of f. 4^v]

    E: Pembroke to the

    E: of Essex

[Written along the top margins of the same folio, but upside-down]

    To the most honorable

    the Earle of Essex

The text of the letter is on f. 3^r; f. 3^v and 4^r are blank. Two words have been inserted: 'better' above the line and 'sort' in the left margin. Those insertions may suggest that the countess transcribed the letter from a rough draft and then corrected it. The letter also appears formerly to have been bound into a volume since it bears holes and impressions of thread along the fold, and the number '93' in pencil in the upper left hand corner of f. 3.

VI. Mary Sidney Herbert, Countess of Pembroke, to William Cecil, Lord Burghley

'Messynger', who delivered the letter, was the Earl of Pembroke's secretary, Arthur Massinger, father of the dramatist Philip Massinger.

The Pembrokes were promoting a match between their son William, then 17 years old, and Bridget de Vere, daughter of Anne Cecil and Edward de Vere, Earl of Oxford. Lady Bridget was the granddaughter of Burghley and niece of Robert Cecil, both of whom were active in the marriage negotiations. Pembroke also wrote to Burghley on 16 August, noting that Massinger had brought to him at 'fallerston' 'my wifes letters reporting my sonnes liking of your daughter'. Pembroke was therefore ready to proceed with the financial settlement and noted that Massinger had 'alreadie acquainted you with my meaning in some things: and of anithing else your Lordship shall desire to be further informed, upon hearing thereof from your Lordship I will speadily ... advertize you' (Pembroke to Burghley, 16 August 1597, PRO SP 12/264/84). On that same day the Earl of Pembroke also wrote to Robert Cecil, to thank him for showing kindness to William when he was at court and for promoting his welfare with the queen, proudly asserting that 'He is by nature born, was by me brought up, and is in his own affection, vowed to her service' (Earl of Pembroke to Cecil, 16 August 1597, *HMC Salisbury*, VII. 354). Some time that month young William dutifully thanked Cecil as well (William, Lord Herbert to Cecil, August 1597, *HMC Salisbury*, VII. 374).

VII. Mary Sidney Herbert, Countess of Pembroke, to Sir Robert Cecil

Robert Cecil was seeking the title 'Viscount Cranborne', which he was finally awarded by King James in August 1604. Cecil had heard rumours that his title had been blocked by the Earl of Pembroke, an irascible man who may well have said something unwise which his more tactful wife had to disavow.

At the beginning of September, Pembroke answered Burghley's questions about the match between William Herbert and Bridget de Vere in a lengthy letter delivered by Massinger. Although Bridget was then only 13 years old, the marriage would still be binding, but the couple would not immediately cohabit: 'their long continuance together may be deferred until you think good', Pembroke said. Proposing the aristocratic custom of early marriage and delayed cohabitation by sending the young bridegroom off to the Continent, he suggested that after the wedding 'your daughter should remayn with my wife; whose care of her shall answer the neernes wherbi she shall then be linked unto her' (Pembroke to Burghley, 3 September 1597, PRO SP 12/264/106).

Despite the Countess of Pembroke's efforts, the match between William Herbert and Bridget de Vere was broken off. Bridget de Vere married Francis Norris, Earl of Berkshire. In 1604 William Herbert's younger brother Philip 'was privately contracted to my Lady Susan [Bridget de Vere's younger sister] without the knowledge of any of his or her friends' (William Herbert, Earl of Pembroke, to Gilbert Talbot, Earl of Shrewsbury, 16 October 1604, Lambeth Palace MS 3200/225). Their wedding, recounted in detail in a letter from Sir Dudley Carleton to John Chamberlain, was the most glittering social occasion of the early Stuart years (7 January 1605, PRO SP 14/12/6).

chaling, n. Obsolete spelling for 'challenge'.

IX. Mary Sidney Herbert, Countess of Pembroke, to Queen Elizabeth

The queen had welcomed young William, Lord Herbert to court 'for her sake that bare him' (Queen Elizabeth to Pembroke, 2 July 1599, *HMC Petyt*, 182, now Inner Temple MSS). In her appeal for the queen to take William into her service, the countess alludes to her own brief service at court, from the death of her sister Ambrosia in 1575 until her own marriage in 1577. In an unusually warm letter, Queen Elizabeth had invited Sir Henry Sidney to send the 14-year-old Mary, his sole surviving daughter, to court under her 'speciall care' (Queen Elizabeth to Sidney, 1575, PRO SP 40/1/83).

X. Mary Sidney Herbert, Dowager Countess of Pembroke, to Sir Robert Cecil

Under the terms of her husband's will, the Dowager Countess of Pembroke held the Castle and borough of Cardiff until the majority of her son William. This letter to Cecil and the following letters to Sir Julius Caesar and to the Earl and Countess of Shrewsbury all concern her administrative problems in Cardiff, as the town attempted to throw off the seigneurial hold of the Earls of Pembroke.

She appealed to Cecil because of 'the want of thos frends of myne long since lost'. Since 1586 she had lost most of the male relatives who had served as her 'frends' at court: her brothers Philip and Thomas; her uncles Leicester, Warwick, and Huntingdon; her brother-in-law Sir Edward Herbert; and, just eighteen months earlier, her husband. By 1602 her only close male relatives living were her brother Robert, in Flushing, and her young sons, none of whom were in a position to be of help at court.

Jhon Udales. John Udale wrote to Essex from Wilton on behalf of the Pembrokes on 30 October 1598, recommending their son William, 'this young

Lord Herbert' (*HMC Salisbury*, VIII. 415). This may be the same John Udall who compiled a Hebrew grammar (see Zim, *Psalms*, 255). If so, John Udall may have tutored Pembroke in Hebrew or acted as a source of expert advice on the Hebrew text.

plead. A likely error for 'pleasd'.

XI. Mary Sidney Herbert, Dowager Countess of Pembroke, to Sir Julius Caesar

Julius Caesar had been knighted by King James on 20 May 1603; he continued to serve as Master of Requests.

This letter is the first in a series of complaints against Edmund Mathew of Cardiff and London. Edmund Mathew's older brother, William, had married the sister of William Herbert, cousin to Henry Herbert, Earl of Pembroke, and had held a seat in Parliament under Pembroke. After William Mathew charged the Cardiff officials with collusion in piracy, Pembroke charged him with collusion in a murder. William Mathew died in prison before he was brought to trial by Pembroke, who was President of the Council of the Marches of Wales. Edmund Mathew eventually inherited his brother's estates—and his quarrel with the Herberts. Probably as a result of his ill will toward her, the Countess of Pembroke fired him from his minor post as steward of Myskyn and gave the stewardship to Hugh Davydd. According to the countess, Mathew unsuccessfully attempted to bribe Davydd and then had him murdered when he was bringing her jewels from Cardiff to London. (Presumably Mathew thought that the jewel theft would appear as sufficient motivation for the murder and thereby not implicate him.) In a convoluted legal battle, the countess charged Mathew with collusion in the murder of Hugh Davydd. Other residents of Cardiff were also charged with defying the countess's authority in Cardiff and setting up an alternative court. The related cases were brought to trial in the Star Chamber in 1604 and 1605. (Cecil Papers, Petition 2301. PRO, Star Chamber Records 8/183/35-6. For the details of these cases, see Hannay, *Philip's Phoenix*, 173-84.)

Lord Wotton. Sir Edward Wotton. Note the letter from Sir Edward's father, Thomas Wotton, and her earlier letter to Sir Edward (cited above), whom she addressed as 'Cossen Wotton'.

She wrote from Windsor, where she and her daughter Lady Anne were present at the Feast of St George on 2 July 1603. At that ceremony her son William, the new Earl of Pembroke, was invested as a Knight of the Garter, along with Prince Henry and several other young men (John Nichols, *The Progresses...of King James the First*, 3 vols. (London: J. Nichols, 1828), I. 193-5).

XII. Mary Sidney Herbert, Dowager Countess of Pembroke, to Sir Julius Caesar

Burnam. Burnham, a town about 8 km. north of Windsor, from which she had written the previous letter.

XIV. Mary Sidney Herbert, Dowager Countess of Pembroke, to Sir Julius Caesar

Because the king would not hear her witnesses at Windsor, she had their testimony recorded for a later presentation. Edmund Mathew claimed, in a letter to Sir Julius Caesar on 21 June 1603, that the examination exonerated him (Caesar Papers. BL Additional MS 12503, f. 38). The countess believed that the examination would convict him. Although records of the eventual Star Chamber trial are extant (see Manuscript Letter XI), the verdict was destroyed by fire.

XV. Mary Sidney Herbert, Dowager Countess of Pembroke, to Gilbert Talbot and Mary Cavendish, Earl and Countess of Shrewsbury

Writing to the Shrewsburys a few weeks before the marriage of her son William to their daughter Mary on 4 November, she first compliments their daughter and then appeals for their help against an unnamed opponent, probably Edmund Mathew, since the letter is written in the midst of her attempts to bring him to trial. Her bitterness is increased because this 'so falce, so curupt and so vile a Creture' had not only injured her with the king, but had also 'devided myne owne from me'.

the deerest part of me. She is probably referring to her son William, in phrasing similar to her reference to him as 'this part of me' in her letter to Sir Robert Cecil, 29 September 1597 (Letter VIII). Two weeks prior to this letter, Robert Sidney had written to his wife that young Pembroke would visit them at Penshurst 'if his mothers being there doe not stay him', suggesting some estrangement between the countess and her son (Robert Sidney to Barbara Sidney, 12 September 1604, De L'Isle MS U1475 C81/111).

Pembroke. After Mary Talbot married William Herbert, she began signing her letters 'M. Pembroke'. Mary Sidney Herbert then changed her signature to 'Pembroke' with an identifying design around her title—the S fermé also used by Mary Sidney, Lady Wroth. For Mary Talbot Herbert's signature, see Lambeth Palace MS 3203/409. Fortunately, her handwriting is quite different from that of Mary Sidney Herbert.

Savoy. The London home of her beloved aunt, Katherine Dudley Hastings, Countess of Huntingdon.

XVI. Mary Sidney Herbert, Dowager Countess of Pembroke, to Robert Cecil, Earl of Salisbury

Ditchlye was a home of Sir Henry Lee, the queen's legendary champion at the tilts, and of his mistress, Ann Vavasour. Anne Vavasour, one of Elizabeth's maids of honour, was imprisoned in the Tower with her illegitimate son, named after his father, Edward de Vere, Earl of Oxford. She was later married to John Finch, a sea captain, and then became the mistress of Sir Henry Lee. After Lee's death, she married Sir R. Warburton, but was charged with bigamy, because Finch was still alive. See Kathy Lynn Emerson, *Wives and Daughters: The Women of Sixteenth Century England* (Troy, NY: Whitston, 1984), 233.

Sir Jhon Gennings was John Jennings, knighted 11 May 1603 at the Charterhouse with more than 130 others. (W. A. Shaw, *The Knights of England* (London: Sherratt and Hughes, 1906), I. 163, II. 107.) In 1607 he was reputedly dying. Pembroke had asked earlier for the wardship of his son (see below) and repeated that request in this letter of 27 July; on 29 August Richard Ouseley also asked for the wardship, but apparently neither he nor the countess obtained it. An inquisition on 2 December found that Sir John Jennings had become a lunatic on 16 August. (HMC Salisbury, XIX. 196, 233, 356.) His death is given as 1611 in HMC Salisbury (XIX. 356) but as 1609 in *Biographical Dictionary of British Radicals in the Seventeenth Century*, ed. Richard L. Greaves and Robert Zaller (Brighton, Sussex: Harvester, 1982–84), II. 139.

Pembroke sought the wardship of his eldest son, 11-year-old John Jennings, who was the child of Jennings's first wife, Anne Brounker, daughter of Sir William Brounker of Wiltshire. John Jennings married Alice Spencer, daughter of Sir Richard Spencer of Hertfordshire, and became Sheriff of Hertfordshire and JP for the county. He was made Knight of the Bath 1 February 1625/6 at the Coronation of Charles I. He served in Charles's fifth parliament as a supporter of John Pym in 1640–2, and died on 5 August 1642, just prior to the outbreak of civil war. (*Biographical Dictionary of British Radicals*, II. 139. According to the *Dictionary*, he 'sired 22 children'.)

Printed Letters Attributed to Mary Sidney Herbert, Dowager Countess of Pembroke

I. Mary Sidney Herbert, Dowager Countess of Pembroke, to Sir Tobie Matthew

Although their authenticity could be proven only by recovery of a holograph original, it is certainly possible that these letters published by Donne had been written by the Countess of Pembroke. The style (allowing for editorial changes in spelling) is compatible with the countess's other letters, especially with reference to her lavish use of commas and parentheses. Her candid confessions of choler, while making the letters an odd choice for models of style, certainly fit the personality of the countess who expressed her 'scorne of so falce, so curupt and so vile a Creture' (Manuscript Letter XV). Like her husband, her uncle Leicester, and her brother Sir Philip Sidney, she had a fierce temper when riled.

Furthermore, the persons, dates, and places fit what we know of her sojourn on the Continent from 1614 until 1616, and the letters mention her residence in Spa. It is also reasonable to assume that she would have written to Sir Tobie Matthew, whom she had known since his infancy. He had been born in Salisbury (within a few miles of Wilton) in 1577, the year of Mary Sidney Herbert's marriage. His father, Dr Tobie Matthew, was a close friend of the Pembrokes and received his positions as archdeacon in Salisbury and then as Bishop of Durham through their patronage. Despite his vehement Catholicism, Sir Tobie maintained literary friendships with English Protestants, exchanging manuscripts with Sir Francis Bacon, Sir Dudley Carleton, and Lucy, Countess of Bedford, as well as with the Countess of Pembroke. If the letters are authentic, they tantalize us by mentioning writings, translations, and portraits of the Countess of Pembroke that have been lost.

John Donne the younger also edited and published poems by Mary Sidney Herbert's son William, third Earl of Pembroke: *Poems Written by the Right Honorable William Earl of Pembroke, Lord Steward of his Majesties Houshold, Wherof Many of Which are answered by way of Repartee, by Sir Benjamin Ruddier, Knight, with Several Distinct Poems, Written by them Occasionally, and Apart* (1660), Wing P1128.

your Other-self. George Gage, Matthew's inseparable companion.

those idle Papers. Cf. her request that Wotton return 'a certain Idle passion' (Manuscript Letter III).

other businesse. Probably Matthew's attempt to gain permission to return to England; he needed to recover one thousand pounds owed him by Sir Henry Goodyer. By the beginning of December, Matthew had heard that his suit had been denied, so that these three letters from the Countess of Pembroke, if authentic, would date from earlier in 1616.

IV. Mary Sidney Herbert, Dowager Countess of Pembroke, to 'her son'

This reference is extant only in William Cory's nineteenth- century account of a letter described to him by Elizabeth A'Court Herbert (d. 1911), widow of Sidney Herbert, first Baron Herbert of Lea (1810–61). In 1865 Cory was the Greek tutor of their son, George Robert Charles Herbert, 13th Earl of Pembroke. Cory himself never claims to have seen the letter and it may well be a forgery or 'a figment of the Lady Herbert's imagination'. (Michael G. Brennan, ' "We Have the Man Shakespeare With Us": Wilton House and *As You Like It'*, *The Wiltshire Archaeological and Natural History Magazine* 80 (1986), 225–7.) Nevertheless, it is tantalizingly accurate in its references to dates, persons, and situations. There is no recorded performance of *As You Like It* at Wilton, but the King's Men, the company of which Shakespeare was a member, was paid thirty pounds to perform before the king at Wilton on 2 December 1603, between Ralegh's trial (17 November) and the date originally set for his execution (13 December). On 27 November Dudley Carleton wrote to John Chamberlain, 'I do call to mind a pretty secret that the lady of Pembroke hath written to her son Philip and charged him of all her blessings to employ his own credit and his friends and all he can do for Raleigh's pardon; and though she does little good, yet she is to be commended for doing her best in showing *veteris vestigia flammae*' (*Dudley Carleton to John Chamberlain, 1603–1624: Jacobean Letters*, ed. Maurice Lee, Jr. (New Brunswick, NJ: Rutgers UP, 1972), 44–5). By quoting Dido's words about Aeneas, '[I recognize] the traces of my old passion', Chamberlain implied a romance that is not otherwise substantiated. Ralegh certainly had close connections to the Countess of Pembroke and undoubtedly knew her well. He had been at Oxford with Sir Philip Sidney, had married the daughter of Leicester's ally, Sir Nicholas Throckmorton, was the cousin of Robert Sidney's wife Barbara Gamage, and was the half-brother of Adrian Gilbert, who reputedly worked with the countess in her chemical laboratory. Perhaps the Dowager Countess of Pembroke and her son did successfully intercede to save Ralegh from execution on that occasion.